John Alden Mason was born in Philadelphia in 1885 and was educated at the Universities of Pennsylvania and California. In 1917 he was appointed Assistant Curator of Mexican and South American Archaeology in the Field Museum of Natural History in Chicago, which he left in 1924 to take up an almost similar post at the American Museum of Natural History in New York. He was Curator of the American Section in the University of Pennsylvania Museum from 1926 to 1955, when he was appointed Curator Emeritus there; he held this post until his death in November 1967. In addition to his Ph.D. he was an Hon.Litt.D.

He went on research expeditions to Texas, New Mexico, Utah, Arizona, California, Canada, Mexico, Guatemala, Puerto Rico, Colombia and Panama. He held office in the Society for American Archaeology, the Eastern States Archaeological Federation, the American Association for the Advancement of Science, and the American Anthropological Association, and he edited *American Anthropologist* from 1945 to 1948. He was a member of the Institute of Andean Research and editor for the New World Archaeological Foundation of Provo, Utah. Much of his work on anthropology has been published. His special interests included archaeology, languages and the ethnology and folklore of American Indians.

THE ANCIENT
CIVILIZATIONS OF PERU

*

J. Alden Mason

REVISED EDITION

PENGUIN BOOKS

PENGUIN BOOKS

Published by the Penguin Group
Penguin Books Ltd, 27 Wrights Lane, London W8 5TZ, England
Penguin Books USA Inc., 375 Hudson Street, New York, New York 10014, USA
Penguin Books Australia Ltd, Ringwood, Victoria, Australia
Penguin Books Canada Ltd, 10 Alcorn Avenue, Toronto, Ontario, Canada M4V 3B2
Penguin Books (NZ) Ltd, 182–190 Wairau Road, Auckland 10, New Zealand

Penguin Books Ltd, Registered Offices: Harmondsworth, Middlesex, England

First published in Pelican Books 1957
Reprinted with revisions 1964
Revised edition published 1968
Reprinted in Penguin Books 1991
3 5 7 9 10 8 6 4

Printed in England by Clays Ltd, St Ives plc

CONTENTS

v

CONTENTS

PART FOUR

Arts and Crafts

vi

CONTENTS

LIST OF TEXT FIGURES

MAPS

TABLE

LIST OF PLATES

PREFACE

IN 1527 a small party of men, Spaniards, gathered on a tiny island in the Pacific off the coast of what is now southern Colombia. In those days sea voyages were no pleasure jaunts. The cramped quarters on the small ships, the stinking water, the monotonous diet of stale food, offered no attractions and barely tolerable conditions for the hardiest of adventurers. These had been several months on the slow voyage of exploration south from Panama where rumours were constantly heard from the Indians of a civilized empire, rich in gold, to the south. But so far the men had seen little but hardships, hunger, and sudden death; most of them were disaffected and mutinous. Now the ship for which they had been waiting had arrived from Panama. The Governor's orders to abandon the expedition and return to Panama were received by most with joy. They, proud Spaniards who had come seeking gold and Indian slaves to wait on them, were in rags, subsisting on the shellfish and crabs that they caught on the shores. Enough of this! There was little wealth or luxury in Panama, but at least the basic necessities of food, shelter, and clothing were not missing.

But for one valiant soul the fleshpots of Panama had no appeal above that of the call of the unknown to action. Francisco Pizarro had not come so far in hopes of imitating Cortés to be turned back by hunger, thirst, wetness, and other such trivial bodily inconveniences. On the sand of the little island he drew a line. 'Behind you,' he said to the men, 'lie ease, pleasure – and poverty; before you, toil, hunger, death, but also Peru and its gold. I go south; who goes with me?' And he stepped over the line. One by one, thirteen other brave fellows followed him, to give their names to history as the fourteen stalwarts of Gallo.

For history certainly records no more sturdy and obstinate persistence towards a distant goal in the face of seemingly insuperable obstacles, and no more incredible example of the success of a patently foolhardy venture. For these fourteen tenacious ones were the vanguard of the 'army' of less than two hundred men who were to conquer an empire of several millions.[1]

But such, for over four centuries, has been the lure of Peru. Colonists and administrators followed Pizarro, seekers for the silver, gold, copper, tin, and other metals that the land yielded,

1. Prescott, 1847.

xi

producers of quinine, coca, and, very recently, oil, exporters of guano, of alpaca wool, and, still later, chinchillas. But not only came those who sought wealth in Peru, but also those who, attracted by its great range of nature, longed to study its flora and fauna, its geology and geography, and to report them to the scientific world. Alexander von Humboldt came, Sir Clements Markham, Darwin and Wallace, to mention only a few of the most prominent.

Inca gold now no longer lures the conqueror, but Inca – and pre-Inca – ruins attract the tourist. The Inca armies and the splendour of Cuzco are gone, but the great pyramids of adobe still tower over the desert sands, and the Quechua Indian still guides his llamas through the narrow-walled Inca streets of Cuzco. In a few short hours the aeroplane carries the tourist from Panama to Lima, over the seas that took many months for Pizarro and his little boats. And in even less time it wafts him from the warmth of arid sea-level Lima over the snow-capped Andes to the cool heights of Cuzco. *Vámonos.*

INTRODUCTION

THE history of pre-Conquest Peru, of the Inca and their pre-decessors – most of the latter nameless and unknown – emanates from sources of two different types. That of the Inca depends primarily on the chroniclers, mainly Spanish, who wrote down, soon after the Conquest, their observations and recollections, and especially the reports of former customs, beliefs, and traditions that they secured from living natives. Later students have based many studies and monographs on these often contradictory accounts. For earlier unrecorded times we must rely upon the work and reports of archaeologists.

Digging in Peru – treasure-hunting for gold ornaments – began with the Conquest; *sub rosa* this still continues. The by-products of fascinating and exotic art objects soon began to grace the cabinets of wealthy men in Peru and Europe. Later, many foreign travellers visited the imposing archaeological sites and described them; and toward the close of the last century professional archaeologists began to dig with a view more to learning about the past peoples than to enriching museum collections. The Germans were leaders in this; the first really scientific excavation in Peru, in which the objects characteristic of certain periods were differentiated by noting their relative depths and superpositions, was made at Pachacamac in 1896 by the late great dean of Peruvian archaeologists, Max Uhle, for the University Museum, Philadelphia (Uhle, 1903). To-day this is the method and goal of all professional archaeological expeditions; art objects of exhibitable value are rare by-products.

The spectacular discovery of Machu Picchu in 1911 by Hiram Bingham awoke popular interest in ancient Peru. Bingham was soon followed by Philip A. Means, who in 1931 published his *Ancient Civilizations of the Andes*, for many years the classic in English on the subject. About the same time Wendell C. Bennett began his researches in Peru; his accidental death at the age of forty-eight in 1953 robbed Peruvian archaeology of probably its most promising student. The dean of native Peruvianists, Julio C. Tello, made his epochal discoveries at Paracas in 1927. But it was not until 1937, with the founding of the Institute of Andean Research by eight American universities and scientific institutions, that archaeological research in Peru took a sudden upswing.

INTRODUCTION

Eight field expeditions to South America were supported in 1941–2, and in 1945–8 six of these institutions collaborated in a thorough archaeological study of the Virú Valley, one of the smaller coastal valleys of northern Peru. The results of all these researches have since been published. About the same time, in 1946, appeared the modern classic of reference, *The Andean Civilizations*, with thirty-four articles by recognized authorities (Steward, Editor, 1946).

Since the appearance of the present book in 1957 (some parts of which were written several years earlier) our knowledge of Peruvian archaeology has increased greatly. Expeditions from many countries in addition to the United States have dug there, including the Japanese, who excavated mainly at Kotosh (Ishida *et al.*, 1960; Izuria and Sono, 1963). A number of young Peruvian, Ecuadorian, and Bolivian archaeologists have begun to investigate their countries' past. Many reports have been issued, and some radiocarbon dates secured. The latter are relatively few and have not altered the overall picture. There is still considerable difference and disagreement in the chronologies preferred by some of the best authorities.

The Peruvian government has continued researches at Chavín, Pachacamac, Ancón, Chancay, and some other sites, and restorations at the former two. The greatest development has been in the pre-ceramic era, with the discovery of a large number of sites. The majority of these have been in the coastal valleys, even in some that are to-day waterless. However, one in the highlands, in a cave at Lauricocha (Cardich, 1960), afforded the oldest radiocarbon date, 7566 B.C. This, like some later coastal sites, was pre-agricultural. The earlier of the horticultural sites on the coast lack maize, the later ones have it. It is now felt quite certain that maize came to Peru from Mexico. At a somewhat later period, about 900–800 B.C., an improved type of maize was introduced. Some of the coastal sites have well-made projectile points, much superior to the simple flaked cobbles made at Huaca Prieta (p. 34). A good number of textiles have also been found, as well as other plant foods. Very recently some sites of about 3800–3000 B.C., earlier than Huaca Prieta, have been discovered (Engel, 1960). These have small subterranean houses but seem to lack cotton, suggesting that Asiatic cotton was introduced about 3000 B.C. to hybridize with the wild lintless native cotton.

Of maximum importance also are recent discoveries in Ecuador, which not only strongly suggest maritime trade with Mexico about the beginning of the Christian era, but also very early (3000 B.C.) trans-Pacific contact, specifically with Japan (Estrada and Meggers, 1961, 1962, Meggers, Evans and Estrada, 1965).

In the highlands, studies of the last decade have laid great stress on Chavín and its art horizon. Close resemblances are noted with Mexico, even before the classic Chavín period; parallels with Mexican Olmec are especially strong. Even the stirrup-spout, so characteristic of the Peruvian north coast, may be a Mexican influence.

The spread of the Chavín horizon on a later level has also been traced more widely, to Early Paracas and Nazca on the southern coast and to Ayacucho in the highlands. On a still later horizon it is coming to be believed that the spread of the Tiahuanaco art style was the result of a military conquest, emanating from Huari, now generally spelt 'Wari' in archaeological literature.

Some ten years ago I wrote 'So dynamic is the state of our knowledge – or lack of knowledge – of Peruvian archaeology, that no book can be published at present with any claim to finality; the picture may be altered decidedly by the time it appears on the book shelves'. This is not quite so true now. Compared with Egypt, Mesopotamia, Greece, and Rome, Peruvian archaeology is still in its infancy; it lags behind Mexico. Many important sites are practically uninvestigated; others will be discovered. There are still relatively few radiocarbon dates, and some of these are incompatible. But the picture is now fairly well in focus.

It has not been possible to revise this book completely and to bring it fully up to date in this edition. Changes from the last (1964) edition are minimal, and almost entirely in Part 2 (pp. 11–37). Most of the more important works that have been published in the last decade have been added to the Bibliography.

J. ALDEN MASON

Philadelphia,
August 1966

ACKNOWLEDGEMENTS

I AM much indebted to my friends the American Peruvianists the late Dr Alfred L. Kroeber, Dr Alfred Kidder 2nd, Dr John Howland Rowe, and Dr Junius Bird, as well as to my colleague Dr Linton Satterthwaite, all of whom read parts of the typescript of this book and made valuable criticisms and suggestions. It must not be assumed, however, that they approve of everything herein, and certainly on some of the more controversial points they are not in entire accord.

I wish also to thank the late Dr Paul Rivet, of the University of Paris Institute of Ethnology, for permission to reproduce Figures 3, 4, 5, and 6; and the Servicio Aerofotográfico Nacional Peruano for permission to reproduce Plates 3, 5A, 6, 9A, and 15A.

Especial appreciation, however, is expressed to the Wenner-Gren Foundation for Anthropological Research, New York, for the grant which enabled me to visit Peru in 1952 and to make the personal acquaintance of the country, its archaeological sites, and its archaeologists, that is indispensable for a work of this type.

Most of the Peruvian handicraft herein illustrated is in the University Museum, University of Pennsylvania, Philadelphia; the photographs are the work of the late Reuben Goldberg, Museum photographer. Most of the photographs of archaeological sites were taken by the author; a few are the work of Sr Abraham Guillén of the Museo Etnográfico, Lima, and a very few are from miscellaneous sources.

PART ONE

THE BACKGROUND

*

Chapter 1

THE ENVIRONMENT

THE native Peruvian, though ignorant of all but his immediate surroundings, might well boast of being a resident of no mean country. For few regions in the world embrace such contrasts of environment, from sea-level to the maximum habitable altitudes, from utterly leafless deserts to the lushest tropical forests, from regions of constant warmth to those of eternal ice and snow. And probably in no other place in the world can the transition be made in so short a space. While the other great early civilizations of the Old World developed in areas of relatively homogeneous altitude and climate, the Peruvian people had to cope with the greatest possible variety. Doubtless this climatic contrast had much to do with encouraging the development of Peruvian civilization.

The great Andean cordillera[1] is the heart of Peru, as of the other nations of western South America. In a past geological age the earth's crust buckled diastrophically, creating a great ridge to the east and a submarine trough to the west so that in only about two hundred miles the surface rises from some twenty thousand feet below sea-level to twenty thousand above. Only in Bolivia is the highland much over a hundred miles in width. The continental divide is close to the Pacific Ocean, in places only about sixty miles (100 km.) from it. On the east side the land rapidly descends to almost sea-level, from which the slow-flowing rivers, affluents of the great Amazon, meander some

1. See Appendix, page 276, for Spanish and Quechua words.

I

three thousand miles to the Atlantic. Even the old Inca capital, Cuzco, is on the Amazon drainage. The rivers to the Pacific naturally are all small and short.

Geographers to-day divide Peru into three radically different climatic areas: the low arid coast, the cool or cold highlands, and the lush, tropical, humid eastern lowlands or *montaña*. The latter, however, is Peruvian only from a political point of view. Geographically it belongs to the Amazonian basin – and we shall not be concerned with it; the old Peruvian civilization never penetrated it deeply, though deriving many valuable tropical products from the nearest parts of it.

Northward from southern Chile, parallel to the coast, sweeps the great Peru or Humboldt Current, bringing cold water far to the north, water that averages some 5° F. (2·8° C.) colder than other waters of the same latitude. It used to be thought that this cold water came from the Antarctic, but now it is believed to be due to upwelling in certain places of the cold water from the abysmal depths of the trough parallel to the coast. Cooled by it, the winds drop their excess moisture at sea, and deposit no rain on the coast. The sun shines constantly through diffused clouds, but in the winter (June–November) heavy fogs are frequent. The normal precipitation increases towards the north. Southern Peru and northern Chile form the region of greatest aridity in the western hemisphere; here years pass without a drop of rain, and there is no visible plant life. At some places in the Atacama desert no rainfall has ever been recorded.

In northern coastal Peru there are occasional rains. In cycles a counter current, locally known as *El Niño* (the boy), flowing south over the cold Peru current, nullifies the effect of the latter, and brings heavy rain to the northern coast. Several times in a century, as for instance in 1925, the rains are torrential and terribly destructive to a country where the entire pattern of existence is based on the absence of rain. Even in the great capital city of Lima there is no apparent provision for carrying off rainwater. Then the desert springs to life, with a tremendous increase in both flora and small fauna. But normally it is a waste of rocky hills and wind-blown sand, without a leaf, not even of cactus. According to the Köppen system, the climate is symbolized as 'BWhn' (warm, desert, foggy). The coastal temperature is about 7° F. (4° C.) below that normal for this latitude.

Normally, on the coast there is naturally little native flora or fauna, except in the river valleys, but the cool sea teems with life – fish, octopus, and sea mammals. This is due to the large amount of nutriment in the cold bottom waters brought to the surface by the Peru current. It is one of the world's great fishing grounds – except in the time of El Niño. For this reason there are also enormous numbers of sea birds who nest on the islands off the coast and have deposited there great thick beds of excrement known as *guano* which for years furnished the world with fertilizing material. When the Niño strikes they fly elsewhere or die of starvation, as do quantities of carnivorous marine animals. Naturally also, then, the fishermen and their families have to tighten their belts.

But as one traverses the coast highway, through interminable uninhabited wastes of sand, suddenly one enters lush green fields of corn, cotton, and rice. Here is a river valley, bringing life-giving water from the mountains. The transition is sudden; above the highest irrigation ditch is absolute arid desert; below it, all is verdant. There are about forty-four of these small streams in present-day political Peru, of which about thirty-one are permanent, the others flowing only in the rainy season in the mountains. About twenty-five of these are of archaeological importance. Owing to the flatness of the terrain and the spread of the irrigation ditches, however, the width of the cultivated valleys is considerable. Here are the modern coastal towns, and here were the villages of the natives from time immemorial.

But the flat coastal strip is quite narrow, and only a few miles from the beach begin the foothills of the majestic Andes. As one traverses one of the roads into the interior, following one of the streams, wild plants begin to appear, at first widely scattered, a stunted cactus thirsting for moisture, then another, and finally, at a considerable altitude, one is surrounded by trees and grass. For altitude is of much more importance in Peru than latitude, and typical Peru is highland.

Much of central Peru is uncultivable, the snow-clad mountains being too high for agriculture or habitation, and rocky steep slopes. But the intermontane valleys are fertile and well watered. The climate is designated as 'Cwb', cool summer mesothermal savanna with winter dry season, the rainy season being from October to May, the warmer 'summer'. (Being south of the equator, 'winter' and 'summer' are naturally reversed.) The annual temperature range, however, is relatively slight, tending towards cool, though freezing temperatures are rare, except in the highest plateaus.

In far northern Peru the highlands are more of the Ecuador type, with greater rainfall and leafy expanses known as *páramos*, but throughout most of the country they are grassy grazing lands known as *punas*. Much of the region is unforested, and pasture for the herds of llamas and alpacas. There is at present little wild life, but the guinea-pig and similar small animals supply the natives with occasional meat.

Hemmed in between high mountain ranges are six major basins which probably contain the larger part of the habitable area of highland Peru, charming great valleys of from eight to eleven thousand feet (2400–3400 m.) altitude, fertile, wooded, with ever-running streams and grassy fields (in the summer rainy season), and numerous towns and villages. These are, from north to south, Cajamarca, Callejón de Huaylas, Huánuco, Mantaro, Cuzco, and Titicaca. The largest and best known of these are Huaylas, Cuzco, and Titicaca.

The Callejón de Huaylas is the most thickly populated and one of the largest of these, some 125 miles long and 25 wide (200 by 40 km.). It contains a number of towns, the largest of which is Huaraz. Nestling between the great Sierra Blanca and the Sierra Negra, it is looked down upon by majestic Huascarán (22,180 ft or 6761 m.). Through it flows the Huaraz River which, cutting through the Sierra Negra and thenceforth known as the Santa, empties into the Pacific in northern Peru, irrigating a large coastal area, the largest of the coastal rivers. Most of the other basins – all except Titicaca – are on the Amazon drainage.

The Cuzco basin, with an average elevation of 11,200 ft (3414 m.), is of course the best known of all, the seat of the Inca Empire.

The highest and most remarkable, however, is the basin of Titicaca in which lies Lake Titicaca, the highest navigable water in the world, 12,506 ft (3812 m.). Even more remarkable than the lake is the relatively large steamboat that traverses it. Fabricated in England, the parts were carried by ship and railroad to the lake and there assembled. Of very irregular shore line, the maximum length of the lake is 130 miles, the width 41 (208 by 66 km.). It is on no drainage system, the excess water flowing south to the marshes of Lake Poopo and then evaporating in the sands. The basin is divided between Peru and Bolivia and contains the great early archaeological site of Tiahuanaco, actually in Bolivia.

The Bolivian *altiplano* surrounding the Titicaca basin – which is a little warmer – is a chill, dreary, treeless *puna*, averaging 13,000 ft (3962 m.) in altitude. Geographers call it a tundra, or cold desert. Too high for corn cultivation, the main dependence is on potatoes, and on the other native plants quinoa and oca. But here is the homeland of the llama and the alpaca, and of their herders, the Aymara Indians.

Chapter 2

PHYSIQUE AND LANGUAGE

No human characteristic is so constant and changes so slowly as the physical type. Though the culture may change radically owing to foreign influence, the physique remains practically unaltered provided that there is no admixture of genes or radical change in the environment. It may be assumed that the present Indians of Peru, who form, according to the 1940 census, about forty per cent of the population, are physically practically identical with their ancestors of four centuries ago.

In early days the dwellers on the coast were probably of a slightly different type from those in the highlands, but the spread of the Inca in the fifteenth century resulted in a more homogeneous native type. At any rate, the modern highland Quechua Indian, descendant of the Inca, may be taken as physically representative of his ancestors.

The Quechua body build is massive, the head short, the face medium short. The stature is also rather low. The mesorrhine (medium broad) nose is often arched and the cheekbones are salient; the forehead is low, and the hairline, coming down quite low on the forehead, makes it appear still lower. The eyebrow ridges are only moderately developed, and the eyes are not deeply set. The length and shape of the nose, together with the beardless face, lend a very characteristic appearance to the Quechua Indian. The chest, shoulders, and hips in both sexes are well developed.[1]

The Quechua are rather short, averaging apparently 5 ft 2½ in. (158·7 cm.) for the men, 4 ft 9½ in. (146·3 cm.) for the women. This is somewhat below the average for South American Indians.

The cephalic index is 80·79, which puts them just into the brachycephalic (broad-headed) class. They are thus a little

1. Steggerda, 1950, from Eickstedt, 1934.

6

below the mean for South American Indians. The nose is mesorrhine, with a mean nasal index of 82.

The highland Peruvians have been described as of 'dark brown', 'coppery', 'dark olive', or 'olive grey' complexion. The eyes are 'chestnut' or 'maroon', with yellowish sclera. The head hair is black, straight, and abundant, seldom turning grey. As usual with American Indians, the face and body hair are very scant.

The outstanding characteristic of the Indians of the Andean highlands is the large size of the upper torso, doubtless related to the unusual size of the lungs. The shoulders are naturally broad, but the thighs and forearms are reported to be short.

Life in high altitudes such as are found in the altiplano of Peru and Bolivia, where the oxygen atmosphere may be only half or less of that at sea-level, requires profound adaptation and bodily changes on the part of persons accustomed to lower altitudes. This applies equally to foreigners and to Peruvians from the sea-coast. Often several months are needed before the stranger becomes acclimatized, and similar acclimatization is required for those who descend from the highlands to the coast. The altitude also affects procreation, and both humans and animals often remain sterile for a long time after moving to the highlands. Yet the tourist, gasping for breath at the slightest exertion, sees the native boys engaged in vigorous sports just as at home; skiing is enjoyed at an altitude of 17,000 ft (5100 m.), and Peruvian aviators from the highlands can ascend to 24,000 ft (7200 m.) without feeling any ill effects from lack of oxygen masks. The highest recorded habitation is at 17,400 ft (5300 m.).

The highland natives whose ancestors have always lived in that region have developed a body build adapted to the oxygen deficiency. This of course applies especially to the Quechua and Aymara Indians. The torso and the lung capacity are much greater than among low-altitude peoples. Monge speaks of the 'remarkable thoracic development and great extension of the chest', 'the very high total capacity of the lungs', and 'the great size of the altitude lung'.[1]

There are equally great differences in the blood, for the cor-

1. Monge, 1953.

puscles must be able to absorb oxygen quickly. The blood volume is almost two quarts or litres greater, and there are many more red-blood cells and more haemoglobin; the amount of the latter is almost double that of sea-level dwellers. The red-blood count is about eight millions, as compared with five millions for the average white person from low altitudes. Also the heart-rate tends to be markedly slow. Adaptation to this blood pattern is of course what produces acclimatization for the newcomer to the highlands.

Studies on the metabolism of the Indians of Peru indicate that, despite the high altitudes, they have metabolic rates well within the limits of those for North American whites of to-day. This applies equally well for both highland and coast. In this respect they differ from almost all other American Indian groups studied, whose metabolic rates are appreciably higher.

When, only a decade or so ago, the distinction in blood groups O, A, B, and AB was discovered, it was thought that these would afford conclusive data on racial migrations and mixtures; these hopes were not fulfilled when it was found that practically all peoples are mixtures of all four; the differences are in their proportions. More recently another set of types, known as M, MN, and N, independent of the O, A, B, AB grouping, was determined. A few American Indian groups consist of only O type; most of them are mixtures. M is of high, N of low, frequency in America. The frequency of the O group is very high almost everywhere. The Peruvians and Ecuadorians seem to follow this general pattern.

The linguistic condition of pre-imperial Peru will never be known; the languages were never written down and almost all have become extinct. There were doubtless some languages that belonged to independent families, related to no other, and certainly many different related languages and dialects. The Inca made their language the official idiom of their empire, and it was widely spoken as a second language. The Spanish adopted it as a second official and written tongue and ignored the local languages. Most of the latter were gradually displaced by Quechua during the seventeenth and eighteenth centuries; a few survived until the nineteenth, and one, Muchik, was spoken until a few decades ago. Two more in the southern highlands, Uru and Atacameño, will disappear soon; only Aymara and Cauqui, in addition to Quechua, will continue to be spoken for some time.[1]

Quechua, spoken to-day by the majority of Peruvian Indians, is the lineal descendant of the Inca language, and has probably altered but slightly. It is a typical American Indian language, functioning on entirely different grammatical principles from European languages, almost all of which belong to one linguistic family, the Indo-European, and have a very similar grammatical pattern. Like all American Indian languages, Quechua has a much more complex grammar, but one strictly conformable to rules.

A few words have been adopted into English from Inca or Quechua, mainly names of native plants, animals, and features, such as llama, condor, guanaco, puma, chinchilla; coca, quinine, guano, pampa. The term 'jerked' meat comes from Quechua *charqui*, through Spanish. Another interesting adoption is French *lagniappe*, from Spanish *la ñapa*, *la yapa*, from Quechua *yapa*, 'overweight'.

1. Mason, 1950.

PART TWO

THE HISTORY OF PERUVIAN CULTURE

*

THE historical viewpoint of a few generations ago is epitomized by statements of eminent historians and essayists to the effect that history is the record of the lives of a few great men, that there is no history apart from biography. History consisted of reigns, campaigns, dates. Fortunately this attitude is gone, and modern historians pay more attention – though still not enough – to the more vital point of the development of culture, to the progress of the common people.

But even if the older point of view were still regnant, it could not be followed for aboriginal America. It is dependent on written records, which are wanting in this continent. Legends and traditions, written down at the time of the Spanish conquest, give some true historical data on the preceding few centuries, but before that historical personages are unknown; in the essential democracy of native America the individual rarely was of great importance anyway. The little that is known of Peruvian history from such traditions pertains to the later Inca empire, and is to be found elsewhere herein.

Throughout the world, the history of pre-literate times and regions is reconstructed on the basis of archaeological investigations, the interpretation of the data obtained by excavating from the ground the remains and traces of former peoples. These may be graves or tombs dug in the earth, edifices covered over by drifting dirt or by the accumulations of later occupations, or debris left by successive habitation. In the Old World the results of archaeological work may be tied in with, or corroborated or contradicted by, written records for several millennia before the present; in America there is generally no such corroborative material, and the archaeological results supply the only data.

In the last half-century archaeology has developed a true scientific technique. No longer do professional archaeologists merely abstract intriguing objects from the ground or uncover buildings without much thought as to their context. Today the location of every object is marked and its spatial relationship to every other one observed. Excavations proceed downward by thin levels, and the changes in the nature of the objects found in each stratum are noted. The associations of objects in and out of graves are recorded, and so their respective ages and the characteristics of the artefacts of each period are determined. When one of these is found as a trade object in another region the respective chronologies can be tied up. Especially important is the lowly potsherd, often neglected by the amateur archaeologist. Pottery is nearly as indestructible as stone, and the possible variations in technique, shape, and especially in decoration are almost infinite. So the potsherd has naturally become the archaeologist's main and standard criterion of cultural periods, and often has supplied the distinctive names for them.

Chronology and Absolute Dating

Until very recently, all dates for the archaeology of preliterate civilizations were subjective estimates without any accurate basis, and the guesses of equally good authorities often differed greatly; they were based on such features as accumulation of debris or overburden, magnitude of cultural change, and similar factors for which there are no standard criteria. Historical records on the other hand can, after long study and comparison, afford rather accurate results; Egyptologists, for instance, feel quite certain of dates as remote as 2000 B.C. within an error of ten years.

Within the last very few years a more perfect tool for the relatively accurate dating of archaeological remains has been developed by the analysis of radioactive carbon, the isotope Carbon 14. These studies were first begun by W. F. Libby of the University of Chicago in 1946, and now (1966) have progressed so far that the dates of many hundreds of archaeological or glacial-age objects of crucial importance from a chronological point of view have been announced.

It is unnecessary here to go into the details of the study and the process, interesting *per se* as these may be. Carbon 14 is formed in the upper atmosphere by the impact of cosmic ray neutrons on atmospheric nitrogen. Like all unstable radioactive substances it disintegrates at a regular rate, having a half-life of 5730 years.[1] That is to say, half of any given amount of Carbon 14 will disintegrate in 5730 years, half of the remainder in the next 5730 years, and so on until all is gone; thus there is none left in Carboniferous-Age cold. Carbon 14 therefore forms a tiny fraction, less than one millionth, of all organic carbon. Careful investigation has indicated that this carbon isotope exists in this standard tiny percentage everywhere in the atmosphere, and has thus existed at least throughout human history. Since all living organisms, vegetable or animal, constantly ingest carbon from the atmosphere, it follows that they all, throughout their lives, contain the same small fraction of this isotope. At the organism's death it ceases to ingest Carbon 14 to replace that which continues to disintegrate. Obviously, then, a measurement of the radioactivity of any organic substance, wood, peat, bone, shell, cloth, etc., will provide data from which the number of years since its death can be calculated within a known margin of error.[2]

Tests on objects of known absolute or comparative ages have convinced both physicists and archaeologists that properly made tests on suitable organic objects will yield reliable results within a small margin of error. Unfortunately, and as should be quite obvious, there is great danger of contamination from present-day organic materials which, naturally, would greatly affect the results; however, the error is always towards less age. Objects to be tested should be gathered and carried with this specific purpose in mind, and many objects of crucial chronological

1. New (1962) revised calculation.
2. See Broecker, W. S., and J. L. Kulp, 'The Radiocarbon Method of Age Determination', *American Antiquity*, XXII, pp. 1–11, July 1956. Also Aitken, M. J., *Physics and Archaeology*, pp. 88–117. New York and London, 1961.

importance were not so treated. To procure a reliable date, several tests should be made on the same material, and the results should be very close; many of the dates secured up to the present are the results of one test, and often on material exposed to contamination. (A considerable amount of material is needed for the test, and this is destroyed in the process.) Generally, therefore, if a date reached by a radiocarbon test seems entirely unreasonable to the archaeological expert, and out of line with adjacent dates, he may decline to accept it and insist on awaiting the corroborative or contradictory results of other tests.

Eras and Periods

It is coming to be realized that, except for minor deviations, practically all of the great ancient civilizations of the world developed along more or less the same lines.[1] A fortunately situated people, on a hunting-and-gathering plane of economy, developed or adopted agriculture. With the increased and assured food-supply that this brought, they became more sedentary and multiplied greatly. While the food-supply was ample the leisure time between harvest and sowing permitted the development of arts and crafts, social and religious institutions, and other concomitants of culture, which culminated in a relatively peaceful 'Golden Age'. Then pressure of population and the resultant competition for the means of food production resulted in violent conflicts between adjacent groups, and mastery by a few of them. Finally one of the latter, impelled by the lust for power rather than by real need for economic security – although generally offering the latter as an excuse – achieved power control over all others within its sphere, establishing an empire. Names such as 'Formative', 'Florescent', 'Fusion', 'Militarist' have been applied to these developmental periods.

While most historians and archaeologists will agree to the above general outline, when it comes to applying it to specific regions, the sequential phases of culture to be placed in each division, and the specific cultural items employed as criteria for

1. Steward, 1948, 1949a.

such classification, there will be great differences in personal opinion and violent disagreement. Considerable Procrustean bed-fitting must be employed to force local divergences into any general scheme.

Even for a single-culture area such as Peru, no such system of cultural development can be proposed that will fit all regions and satisfy all authorities. Except in the rare instances of sudden change, as by military conquest, the slow development of civilization will not permit the assignment of a definite beginning or an ending to a cultural period. 'Cultural lag' in one region will place a cultural phase later in time than a similar cultural phase in another area; thus in any synchronized developmental scheme there is considerable overlap.

Practically every Peruvianist who has published on the general subject in the last ten years has accepted and used this concept of evolutionary cultural periods, and the differences in opinion regarding the criteria for each and the archaeological and cultural phases composing each are not great, but there is yet no standard terminology. For instance, the Wari-Tiahuanaco period is termed by some 'Expansionist', by others 'Fusion'; the Moche or Mochica period is 'Florescent' or 'Mastercraftsmen'. Some combine the Chimú and Inca periods; some eliminate the Cultist period and consider it a phase of the later 'Formative' or 'Experimenter'.

The developmental and evolutionary scheme must therefore be thought of as little more than a generalized skeleton, but it seems the most cogent method for the simple presentation of an undocumented culture history. It is most strictly applicable to the Peruvian coastal regions, especially the northern and central ones, the best known; its application to the highland cultures, less well known in their earlier phases, is largely presumptive, but not refuted.

The archaeological chronological chart on pages 16-17 is therefore given without any claim to finality. The only certainty about it is that it will be changed in some degree within a very few years, as more excavation is done and especially as more radiocarbon dates are determined. Peruvian archaeological knowledge is in such a dynamic state at present that no two such

Eras	Dates	Periods	Northern Coast	Central Coast	Southern Coast	Northern Highlands
CLIMATIC		Colonial	Spanish	Spanish	Spanish	Spanish
CLIMATIC	A.D. 1532	Imperialist	Inca	Inca	Inca	Inca
CLIMATIC	A.D. 1440	Urbanist	Chimú	Chancay black-on-white	Ica	Late Huama-chuco
CLIMATIC	A.D. 1000	Expansionist	Epigonal	Tiahuanaco 'Epigonal'	Nazca Wari	Wilkawain
FLORESCENT	A.D. 600	Florescent	Moche Late Gallinazo	Interlocking Early Lima	Nazca	Recuay
DEVELOPMENTAL	A.D. 200	Experimental	Early Gallinazo Salinar	Chancay white-on-red	Paracas Necropolis	Huaraz
DEVELOPMENTAL	300 B.C.	Cultist	Cupisnique Late Guañape	Early Ancón, Supe Cerro Sechín	Paracas Cavernas Ocucaje	Chavín Kotosh
DEVELOPMENTAL	850 B.C.	Formative	Early Guañape			Early
INCIPIENT	1250 B.C.	Early Agricultural	Huaca Prieta	Asia		Kotosh
INCIPIENT	4000 B.C.	Pre-agricultural		Lomas		Lauricocha
INCIPIENT	9000 B.C.					

PERIODS IN PERU

Central Highlands	Southern Highlands	Cultural Development (Especially applicable to the North Coast)
Spanish	Spanish	The Spanish under Pizarro conquer the Inca empire; the Colonial Period begins
Inca	Inca	The Incas ride to power, conquer all others, and establish a military empire
Early Inca	Colla	Local autonomy with large population centres were a characteristic feature in some area. Clear-cut regional styles in ceramics
Wari	Decadent Tiahuanaco	Apparently a period starting with conquest and political or social unification, breaking down into one of disruption or decadence
	Tiahuanaco	Handicraft reaches its apogee, as do engineering, architecture, and other social features
Chanapata	Early Tiahuanaco Pucara Chiripa	Many new techniques indicate a very dynamic period
		Cultural progress continues. Certain elements common to almost all regions suggest a widespread religious cult—that of Chavin
		Corn and pottery are introduced. Great technical progress is made in all crafts
		Simple agriculture, combined with fishing, hunting, and wild-plant-food gathering
		Hunting, fishing, and wild-plant-food gathering

charts drawn up by any two Peruvianists would agree in all respects, especially as to period names and dates. Some of them object to any presentation by universal culture periods on the ground that this is fully applicable to only one region, the northern coast, the data on the other regions being not so full. Probably some compromising has had to be done herein, but the data have not been controverted. The greatest difference in opinion concerns the dates.

Some Peruvianists prefer another system, an expansion of the formerly accepted division into Early, Middle, and Late, based on the three 'horizon' pottery styles that imply pan-Peruvian influences. John H. Rowe suggests such a classification, the approximate correlation of which with the system herein employed, with his preferred dates would be:

Late Horizon (Inca)	A.D. 1476–1534	Imperialist Period
Late Intermediate Period	A.D. 1100–1476	Urbanist Period
Middle Horizon (Tiahuanaco)	A.D. 800–1100	Expansionist Period
Early Intermediate Period	A.D. 150–800	Experimental and Florescent Periods
Early Horizon (Chavín)	700 B.C.–A.D. 150	Cultist Period
Initial Period	1400–700 B.C.	Formative Period

Chapter 3

THE INCIPIENT ERA
c. 9000–1250 B.C

THE history of Peru begins, of course, not with Pizarro nor with the first Inca, but with man's – and woman's – first invasion of the soil that was later to become the Republic of Peru. This was, according to the best modern consensus, over ten thousand years ago. He was a hunter of the wild game and a gatherer of the wild produce of land and sea, doubtless a man of simple culture. In physical type he may have differed somewhat from the modern Indian. For over five thousand years the improvement was slow; then he discovered or invented agriculture and life became easier, but it was another thousand years or more before he had mastered that art, the prerequisite of civilization. We therefore divide the Incipient Era into two periods, the Pre-agricultural, and the Early Agricultural.

Peruvianists see four important events in the very early history of Peru and are inclined to date coastal archaeological sites on the basis of their culture in order of increasing age, as pre-pottery (*c.* 1250 B.C.), pre-maize corn (*c.* 1400 B.C.), pre-cotton (*c.* 3000 B.C.), and pre-agriculture (*c.* 4000 B.C.).

Pre-Agricultural Hunting and Gathering Period
c. 9000–4000 B.C

Until a very few years age the history of this long period in Peru was purely hypothetical; no site had been excavated and published. Of course they are not obvious; early man left few imperishable objects around his camps, and the latter had to be changed frequently to follow the game and the ripening wild plant foods. Recently, however, several archaeologists have centred their researches on this topic and a number of very early dwelling sites have been discovered and excavated and a few of them published. Most of these are on the coast, a few in the highlands.

Cultural progress in this long period was slow, and possibly never rose much if at all above that of the present aborigines of Tierra del Fuego. It is quite possible that in those days the highland peoples were in the cultural van, the coastal fishermen backward and peripheral. There is some evidence that at this period the precipitation in the highlands was greater than at present, with a consequent larger amount of vegetation and game.

ORIGINS

The problem of the origin of the Andean peoples and of their high civilizations is of course basically one phase of the question of the origin of the American Indian and of his varied cultures. The American anthropological 'Monroe Doctrine' of a few decades ago, holding that all the ancestors of all aboriginal Americans developed their cultures without any influence from the Old World, is no longer unquestioned; there are too many apparently trans-Pacific cultural resemblances to be explained away. But other alternative or subsidiary hypotheses open up an equal number of problems. Whatever other elements – if any – there may be in the Andean populations, the great bulk of the blood is that of Asiatic Protomongoloids, and the major part of the high culture was developed *in situ* from primitive original elements. This is the standard theory today.

Man did not originate in America. There are not – and never have been – in that continent any of his nearest relatives, the anthropoid apes. No remains of early and primitive human species have been found here, nothing but *Homo sapiens*, and apparently none that could not be duplicated today in some American Indian group. And none has been found of an age anywhere near approaching that of paleolithic man in Europe and Asia, probably nothing older than the latter part of the last glacial period. America was the 'New World' not only to medieval Europe but to mankind.

A detailed discussion of this question need not concern us here. The American Indian physical type is fundamentally similar to the Asiatic and obviously a sub-group of the latter. His ancestors must have emigrated from Asia, and probably via Bering Strait in late glacial times.

The time of this migration to America is not known with any accuracy, but recent radiocarbon dates afford approximate data. Sandals found in a cave in Oregon appear to be about 9000 years old, a relatively short time after that ascribed to the melting of the last great ice-cap in northern Wisconsin, 11,000 years ago, and but little before the occupation of a cave near the southernmost tip of South America, to which an age of 8639 years is ascribed, about 6700 B.C.[1]

Transoceanic migrations to America have always been a favourite creed of those with the will to believe, but until quite recently anathema to all reputable American anthropologists; they still are to many or most. No theory of trans-Atlantic migration – or even of influence – has ever received any consideration from scientists of repute; it is supported by no credible evidence.

However, ignoring the mythical 'Lost Continent of Mu', evidences of trans-Pacific contacts are strong enough to be convincing to many good anthropologists. Their time, extent, route, nature, and effect are still so little known that no cogent, comprehensive picture of them has yet been proposed. But there are many curious and close resemblances in cultural elements between several regions in mainland America and Polynesia, Melanesia, and south-eastern Asia that are difficult to account for on other grounds than historical contact.[2] The evidence seems to indicate voyages across the Pacific at several different times or on several different horizons, some of them surprisingly early, but mostly relatively late, and to and from several different regions.

1. Recent radiocarbon determinations have suggested enormous increases in the age of man in America, such as to more than 38,000 years at Louisville in north-central Texas, and to 29,500 years on Santa Rosa Island, southern California. Unfortunately, the validity of these dates is still under discussion. (Krieger, 1964).

2. Ekholm, 1950, 1964.

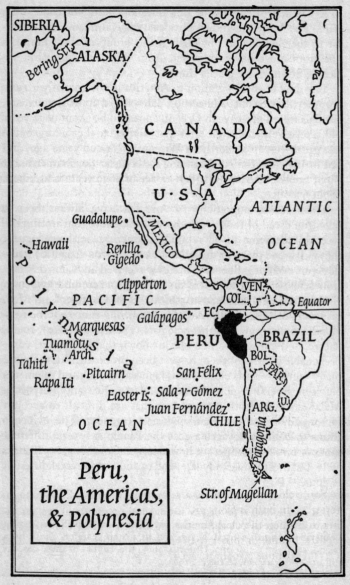

SIBERIA

Bering Str.

ALASKA

CANADA

U·S·A

ATLANTIC

Guadalupe·

MEXICO

OCEAN

·Hawaii

Revilla
·Gigedo·

Clipperton

PACIFIC

VEN.

COL.

Equator

Galápagos''

EC.

·Marquesas

Tuamotus
Arch.

PERU

BRAZIL

BOL.

PAR.

Tahiti

·Pitcairn

San Félix

Rapa Iti

Easter Is.·

Sala-y-Gómez

U.

Juan Fernández·

ARG.

CHILE

OCEAN

Patagonia

Str. of Magellan

POLYNESIA

Peru, the Americas, & Polynesia

In fine, the resemblances between certain cultural features in America and in Polynesia, Melanesia, Indonesia, or south-eastern Asia are too great and too close to be all explained away as parallel developments. It is altogether likely that certain elements of Oriental origin were introduced from time to time over a long period into America, but their effect on the general American cultural pattern was apparently relatively unimportant. Similarly, some American cultural traits may have been carried to Polynesia, Malaya, or south-eastern Asia.

Aboriginal American cultivated cotton has recently been indicated to the satisfaction of botanists to be a hybrid between Asiatic cultivated and American wild cotton. Cotton was present in early agricultural, pre-ceramic horizons of coastal Peru. Carriage by human hands across the Pacific at this early period would appear to be the only explanation. The other agricultural products found in this earliest Peruvian agricultural horizon, beans, and cucurbits (squashes and gourds), are also of widespread occurrence in both the Old and New Worlds.

On the coast of Chile characteristic stone implements have been found which must have come from Easter Island.

The pan-pipes of Peru and of early China show some astonishing similarities, such as use in pairs, connected by string, with alternate notes of the scale on alternate instruments.

In both regions a narcotic is chewed, betel-nut in the Pacific, coca in the Andean region, and the alkaloid is released by mixing the quid with lime. The gourd containers and the lime spatulas are of the same basic forms.

Bark cloth is made of the same or a similar bark by a very cognate process in Polynesia and South America, and the product has a very similar appearance. In both regions feather mosaics were important and had a very like appearance, made by analogous processes.

Some close resemblances are found in weaving. Especially interesting in both regions are the several processes of resist dyeing, by which the cloth, or the yarn from which it is woven, is tightly bound or otherwise protected before dyeing, so that certain portions remain undyed.

The sweet potato, a plant of unquestioned American origin,

was found by the earliest European explorers under cultivation in Polynesia where it was known by the same name as in Peru, *kumara*.

In Nuclear America gold ornaments were cast by a very complicated technique known as the lost wax process, which was also the one employed by European medieval goldsmiths, as well as recently – or today – in India.

One of the most interesting and significant discoveries in the field of transpacific relations is a most recent one.[1] Pottery of an unusual type, unknown elsewhere, was dug up in a small area on the coast of Ecuador. Radiocarbon tests indicated an age of 3000–2500 B.C., which is over a thousand years earlier than Guañape, the oldest known pottery on the Peruvian coast. Moreover it is ceramics of a high quality, sophisticated, not experimental, and much superior to the relatively crude Guañape ware. Also it was associated with a non-agricultural people who lived principally upon shellfish. In shapes, decoration, and other peculiarities, the pottery shows many points of resemblance to Middle Jomon ceramics which was the ware in vogue in Japan in 3000–2000 B.C. The evidence seems convincing to some Peruvian specialists. Apparently, however, this group of shipwrecked Jomon Japanese fishermen had no permanent effect or influence on the culture of the natives of Ecuador.

Whatever cultural influences possible trans-Pacific voyages and migrations may have had, they had little effect on the blood or physical type, which is predominantly Protomongoloid. Anthropologists are pretty well agreed that America was populated by peoples of this type who came via Alaska during a favourable time toward the end of the last glacial period when so much water was tied up in the ice-caps that the sea-level was lowered some three hundred feet, making a broad isthmus at what is now Bering Strait.[2] Despite the great ice-cap elsewhere, the geological evidence is that the region of the Strait and of the Mackenzie River Valley was unglaciated. Gradually the migrants spread south, filtering through Panama and reaching Patagonia

1. Estrada and Meggers, 1961; Meggers, Evans, and Estrada, 1965; Meggers and Evans, 1966.
2. See Sellards, 1952, Wormington, 1949, 1953, and Macgowan, 1950.

after many centuries or several millennia. They were a marginal or peripheral people, hunters, fishermen, and food-gatherers, in a primitive hunting stage of culture, a stone age, with a poorly developed technology.

Recently some archaeologists have suggested, on grounds of their absence at some very ancient sites, that the oldest inhabitants of America had a 'Pre-projectile-point' lithic culture and were unable to make pressure-flaked spearheads.[1] The present evidence for this is weaker in South than in North America.[2]

The oldest traces of man so far found in South America have been in the Andean highlands, the highlands of east Brazil, and in southern Patagonia; none has yet been discovered in the forested region, though it must be remembered that the latter area is still slightly known, and difficult of exploration.

Four discoveries of human remains are of outstanding importance. In 1844 the Danish explorer Lund excavated a number of caves in the Lagoa Santa region in the state of Minas Geraes, Brazil, and secured eight human skulls and other remains, in association with the bones of the great ground sloth and other extinct animals, and in an approximately equal state of fossilization.[3] The skulls are definitely archaic, having the lowest known average cranial index in South America, 71·7, and showing some non-Mongoloid characteristics. In 1933, renewed investigations in this region produced another cranium of similar type, known as the Confins skull, associated with the bones of mastodon, great ground sloth, and horse.[4] This skull had the lowest of all these cranial indices, 69·1. A series of eleven crania from rock shelters near Paltacalo[5] in southern Ecuador have almost exactly the same low cranial index, 71·4, and other archaic characteristics similar to those of Lagoa Santa; though these skulls seem to be only a part of a larger group, the overall average was certainly very dolichocranic. Also, at Punin in Ecuador,[6] a skull showing Australoid-Melanesoid physical characteristics in a much higher

1. Krieger, 1964.   2. Bird, 1965.
3. Lutken, 1884; Ten Kate, 1885.
4. Walter, et al., 1937.
5. Rivet, 1908.
6. Sullivan and Hellman, 1925.

degree than expectable among American Indians was found close to a Quaternary fossiliferous bed in 1923.

We have seen that the Lagoa Santa and Confins remains were found in association with the bones of the extinct great ground sloth, horse, and mastodon. In Palli Aike cave near the Straits of Magellan, Bird found long-headed human skulls and artefacts associated with bones of the sloth and the horse, which latter was extinct in America at the time of Columbus. This cave is given a radiocarbon age of about 8600 years. The one measurable skull is long-headed and somewhat resembles the Lagoa Santa type.[1] The condition of the remains of a mastodon found near Quito in Ecuador suggests that it had served as a meal for men of that time.[2] In 1952, prominent United States archaeologists, invited to the site, witnessed the excavation of a mammoth skeleton in indubitable association with stone projectile points and knives in the Valley of Mexico.[3] However, these evidences of man's contemporaneity with extinct animals are no proof of great antiquity, for all the data indicate that the animals survived in America to a much later time than formerly believed.

And so our primitive aborigines finally reached Peru after their ancestors' long journey from Alaska. They probably lived in small kin groups, knew how to make fire, and flint knives, scrapers, and projectile points by pressure flaking, and how to cut and shape bone into awls and other implements. They hunted with spear and spear-thrower, for it would be many millennia before the bow and arrow would be introduced or invented. The virtual universality of certain traits in America indicates that they believed in supernatural beings and witchcraft, had shamans or medicine men who cured illness by sucking out the pernicious object, and believed in the evil influence of menstruating women, sequestering them, with special emphasis on the pubescent girl. On this primitive basis the American civilizations of Mexico and Peru were built.

For many thousands of years there was no major change in the

1. Bird, 1938.   2. Uhle, 1928.
3. Aveleyra Arroyo de Anda, 1952. A second mammoth was later discovered at this site of Santa Isabel Iztapan. See Aveleyra in *American Antiquity*, vol. 22, pp. 12–28, 1956.

life of the people. They became adapted to their varied environments and developed their various cultures to fit these. Except for elaboration of their social and religious life, some of the more backward living American aborigines never got much further, still remaining in a hunting, fishing, and food-gathering economy.

Agriculture is the basis of all civilization. On a hunting plane there are seasons of plethora and seasons of want. Domiciles often have to be temporary in order to follow the migrating game. The man's time is rather fully occupied in the search for food. A communal pattern of life is almost necessary, for the lucky hunter cannot deny his hungry neighbours food, or his family will starve the next time his luck is bad, so there is no incentive for the industrious man to labour any harder than the lazy one. The farmer, on the other hand, settles on his land, builds his permanent house, plants his tubers and seeds, and then has some leisure time before the crop matures. After harvest is in, he has even more leisure until the next planting season, and this he can spend in intellectual and cultural pursuits, in building temples and taking part in ceremonies, in creative art and all other elements of civilization.

Although most of the great early civilizations, Mesopotamia, Egypt, Mexico, Peru, reached their apogees in arid regions under the influence of irrigation, nevertheless the most ratiocinative of modern agronomists believe that the origins of agriculture must have been in clearings at the edge of wooded regions, especially in temperate mountain valleys.

Some six thousand years ago at a reasonable estimate, some of the American Indians began to plant tubers and seeds around their houses instead of merely gathering them from wild occurrences. The idea is a perfectly natural one that might have presented itself to any people, and possibly it occurred to several independent groups at more or less the same time; on the other hand, the suggestion may have come from across the Pacific. The labour in gathering the crop was much less, and soon the natives found out that by eliminating the weeds, and by cultivation, fertilization, and other agricultural methods the yield could be greatly increased. Soon, too, they realized that some individual plants were more vigorous than others and afforded a better crop;

they began to save and plant the roots and seeds of these superior plants and their quality began to improve. Naturally each group tended to plant first the crops that they were familiar with as native wild food plants, but also adopted those of neighbouring areas, especially if the latter were superior. The best of these soon spread to the limit of their natural environment, and ultimately, by long cultivation and selection and slow evolution, types developed adapted to environments much different from those tolerated by their wild ancestors. Botanists believe that several millennia of such cultivation and selection were required for native American food plants to have developed from their original wild forms to the varieties cultivated at the time of the Conquest.

The three great American food products, corn (maize), beans, and squash, thus eventually spread over the greater part of North and South America, in a great many varieties adapted to various climates. Some botanists believe that the American food plants that are known in only one species, such as corn, sweet potatoes, chilli peppers, peanuts, manioc, and tobacco, had a single centre of domestication, while those that exist in several species, such as squash, beans, tomato, and cotton, were independently developed from different wild ancestors in several different regions – or possibly one of the forms was introduced from abroad. Further, almost every region had its own local plant foods of limited distribution, plants that tolerate only a special environment, or, possibly, ones of rather recent domestication. Most of these are found in Middle America and Peru, the two great and earliest centres of plant domestication.

Maize or corn, which became the great staple food of much of aboriginal America and a great world crop, is generally admitted to be the most domesticated of all plants, without known wild relatives, and incapable of self-propagation. The origin of corn has been hotly disputed for years, and the best agronomists held conflicting opinions. Only a few years ago one of the best of them could write that the original home of maize was a greater puzzle than ever before.[1] Archaeologists had discovered very primitive types of corn, tiny ears with highly developed glumes, pop-

1. Sauer, 1950b.

corns, and pod corns, but not an extreme type of pod corn. Such corn, found in Bat Cave, New Mexico, has been given a radio-carbon age of 5605 years (i.e. 3650 B.C.), with a plus or minus possible error of 290 years.

The situation had been greatly clarified, however, by the recent and sensational discovery of maize pollen in drill cores in the Valley of Mexico from a depth of over 200 ft (over 60 m.). On the basis of currently accepted glacial chronology, this is at least 60,000 years old. The corn must have been a wild variety, the ancestor of modern corn. This discovery has impelled Mangelsdorf[1] to announce the following conclusions as estab-lished: maize is undoubtedly an American plant; its ancestor was wild maize. This was a popcorn, and a form of pod corn, but not the extreme type known today. It had at least one centre of origin in Middle America. Later it hybridized with Tripsacum or teosinte to produce new types.

More than one hundred food plants were cultivated by the American Indian, of which, of course, each region possessed only a part; Peru, with over thirty of them, was probably in the forefront. (See pages 76, 141.) Of these, only very few, such as gourds, cotton, sweet potatoes, possibly plantains, peanuts, and coconuts, have close enough relatives in the Old World to sug-gest importation (and the sweet potato almost certainly was of American origin); the great majority have no foreign congeners, but rather close wild relatives in America.

In the older discarded theories of cultural evolution the pastoral stage was presumed to have preceded the agricultural economic one. However this may hold for the Old World – and even there it is generally discredited today – it does not fit America at all. Only in Peru were there large animals susceptible of domestication, the llama and alpaca, native to the highlands. Whether plants or animals were domesticated first in this high-land region is a moot question, without any present evidence; possibly they were always, as today, contemporary. At any rate, the llama and alpaca have both played a most important part in Peruvian native economy since very early cultural history. The bones of a llama were found in an early agricultural level in the

1. Mangelsdorf, 1954.

Virú Valley; the domesticated animal must have been brought to the coast from his native highlands. However, this was a long time – probably at least a millennium – after the earliest agriculture on the Peruvian coast.

On the Peruvian coast there are evidences of camp sites indicating that men visited that region at least 10,500 years ago[1], but the earliest preagricultural settlements have an age of about 7000 B.C. These were in what is now uninhabitable desert, but precipitation was probably a little greater in earlier days. In certain parts of the central coast the fogs carried enough moisture in the winter to nourish plant life that sprang up in the 'fog meadows' called *lómas*. Due probably to alteration in the Peru Current, the lomas thrived in larger quantity and at lower altitude than at present. Groups of men then came, probably from the highlands, and made their rude winter camps there, gathering seeds and other vegetal foods such as wild potatoes that grew there, and hunting snails, lizards, birds, and occasional deer and guanaco. There was slight dependence on the sea, which was often at some distance. Milling stones were made to grind seeds to flour, but hunting implements are uncommon. It is questionable whether the bottle gourd *lagenaria* was cultivated or gathered wild; certainly nothing else was grown. Pottery and cotton were lacking.

Different camps were made every winter so that cultural development may be traced for 4500 years with slow and slight change. Five periods are distinguished. There was increased reliance on gathering. In the earliest period the flaked tools resembled those at Lauricocha (q.v.). There is no clear evidence of pressure flaking; cobble tools are common.

About 2500–2000 B.C. the lomas dried up, probably owing to some change in the Peru Current, and the dwellers had to leave. They apparently moved to the shore where the sea provided the primary food source, but then they began to raise cotton, and probably beans, squash, and gourds on small garden plots. This horticulture forced them to establish permanent villages and thus to initiate civilization.

1. Lanning, 1963, 1965.

Cave and cliff-shelters have always been more or less permanent residences of primitive hunters, so it is to be expected that the best archeological record of the most ancient human life in Peru would be found in a cave. That of Lauricocha in the northern highlands near Huánuco at 3–4000 metres elevation gave a continuous history from 10,000 years ago to the Colonial period.[1] The lowest stratum, which yielded seven human burials, gave a radiocarbon age of 9525 years or 7566 B.C.; the occupation may be roughly dated at 8000–6000 B.C. The cave dwellers were hunters, subsisting principally on highland deer which they probably killed with spears and spearthrowers. They had a rather crude lithic industry, with many flakes, fewer points and scrapers. Horizon 2, probably about 6000–3000 B.C., shows an improvement in the manufacture of flint tools with excellent pressure flaking. The inhabitants ate fewer deer, but more of the cameloids – llama, vicuña, and guanaco. Horizon 3 is estimated to be about 3000–1000 B.C.; this is presumably in the Early Agricultural period, but no evidence of horticulture was preserved. Like the earlier periods it was preceramic, lacking pottery, and is characterized by implements of bone. Horizon 4 was certainly agricultural as it contains Chavinoid (q.v.) potsherds. Period 5 and last is recent.

A number of preagricultural and preceramic sites are now known from the highlands. The early hunters lived well, if simply; apparently there was ample game for them.

Early Agricultural Period
c. 4000–1250 B.C.

Even a hunting and gathering people is seldom truly nomadic; it has certain preferred places for residence. And seacoast dwellers, near a sea yielding ample quantities of marine food, fish, shellfish, and marine mammals, could build and inhabit large and rather crowded permanent settlements, with their ceremonial centres and personnel. Such were the early villages on the coast of Peru by 4000 B.C. or earlier, at first preceramic and preagricultural.

1. Cardich, 1959, 1960, 1964.

Apparently in the fifth millennium B.C. the people became plant-conscious and began to plant and cultivate seeds and tubers. It is believed by some good agronomists that agriculture in western South America was an influence from the Amazonian forests. The earliest cultivated plants were apparently gourds, with lima beans nearly as early, followed by squash and peanuts. Cotton appeared about 3000 B.C. The cotton and gourds were used primarily for fishing nets. With little doubt, women did the cultivation on small garden plots near swampy places in the river valleys; a family's garden plot might be at some distance from the home.

By the third millennium B.C. plant domestication had reached its maturity, and took a sudden advance with the introduction of maize corn, which apparently reached the Peruvian coast about 1400 B.C. There is no question now that corn originated in Mexico. At first, however, it was merely another plant food.

Our information on the Early Agricultural period comes mainly from the coast since objects of organic materials are so much better preserved there; one important highland site is now well known, however. Actually most of our data come from two sites, Huaca Prieta[1] and Asia,[2] for, although some fifty pre-pottery and pre-maize sites are now known on the Peruvian coast, these two are the most fully reported. While differing considerably in time and details, that at Huaca Prieta at the mouth of the Chicama Valley may be considered typical. It was carefully examined by Junius Bird in 1946, and it affords our best – and a very good – picture of life on the Peru coast in this remote period.

A sample of charcoal taken from the lowest level of the Huaca Prieta mound and resting on bedrock was analysed by the radio-carbon method and ascribed an age of 4298, plus or minus 230, years. This date is acceptable to Dr Bird, who further calculates that the age is probably between 4320 and 4528, the latter being the radiocarbon maximum age. This would mean that the sample dated from between 2370 and 2578 B.C.[3]

At that remote time, conditions at the mouth of the Chicama Valley were probably somewhat different from the present. Probably the river carried more water and there were lagoons

1. Bird, 1948a, 1948b.   2. Engel, 1963.   3. Bird, 1951.

and swamps, more lush vegetation, a larger area available for agriculture, and consequent greater amount of animal life, especially of birds.

The people lived, like the Indians of the eastern coast of the United States, by an economy that included fishing and wild-plant gathering together with simple agriculture. The population, although sparse, was probably about the maximum that could be supported under these conditions. Probably the major part of the dietary consisted of fish caught in nets, as the place was not well adapted to hand-line fishing; the latter practice was known, however, as indicated by the discovery of small fish-hooks of shell or thorn, suitable only for small fresh-water fish. Hunting, either for sea mammals or land animals, played a very minor part in the economy, for no weapons whatever were found, nor any remains of land animals; a few bones of sea lion, porpoise, and sea birds indicate that these were occasionally eaten, if not hunted. Since land game was still hunted in the later Moche period, it could hardly have disappeared; apparently, except for the simple agriculture, the orientation was exclusively toward the sea. The dietary was mainly maritime – fish, mussels, clams, crabs, and even sea-urchins and starfish. It is very interesting that the mussels were of a deep-water variety rarely found in less than fifteen to twenty feet of water, indicating that the men must have been good swimmers.

Wild plants provided additional food in the form of roots of the cattail, tubers of a rush and a sedge, and several native wild fruits.

The agricultural complex of course is of especial interest. Corn or maize, later to become the staple food, is missing, and most of the cultivated plant foods discovered in the excavations are of world-wide occurrence; several varieties of beans, bottle gourds, squash, chilli pepper, achira (canna), and cotton were cultivated. It is not impossible, of course, that some of these grew wild.

The cotton is apparently the 26-chromosome *Gossypium barbadense* variety, believed to be an Asiatic-American hybrid. The beans are of at least three varieties, and the cucurbits, consisting of both *Lagenaria* and *Cucurbita*, are of considerable interest.[1] The

1. Whitaker and Bird, 1949.

33

former is represented by *Lagenaria siceraria*, the bottle gourd, which was used for a number of purposes in addition to – or possibly not including – food, as ladles, containers, and floats for fish-nets. It is practically identical with the bottle gourds found in Polynesia and may have been introduced from there. The cucurbita are *ficifolia* and *moschata*, squashes presumed to be of American origin.

Food was apparently cooked with the aid of small hot stones, possibly by dropping them into containers of water together with the food, as was done by most of the Indians in the United States.

The houses were small, single-room, and semi-subterranean, the walls lined with small boulders or cobblestones. In another Early Agricultural site, where stone was less accessible, they were composed of rectangular adobe bricks. The roofs were made of timbers and whale bones resting on posts. The very oldest graves were merely dug in the ground, but slightly later they were small chambers, lined and capped with small boulders.

The paucity of handicraft found in the excavations illustrates the simplicity of the life. Pottery was absolutely absent as were all ground stone tools, and knives and projectile points made by pressure flaking. The absence of the latter is most surprising, for the technique of pressure flaking is one of great antiquity in the Old World, and the most beautiful pressure-flaked tools ever made in America, the so-called 'Yuma' points of the western United States, are given a radiocarbon age of about 7500 years; the Huaca Prieta artefacts are of paleolithic type.

The only tool made of bone that was found was a small awl, and the sole wooden artefact a paddle-shaped stick, probably used for digging. There were no beads or other ornaments, and only a half-dozen of the thousand of objects found, such as fragments of easily decorated gourds, showed any attempt at ornamentation, and these were very crude; the people obviously were not aesthetically inclined.

'Cloth' was made of pounded bark, a rather surprising feature, for this is an element of the culture of the tropical forest region, not of the Andean. As might be expected, mats and baskets were made of twined rushes and reeds. But probably the most interesting manufactures were the woven cloths, of which about three thousand fragments were found.

Wool was unknown – here, at least – at this time, and practically all the textiles were of cotton, a very few of bast – some local plant fibre. About three-quarters of them were made by twining, a very old process of wide distribution. Netting, looping, and coiling, used in the manufacture of wide-meshed fish-nets and bags, accounted for most of the remainder, but nevertheless there were a number of pieces of true weaving.

The twined cloths may have been made without even a frame, with merely warp strands hanging from a stick. The weft was not continuous; it crossed the warps only once and was then knotted at the selvedge. Designs of birds and serpents were neatly woven in twined fabrics by means of floating warps.

The woven fabrics are obviously examples of very early and primitive weaving. Though a true loom was necessary, it probably had no heddle, the picking of the warps being done entirely by hand. All the cloths are quite small, almost never more than eight inches (20 cm.) in width and about double that in length. Every piece is in some way combined with twining, sometimes twined rows between woven areas, or other variations. Sometimes, as with the twined cloths, the wefts are short yarns that cross the fabric only once. The warps outnumber the wefts so that the cloth is of the 'warp-faced' type, with the warps prominent on the surface. Sometimes short sections of warp were left free or floating on the surface, creating designs. Blue was the only colour found.

The over-all picture of this very early sedentary Peruvian population is therefore that of a simple, peaceful people living in a small cultivable oasis by the sea, fishing, raising a few food crops, living in small, simple, non-masonry houses, and making the objects necessary for their economic and household life, with slight attention to art. The occupation of Huaca Prieta ceased about 1200 B.C.

Naturally, the date for the beginnings of horticulture, when native plants began to be cultivated, is difficult to determine. Cotton was introduced about 3000 B.C. on the coast of Peru, corn about 1400 B.C., and pottery about 1200 B.C., but some habitation sites at Chilca on the southern coast give ages of some 3800 and even *c.* 5000 B.C.[1] and contain evidence of beans of several varieties and gourds; doubtless they were grown there. The site is ordinarily very arid but the neighbouring stream-bed would have permitted floodland farming. Chilca was a village of probably 100 families and 500 population, three kilometers from the sea which supplied the greater part of the dietary in the form of shellfish and crustaceans, fish, marine mammals, turtles, and birds.

The houses were small and of beehive shape, partly sub-terranean, made of cane and thatched with junco grass, sometimes braced with whale ribe; they are the earliest artificial shelters so far found in Peru. The cane and junco grass indicate that there were marshes nearby in occupation days. Utensils and posses-sions – at least those that have survived for more than five millennia – are simple: stone mortars and *manos*, knives and projectile points, implements of bone, shell beads, awls, axes, pins, needles, fish-hooks, spears and lances. Mats and twined bags were made, and gourd dishes. There were hides, wool, and yarn of vicuña.

Another early agricultural village that has been well published[2] is at Asia in the Omas River Valley, about 100 km. south of Lima. Asia is a typical late preceramic occupation site, dated by radio-carbon at 1225 B.C., and presumed to date from just before the introduction of pottery. The inhabitants were fishermen, gatherers, hunters, and farmers. Cotton and beans were found in the lowest occupation level; cucurbits and pepper were also cultivated. Horticulture was probably by flood-farming. Fish were caught with both hooks and nets, shellfish gathered and sea mammals captured. The occupation site was an architectural compound with walls of fieldstone and mud. A rectangular house lay in the centre. Many fabrics and bags of cotton were made, mostly twined, weaving being rare, and with loomed designs.

Doubtless the most ambitious and productive of important results of the expeditions of the past decade has been that of the Japanese[3] archeological investigations and excavations at Kotosh in 1960–62. Kotosh is on the eastern slope of the Andes in the

1. Donnan, 1964.   2. Engel, 1963.   3. Isumi and Sono, 1963.

northern highlands, 5 km. from Huánaco. A large mound that covered – and resulted from – the debris of an old temple was entirely excavated. Few dates are given but possibly 2000 B.C.–A.D. 500 might be a good guess for the occupation period. Six periods are recognized, the first three preceding Chavín and the first two falling within the time of the Early Agricultural period.

In the first period neither pottery nor evidences of agriculture were found and both may have been wanting. The second period gave no evidence of cultivated crops (such are seldom preserved in the highlands) nor of milling stones. However, plenty of potsherds were found. These are of high-grade sophisticated wares, by no means primitive, and of many types, evidently the result of a long developmental period. They most resemble wares from the neighbouring forests to the east, thus strengthening the theory that much of Andean culture came originally from the Amazonian region. The most surprising feature, however, is the radiocarbon date, 3500 years old, or 1850 B.C., making it some 600 years older than the much cruder pottery of the not-so-distant Guañape. Could the influence have taken so long to reach there?

Surprising also is the size and elaboration of the early temple which, although undated, probably is older than 2000 B.C. It predated by centuries edifices of similar complexity in Mesoamerica.

No proof of agriculture was found at Kotosh in the early periods, and no metates or manos, but it is altogether likely that horticulture was practised, since it had been pursued for possibly several thousand years on the coast. Small objects of stone, bone, and clay were well made.

Chapter 4

THE DEVELOPMENTAL ERA

c. 1250 B.C.–A.D. 200

AT least a millennium seems to have elapsed between the later stages of the simple potteryless farmers of Huaca Prieta and the time when Peru practically reached its apogee of culture and most of the techniques had been perfected. This era might properly be termed 'Developmental'.

Almost all our data on this epoch refer to the coastal people, mainly in the north, and the adjacent northern highlands, as it is in these regions that the most intensive archaeological studies have been made, and only towards the end of the era that any contemporary sites from the central and southern highlands are known. This is more likely due to the better state of preservation of coast materials than to any great difference in cultural level.

During this era there was a gradual change – on the coast at least – from a subsistence economy based mainly on sea food to one with the main dependence on agriculture. The population increased slowly but there were no large centres; the village was apparently the political unit. It was a time of early cultural development.

Probably for centuries the two ways of life, maritime and agricultural, competed in the settlements on the coast of Peru. As both methods and yield improved, horticulture instead of maritime products became the primary source of nutrition, acreage increased, and probably the man soon became the farmer. He found the distance too far from his seacoast town home to his country fields, and moved his habitation to his farm. The total population became larger with intensive agriculture, but more dispersed. The large littoral towns were eventually abandoned. Later, with further improvement in horticultural technique, large towns again sprang up, but these were at some distance inland in the river valleys, not on the coast.

Intensive agriculture began with the introduction of maize corn on the coast about 1400 B.C., and received an impetus with the introduction of an improved variety of corn at about the end of the Formative period, 900–800 B.C. For some time fields were watered by floodland farming, but soon extensive irrigation works were constructed. This, naturally, could not be done until responsible governments were established, able to apportion labour and land and compel obedience to decisions.

The era divides naturally into three periods, 'Formative', 'Cultist' and 'Experimental'.

The Formative period begins with the introduction of pottery and ends with the beginnings of Chavín influence which introduce the Cultist period. The Experimental period then takes us up to the time of the great early high cultures.

The Formative Period
c. 1250–850 B.C.

The long-occupied mound at Huaca Prieta in the Chicama Valley, the best-known site of the maizeless, potteryless, early farmers, was abandoned before the culture of its habitants had improved greatly, and the best data for the ensuing period come from excavations in the Virú Valley, a little to the south, where also is found a less-known site of the Early Agricultural Period, Cerro Prieto.[1] The period is also sometimes termed Guañape, from the near-by little fishing village of that name, where sites of this archaeological period were discovered and excavated.

Plain pottery, both black and red, was found in the earliest Guañape levels, but it is believed that the two colours were merely due to inefficient control of firing. While of a poor quality and lacking decoration, the ceramic could hardly be termed experimental, and, while doubtless of local manufacture, it is doubtful if it was a local invention, though this is not impossible. It was, of course, hand-modelled and probably built up by the coiling process. In the later periods other and better pottery types were developed and soon displaced this inferior form.

1. Strong and Evans, 1952.

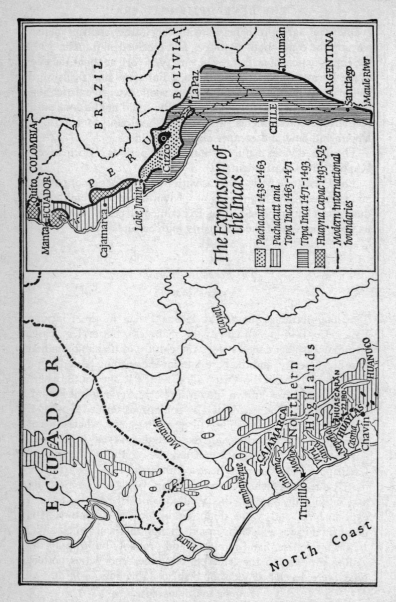

The Expansion of the Incas

Pachacuti 1438–1463
Pachacuti and
Topa Inca 1463–1471
Topa Inca 1471–1493
Huayna Capac 1493–1525
Modern international
boundaries

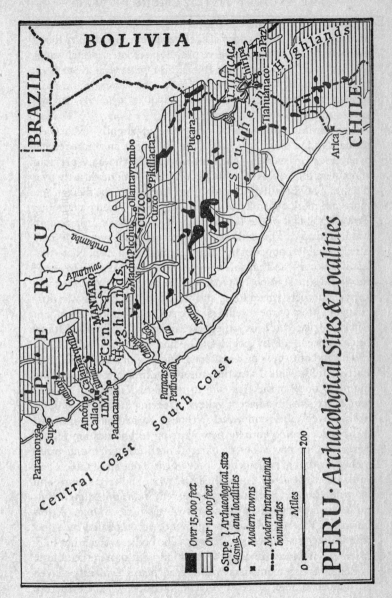

PERU · Archaeological Sites & Localities

Guañape pottery, dated at 1200–1000 B.C., is the first ceramic on the Peruvian coast, and is of such relatively poor quality that it was believed to be the primitive prototype of later coastal wares. Such it may have been, but the earliest pottery at Kotosh (p. 37), six or eight centuries earlier, is of a far superior and more sophisticated type, and it is strange that its example had not spread to the coast much sooner.

The earliest Guañape vessels were apparently exclusively utilitarian and show no decoration. But what an improvement over the gourd vessels that were apparently the only previous containers for liquids! Cooking could now be done directly over the fire. The sea still produced the greater part of the dietary, but more and more dependence was coming to be placed on farming. Toward the end of the last period, about 1400 B.C., maize corn was introduced. This earliest corn was a primitive type with small ears, probably a popcorn but definitely not a pod corn. Nevertheless it was corn, and capable of developing – as it did – into one of the world's most important food plants. But for a long time it was merely another vegetal food, and the life of the people was little changed. Most of the dwellings were still semi-subterranean, but – in some places at least – they were lined with cylindrical adobe bricks instead of by cobblestones and water-worn boulders.

Throughout the long Guañape period, which is divided into Early, Middle, and Late, the culture continued to develop and improve, both at the type site in the Virú Valley and in contemporary sites in adjacent valleys. Weaving improved, and entirely woven fabrics appeared, although twined ones continued to be made; some entirely new weaving techniques are found. Several other new types of objects, both utilitarian and ornamental, weaving implements, stone bowls, bone snuff tablets and snuff tubes, beads of bone, shell and stone, pottery stamps and figurines, and jet mirrors now appeared, indicating quite a cultural advance and a development of aesthetic feeling. A few burials of this period have been found, accompanied by a few simple objects as funerary offerings. The bodies were either fully extended or placed in a seated position with outstretched legs.

Religious ceremonialism with sacred places evidently played an important role, since at Aspero, in Supe, a rude structure which probably served this purpose has been discovered. It consists of one large and two small rooms, connected by doors; the low walls are of natural stones laid in mud plaster and the floors are of clay. A platform occupies the centre of the main room. Here were found llama bones and corn, both probably imported from the highlands. Sacrificed llamas were also found in a rude temple in the Virú Valley.

The Guañape period was a long one. On the basis of radiocarbon analysis, the beginning, with the appearance of the earliest pottery, is calculated to have been about 3200 years ago, that is, about 1250 B.C. The radiocarbon age for the end of the period, with the introduction of the first high-grade ceramics, the beginning of Cupisnique, is about 2800 years, or about 850 B.C. The period, therefore, apparently lasted about 400 years.

Like the Early Agricultural period, the Formative is known mainly from the north coast, the Early Guañape. We still know almost nothing of highland life and culture at this time because of the lack of preservation of organic objects. Presumably animal husbandry and horticulture were both fairly well advanced. However we have seen (p. 37) that at Kotosh three periods preceded the Cultist, and that in the second, about 1850 B.C., excellent pottery was found. The next, of Formative age, about 1000 B.C., has typical Formative-type ceramics, and definite cultivation of corn, uncertain at an earlier date. Apparently the adoption of the bow and the sling both postdate that of pottery.

The Cultist Period

c. 850–300 B.C.

The so-called Cultist period brought a great and rather sudden cultural advance. By some Peruvianists it is counted as beginning with the introduction of pottery and maize, and therefore including the transitional Guañape period with its rather crude ceramics. But the era truly begins with the highly developed and characteristic Chavín de Huántar horizon style, and with its aspect on the northern coast, the Cupisnique; it is so regarded herein.

The Chavín was the first of several 'horizon styles' that, at widely separated periods, were of the greatest importance in Peru and had very widespread influence. The other later ones, the Wari-Tiahuanaco and the Inca, were pan-Peruvian, affecting all parts of the land and, at least as far as the Inca were concerned, spread by population movements. The Chavín influence never reached the southern highlands and was very attenuated in the central highlands and the southern coast. It was primarily an art style, probably spread by the vogue of a new religious cult.

While the Wari-Tiahuanaco and Inca periods have always been accepted as major epochs in Peruvian archaeology, the Chavín period and its importance have been recognized only within the last forty years, mainly owing to the researches and concepts of the great dean of Peruvianists, the late Dr Julio C. Tello.[1] Wherever found stratigraphically, Chavín underlies the remains of all others of the higher cultural periods.

Chavín takes its name from the site of Chavín de Huántar in the northern highlands on the east side of the continental divide on a small tributary of the Marañon River, just across the divide from the Callejón de Huaylas. It is not a large site, and Peruvianists believe that it was only one of several ceremonial centres of the Chavín cult. But at any rate it is the most important of the few known typical sites, and the largest one on which detailed reports exist. However, nothing but very superficial excavations have yet been made there.

The land available for agriculture in the small valley surrounding Chavín is limited and could never have supported a large population; it was not the centre of a populous district. Nevertheless, a considerable body of men must have been occupied for a long time in its construction. Although it contains many rooms, they were not well suited for habitation, and the buildings were almost certainly not residential; they may well be compared with the stone buildings of the Maya of Middle America, composing a ceremonial centre.

The complex covers a considerable area.[2] For a space of over eight hundred feet (250 m.) square, the surface is completely landscaped, with a sunken court, raised platforms, terraces, plazas, and stone edifices, oriented to the cardinal points, prin-

1. Tello, 1929, 1943.　　　2. Bennett, 1944.

cipally east-west. Though there are a number of buildings, one, known as the Castle (*Castillo*), far exceeds the others in size and importance. Fortunately it is – or until recently was – rather well preserved, for it is unique – much the largest of the few known similar structures of this ancient period. In this highland region old buildings were neither torn apart by lush tropical vegetation as were the Maya structures, nor covered with drifting sands as in the Near East.

For one of the earliest-known large stone edifices in Peru, the Castillo is remarkably advanced architecture, and there can be no question that a long period of architectural development in masonry lay behind it somewhere. The plan is complex and it must have been built from the first stone with the finished structure in mind, if not according to a drawn plan or a model. It consists of three floors – more than were built at any later period in Peru – all of dry stone masonry. The building even contains a system of ventilating shafts, both vertical and horizontal, so efficient that it is said they still provide fresh air for the interior rooms – surely the work of no amateur masons. However, the walls are massive and thick, faced with selected split stones, and filled with rubble. The outer walls are faced with large rectangular dressed stones laid in courses of various widths, alternately thick and thin.

The Castillo is an immense complex building, large and square, about 245 by 235 ft (75 by 72 m.). It is still about 45 ft (13 m.) high at one corner. The outer walls are slightly battered, i.e. slope inwards towards the top, where also they are set slightly back in several narrow terraces. Originally there was a row of large projecting carved heads, inserted in the walls by means of tenons, which encircled the building below a decorated cornice; a few of these heads still remain. The interior consists of a maze of walls, galleries, rooms, stairs, ramps, and ventilating shafts on three floors. The rooms and galleries are rather low, about six feet (1·8 m.) high, the galleries only about a yard or metre wide, the rooms from about six to sixteen feet (2–4·5 m.). There are no external windows or doorways except for the main entrance to the first floor, reached by a stairway of admirably cut rectangular blocks (Plate 1A).

Figure 1. *Drawing of the Raimundi Chavín sculptured stone monument*

46

The edifice is massive as well as immense; the rooms and galleries are of less cubic area than the walls and other masonry. They are dark, without any lighting. Great broad slabs form the ceiling of the room below and the floor of that above, and the roof slabs are covered with earth which formed the foundation for several small rectangular masonry houses that were built upon them. In one of the galleries a large, tall vertical carved stone known as the Lanzón was discovered (Plate 36).

The status of archaeology in Peru and the immense amount of work that remains to be done there may be judged from the fact that this great, significant, and almost unique edifice has never been carefully studied. No detailed plan exists; in fact many of the rooms and galleries have never been entered, for many – or most – of them have never been cleared of the stones and debris with which they were apparently filled in ancient unrecorded times. Sad to report, such studies may now have become impossible or prohibitively expensive, since the structures were largely covered by a great landslide only a few years ago, in 1945.[1]

Though overshadowed by the Castillo, the Chavín de Huántar complex consists of many more features such as plazas, platforms, terraces, and mounds. The mounds, and apparently also the platforms, seem, like the Castillo, to be masonry constructions, honeycombed by galleries.

Chavín influence extended quite a distance to the north, since several little-known sites, such as Kuntur Wasi and Pacopampa in the Department of Cajamarca, show rather definite Chavín characteristics in architecture and sculpture.

Kotosh in the northern highlands is the archaeological site most often compared with Chavín. It is much older (p. 37), with three periods before the one equated in time with Chavín. This period (Kotosh-Chavín) contains 'typical classic Chavín pottery of superb quality'. This ceramic had a short vogue, appearing and disappearing suddenly. As in all highland sites, data on agriculture are difficult to secure, but some metates and manos were found, and other evidences of corn cultivation. In the later post-Formative periods good work in metallurgy, principally in copper, is

1. It is now (1956) being cleared by the national Dirección de Arqueología.

47

found, good textiles and pottery vessels. The masonry and sculpture, however, cannot compare with those of Chavín de Huántar.

However, the Chavín horizon is best known in its manifestations on the northern coast where sites and cemeteries of the period have been excavated, affording better data on the life of this time than can be secured at the highland sites. The phase best known is that of the Cupisnique graves in the Chicama Valley, but edifices and graves in the Casma, Nepeña, Virú, and Lambayeque Valleys, the debris in the lower levels in shell-heaps at Ancón and Supe,[1] and certain other sites from Piura to Lima show Chavín traits. Chavín influence also seems to be present at the earliest known sites on the southern coast, those of Paracas Cavernas and Ocucaje,[2] showing the widespread ramifications of this culture. The resemblance is seen in the ceramics, in shape, decorative technique, and motifs. Some Chavinist enthusiasts see these influences extending to Ecuador, Bolivia (Tiahuanaco), Argentina (Barreales), and northern Chile (Pichalo), but these are not accepted by the best authorities. In some places, such as Cerro Blanco and Punkurí in the Nepeña Valley, and Moxeke and Pallca in Casma Valley, the resemblances are seen in masonry temples or terraced pyramids; in the others they are recognized in the pottery and other grave furniture.

The coastal Chavinoid architectural sites were recently discovered and are not well known. None has been well excavated or described, and of most of them little is known. Several, especially Cerro Blanco in the Nepeña Valley, have mud-covered walls painted with Chavinoid designs in several colours.

A very important site which has been the cause of much dispute among archaeologists is Cerro Sechín in the Casma Valley. The unusual and striking feature is a line of erect, large, flat, unshaped stone slabs carved with large human figures and human heads in outline or low relief. The poses are rather dynamic and naturalistic, and they have been compared with the 'dancing' figures at Monte Alban, Mexico. The art, however, is very different from the Chavín-Cupisnique style. Though ap-

1. Willey and Corbett, 1954.   2. Kroeber, 1953.

parently on the Chavín horizon – probably, in fact, a little earlier – Cerro Sechín seems to be a sub-culture *sui generis*, like nothing else yet known.

The Southern coast boasts of no great masonry or adobe structures to attract attention. The stupendous masonry ruins of the Peruvian highlands and the immense adobe pyramids of the north coast have always been famous, but the ancient civilizations of the south coast, in the valleys of Pisco, Ica, and Nazca, without any impressive structures, were almost unknown until the present century. The cemeteries of the Nazca period with their extraordinary polychrome pottery were discovered by Max Uhle in 1901, those of Paracas with their even more splendid textiles by Julio C. Tello in 1925. In this region it can almost truly be said that it never rains, and the objects buried with the dead in the desert sands are incredibly well preserved. All surface indications of these cemeteries have long since been covered or erased by the drifting sands, and they are found today only by the spade of the archaeologist or the probe of the native treasure-hunter.

The Paracas Peninsula, lying about eleven miles (18 km.) south of the port of Pisco, is the seaward extension of a line of low sandy hills known as Cerro Colorado. The red sand is absolutely bare of all vegetation, not a leaf, not a living thing; no stream enters the ocean near by. The nearest human habitation is several miles away where wells tap underground water and a few sedges line the beach. It is the epitome of loneliness and desolation. Yet beneath these sands are found the desiccated bodies of a people unknown to history, together with some of the most magnificent cloths that the world has ever seen. Today their bones lie scattered on the surface, and the winds alternately cover and uncover fragments of the coarser fabrics, discarded by the diggers, still soft and strong after nearly two millennia. For the 'mummies' have been removed from the discovered cemeteries, and either carefully preserved by archaeologists, or rifled and only the presumably saleable goods kept by native *huaqueros*.

Two types of burials, known as Paracas Cavernas, and Paracas Necropolis,[1] were found in this region by Julio C. Tello

1. Carrion Cachot, 1949.

between 1925 and 1930. They differ greatly in nature and in contents, Cavernas being characterized by a remarkable type of polychrome incised pottery and textiles of average quality, Necropolis by magnificent cloths and simple unpainted pottery. The former shows some Chavín elements; the latter is obviously related to the Nazca culture, demonstrably later by stratigraphic proof. The great diversity of Paracas Cavernas pottery shapes, the occasional use of negative-painted designs, and the post-fired painting strongly suggest a dynamic experimental stage rather than a static standardized one. Cavernas has therefore always been considered the older and has been assigned to the Cultist period, Necropolis to the Experimental.

Paracas Cavernas was so named because the bodies are found in communal bottle-shape chambers excavated in the rock at the foot of vertical shafts, at a depth of approximately twenty feet (6 or 7 m.). Many of the tombs also have a stone-lined upper chamber at the surface. As many as fifty-five bodies were found in one of these sepulchres, of both sexes and all ages. The heads were artificially deformed, and a large proportion of them had been trephined. The bodies were wrapped in coarse cotton cloths and accompanied by mortuary offerings. It has been suggested that the tombs might have been family vaults. The considerable variation in the quality and quantity of the grave goods placed with the dead suggests a similar difference in economic conditions during life.

Paracas Cavernas pottery is of superior type and very distinctive; good collections and even single vessels are rare outside of Peru. A Chavín-Cupisnique influence is noticeable; incised lines delimit the designs and the coloured areas, and the feline motif with characteristic elements is common.[1] The pastel colours are, however, rich and polychrome, red, green, yellow, and dark brown; the polychrome pottery set the pattern that was further accentuated in the later Nazca period. The pigments are thick, glossy, and resinous, like a mastic. They were applied after firing and are disintegrated by damp earth. The majority of the decorative designs are highly conventionalized and stylized biomorphic, producing a distinctive art of high quality.

1. Kroeber, 1953.

The variation in form is very great and there cannot be said to be any standard or predominating forms. Simple-silhouette vessels such as bowls and ollas are probably most common, and double-spouted vessels with bridge handle are frequent, though not the stirrup-spout. There are a number of effigy forms, but these are not so realistic as those of Moche or Salinar. Unique are double-bottom bowls with a rattling pellet between.

The textiles are well made but far inferior to those of the neighbouring Paracas Necropolis. The gauzes are especially outstanding. As would be expected for an early culture, the single-element techniques such as netting, knotting, knitting, twining, and plaiting are especially prominent, though brocade, weft-patterns, embroidery, and painted cloth were made. Cotton, wool, fibre, and human hair were used in weaving.

The fabrics found at Paracas Cavernas indicate that the costume was of the usual coast pattern, including loincloths, waist-bands, shirts, shawls, turbans, head-bands, and bags with straps. Doubtless more and heavier clothing was worn in the highlands. The people made and used baskets and mats. Bone flutes and clay pan-pipes are preserved, but it is likely that the latter were funerary replicas of the more common pipes of reeds. Among the most characteristic objects of the culture are gourds decorated with pyrographic burnt designs. The craftsmen knew how to make ornaments of thin gold but silver was apparently not yet known, though objects of pure copper have been found.

The type site of Paracas Cavernas is the only one so far found of its nature, and the peculiar shape of the graves was doubtless due to the local conditions, a hard surface stratum overlying softer rock. Graves containing pottery of similar type, and obviously of similar culture, are found fifty to eighty miles further south at Ocucaje and several other sites in the Ica Valley, but these are rectangular tombs in the sand. The bodies were obviously brought to Paracas for interment either because the sites had some sacred importance or on account of the preservatory aridity of the regions which, lacking water, are unsuited for human habitation. It may have been the local custom to carry the dead to seaside cemeteries.

The nature of the Chavín horizon has long been a mooted

point. The native Peruvianists have thought of it as a cultural entity, possibly even a pre-Incaic empire, at any rate a 'civilization'. Tello, its principal protagonist, thought that it was brought to the coast by a migration from the Andes, and that it originated in the Amazon region. Larco Hoyle believes that it began with the Cupisnique people on the northern coast and was carried by them to Chavín de Huántar and other highland parts. The opinion of United States Peruvianists, as formulated in a masterly paper by Gordon Willey,[1] is that it was not a homogeneous culture, but the expression of a widespread and rapidly diffused religious cult.

While these sites on the Chavín horizon show a basic cultural similarity, they differ considerably in detail, more than would be expected of a homogeneous culture. The common possession, the determinant feature of Chavín, is a similar art style. This emphasizes a feline – jaguar or puma – treated in a characteristic stylistic manner. It is, epitomized by Willey, 'a matter of line, of composition, of emphasis. It is the curvilinear forms, the massive heads, the intricately disposed small heads, the locked and curved fangs, the claw feet, the prominent nostrils, and the eccentric eyes.'

Presumably this feline being was a deity whose cult, with its characteristic stylized representation, spread over the region of Chavín influence. Apparently it carried with it no technological concomitants, and almost certainly was carried by no proselytizing crusaders, at any rate by no vanquishing ones. The Chavín *tradition*, however, persisted almost throughout all of Peruvian history; the feline element in art – and probably in religion – was a strong feature in both the Nazca and Moche regions and periods, in the Wari-Tiahuanaco pan-Peruvian horizon, and even later.

The radiocarbon date for the beginning of the Cupisnique period is 848 B.C. with a plus or minus error of 167 years. The ending lacks a definite radiocarbon test and two equally respected Peruvianists estimate it as 500 and as 100 B.C.; a mean of 300 B.C. is here accepted.

Although the earliest, the Chavín is generally regarded as the

1. Willey, 1951b.

greatest art style evolved in Peru. It is unfortunate that examples are not many and known to few but Peruvianists. It is seen to best effect in the stone carvings, either in the round or in relief. The figures are mainly feline, human, and monstrous or demoniacal, though the condor, snake, and some other animals are depicted. Far from being naturalistic and pictorial, the art is decidedly stylized, conventionalized, and symbolical. The effect is massive and strong, and sometimes even dreadful. The lines are almost always curvilinear. Many of the details on the figures are extraneous from a naturalistic point of view, and evidently symbolical (Plate 37A). Considerable resemblance to the art of the Olmec of south-eastern Mexico has been pointed out.

Our picture of life on the Chavín horizon is afforded by excavations and grave contents in sites of this period on the northern coast; needless to say it must have differed considerably in detail – though probably not greatly in general nature or quality – in the ecologically different highland region. There were also considerable differences between the cultures of the various sites of the Chavín period, and between the temporal subdivisions of this horizon, though on a rather uniform basis. Future researches will differentiate and characterize these subdivisions.

Agriculture had improved immeasurably and now was the main source of food supply; fishing, hunting, and wild-food gathering were of less importance. About 900–800 B.C. an improved variety of corn had been introduced to assume its place as the staple food, and the beans and gourds of the earlier population were now relegated to minor roles. With the superior corn came also warty squashes, avocados, and manioc or yucca. And, of even more importance, with these improved agricultural conditions came the post-harvest leisure time that horticulture affords, time in which to develop and improve technology, art, and the higher aspects of culture. Sea food, however, continued to be of importance here – as it is yet – as evidenced by the large shell-heaps and middens containing refuse of this period, middens, by the way, from which come many of the archaeological objects that afford us the data for reconstruction of the life.

Some llamas had been brought down from the highlands, but their herding probably had not yet become an important element of native life. The dog may have been introduced at this time, but it is not certain; strange to say, there is no evidence of his presence in this region at any earlier period.

The locations of the habitation sites of this period on the edges of the fertile areas at the mouths of the rivers imply that agricultural engineering was still in an incipient stage. Irrigation and drainage were primitive, and doubtless much of the watered land was swampy or overgrown with brush or weeds. The cultivable area was not great, nor was the population.

The houses of the people were apparently small, one-room, rectangular structures with thatched gable roofs. It is doubtful whether they were grouped in the settlements according to any plan with regular streets. They stood on raised stone-faced platforms, but the walls were generally of mud, made into conical adobe (sun-dried) bricks. These were laid with the flat end to the outer surface, the interstices filled with mud, and a smooth mud plaster given to the wall faces. In some places the walls were apparently made of stone, probably where suitable stone was easily available.

Religion had obviously reached an advanced, formalized stage, for the larger and more elaborate buildings were presumably temples. While conical adobes were much used in the construction of these, stone masonry is also common, the stones being set in a kind of mortar. These temples are well planned and built, quite large, with numerous rooms, platforms, and steps. The smooth plastered walls are adorned with frescoes in polychrome, or decorated with clay relief or incised designs.

The religious aspect is also present in the treatment of the dead. The Peruvian pattern that prevailed from earliest to latest agricultural times was followed. The dead were interred in the arid desert in relatively deep graves, and provided with mortuary offerings, presumably for their use in the after-world; at Cupisnique these included jewellery and other ornaments, and pottery vessels containing food and drink. Coastal graves were almost always deep in Peru, because the desert sands were easily excavated and because the people wished to place their dead below the reach of dampness from the occasional rains. The Cupisnique graves, however, were relatively shallow. The dead were interred, probably in their best clothing and with their favourite ornaments, in horizontal position, the limbs generally flexed. Most commonly the bones were covered with a red powder or pigment, probably cinnabar, a practice that is found sporadically in America from here to Maine and which suggests that the burials were secondary, i.e. that the bodies were not placed in their final graves until the flesh had decayed. The Cupisnique graves lay at depths from $2\frac{1}{2}$ to 6 ft (80 c. to 2 m.), and neither the graves nor the bodies seem to have been oriented to any particular direction. Much of the grave furniture was ornamented with theistic symbols, especially the ubiquitous Chavín feline. However, the Cupisnique graves seem not to be typical of the period. Those in other coastal sites of the Chavín horizon contain little grave furniture and few pottery vessels, and little or no food placed in them. Owing to their comparatively great age and to the greater amount of precipitation in this northern coastal region, textiles and other objects made of perishable organic substances are rarely preserved. However, the middens at Ancón and Supe preserve such perishable objects as nets, bags, baskets, mats, gourds, and textile clothing of the Chavín horizon.

The Cupisnique, and probably all other men of the northern coast on this horizon, apparently ordinarily wore nothing but a loincloth and cap; the attire of the women is not known. Bone ear-ornaments and finger rings, bracelets, wristlets, crowns, and necklaces of stone beads were worn by one or the other or by both sexes, as well as feather headdresses and capes. Stamps found in the graves suggest that the body was decorated with paint. As frequently in later periods in Peru, skull deformation was a common practice.

The potters of the Chavín horizon had reached a high plane both as craftsmen and as artists, but the industry was still too new to have achieved technical excellence. Naturally each region or site had its specific types, and within these the fashions varied from generation to generation. From the type site of

Chavín only potsherds are known, but they are of technically good quality. They represent simple shapes, mainly open bowls with thickened rims, but vessels with stirrup spouts, so characteristic of the coast, seem to be lacking. The ware is polished red, black, or brown, or combinations of them. Decoration is mainly by incised lines, with a little low relief and modelling but no true painting. Very similar potsherds have been found in the lowest levels at the shell-heaps of Ancón and Supe.

The best-known ceramic of this period is that from the Cupisnique graves of the Chicama Valley; it bears but slight resemblance to the pottery of Chavín. These vessels are, of course, mortuary furniture, the utilitarian ware being less attractive. Cupisnique pottery was not discovered until 1939, and is poorly represented in all museums outside of Peru. Although giving an impression of technical mastery, it both looks and is heavy, with thick walls. The control of the firing had not been perfected and the vessels were baked at a low temperature with a reducing atmosphere so that the surface is black, brown, or red. Toward the end of the period a few vessels of lighter colour appear. The most common shape, at any rate among the mortuary furniture, is the stirrup-spouted jar, a form that is very characteristic of Peru and which retained its vogue in the northern coastal region throughout Peruvian history (Plate 23). Two curving tubes rise from the quasi-spherical body of the vessel and coalesce into one vertical tubular spout, thus serving as a handle. The body of the vessel is altered into effigy shape or decorated.

Since dark surfaces do not lend themselves to painted decoration it is not surprising that there is little of the latter in Cupisnique ceramics. However, the beginnings of painting are seen in the occasional colouring of the designs enclosed within incised lines.

Some Cupisnique pottery vessels are said to bear impressions of moulds or even to be entirely mould-made, a process that became common in the later Moche[1] period. Quantity production

---

1. American Peruvianists prefer the new term 'Moche' to the old standard 'Mochica'. We do not know if they spoke Mochica, the language in use here in Colonial days, but we do know that they erected the structures at Moche.

at such an early cultural stage would not be expected and would indicate a surprisingly rapid advance in technique.

The decorations are on the whole simple, generally curvilinear geometric, but the feline, the determinant art element of the horizon, is frequent. Effigy vessels were modelled or moulded in the form of animals, plants, human beings, and even houses. A human portrait jar and a nursing mother are outstanding individual pieces.

In the Cupisnique graves only enough textiles have been preserved to assure us that weaving was practised, but better-preserved examples found elsewhere show that, while by no means all techniques later found were known, the art had progressed greatly over the simple fabrics of Huaca Prieta. The use of the heddle is indicated. Tapestry and embroidery were made, as well as plain weaves, a lace-like gauze, and gingham, all embellished with fringes and tassels. All seem to have been of cotton.

Although no metal objects of the Chavín period have been excavated under controlled conditions, three groups of gold ornaments are known which, judging from their art style and other circumstances, are ascribed to this horizon.[1] Two of these came from graves at Chongoyape; the provenance of the third is unknown. One of these groups apparently consisted of a man's, another of a woman's ornaments. They are probably the oldest known examples of metallurgy in America. Some are of pure gold, one is seventy-four per cent silver, and the others consist of a large proportion of gold, a small proportion of silver, and a little copper; the three metals were probably not intentionally mixed. Most of them were made of thin hammered gold, for casting, later the principal metallurgical technique, had apparently not yet been invented. The techniques employed, however, demonstrate the rapid advance of the goldsmith's art, for they include hammering, embossing, annealing, welding, soldering, strap joining, incising, champlevé, cut-out designs, and the manufacture of bimetallic objects. One pin has a gold head and a silver shaft.

For all that we know to the contrary, metallurgy and all the

1. Lothrop, 1941, 1951a.

57

above goldsmithing techniques may have been invented in this northern coastal Peruvian region – or they may have been introduced from we know not where. The discovery that gold and silver nuggets are soft and can be cold-hammered into thin plates must have been the first discovery; the various methods of decorating these sheets followed quickly. Later the use of heat was discovered, and metallurgy was on its way to the heights of technique and art that it later attained.

The Chavín-horizon gold ornaments are really dainty and exquisite and include a large range of objects, pendants of many different types, tweezers, staff-heads, crowns, ear and nose ornaments, cuffs, pins, plaques and disks, gorgets, ear-spools, spoons, and beads. Some human or animal figures in the round are naturalistic, but the more common repoussé ornamentation is either geometric or very conventionalized naturalistic, including elements that are typical of Chavín stone carving, especially the feline motif. Strange to say, much of the gold was painted with coloured pigments.

The Cultist-horizon peoples were also master artisans in minor media such as semi-precious stones, bone, shell, and wood. Beads, pendants, rings, combs, and similar ornaments were made of turquoise, quartz, lapiz lazuli, and other hard stones – a protracted task for a people without metal implements – as well as of bone and shell. Pyrite and jet provided materials for polished mirrors.

Among the utilitarian objects made on this horizon may be mentioned hammer-stones, club-heads, grooved stones, projectile points, mortars, pestles, bowls and boxes of stone, awls, spatulas, needles, daggers, spoons, and spear-throwers of bone or wood (or both), nets and netted bags, twined baskets, mats of *totora* reed, carved gourd containers, and clubs and boxes of wood. An object of *chonta* palm wood, found at Ancón and claimed to be a bow, is of considerable interest as showing the possible use of this weapon at this early period; in the United States its first appearance seems to have been at a much later time. Nevertheless, the Cultist hunter and warrior certainly relied much more on the spear and spear-thrower.

Large sculpture in stone was an important culture element in the highlands but unknown on the coast, except at the site of Cerro Sechín which, as we have seen, is rather a cultural anomaly, possibly of an earlier period.

The over-all picture of life on the Cultist level, the earliest Peruvian culture that could be considered a civilization, as illustrated on the north Peruvian coast, the only region from which we have sufficient data, is that of a simple sedentary people whose activities were still devoted mainly to acquiring the means of existence, food, and shelter. Nevertheless, the leisure time afforded through their main dependence on agriculture permitted the community erection of temples and other religious structures. A religious cult in which a feline deity, puma or jaguar, played the most prominent role was the common element, for otherwise the small villages apparently had no political bond, and the local cultural variations from valley to valley were considerable. Both trade and warfare were apparently of little importance. The small settlements were probably based mainly on blood relationship. Ancestor-worship and the cult of the dead had apparently hardly begun the vogue that they later reached in Peru.

It has been suggested that such great structures as Chavín de Huántar were shrines to which pilgrimages were made from a large surrounding region, and centres in which the entire population gathered on definite occasions for ceremonial celebrations and for markets. This is a Peruvian – and a nuclear American – cultural pattern of long standing, as exemplified, for instance, by the great pan-Peruvian shrine at Pachacamac, and today by the great annual *romería* at Copacabana, Bolivia. It was probably at these times that the assembled multitudes built – or at least assembled the great amount of materials necessary for – the immense structures and edifices. A small number of trained architects and masons could then work during the long intervening periods, while the great body of the people, returning to their villages, disseminated the new cultural developments – together with the gossip – that they had learned during their pilgrimage.

The Experimental Period

c. 300 B.C.–A.D. 200

The term 'Experimental' aptly characterizes the period between the 'Cultist' (Chavín-Cupisnique) and the 'Florescent' periods. It was a time of development, of improvement, of invention. In fact, the Experimental might be considered the earlier, incipient, developmental phase of the full-blown Florescent which, without any sudden break, followed it. As is inevitable in such cases, it is a question of personal opinion as to when the first ended and the second began, and whether a transitional phase should be placed in one or in the other.

Cultures on the Experimental horizon are found in almost all parts of Peru, being the earliest known in some regions, though certainly not actually the first. However, as in the earlier periods, almost all our data come from the coastal peoples. No outstanding civilization, culture, art, or technique characterizes the period, and the local phases are little known and of interest to few but archaeologists. The period lacked any over-all unity.

It must constantly be kept in mind that all these peoples and cultures of early Peru are unknown to history. Archaeologists separate the main periods and give designating terms to them, generally the modern name of the region with some temporally qualifying adjective, but we do not know what name the people applied to themselves or what their neighbours called them, what language they spoke, what their gods and chiefs were named, what inventions they contributed to mankind or what evils they perpetrated on their neighbours. For there are no written records and no traditions.

The Cultist art with its emphasis on the Chavín feline, the one unifying bond of that period, suddenly disappeared, and with it all traces of former cultural homogeneity. Probably the religious cult waned, and possibly former unifying pilgrimages were abandoned. Apparently the people became more locally minded, and each valley began to develop the local characteristics that it had begun in the Cultist period. All, however, were on practically the same cultural plane, with many common elements. Among these were two horizon styles of pottery decoration, traits that must have spread from centres. For the greater part of the period the characteristic pottery decoration of most regions was of designs painted in white on a red surface, and this has been employed as a term for this sub-period in several of the areas: 'Chancay White-on-Red' on the central coast, and 'Huaraz White-on-Red' in the northern highlands; the white-on-red style is also found on the northern coast, where it is known as Salinar. Towards the end of the period negative-painted pottery appeared in these three regions, as well as on the southern coast.

White-on-red ware is unattractive. The shapes are simple, bowls and cups with flaring sides and rims, and bottle shapes being the commonest forms. There are few effigies and no stirrup-spouts, though double spouts are found. The decoration is usually of simple rectilinear geometric designs with rather thick straight lines, parallel, hatched, or cross-hatched, dots, and circles; pictorial designs are missing, and incising and modelling rare. In a variant type of this ware either the entire vessel or large zones of it are painted white.

Although the break between the Cultist and the Experimental periods is a rather sharp one, it was apparently cultural rather than political in nature. In only one place the Cultist tradition apparently lasted into and through this period, for the Chavín feline appears again in the Moche art of the following Florescent period, though practically missing in the intervening Salinar culture of the Moche region. A very few unusual and untypical designs on Salinar bone spatulas are the only Experimental period objects that betray any Chavín influence.

A comprehensive description of the culture of the period is difficult because of the great degree of local variation. It was a period of development and experiment; archaeologically this is best seen in the technology. On the whole, although the technology is superior, the art and the aesthetic feeling are not equal to those of the preceding Cultist period.

Information on the culture of the Experimental period is derived from graves, cemeteries, from refuse deposits of dwellings, and from fortresses and shrines, the first three mainly from coastal sites, the latter two from the highlands.

As in the former periods, the coastal settlements were on the margins of the river valleys or on the coast. While there was still great dependence on sea food, the progress in agriculture had been great; irrigation was practised and a number of new cultivated plants had been introduced. Among the latter were the frijol bean, quinoa, and several other plants known only in Peru. Terraces were built to utilize better the small amount of irrigable land available. Coca, the narcotic plant of the highlands – of the greatest cultural importance in later times as today – was grown or known, and chicha, the beer made of corn, seems to have been made. Meat was apparently preserved by drying, and grain was stored. Llamas were common in the highlands and well known on the coast. Some edifices were of stone masonry but most were of adobe, the latter being of different shapes in the three main sections of the coast: northern, central, and southern.

In socio-political matters there seems to have been little change from the preceding period. The groups continued small, and the basic social cluster was probably still the family, without any marked political or religious unity. There is little evidence of any class distinctions, the pattern being essentially democratic. Though more attention was paid than formerly to the dead, community religion seems to have been of slight importance.

The local phases of the culture of this period that are best known are, as usual, those on the coast, owing both to the better preservation of the materials and to the greater amount of archaeological excavation that has been done there. Best known of all, probably, are the cultural phases of the northern coast, especially the Salinar and the Gallinazo cultures.

Salinar is a recently discovered culture, first found by Rafael Larco Hoyle in 1941,[1] since which time several hundred graves have been excavated in several large cemeteries in the Chicama Valley. Burials at Puerto Moorin in the Virú Valley are obviously closely related culturally, and it is likely that careful search would reveal similar but slightly variant cultural remains in other valleys of the northern coast. As commonly, the cemeteries were

1. Larco Hoyle, 1944, 1945d, 1946.

placed in the desert hills bordering the cultivated areas. Strati-graphical observations prove that the Salinar followed the Cupisnique (Cultist) and preceded the Moche (Florescent) periods. It takes its name from the small place in the upper Chicama Valley where the largest cemetery was found.

The Salinar people cultivated corn, squash, and gourds in addition to several plants unknown outside of Peru, and gathered shellfish and other local animal life. No house remains are known, but an effigy pottery vessel affords an illustration of one, and other pots give some idea of the costume of the people. The houses were apparently rectangular, with an open front and a sloping roof. Some clothing in addition to a loincloth was certainly worn, and the use of a cap was common. The hair was cut, though not short, and ornaments in the form of ear and nose pendants, finger rings, bead necklaces, and bracelets were worn. Skull deformation was practised, and apparently also tattooing.

Many pottery vessels of distinctive types were found in the graves; these, of course, were mortuary offerings, and the utilitarian ware is not well known. Most of these have a red paste and surface. This red colour indicates a great technical advance, for the vessels must have been fired in a very hot 'oxydizing' fire instead of in the relatively low-temperature 'reducing' fire that produced the black or dark Cupisnique ceramics. Possibly the kiln had now been invented; at any rate, temperature control had improved greatly. A small minority of vessels have the dark colour of Cupisnique pottery.

The paste of Salinar pottery is superior, with more even tempering than in Cupisnique ceramics. Jars with vertical spouts and ribbon handles are common, handleless vessels being rare. The white colouring was apparently applied with a brush on the untreated surface, without the basic slip that later became almost universal. The eyes are treated in an unusual characteristic style, and the details of the facial expression are especially notable. Appliqué relief is slight and low.

The 'stirrup' jar with tubular spouts continued to be the most common shape; the body of the vessel was either modelled in effigy form, or decorated with incising, painting, or relief, or both.

The effigy vessels, at least, were made in moulds; humans, animals, birds, plants, and other objects are portrayed. The incised and painted designs are simple and geometric. The beginnings of painted pottery, later to become almost universal in Peru, are here seen. This represented another important step in cultural advance. The colouring is generally white, but a little red paint was also employed. The pictorial representations are slightly stylized, lacking the perfect realism that the later Moche pottery in this region achieved. A few of the effigy vessels are erotic, though none depict practices of perversion. This is significant in view of the slight interest in sex generally characteristic of aboriginal American art and religion, and of its importance in the later Moche ceramics.

Not enough of Salinar fabrics have been preserved to afford much information on the subject of textiles. Bone spatulas bear incised designs that connect them with Cupisnique art motifs. Fewer Salinar gold ornaments have been found than from the Cultist period and no new techniques are known, except possibly gold-copper alloy, but there is no reason to think that the goldsmith's art had deteriorated.

The better care for the dead indicates a belief in the after-life, and probably early phases of the cult of ancestor-worship which later became of maximum cultural importance. The bodies were interred wrapped in or covered with textiles, and provided with pottery vessels and gourds containing food and drink. They wore their ornaments, and a piece of beaten gold was often put in the mouth. Dogs were sometimes placed at the feet, together with pieces of chalk, quartz, and other stones, generally of a white colour. Red powder (cinnabar?) was found in most of the graves. The body was almost always laid at full length, on the right side, in elliptical graves covered with great stone slabs. No exact orientation was observed in the making of the graves, but most of the dead had the head in a westerly direction.

Large stone sculpture was apparently unknown.

On the north coast the Salinar culture was succeeded in the latter part of this period by a slightly different and more developed phase, the Gallinazo. This was probably the result of a highland influence on the Salinar people. Gallinazo is so named from a site in the Virú Valley where the culture was first identified and where it appears in strongest form. Some, believing that the culture originated in this valley, and disliking the name Gallinazo (Vulture), term it the Virú Culture.[1] Its characteristic pottery type, decorated with negative painting (see page 266), is found in some other valleys of the north coast. This negative painting is typical of the Callejón de Huaylas in the northern highlands, especially of Recuay, in the next period, and is doubtless related to, and possibly an influence from, the cultures of highland Ecuador and southern Colombia, where this technique was in great favour. Since it is also found in the Paracas Cavernas pottery on the south coast and, a little more frequently, on the central coast, it is a quasi-'horizon style', diagnostic of this time.

The Gallinazo was a period of probably several centuries duration, in the Virú Valley at least.[2] Civilization had progressed greatly and was only slightly inferior to that of the Moche in the next great period. The communities were well organized so that large pyramids, doubtless religious structures, were built of adobe bricks which were formed in moulds made of cane. Intensive agriculture, produced by irrigation, was the basis of life. Llamas seem to have been plentiful. Fishing and hunting were now of slight importance, with little dependence on the sea. Weaving was highly developed, as was metallurgy.

When first identified, the Gallinazo culture was believed to be of a much later date, following the Moche period, but the stratigraphy of recent excavation indicates its earlier position.

The pattern of economic life in the central and southern coastal regions probably differed but slightly from that of the Salinar and Gallinazo peoples, but information is scanty. Excavations at Cerro de Trinidad and Baños de Boza in the Chancay Valley show a period characterized by a rather unattractive type of pottery painted in white on the red paste; for this and other reasons it is correlated with the Salinar period. The painting is generally rude, careless, simple, and geometric; effigy vessels are rare. In fact, throughout Peruvian history, the ceramics of the central coast were aesthetically much inferior to those of the northern and southern coasts. The other objects found in the

1. Larco Hoyle, 1945a.   2. Strong and Evans, 1952.

graves differ only in minor details from those of Salinar, and include gold, cloth, pottery figurines, pan-pipes, and spindle whorls. The bodies are generally flexed in graves covered with poles, though some are covered with stone vaults.

Remains of edifices of some type, made of large hemispherical adobe bricks, are found in this region.

On the south coast the cultures of this period centre in the valleys of Pisco, Ica, and Nazca. Since rainfall, even in the mountains, is deficient in this region, the rivers are not large, though they may have carried more water in earlier days.

At Paracas, just south of Pisco, Tello discovered in 1927, close to the Cavernas tombs, a burial area of very different type and known as the Necropolis, already briefly mentioned. This was surrounded by a stone wall and contained 429 'mummy' bundles. Most of these – mainly the smaller and poorer ones – are still unopened in the Archaeological Museum in Lima. The bundles are large and of conical shape, the largest about five feet (1·5 m.) high and wide, the body having been wrapped in quantities of cloth. While probably no embalming process was employed, the viscera were apparently removed and the body allowed to dry naturally in the arid sand.

The Necropolis, a large enclosure in the midst of semi-subterranean houses and refuse-pits, was evidently a cemetery for a special class and differed in many respects from the Cavernas. The bodies were all of elderly men, probably chiefs or priests. The skulls were deformed, but in a different manner from those in the Cavernas vaults; none of them was trephined. The bodies were well preserved, in contrast to those in the Cavernas.

The nude body was placed in a seated position in a basket, and long cotton cloths wound around him. These shrouds of cotton cloth are not so well preserved as the woollen textiles, but are remarkable for their size. Whereas cloths wider than about four feet, the span of a weaver's arms, are practically unknown elsewhere in Peru, these are sometimes thirteen feet (3·9 m.) in width and eighty-four feet (25·5 m.) in length.[1] The wide loom may have been manipulated by several women. Many of the bundles

1. O'Neale, 1936.

showed that they had been completely wrapped and finished several times by adding new layers, probably at several successive ceremonial occasions.

Tucked into the bundle were articles of clothing, generally new and unworn, as well as ornaments, weapons, food, pottery vessels, pet animals, industrial materials, and similar objects. Miniature clothing, feather fans, ornaments of sheet gold, smooth sticks or batons, gourds, and a few pottery vessels were among these objects. Among the food placed for the dead were corn, beans, peanuts, yucca, and sweet potatoes. The four standard articles of clothing were cloak or mantle, short cape, skirt, and headband, but in the richer bundles many other articles were added such as small ponchos, kilts, turbans and other headgear, veils, and slings; these were mainly of llama or vicuña wool and very well preserved. Of the magnificent mantles we will speak later. As many as one hundred and fifty articles of clothing and other offerings were placed with the larger bundles.

The pottery of Paracas Necropolis – always our best criterion – differs considerably from that of the Cavernas, with thin walls, of a light colour and without painted decoration, the shapes of the mortuary ware variant but relatively simple, with some effigy shapes and biomorphic relief. The goldsmiths in this region seem not to have yet learned the technique of casting, but work of a high aesthetic and technical quality was done in ornaments of thin beaten gold with repoussé ornamentation.

But it was in the field of textiles that the Paracas craftsman excelled; the name 'Paracas' means to the archaeologist and the artist magnificent cloths. This renown is due to their large size, their wonderful state of preservation – some of them being practically as soft and brilliant as the day they were woven, and the harmonious beauty of their colouring. The techniques employed are few – mainly embroidery, and finer work was done in other periods, but for general over-all superb effect, Paracas Necropolis textiles rank with the world's best.

The magnificent Paracas mantles must be seen to be appreciated, for no description can do justice to them. They are large, averaging four and a half by eight feet (1·3 by 2·5 m.). The background is a loosely woven wool or cotton cloth on which are embroidered figures in wool in soft harmonious polychrome tones. Four to six colours were generally employed, and both the colours and the figures themselves bear an obvious close relationship to those on Nazca pottery. The embroidered figures are small and repeated many times in various colour combinations, in horizontal and vertical bands, or in chequerboard pattern. Anthropomorphic animal deities, probably mythological beings, with stylistic animal characteristics, more naturalistic animals, and occasionally geometric motifs are employed. Fish and bird deities seem to be the most popular. The workmanship is perfect, and the effect, both macroscopic and microscopic, is colourful, and – to us – exotic (Plate 49).

These magnificent textiles seem to have been made purely for mortuary purposes. The amount of work on them is marvellous, for some are almost completely covered with a veneering of embroidery, meticulously done. The stitching closely follows the weave, each stitch enveloping one warp or weft strand.

The occupation sites, the towns, of the people who buried their dead in the Paracas Necropolis have yet to be found; they may have been those of the population of the Pisco Valley, whose habitation sites seem not to have been discovered yet. The Necropolis cemetery was obviously for men of high rank who were probably brought there from some distance, as the region of the cemetery is absolutely unsuited for human existence, at least at present.

The fact that the temporal relations of the two cultures of Paracas are still a question for discussion well illustrates the present uncertainty on many vital points of Peruvian archaeology. The reports from Dr Strong's 1952 expedition indicate that in the Nazca region the refuse of that period is underlain by, in places, ten to thirteen feet (3 to 4 m.) of deposits containing pottery and textiles of both Paracas types intermingled, together with some other types heretofore unknown. This would suggest the contemporaneity of the two Paracas cultures. Most Peruvianists, however, remain unconvinced and, on other grounds, believe in the greater antiquity of the Cavernas phase.

The cultures of the highlands in the Experimental period are far less known than those on the coast, largely owing to the fact that the objects are much less well preserved, and – as a natural concomitant – much less excavation has been done there. In the northern highlands little more is known than the type of pottery, rather rude and painted with white geometric designs on the red surface; the type site is at Huaraz in the Callejón de Huaylas. The houses were semi-subterranean. The white-on-red is a horizon ceramic style linked with Salinar on the north coast and with Chancay white-on-red on the central coast, but it is missing in the south and in the central highlands.

At Chanapata, near Cuzco, excavations in 1941 revealed the occupation sites of a pre-Incaic population.[1] While only its precedence to the Inca is certain, for cultural and other reasons it is generally assigned to the Experimental horizon. Chronologically it hangs in the air, without identified antecedents or descendants. It was certainly pre-Wari-Tiahuanaco and presumably relatively early, showing some Chavín influence, though probably not as early as the latter.

The culture of the place and period was incomparably inferior to that of the Inca who later made this region the cultural centre of South America. Masonry of plain uncut field stones was employed in semi-subterranean houses and in the walls of agricultural terraces. Very little attention was paid to the dead, who were buried in unlined pits in refuse-heaps, apparently without any mortuary offerings. Metal seems to have been unknown – at least none was found – but implements and ornaments were made of stone and bone.

The pottery is *sui generis*, slightly known, and of no aesthetic or technical interest. It is mainly either incised polished black or painted white on red, with a little red on white. Flaring bowls, plates, ollas, and bottles are the typical shapes. Most of the decoration is incised, but punctate designs and appliqué are also found. Most of the decorative designs are rectilinear geometric, but some biomorphic motifs were employed, especially a feline which, however, is stylistically very different from the Chavín cat.

In the southern highlands also a site has been discovered and excavated which is ascribed to this period; in this case strati-

1. Rowe, 1944.

graphy indicates that it was pre-Tiahuanaco in age. This is at Chiripa on the Bolivian side of Lake Titicaca and therefore not far from Tiahuanaco.[1] Probably, as in all such cases, the unknown people who lived there also occupied similar settlements throughout this region, but only one small site in addition to Chiripa has been discovered so far. Here the village was composed of fourteen rectangular houses in a circle surrounding a central court. The lower part of the walls was made of small stones embedded in clay, the upper part of rectangular, sundried, large mud bricks (adobes), and the roofs were apparently thatched. The walls had two unique and interesting features: they were double and the space between them was utilized for storage, very much as cupboards in some modern houses. However, they were apparently used as storage bins for food, and access was through windows in the interior walls instead of doors. Even more interesting are long narrow slots left in the wall masonry at the door jambs; undoubtedly sliding doors fitted into these.

Agricultural terraces with masonry supporting walls were used in this region also at this time. The dead were interred in stone-lined box graves under the floors of the rooms. The depth of the refuse deposits indicates that the site was occupied for a very long time.

Chiripa ceramics are rather rude, with simple geometric designs painted, generally in broad lines or bands, in yellow on a red slip; the painted areas are sometimes outlined by incised lines, a technique found also in Chavín and Cupisnique, Paracas Cavernas and Ocucaje, and in the neighbouring and slightly later Pucara. A feline figure made in appliqué relief is a frequent element. The most common shape is a bowl with flat base and straight vertical sides. The utilitarian objects found include stone mortars, hammers and similar tools, bolas, bone needles, awls, spear-throwers, chisels, daggers, knives, etc. A few objects of pure copper have been found.

In the southern highlands, resemblances in ceramics and some other features indicate that the Experimental Chiripa culture developed into several later phases, among them the Pucara and

1. Bennett, 1936.

the Early Tiahuanaco. All three of these are now (1966) considered as pertaining to the Experimental period.

Pucara is a site in the Department of Puno, Peru, between Cuzco and Lake Titicaca; the architecture, ceramics, and sculpture are characteristic and unique.[1] As is the case with all the Peruvian cultures up to at least this time, we know nothing of the history of the people who lived there, not even their name or language. Inca traditions do not mention them; our knowledge is restricted to the data derived from digging, and the deductions made therefrom.

Pucara has the basic elements of the earlier and neighbouring Chiripa plus a strong influence of the Tiahuanaco region. The structure excavated by Alfred Kidder II, built of very good masonry of dressed stone with some use of adobe, was almost certainly a temple. A sunken central court is surrounded by walls forming a horseshoe-shaped group of small rooms. In this central court four burial vaults, made of dressed stone blocks and entered by means of a doorway and steps, were found. Each of these vaults contained a stone altar.

Stone sculpture is a characteristic element of Pucara. This is much better made than the stone carving of the northern highlands. Human and animal figures are found, as well as carved stelae and slabs (Plate 18B). The pottery, in form and motif, is of Tiahuanacan type, with wide-mouth bowls and goblets predominating. These, however, are painted in yellow and black on a red slip with the outlines incised. Many of the vessels are further decorated with a large feline head in high relief, the body in flat profile. The ceramic has some resemblance to the earlier Chiripa, and a little to the Early Tiahuanaco.

Probably contemporary with Pucara was Early Tiahuanaco. This is little more than a pottery type which was found principally in the lowest stratigraphical cuts at Tiahuanaco; it differs markedly from Classic Tiahuanaco in shape and design. It occurs in the refuse-heaps of dwelling sites which probably stood on the site of Tiahuanaco before this was made into a great ceremonial centre. No architecture or sculpture has been identified as belonging to this period, though a few statues in Bolivia

1. Kidder, 1943, 1948.

that bear some resemblance to Pucara are assigned to the Early Tiahuanaco culture and period. In addition to pottery fragments many implements of stone, bone, copper, and other similar materials were found in the excavations.

Early Tiahuanaco has a small area of distribution. Decanters and bowls are the most frequent of the few simple shapes. The painted decoration is either red on buff, or polychrome with black, white, red, brown, orange, and yellow, the designs mainly rectilinear geometric, but with some animal motifs. There is little or no modelling but a little incised decoration. The surface is highly polished.

The general picture of the Experimental period is one of small discrete local groups, on more or less the same cultural plane, but without any political or religious bond, and with considerable local variation. The emphasis was on agriculture, and on the development and improvement of techniques in economic life and in handicrafts. Formalized religion apparently played a small role in native life at this time; shrines and temples seem to have been few.

As before remarked, the division between the preparatory Experimental and the full-blown Florescent periods is a vague, indefinite one, for the transition was slow, even, and unbroken, and intermediate phases may be placed in one or the other, according to the opinion of the individual. Diagnostic pottery styles evolved into others: White-on-Red into Interlocking at Chancay and Pachacamac, Chiripa into Pucara and Early Tiahuanaco. Most of these later phases could be placed in either period, and Pucara and Early Tiahuanaco, as well as Paracas Necropolis, are now generally placed in this Experimental period.

The length of this Experimental period is a most controversial question, and the estimates vary greatly. According to the chronological scheme adopted herein, it lasted about five centuries, from c. 300 B.C. to A.D. 200. Other 'guess-dates' are from 400 B.C. to A.D. 400, a period of eight hundred years.

Chapter 5

THE FLORESCENT ERA

c. A.D. 200–600

By the close of the Developmental Era and the Experimental period, an epoch represented by Salinar and Early Gallinazo on the north coast, and by Paracas on the south coast, Peruvian civilization, at least as expressed in technology – weaving ceramics, metallurgy and other handicrafts – had passed its adolescence and was prepared to enter the classic stage. The crafts had a firm basis, and most of the techniques had been developed. Later periods saw a refinement of these, a great increase in quantity production, a florescence of art, a development of social institutions and civic patterns, but little change in economic or technical methods. In fact, the apogee of the latter was certainly reached in these times.

This era is therefore termed 'Florescent' because in it Peruvian culture, as represented in economy, technology, and art, flourished to achieve its maximum. It was a relatively long era, probably encompassing much of the first millennium of the Christian epoch. It consists of only one period, the Florescent. As generally believed by archaeologists, it was a period of about four centuries, during which the Peruvian cultures attained and retained a high level of excellence. There was no uniformity, no ubiquitous 'horizon style' to tie the various regions together. As in the preceding periods, we know nothing historically of the various peoples, their languages or wars; all our data have been supplied by the spade and trowel of the archaeologist.

These excavations indicate that, for a period of several centuries, artefacts and handicraft of a technical and artistic quality that was not later surpassed were made in most parts of Peru, but especially on the coast. The period ends, not with any catastrophic war, as did most Old World eras, and not with any 'dark age' of cultural retrogression, but with the appearance of the

Wari-Tiahuanaco 'horizon style', a pan-Peruvian influence, which affords a convenient time-marker. The many peoples with their minor variant cultures continued their lives untrammelled except for adopting and adapting to their cultural patterns the Wari-Tiahuanaco art style.

The period was characterized by admirable craftsmanship in textiles, ceramics, metallurgy, and minor arts, by high development of art styles, and, in most places, by the erection of massive architectural structures. Agricultural techniques, the basis of existence, were highly advanced with their concomitants of extensive agricultural engineering features.

Dwelling-houses were now relatively comfortable, permanent structures of adobe bricks or stone, and immense public works, temples and forts, were built in most regions, except the south coast. Skull deformation was a general practice, and trephining was very common, especially on the south coast.

Religion had apparently become highly developed, theocratic, and organized with a priesthood and a pantheon in which anthropomorphic deities, especially a feline, were prominent. Nature- and ancestor-worship seem to have been rather universal, as were human sacrifices and the taking of trophy heads. Worship was probably largely by ritualistic ceremonies and dances.

The increase in population must have been great, but competition was not so great as not to afford plenty of leisure time which the various groups utilized in cultural development according to the local pattern, in rest and relaxation, and in improvements in technology.

No cultural remains of this period have yet been identified in the central highlands, later to become the cultural centre of Peru in the Inca period, but in both the northern and southern highlands there were culture centres that are ascribed to this horizon. Apparently, however, the major civilizations continued to be on the coast. In addition to this fact, the objects there are much better preserved, and consequently much more excavation has been done there, both by native *huaqueros* and by archaeologists.

In this period flourished the two native cultures that have probably furnished the major part of the outstanding Peruvian ceramic art products that today grace the museums of the world and awake the admiration of artists and craftsmen: the Moche of the northern coast, and the Nazca of the southern coast.

The Moche culture has been known, mainly by its extraordinarily naturalistic ceramics, for a long time, but it was formerly termed Proto-Chimú or Early Chimú, since it preceded the historically known Chimú empire in the same region. The civilization centred in the valleys of Chicama, Moche, Virú, and Santa, and also extended southward to Nepeña and Casma, and northward to Pacasmayo. It had almost certainly been extended by military conquest. The irrigable areas of these valleys were utilized for agriculture while the temples and the great graveyards from which quantities of exquisite pottery and other artefacts have been extracted were placed on the desert edges of the cultivated fields; this was generally true of the villages also.

Moche culture – at least as far as ceramics are concerned – developed out of Cupisnique without being affected by Salinar and Gallinazo, cultures of lesser geographical and historical extent. Its beginnings went back into the Experimental period.

Terrestrial wild animal life was still present but was probably of slight economic importance to the Moche, though they took as much advantage of it as possible, using nets, javelins and spear-throwers, and blow-guns. Judging by the scenes depicted on the pottery, however, hunting had largely become a sport of the privileged classes. The domesticated llama and guinea-pig provided most of the meat diet. Naturally, sea food, in the shape of fish, shellfish, and even sea lions, was a welcome addition to the vegetable diet, and its procurement was an important, though doubtless unspecialized, industry. Small one-man boats or *balsas*, probably identical with those used today, were made of *totora* reed. Men ventured in these a considerable distance to sea, to fish with lines and hooks without barbs, or with harpoons, or to spread their nets supported by gourds. Large *balsas* holding several persons, like those used today on Lake Titicaca, were apparently also made.

The basis of existence, however, was agriculture, and this had been brought to technical perfection. Irrigation works, most of them now long since abandoned but a few still in use, watered almost every possible acre of land and doubtless supported a much larger population than live in these valleys at present. In some places, however, potentially fertile land seems to have been unused, indicating that the population had not reached its maximum and that the pressure of population was not very great. Aqueducts and canals were made in every valley, some of them immense engineering projects that required not only an enormous amount of labour to carry out but a high degree of knowledge and experience to plan. Thus La Cumbre canal, still in use today, conducts water from the headwaters of the Chicama River to near the mouth, a distance of about 75 miles (113 km.). Aqueducts were built to carry these irrigation canals across intersecting ravines. The aqueduct at Ascope, also in the Chicama Valley, is one of the great engineering triumphs of ancient Peru nearly a mile (1400 m.) long, fifty feet (15 m.) high, and has a cubic content of over a million cubic yards (785,000 cu. m.) of earth.

By this time all the known Peruvian food plants had been brought under cultivation and developed to practically their final stage of perfection. The major crops were corn (maize), beans, peanuts, potatoes, sweet potatoes, chilli peppers, yucca (manioc), pumpkins, gourds, cotton, and coca, as well as avocado, tuna, granadilla, chirimoya, guanábana, tumbo, papaya, pineapple, and the lesser-known pacai, lúcuma, jiquima, yacón, achira, pepino, quinoa, oca, mashua, lupin, ulluco, and cañahua. Some of these were unknown previously. The latter six are not found on the coast but restricted to the highlands. The fermented beer, chicha, was made from corn, probably exactly as it still is today. Guano fertilizer was employed, and the agricultural tools, the digging stick and the hoe, were the same as those used by the Inca many centuries later.

Our information on the Moche culture is rather fuller than that on other civilizations of this early period because, in addition to the many actual objects found in the graves, the very naturalistic modelled pottery, and the dynamic scenes painted on some of it, afford much data on many phases of native life.

Civic planning was not yet a cultural feature, and the Moche villages were groups of houses arranged haphazardly. The houses, judging by pottery models of them as well as by the actual remains, were rather small but consisted of several rectangular rooms. Some were built on terraces and some had open patios. The roofs were gabled and thatched with straw, supported by wooden posts and with opening for smoke and ventilation. The walls were of large rectangular adobe bricks made in moulds, the surface frequently decorated with arabesques, but the lower foundations were generally of rough stone.

The Moche erected enormous temples, the most impressive of these being the great twin pyramids at Moche, not far from the present city of Trujillo; they are locally known today as the 'Huaca del Sol' (Temple of the Sun) and the 'Huaca de la Luna' (Temple of the Moon). Both consist of terraced platforms, and the larger, that of the Sun, is surmounted by a terraced pyramid, all solidly built of adobe bricks in astronomical numbers. The Huaca del Sol is the most stupendous structure on the coast. The base platform measures 750 by 450 ft (228 by 136 m.) and is 60 ft (18 m.) high, rising in five terraces. A causeway 20 ft (6 m.) wide and nearly 300 ft (90 m.) long leads to the north end, and a stepped pyramid 340 ft (103 m.) square and 75 ft (23 m.) high surmounts the southern end of the platform. It has been estimated to contain 130 million adobe bricks. The Huaca de la Luna lacks the pyramid and the platform is smaller, 260 by 195 ft (80 by 60 m.), and 70 ft (21 m.) high. On the top are remains of a few rooms whose walls bear traces of frescoes painted in black, white, red, yellow, blue, pink, and brown in typical Moche design motifs (Plates 1B, 2A).

Smaller isolated pyramids of adobe bricks are found at most of the other Moche sites; some of them are decorated with arabesques in clay relief. Murals painted in colour and showing human figures very similar to those found on painted Moche pottery vessels have recently been uncovered at Pañamarca. These great sub-structures certainly served as foundations for temples, traces of some of which still remain. Other large structures are presumed to have been forts since they are located in strategic places, are often surrounded by walls, and are entered by narrow, steep stairs. Roads of a standard width of 33 ft (9·8 m.) seem to date from this period, and platforms at intervals along them suggest that the later Inca pattern of relay messengers was already in vogue.

The effigy figures on the pottery vessels as well as the objects found in the graves give us a good picture of dress and adornment in the Moche period. As among most early peoples – and as in nature – the male was much more gaily attired than the female. Women generally wore nothing but a long shirt and simple ear pendants. Presumably, when at work, the ordinary man wore only a loincloth, but the effigy figures of men, doubtless garbed in their 'Sunday best', show a great development of clothing and ornament, probably distinctive of rank or occupation. In addition to the ubiquitous breechcloth, they wore undershirts and underskirts beneath the more ornate shirts and skirts. All were, of course, rectangular pieces of woven cloth, never cut or tailored, which were fastened around the waist by woven belts. The headdresses were very varied, some just simple turbans, others very large and sumptuously decorated; the latter apparently varied according to, and indicated, rank or office. Doubtless bright-coloured feathers, and apparently even stuffed birds and ornaments of gold and silver were attached to them. Ear and nose ornaments, necklaces and finger rings were probably more or less standard adornment for any man of any social position; they were made of precious metals, semi-precious stones, shell, bone, or almost any other suitable substance.

Apparently the Moche wore no foot coverings, but painted their feet and lower legs in a fashion that recalls boots, and also sometimes painted the face and body with designs that apparently indicated rank or occupation. There is no evidence of tattooing, however.

The effigy pottery vessels indicate that amputation, bonesetting, and circumcision were practised by the Moche, and that diseases were treated by the almost universal American Indian custom of sucking out the tangible object believed to be the cause of the illness.

Owing to the occasional, though rare, heavy rains in this northern coastal region, and also the amount of saltpetre in the soil, very few Moche textiles have survived even sufficiently to afford a good idea of the techniques, though the effigies and painted scenes on the ceramics indicate that it was a highly developed industry, and possibly even made on a quantity-production level. Probably it was on the same high level of competence as in the other regions on this horizon, with the exception of the south coast, where the work was especially good. All the usual techniques such as tapestry, embroidery, brocade, gingham, and twill were known. Plain weaves made of cotton predominate, and wool fibre seems to have been rare.

Considerable progress had been made in metallurgy and Moche goldsmiths were capable craftsmen. Embossed ornaments of thin gold were still in the majority but casting (doubtless by the *cire per due* process), soldering, annealing, and gilding were common practices. Bronze was still unknown, but other alloys of gold, silver, and copper were made. As in the Old World Bronze Age, the Moche made heavy implements of solid copper; elsewhere in Peru at this time all metals served mainly ornamental purposes (Plates 62, 63).

Gourds were artistically decorated, and the graves contain many art, as well as utilitarian, objects of carved wood, shell, and bone, inlaid shell mosaics, stone club-heads and axes, staff-heads, baskets, and many other objects. Musical instruments of a number of types have been found: percussion instruments such as drums and tambourines, rattles, clappers, and gongs; trumpets; and several of variable tones, such as flutes and pan-pipes.

But it is in the field of ceramics that the Moche excelled as artists and craftsmen; the perfection of their realistic modelling has nowhere been exceeded, and rarely equalled. Quantities of tastefully moulded vessels were buried with the dead, and today large groups of them grace many museums and private collections. Specialists divide Moche pottery into five periods, two formative, two climactic, and one decadent under pressure from the Wari Tiahuanaco culture. Though made in moulds, duplicates are rare. The shapes are simple and few, but with countless variations, the stirrup-spout vase being most characteristic. In most of these the body may be modified into almost every conceivable form, humans engaged in many activities, animals, vegetables, and objects such as houses and boats. Deformation, mutilations, punishments, and captives are portrayed. Erotic scenes – elsewhere in America a rare art element – are characteristic, and modern collector's items. The acme of realism was achieved in the so-called portrait vases, so lifelike that they doubtless were representations of definite individuals (Plates 24, 25).

Only single figures are ordinarily represented in this ceramic modelling, which is representational rather than symbolic. Posture and expression are admirably portrayed. The technical craftsmanship is excellent also, the vessels being painted in red or black on a cream slip, well baked and polished; black vessels are rare.

In a second group of stirrup-spouted vessels the upper part is plain but the body painted with realistic scenes such as war, hunting, fishing, and ceremonial or diplomatic gatherings. Here the representation is of groups of persons, always shown in profile, and in rapid dynamic action, generally running. While very much stylized and not approaching the modelled relief in realism, they afford much data on the life of this early time, of which we have not the slightest historical or traditional record, and which could be secured in no other way. The ceramics have been aptly termed a picture-book of the culture (Figure 2).

There is considerable evidence – though still not enough to be convincing to most students – that the Moche had developed some system of 'writing' or, let us say, non-verbal communication.[1] It was certainly not alphabetic, phonetic, syllabic, or probably even pictographic, and probably most nearly resembled in kind the *quipu* of later periods. The message, however, was apparently incised on lima beans and could be interpreted only by a special class of persons trained in such decipherment. How standardized were the ideograms we have no means of knowing. They were probably limited to factual data; no philosophical discussions could have been thus transmitted. And probably the reader had to be familiar with the idiosyncrasies of the writer.

Data on this question are derived almost exclusively from scenes on the painted vessels which show runners with a certain type of attire, probably messengers, in dynamic attitudes, carrying small bags. Other vessels portray beans painted in dozens of different designs, and still others are modelled in the form of

1. Larco Hoyle, 1942, 1943.

persons, again with standardized characteristics and attire, who seem to be studying the beans; these men are presumably the decoders. Similarly, apparently painted beans on Nazca vessels suggest that the latter people may possibly also have had the same or a similar custom.

The picture of the Moche afforded us by the archaeologists is that of a dynamic, almost aggressive, people, far along the road to civilization. They had evidently passed beyond the simple democratic stage and had evolved a status society in which a small aristocratic class directed or commanded the life and labour of the masses. There was also great division of labour and specialization of occupation and crafts. While we cannot be sure whether a potter or goldsmith, for instance, worked at his craft the year round or only in the agricultural off-season, there were probably priests, physicians, and similar full-time practitioners who did no farming. There may have been a slave class, and there almost certainly were aristocratic, noble, or regal classes. In the pottery effigy vessels and paintings, definite attire, accoutrements, paraphernalia, or symbols indicate the various classes and crafts, and these are often shown in zoomorphic form, such as birds, centipedes, or dragon-flies for messengers, foxes for savants, jaguars for men in authority.

The great differences in the quality of the costumes worn by different personages in the pottery effigies indicate differences in social status, as do grave contents. The paintings show certain persons on raised platforms under arbours receiving obeisances of others, or carried in litters; these obviously were leaders or rulers. They also sit at higher levels at meals. Servants are often depicted as lizards. Since there seems to have been no differentiation between secular, military, and religious leadership, it is rather obvious that the political system approached a theocracy. Strict authority is also shown by effigies of persons who have evidently undergone punishment, such as mutilation, or scenes depicting execution or stoning.

Warriors seem to have been especially highly honoured, which indicates an aggressive or militaristic pattern, for effigies of warriors in full panoply are especially frequent; they carry maces, battle-axes, spears and spear-throwers, and shields. Conquest of neighbouring peoples had probably already begun. Prisoners are depicted as nude with ropes around their necks, but even here class distinction lifts its ugly head, for some prisoners, probably war captives, are shown carried in litters. Though if some observers might prefer to consider them wounded enemies, borne off by primitive Red Cross stretcher-bearers to a first-aid dressing station, none can deny it, though such was not the aboriginal pattern!

The Moche world was obviously man's, and women definitely

Figure 2. *Drawing of a scene from a Moche pottery vessel. Chief in house receiving captives borne in litters*

occupied an inferior position. No women are ever shown in scenes of ceremonies, but only engaged in domestic tasks.

The authoritarian pattern of the Moche, when applied to the large population with leisure time in the agricultural off-season, naturally resulted in immense public works such as the great engineering irrigation features, and especially in the enormous temple pyramids.

Whether by military conquest or not, at the end of the period the Moche culture succumbed to pressure from the all-pervading highland Tiahuanaco influence from Wari which, however, dominated no farther north than Chicama. After several centuries the Moche tradition was carried on by the Chimu (q.v.).

Culturally and economically, the life of the inhabitants of the central coast valleys probably differed little from that of the Moche, but, since their products were not outstanding, less attention has been paid to them, though considerable excavation has been done in this region, especially at the great cemetery at Ancón and the famous temple at Pachacamac. No effigy vessels or painted scenes give information on the life of the people. As in the northern region, immense pyramids of adobe were built, evidence of community activity under direction or authority. Handicraft was good but not impressive. Ceramics were aesthetically unimportant as compared with the products of the north and south coasts. The sequential temporal phases are generally known by the pottery types characteristic of them, of interest and importance to few but professional archaeologists.

The valleys of Chancay, Rimac, and Lurin fall together culturally – and probably historically – and are considered as forming the Central Coast culture. The valleys of Supe, Paramonga, and Huarmey to the north are also generally included in this group, but are not so typical, nor so well known for the early periods.

Little is known of cultural developments except the changes in the ceramic types that characterized them and by which the sub-periods are known. Following the Chancay White-on-Red of the Experimental period, the Intermediate, Interlocking, and Early Lima periods are distinguished. The not-very-well-chosen name 'Interlocking' was selected because the most frequent decorative motif is a very conventionalized fish, obviously adapted from textile design, repeated in an interlocked pattern and painted in black and white on a red base. The change from White-on-Red pottery to Interlocking was one of fashion, for the change was gradual, and intermediate forms are found; it was obviously not accompanied by a change in population. The Interlocking style is generally ascribed to the Florescent period. The immense adobe pyramid of Pachacamac was probably begun in this period, since Interlocking is the earliest major ceramic type found there; the great site of Cajamarquilla close to Lima may have been begun at about the same time. At Pachacamac Interlocking is associated with a type of negative-painted ware.

Early Lima is a slightly later pottery style found at the type site of Nievería near Cajamarquilla, at Pachacamac, and at other sites in the Lima region. The shapes are more graceful, with some life forms, and the painted decoration more pleasing, predominantly white on a dark red surface. Spheroid pitchers with short vertical spouts are especially common (Plate 29B).

While the stratigraphical evidence in the Nazca Valley, more than a hundred miles south-east of Paracas, indicates clearly that the Paracas cultures preceded the Nazca and possibly gave birth to the latter, the temporal difference cannot be great. Paracas textiles show demoniacal figures very similar to those on Nazca ceramics. It is likely that the Paracas Necropolis culture was contemporary with the earliest phase (A) of Nazca, though regional differences exist, as would be expected.

The Nazca culture was unknown until 1901 when it was discovered by the old master of Peruvian archaeology, Max Uhle. Before that time only five of the beautiful Nazca polychrome pottery vessels, of unidentified provenance, were known in museums. A decade later practically all the graveyards had been almost completely looted and all great museums boasted of large collections of Nazca ceramics.

While of coastal type of culture, the Nazca were not a littoral people. The fertile valleys in this region are some fifty miles inland, the intervening area being occupied by a desolate arid range of hills and sand in which the rivers disappear.

Until 1952 no extensive excavations had been made in the Nazca region, except by treasure hunters, and practically nothing was known except the association of grave contents. Brief reports have clarified the picture greatly.

The Nazca culture developed directly out of the Paracas, apparently without change of population. The evolution may have taken place in the Nazca region where Nazca sites are underlain by ten feet (3 m.), at times, of typical Paracas refuse, with intermediate stages. No large structures were built of adobe and there was no stone masonry of this period, but small houses were built with adobe walls. While there were no known large towns, the houses tended to cluster in small village-like groups. Also prominent natural features were covered with adobes, making small pyramids and terraces. The adobes used in construction were variable in size and form, from conical to pancake shape, and were combined with wattle-and-daub to build the houses. There was apparently great building activity in the earliest Nazca period.

Owing to the absence of effigy vessels and painted scenes, our knowledge of Nazca life and customs is far less than that of the

Moche, its northern contemporary. But the general picture seems to be one of a sedentary democratic people without marked class distinctions or authoritarianism, possibly without an established religion. There is less difference in the 'richness' or poverty of the graves, and women seem to be on an equality with men in this respect. The apparent absence of great public works, of extensive engineering features, and of temple pyramids implies a lack of authoritarian leadership. Instead, the leisure time of the people seems to have been spent in individual production, especially in the making of quantities of perfect, exquisite textiles and pottery vessels. This seems to indicate a strong cult of ancestor-worship. Cloths on which an incredible amount of labour was spent were made especially for funerary offerings and interred with the dead. The orientation seems to have been towards individualized religion rather than towards community participation, dictation, coercion, and aggression.

The Nazca graves are generally bottle-shaped with a shaft running down to a chamber which may be at a depth of anywhere between close to the surface and fifteen feet (4·5 m.). Many of the skulls show longitudinal deformation, and the bodies give evidence of the practice of tattooing. The flexed bodies were wrapped with cloths which are well preserved and of excellent quality, though not equalling the exquisite products of Paracas. Many beautiful polychrome pottery vessels and other objects of mortuary furniture were placed in the graves.

'Lovely' best describes Nazca ceramics. The shapes are few and usually simple with little relief, though some effigy modelling is found; in contrast to Moche, the emphasis is on polychrome painting with polished surface (Plate 28). As many as eleven soft harmonious pastel colours may be employed on one vessel: black, white, violet, grey, flesh-colour, and two shades each of red, yellow, and brown; the absence of blue and green is noteworthy. The motifs seem to fall into two main categories, naturalistic biomorphic and mythological. The former are repeated figures of birds, fish, insects, vegetal products, and similar objects. They are obvious yet stylized, naturalistic but not realistic or pictorial. Other designs depict monstrous or anthropomorphic animals, presumably deities, in which the characteristic features are emphasized; one of the most frequent of these is a feline. Bowls are the commonest forms, also spheroid vessels with two short vertical spouts connected by a bridge.

Nazca ceramic styles are seen in four sequential stages, Early, Middle, Late, and Nazca-Wari, though the differences are not clear cut and the criteria rather subjective. Early types tended to be simple, often with repetitions of natural objects such as vegetables, birds, or fish. Vessels of the Middle period became more abstract and symbolic, the natural motifs more conventionalized or anthropomorphic. In the late period effigy forms became more common, the anthropomorphic designs more complicated. Vessels of the Nazca-Wari late period were a little decadent with more careless workmanship, as well as characteristic period shapes such as tall cups or beakers.

Nazca textiles are lovely and admirable. Progress is shown by the larger number of techniques; in fact, practically every one of the many Peruvian textile processes was known to the Nazca weaver; no important one was later invented. Embroidery, tapestry, brocade, gauze, and warp or weft patterns were the most common. Painted cloths are also found. Three-dimensional needle-knitting was popular. Wool, imported from the highlands, was more used than the native cotton. As with the ceramics, the range of colours was enormous and amazing. As many as 190 tints on the scale in seven main colours have been identified in early Nazca fabrics, though some of these may be due to differential fading. The design motifs also bear some resemblance to those on the pottery vessels.

Metallurgy, on the other hand, was retarded, being far less developed than in the Moche region. Only gold was known, and the people seem to have been ignorant of – or untrained in – the technique of casting. Dainty ornaments were made, however, by the old process of hammering the metal into thin sheets, cutting it into graceful shapes, and decorating it with embossed or repoussé designs.

The taking of human heads – probably from enemies in combat – was a striking element of Nazca culture. These are depicted in ceramic and textile designs and have also been found in the tombs, flattened, painted, and attached to slings for carrying.

The largest Nazca site, or most thickly occupied area, the puta-
tive 'capital', is at Cahuachi on the lower-middle Nazca River
just before it enters the first gorge in the sterile hills. The word
'enormous' is applied to it, but its actual area is not on record.
Just at the gorge is a remarkable site known as 'La Estaquería',
Spanish for 'the place of stakes'. This has been aptly termed a
'wooden Stonehenge'. On a level sandy area quantities of trunks
of trees, *algarrobo* and *huarango*, have been planted in orderly
rows and masses. The greater number are in a quadrangle of
twelve rows of twenty posts each, about seven feet (2 m.) apart
and there are lines of posts, and a few posts of much larger size
adjacent. Although the aligned posts are merely columns, most
of the single ones have forked tops and almost certainly supported a roof or canopy. The wood is still hard and firm – and
after at least a half, and probably a full millennium or more! For
the structure is clearly pre-Spanish, and the surrounding graves
are of Nazca period. Presumably they are late, probably Nazca-
Wari, but they may be much older; there is no evidence (Plate 8B).

In the absence of any written records or historical traditions
we can know little or nothing of the degree of scientific knowledge of the more ancient peoples of Peru, such as, for instance,
their knowledge of astronomy. But celestial phenomena have
always been of the greatest importance to early peoples, especially to farming folk who needed to know the progress of the
seasons, irrespective of the vagaries of the weather, in order to
plan their times for planting and harvest. The surprisingly accurate astronomical and calendrical knowledge of the Maya is
revealed to us almost in its entirety mainly by one old book or
codex that luckily escaped the holocausts of the Spanish Conquest. Although the Peruvians were apparently not so calendrically minded as the Mesoamericans, it is likely that all the more
highly cultured peoples of America were not much inferior to the
Maya in their astronomical erudition, and were far better informed than is generally credited.

Just as, in a number of other regions, the orientation of
edifices and other structures has thrown some light on the astronomical knowledge of their builders, so in the Nazca region the
ancient peoples left on their land tangible and intelligible evi-

dences of their interest in and knowledge of this subject. This has been one of the most interesting, surprising, and unique discoveries of recent years in Peruvian archaeology, and a direct result of aeroplane observations.[1]

In the Nazca region, at some distance from the sea, and mainly on both sides of the Palpa Valley, is a stretch of tableland, free of the sand that envelops the coastal region, and covered with small broken stones. It is about forty miles in length, a mile or more in width. Rain is unknown and the sunshine is practically eternal. Locally it is called a *pampa*, though not a blade of vegetation can be seen. The changelessness of the region is incredible. Marks furrowed on the surface several years ago look as though they had been made the day before; a bit of paper lost by a previous expedition seems to have just been dropped.

The small stones that cover the surface probably contain iron, and the suns of many millennia have formed a dark patina on their upper faces. These stones were removed from certain areas by the ancient peoples and piled at the edges of these places, leaving designs in the lighter-coloured sand and gravel below. Long straight narrow lines radiate from hills, mounds, and other strategic points. Many lines are parallel; others cross and crisscross. Large rectilinear trapezoidal spaces were also cleared, and there are furthermore a number of spirals, and large figures of animals (Plate 9A). These latter give clear proof of the identity of their makers, if more evidence were needed other than the region and the occasional fragments of typical Nazca pottery found on the surface, looking as though the vessel had just been broken. For the great figures on the surface of the land, probably representing divinities, are in the same art style as those on the surface of the potsherds, typically Nazca.

These figures, it must be remembered, are very large and made on flat ground. There is no near-by elevation and they can be seen to good advantage only from the air, from an aeroplane or balloon. Doubtless they were made to be seen by celestial deities. Their delineation, however, brings up some intriguing suggestions and possibilities. How were they made so perfect without being seen in proper perspective? The makers must have

1. Reiche, 1949; Kosok and Reiche, 1947, 1949.

known much about proportions. Could they have worked from a small model on a grid?

The lines and figures are now being carefully studied and measured, but no final definitive report on them has yet been issued. Some of the straight lines, at least, seem to verify the presumptive hypothesis that they were astronomical, pointing towards solstitial and equinoctial points, or towards other important rising or setting places. As such, they could have served as a farmer's almanac or calendar, indicating the seasons. The problem is a very difficult one, owing to the great number of such lines. However, the measurements of the lines apparently indicate the linear standards of these people. A report from Miss Maria Reiche is to the effect that, from one centre ten feet (3 m.) square, twenty-three straight lines radiate; two are solstitial lines, one equinoctial. Most of them are 595 feet (182 m.) long. Some lines are found of half or quarter this standard. Another frequent measurement, perhaps another standard, is eighty-five feet (26 m.).

Throughout the early periods, information concerning the Peruvian highlands is far less than that concerning the coast, largely because, on account of the rains, objects of organic materials are not preserved, and therefore little digging has been done by natives. Scientifically controlled excavations have also been fewer than on the coast. The little evidence seems to indicate that the culture in the two regions was about equally high, though naturally the economic life differed considerably. Less is known, of course, about the cultural evolutionary development. The sequential phases are placed in the several periods mainly on the basis of the coastal evolutionary periods with which they seem to correspond in time. This is admittedly unproved.

In the northern highlands, toward the end of the Experimental period, the interesting ceramic technique of negative painting was introduced and later came into great vogue. This also is considered a horizon style, since it was known in all the coastal cultures. It became of maximum importance, however, in the northern region, especially in the northern highlands where it is the characteristic ware of the Recuay culture, generally assigned to the Florescent period. This Recuay ware, one of the better-known types of Peruvian pottery, is of many varied shapes, many of them modelled life-forms somewhat similar, though much inferior, to Moche pottery. The surfaces are often decorated with very stylized rectilinear animal designs, in which the jaguar predominates. There is also another type of Recuay ware, known as Recuay B, painted in positive designs; this seems to be on the whole later than the negative-painted Recuay A (Plate 29A).

The vertical extent of the architecture that was a characteristic of this region in earlier days probably continued into this period, that is to say, two- and three-storey temples with heavy slab roofs, and subterranean houses and galleries with as many as two storeys underground, built mainly of stone slabs and entered by vertical shafts. Stone sculpture, missing on the coast, is also very characteristic of this region and period. The figures are probably those of deities, but are decidedly ungraceful and archaistic, being massive, and columnar or ovoid, with low relief and vestigial limbs. There are also carved slabs and lintels in a rather different art style.[1] Ornaments and tools of copper have been found in the graves, but of course textiles and other objects of organic materials have long since disappeared.

Strange to say, no important site of this period has yet been identified in the central highlands. Such sites must of course exist, and remain to be discovered or identified.

An horizon art style dominates and characterizes this period. This style apparently emanated from the highlands and is best typified at the great site of Tiahuanaco, from which it takes its name. The influence, probably that of a religious cult that had its centre at Tiahuanaco, spread to almost all parts of Peru and is obvious in the art styles of the various regions. It thus recapitulates the influence of the much earlier Chavín cult. It apparently originated and reached its apogee in the highlands in the earlier part of this period; later it reached the coast, where the style is sometimes known as 'Epigonal'. For reasons to be explained later, this horizon art style is now known as 'Wari-Tiahuanaco'. The horizon is often termed the 'Middle Period'. The classic Tiahuanaco of the highlands apparently did not develop from

1. Schaedel, 1948b, 1948c.

the 'Early Tiahuanaco' of that region; the styles are considerably different.

While a Tiahuanaco or 'Megalithic' Empire is no longer generally credited, some loose political force probably accompanied the spread of the Tiahuanaco cult. At any rate it seems to have been a period of unrest, with an increase in expansion, aggression, and conquest, and some warfare between neighbouring local groups. This was probably a result of a strengthening of political organization and more centralized power within the groups. It was apparently not due to population pressure, for there seems to be some evidence of a decrease in population, at least on the coast, although it was still large.

The Tiahuanaco influence, while strong, was not an engulfing or permanent one. The local regions retained their individualities, and, towards the end of the period, the rather uniform art style disappeared, like a fashion, and the local cultures re-emerged as quite separate entities, each with its own peculiarities.

TIAHUANACO

Mystery and glamour have always hung about the ruins of Tiahuanaco (Plate 10). It has been claimed to be of immense age, the place of origin of all American, if not of all world, civilizations.[1] Some fanatics even have it originally on an island, then sunk beneath the Pacific, and finally uplifted, together with the Andes, intact to its present height! Even solid scholars have until recently believed it the seat of a great forgotten Megalithic Empire. Discarding all such theories, silly or plausible, enough of mystery remains to intrigue and puzzle the unimaginative archaeologist.

Tiahuanaco lies at a height of about 13,000 ft (c 4000 m.), an altitude exceeded by few Alpine peaks and by only a very few in the United States; it is thirteen miles (21 km.) south-east of Lake Titicaca, the world's highest navigable lake (12,506 ft). Bleak, chilly, a practically treeless *puna*, too high for intensive agriculture, it is the last place in the world to expect a great stupendous archaeological site. No wonder many mystics have felt sure

1. Posnansky, 1946.

that the climate and environment must have been much less rigorous when it was in its prime. No credible traditions refer to it. Today the scattered families of Aymara Indians pasture their llamas and alpacas and raise their potatoes in the more fertile parts of the region – a stolid, taciturn people with no high degree of culture. Did their ancestors quarry, transport, and erect these massive stone blocks so perfectly cut and fitted?

The major structures occupy about a sixth of a square mile (1475 by 3275 ft or 450 by 1000 metres), and consist of four principal units and a number of minor ones. Tiahuanaco is a unique site. While, as usual in the highlands, no adobe was employed in the constructions and all the ruins are of stone, there are few walls, and none of any height. It was obviously an important ceremonial site rather than an occupied town, and bears considerable superficial resemblance to Carnac, with long lines of megalithic monuments, though, of course, much more carefully carved. The masonry, in fact, is among the most skilful in the Andean region, as well as among the most megalithic.

The largest unit, known as the Acapana, is a terraced pyramid about 50 ft (15 m.) high, originally faced with stone. Of irregular ground plan, it is roughly 690 ft (210 m.) on each side. The remains of a large reservoir with an overflow canal, and foundations for houses, suggest that it might have been a place of refuge in case of attack.

The Calasasaya is a large square area about 445 by 425 ft (135 by 130 m.) delimited by upright monoliths which apparently originally formed part of a continuous wall. The interior is raised, and within this is a sunken court entered by a megalithic stairway. Associated with the Calasasaya is the most famous monument at Tiahuanaco, the great monolithic gateway known as the 'Gateway of the Sun' (Plate 10B). This enormous sculpture, carved of a single block of andesite, is about ten feet (3 m.) high, twelve and a half feet (3.75 m.) wide, and is estimated to weigh about ten tons. A man can easily pass through the rectangular doorway cut in the centre, above which is a low frieze in typical Tiahuanaco style. In this, a large central figure, certainly a god and possibly Viracocha, is flanked by forty-eight small rectangular figures, running toward him. It is one of the archaeological wonders of America. For centuries broken and askew, it was restored to proper position in 1908.

Two smaller enclosures are the Palacio and one termed Puma Puncu; the latter is another platform structure. Both of these contain large stone slabs and blocks, well dressed and fitted, some of them estimated to weigh more than one hundred tons. Smaller broken monolithic gateways are also common. A few well-built subterranean chambers have been found.

Both basalt and sandstone were used in the construction of Tiahuanaco, and the nearest quarries of the latter are three miles (5 km.) from the site. The stone-work is unusually well done, with smooth faces, the great blocks perfectly fitted together. They are sometimes held together more firmly by notches, or – something new and unique in Peruvian masonry – by copper cramps. T-shaped depressions were cut into adjacent sides of two stone blocks where copper objects made to fit were hammered in.

Tiahuanaco is also famed for its great human statuary. The largest of these was unknown until 1932 when it was discovered by the American Peruvianist Wendell C. Bennett[1] in the course of his excavations; it was carried to La Paz and erected in a plaza there. This tall forbidding figure of red sandstone is over twenty-four feet (7.3 m.) in height, and from forty-two to fifty inches (1.05 to 1.27 m.) in width and thickness. The low-relief art is symmetrical, stiff, and very characteristic of the site and period (Plate II).

It has been suggested that the site was a great ceremonial centre, to which came a large part of the population of the region on regular rare pilgrimages, at which times they worked, under expert supervision, on the constructions; this implies a well-organized and regulated society with limitless manpower, approaching that of the later Inca. The structures were apparently still uncompleted when work on them ceased.

Few excavations have been done at Tiahuanaco or in its general region. Though textiles are not preserved here, those of this period and type found on the coast suggest that the art was on a high plane, especially in the making of tapestries. Much of

1. Bennett, 1934.

the stone carving in relief is in textile motifs. High-class work was done in gold, silver, and especially in copper.

The classic Tiahuanaco pottery of the great period is most characteristic and a great art. It is a painted, not a modelled style, with relatively few and simple shapes and very diagnostic designs. A goblet with flaring sides is probably the most characteristic shape, next a container made in the shape of a puma or llama, with relief head; bowls and vases of various proportions are common. The designs are, like the Nazca, in many tints and highly burnished, with rich, blending colours, prevailingly dark; black, white, yellow, grey, and brown are the commonest. The most characteristic design is the puma, always shown in profile, but this is very much stylized and conventionalized; condors are frequent, as also are purely geometric elements (Plates 27, 30B).

Almost nothing is known of the daily life of the people of Tiahuanaco, but it probably differed only slightly from that of the highland peoples of later periods; they doubtless grew potatoes and other highland food crops, and bred and used llamas and alpacas.

The tangible evidence of the influence is in the art style of textiles and ceramics. Practically everywhere in Peru – except apparently, strange to say, in the Cuzco region – the local art styles, especially as expressed on pottery, became modified by the adoption of elements obviously related to those found at Tiahuanaco.

In most Peruvian archaeological sites of this period are found flat-based, flaring-sided goblets and bowls painted in four or more colours and highly polished. The motifs are also those of Tiahuanaco: stylized geometric profile pumas, condors, and other figures; the same unmistakable elements are found in the textiles. Every region, naturally, had its characteristic style, its ways of employing these elements and of combining them with the existing local styles.

In the absence of reliable radiocarbon dates, estimates of the date and length of the Classic Tiahuanaco phase vary greatly from the A.D. 200–600 accorded it herein. Some good authorities place it much later, such as A.D. 800–1000.

Lest the reader, who may have thought of all pre-Columbian Peruvians as Inca, be surprised at the number of apparently independent and unique cultures in prehistoric Peru, it may be stated that possibly as many other cultures still remain to be discovered. Relatively few scientific archaeological excavations have been made in Peru, and large parts of the country are practically unknown archaeologically because the paucity of saleable objects that might be recovered has not tempted natives to dig. Future excavations in new sites may be expected to reveal many new cultures, each with its specific type of architecture, ceramics, and other artefacts. Doubtless their languages, religions, and social customs were equally different; of these we will never know anything. The economic basis of life, however, was probably practically the same throughout the highlands at any given time; the same is true of the coast.

Chapter 6

THE CLIMACTIC ERA

c. A.D. 600–1532

THE Climactic Era comprises the final periods of Peruvian culture history. Material culture had reached its maximum development, and probably government also. The pattern of life was urban, militaristic, probably socialistic. Most of the groups and tribes were probably united into a few large nations or empires between which there was violent competition if not war. Beginning with the Expansionist period preceding the Urbanist period with a few such large nations, it closed with the Imperialist period of the all-embracing Inca empire. A final Colonial period, following the Spanish Conquest, might be added.

The Expansionist Period

c. A.D. 600–1000

Tiahuanaco style is found in its classic form only in the area of Tiahuanaco itself; the phases from the coast and the northern highlands are in a slightly different, evolved, but readily recognizable style, and presumed to date from a somewhat later period. It was long surmised that this later coastal Tiahuanaco style must have spread from some focus in the highlands nearer the coast than Tiahuanaco itself; recent studies have suggested that this may have been the site of Wari, and, to indicate this, archaeologists today refer to the Wari-Tiahuanaco influence or style.

The present status of archaeological research in Peru is well exemplified by Huari or Wari. Though mentioned by Cieza de León in 1554 as a pre-Inca site, under the name of Vinaque, it was forgotten until rediscovered by Tello in 1931; only in the last decade has it been investigated.[1] Wari is a large site in the pro-

1. Bennett, 1953a; Rowe, Collier, and Willey, 1950.

vince of Huanta, department of Ayacucho. The ruins may cover as much as four square miles, with quantities of walled enclosures and the remains of buildings and houses. Some of the walls tower to a height of twenty-five feet (7 to 8 metres). All are of masonry made of rude field stones laid in mud and originally faced with mud plaster. The buildings seem to lack both doors and windows and, in this respect, as well as in the type of masonry and general appearance, the site bears much superficial resemblance to Pikillacta, near Cuzco. Only a very little cut stone was used here, in great contrast to Tiahuanaco. A number of carved stone statues, however, have been found; these resemble those of Tiahuanaco more closely than any others, but there is considerable difference. Obviously here was a great residential city, not mainly a ceremonial site.

As usual, it is the ceramics that afford the clue to the temporal placing of Wari. There are a number of types, covering a considerable time period, but two groups of polychrome ware bear a very close resemblance to Coast Tiahuanaco pottery, and to the Late Nazca Wari type, presumed to date from the Tiahuanaco period. Probably, therefore, the Tiahuanaco influence spread to the coast from Wari. Logically, however, large cities like Wari and Pikillacta should belong in the next, Urbanist, period.

The best picture of the Expansionist Wari-Tihuanaco-horizon period is, as usual, secured from the coastal sites where the preservation of material objects is best, and where cemeteries are found. No great edifices were erected, but use of the older ones continued. Excellent textiles of wool and cotton continued to be made, and the tapestries of this period are the finest ever made in Peru; that had become the most popular technique, but many others were known and practised. Some new metallurgical methods, such as silverplating, had been developed.

Wari-Tiahuanaco influence, as evidenced mainly by the horizon art style, is found in all the coastal areas as far north as Chicama (but not in Lambayeque), especially at Chicama, Moche, Virú, Supe, Chancay, Ancón, Nievería, Pachacamac, Cañete, Chincha, Ica, and Nazca. The impact on the peaceful Nazca culture was strong, practically absorbing it, while it affected only slightly the vigorous Moche who soon threw it off and re-established their own pattern.

Archaeologists divide the Coast Tiahuanaco or 'Middle' period into two sub-periods, 'A' and 'B', characterized by pottery styles. 'A' is the Wari-Tihuanaco-influenced polychrome style, generally known on the coast as 'Epigonal'. At Ancón it is known as 'Middle Ancón I'. Each site had its particular modification of this ware. The shapes of coastal Tiahuanaco vessels, however, differ much from those of the highlands; only the goblet and the cup are similar, and vessels with long upright spouts, especially double-spouts, are common. Epigonal pottery is very well made, highly polychrome, with rather elaborate designs (Plate 31A).

The influence of Tiahuanaco ceased with the Epigonal style, for the succeeding 'B' style, known to Peruvianists as 'Black-White-Red', is very different; local variations of it are known as 'Middle Ancón II' and 'Late Ancón I'. The latter is a quasi-horizon style, found over much of northern Peru. It has no congeners, however, in the central and southern highlands. The ware is definitely decadent, softer, unpolished, with simple, poorly executed designs in fewer colours. The shapes are also simple with little if any modelling in life-forms, and the painted decoration is almost exclusively geometric (Plate 31B).

The influence has not been definitely recognized in the central highland, Cuzco, region, but can hardly fail to have been present. As we have seen, the site of Pikillacta near Cuzco, of still unidentified period, bears some resemblance to Wari, definitely of the Tiahuanaco period.

In the northern highlands are small sites in the Chavín architectural tradition but assigned to this period because of the associated ceramics. Wilkawaín, near Huaraz, the most important of these, consists of a stone temple and a number of other one- and two-storey stone houses.[1] The temple is a small replica of the Castillo at Chavín, with three floors, interior staircases, ramps, galleries, rooms, and ventilation shafts; there are seven rooms on each floor. The great roof slabs are placed sloping so as to form a gable roof, but this is covered with dirt and stones to form a sort

1. Bennett, 1944.

of dome. The temple measures about thirty-five by fifty-two feet (10·7 by 15·6 m.). It is much less known even than Chavín, and few of the rooms have been entered, for most of them are filled with stones and other debris which must have been brought there for this purpose. The principal rooms are large, measuring more than seven by twenty-two feet (2·25 by 6·8 m.), and over six feet (1·8 m.) high.

A very distinctive pottery type of which more should be known is what is called the Marañon style. The characteristic shape is a tripod plate, rather flattish and supported on three long conical feet. This form, so common in Mexico and Central America, is otherwise practically unknown in Peru. Shallow bowls are also found, both types painted on the interior in rather fine lines of reddish tints, generally curvilinear, and depicting demoniacal animals as well as geometric elements. The ware is often also termed Middle Huamachuco, as it is found also in the far northern highlands, near Huamachuco and Cajabamba.

In the southern highlands, following classical Tiahuanaco times and the Middle Period, the ceramics became poorer, just as on the coast, and are known as Decadent Tiahuanaco. The designs are carelessly made, the colours fewer, and dull. The classical Tiahuanaco design elements are retained but employed separately, independently, and not as parts of complete designs, such as pumas.

The four centuries here allowed for the Expansionist period, A.D. 600 to 1000, is longer and earlier than that accorded it by good authorities of another school of thought, A.D. 900 to 1200.

The Urbanist Period

c. A.D. 1000–1440

Toward the end of the Expansionist period whatever unity or homogeneity of culture the highland influence from Wari or Tiahuanaco might have produced began to lessen, and local differentiation soon eliminated practically all traces of it. The populations had now probably reached their maxima, civic organizations were well developed, and contentions for land, power, and dominance began. Fortified refuge places were built.

Villages probably contended for mastery and formed alliances and coalitions which in turn fought for domination until at last a few large commonwealths of considerable extent emerged. This was the pattern in many other parts of the world at similar stages of development, but in other times.

These minor nations might well be likened to medieval kingdoms; they set the pattern for the Inca empire that soon conquered and consolidated all of them. For, contrary to the usual American Indian democratic proclivity, there was apparently great stress on social stratification, with noble and aristocratic classes, and reverence for the chief, leader, or 'king'.

Most of our data for this period, both historical and archaeological, refer to the coastal peoples, especially to the Chimú of the northern coast, for the big fertile irrigated river valleys there supported a large concentration of population, whereas in the highland regions, more uniformly watered, the people probably remained somewhat more rural. Nevertheless, even in the highlands, this seems to have been a period when the natives tended to gather into large urban centres, with city planning. It has therefore sometimes been termed the 'City Builder Period'.

Owing to the heavier rainfall on the north coast and the consequent larger size of the irrigated valleys with their greater populations, the largest and most important of the 'kingdoms', that of Chimú, developed on that coast and controlled a great area from Piura in the north to Paramonga in the south (Plates 5B, 6). There is little doubt that military conquest extended the sway of the Chimú north to the Lambayeque and Piura Valleys, and south at least to Casma (Plate 5A). Every valley had its urban centre, but the capital of the Chimú was Chanchán, in the environs of the present city of Trujillo.[1] Chanchán is a stupendous site – and sight. The ruins cover about six square miles, filled – the major part at least – with great tall boundary walls, smaller house walls, streets, reservoirs, pyramids, and other edifices and features expected of a great metropolitan centre. All are built of large rectangular adobe bricks. The occasional torrential rains have eroded the tops of the great walls and covered their bases, but they still tower to a height of some thirty feet (9 m.). When

1. Holstein, 1927.

the lower walls are cleared of the earth that covers and protects them, many of them are found to be covered with arabesque decorations in low relief and probably made by impressions of moulds (Plate 4). The designs are of small, identical repeated motifs, in rows, and apparently derived from textile designs, mainly geometric, but also with conventionalized animals. When cleared – and unless protected – these arabesques, of course, are ruined in the next heavy rain. There are also some wall paintings.

Today the great city is deserted except for the occasional tourist's car traversing the narrow, humpy streets. For the city was planned like a modern one with long straight streets meeting at right angles. The visitor blessed with imagination can visualize them teeming with busy people, the gable-roofed houses full of the domestic sounds of women and children. The aboriginal population is estimated to have been about 50,000. In those days the city was probably green with trees, but today, the irrigation ditches filled up, not a tree grows for miles around.

The city was apparently composed of ten large units, generally rectangular, each, probably, the locale or ward of a clan or some other social group, and the domain of a sub-chief. Each unit is surrounded by one or more great high walls, within which is a gridiron of streets with many small houses, large pyramids – probably for temples, reservoirs, gardens, and cemeteries. In between the wards there were apparently irrigated and cultivated areas, marshes, cemeteries, and some isolated small structures. Some of the units are said to be as large as 1100 by 1600 ft (355 by 480 m.), or about forty acres (Plates 2B, 3).

Similar, though smaller, cities are found in each of the valleys; typical larger ones are Pacatnamú (Pacasmayo) and Purgatorio in the northern valleys. Each had its planned streets, houses, pyramid temples, reservoirs, and similar civic features. It was an urban period, and we may conceive that there were many of the facilities, functions and functionaries, and utilities of a modern city, such as jails, magistrates, and possibly even police and traffic laws!

In the absence of any wheeled vehicles, or any methods of transportation except the backs of llamas and men and women,

provisioning, disposal of garbage and refuse, and similar muni-
cipal problems must have been difficult in such large and
crowded population centres. Trade and commerce were doubtless slowed by the probable lack of any standard currency. The
slight evidence also indicates the absence of any formalized
religion.

The Chimú culture was, in its later phases, contemporary with
the Inca, and indeed persisted throughout the Inca empire so
that some authorities consider the late Chimú period to have
lasted until A.D. 1600. The history of the later days of the Chimú
empire, and traditions of earlier times, were therefore well known
at the time of the Spanish Conquest, and were written down by
some of the chroniclers. Miguel Cabello de Balboa[1] recounts the
traditions of the dynasty of Naymlap of the Lambayeque region,
and Antonio de la Calancha[2] speaks especially of the Pacasmayo
area. They portray a high culture and an aristocratic and autocratic court. The Chimú language, known as Yunga, was probably entirely distinct from the Quechua spoken by the Inca, and
a few words of it are still – or until very recently were – remembered by some of the coastal fishermen, especially by those of the
village of Eten, near Chiclayo.

Archaeological evidence corroborates historical tradition in
indicating a strong development of political and social organization. The great cities themselves suggest such a fact; such immense concentrations of populations in orderly city blocks need
a centralized and efficient government. The building of the walls,
edifices, and the large adobe pyramids required organized
labour under experienced supervision. The division of the cities
into wards, each a town in itself with all necessary public
buildings and utilities, moreover, indicates social subdivisions.
Also the great variation in the size and quality of the houses
suggests social classes, based on wealth or birth, and the same
is indicated by the differences in the quality of the burials. Some
of these are simple, with few and poor gifts, while others consist
of large subterranean chambers with quantities of pottery vessels, textiles, ornaments, and similar grave furniture. These,
naturally, being much younger, are found in a much better state

1. Cabello de Balboa, 1840.   2. Calancha, 1638.

of preservation than the buried objects of the preceding Moche period.

Everywhere in the Urbanist period craftsmanship had reached a high level of technical accomplishment and tended to become static and standardized; the emphasis was on quantity rather than on quality. There were few new inventions, and the art products were uninspired. Textile and painted designs were typically in orderly bands and rows, with a standard sequence of a few colours, and generally consisted of repetitions of small geometric motifs and conventionalized animals.

The Chimú produced no outstanding ceramic art. Like the Inca, it was standardized and lacked creative imagination. Similarly, it is very characteristic and easily recognized. As with Moche, it was produced in great volume, mainly in moulds, and is well represented in most large collections of Peruvian ceramics. Duplicates are common. The technique of manufacture had returned to the earlier 'reducing' process of firing, so that four-fifths of the vessels are of black ware. Few vessels are painted, and these very rudely. Most of the shapes are similar to those of the Moche, the stirrup-spout predominating, but many other Moche forms had been given up. Many vessels are effigies, depicting life-forms and activities, but far less realistically than those of the Moche. Scenic painting is gone. Very characteristic are double vessels. Each of the connected bottles has a spout, and one of them is equipped with a whistle so that when the vessel is tilted and the liquid flows from one to the other, air is forced out and a whistling sound produced (Plate 26).

Chimú pottery also retains some Coast Tiahuanaco elements, but is basically rather degenerate Moche, more stereotyped, and lacking the realistic, photographic, and imaginative quality of its greater predecessor.

For the first time on the northern coast, textiles are well preserved. Painted and tie-dye cloths, double-cloth, brocade, gauzes, and pattern weaves were the popular techniques. Metallurgy had reached a high stage of development, and copper, bronze, gold, and silver were now worked. Alloying to form bronze was a new process, as was the casting of copper and bronze. Large utilitarian copper implements such as picks, knives, and awls were made, but most of the smith's skill was still employed in fashioning ornaments. Calabashes decorated with pyrographic ornamentation were common, and feather mosaic objects are often found.

While the best known of the 'empires' of this period was the Chimú, similar large groups occupied the rest of the habitable coast to the south. The valleys of the central coast such as Chancay, Lurín, and Rímac constituted the Cuismancu empire and formed an archaeological sub-culture. Each of these and other valleys had its large urban metropolis as well as some smaller ones. Pachacamac with its great famous temple pyramid was one of these; another of the largest was Cajamarquilla, a great ancient site a short distance up the river from the city of Lima. Cajamarquilla cannot compare with Chanchan in size, nor do the adobe walls tower as high, but the large congested area of house walls, streets, and raised temple (?) sites gives the visitor a memorable impression (Plate 7). All are built of puddled mud.

The great pyramid temple of Pachacamac overshadows the city in the Lurín Valley and was a famous shrine in Inca and pre-Inca days. So great was the veneration for Pachacamac and his shrine that the Inca permitted a continuation of his worship together with that of the Sun, and at the time of the Spanish Conquest Pachacamac was the Mecca of Peru. Pizarro, learning of it on his way to Cuzco in 1533, and desiring to seize the golden treasure reported to be there, dispatched his brother Fernando thither. Fernando destroyed the idol of the god, but most of the treasure had been hidden; a part was recovered. Pachacamac was also the scene of the first scientific archaeological work in Peru, and the first excavation of the old dean of Peruvianists, Dr Max Uhle, on an expedition for the University Museum of Philadelphia. By careful excavations, Uhle distinguished graves of the Inca period from earlier ones, and determined the types of artefacts diagnostic of the several periods.[1] Uhle's work was continued by the great Peruvian archaeologist Dr Julio C. Tello, and a part of the ruins of the Inca period have been restored, making the site, within easy reach of Lima, one of the 'must' sites for the tourist to Peru.

1. Uhle, 1903.

The Cuismancu empire is not so well known historically – or rather by tradition – as the Chimú, and, although the excavations at Ancón, Pachacamac, and other sites are famous, the artefacts are also not so well known. The great aboriginal cemetery at Ancón, only an hour's ride from Lima and now being developed as a suburban watering-place, has been dug in for centuries, first by native looters and later by archaeologists, and is still yielding quantities of 'mummies' to the spades of government scientists.[1]

Life on the central coast in this period was doubtless much like that in the Chimú region, and the handicraft was basically similar, though differing in detail from place to place and time to time. Most characteristic and diagnostic, as usual, is the pottery. The most striking and interesting of these styles is the Chancay Black-on-White, especially typical of the site of Chancay but also known as Late Ancón II. The ware is thin, porous, hard-baked, and red, covered with a creamy white slip on which are painted designs in boldly contrasting sepia. The shapes are generally simple-silhouette, especially large, tall, oval vessels with small orifices, and bowls. Very large pottery human figures are also characteristic. The designs are most frequently geo-metric, straight or wavy lines, cross-hatching, or fields of dots, but small animals or birds in a textile pattern are also found (Plate 32).

According to the chronicles, a small empire, the Chuqui-mancu, occupied the Mala, Chilca, and Cañete Valleys, but these are not so well known archaeologically, and they appar-ently did not compose a cultural entity. Nor is much known of their history.

The lesser rainfall and consequent smaller valleys on the south coast did not permit such large populations as farther to the north, but the inhabitants of the irrigated valleys were doubtless more urbanized than in the preceding periods. These valleys, Chincha, Pisco, Ica, and Nazca, composed the Chincha empire of the period immediately preceding their conquest by the Inca. The regions constitutes an archaeological entity that is known as the Ica culture. While no great cities are known,

1. Reiss and Stübel, 1880–7.

smaller sites, such as La Centinela and Tambo de Mora in Chincha Valley, and Tambo Colorado in Pisco Valley, are remarkable for their extraordinary preservation in this almost totally rainless region. Tambo Colorado in particular is the best-preserved adobe ruin in Peru; little is missing except the roofs. Many of the walls and especially the niches still preserve their original red and yellow paint. It was doubtless an administrative centre with storehouses and quarters for couriers and troops as well as for permanent officers, and was built either in the late Ica or the Inca period (Plate 8A).

Archaeologists divide the Ica period into four subdivisions, based on pottery styles. The ceramics differ radically from both Chancay and Chimú, and almost as much from their Nazca predecessor, although there was no break between Nazca and Ica. Gone are the polychrome vessels with their large naturalistic and demoniacal decorations. There is even less modelling in naturalistic or effigy shapes, and the forms have become limited to a few characteristic shapes such as bowls with relatively straight converging sides and almost flat bottoms, and spheroid vessels with small orifices. In the earliest (Epigonal, Early Ica) period, designs were rudely painted Wari-Tiahuanaco elements, but soon the very characteristic Ica type of decoration developed, the vessel being practically covered – the upper part at least – with rows and bands of repeated small elements, geometric motifs or small conventionalized birds or fish, painted in black, white, and red, evidently in imitation of textile patterns (Plate 30A). The cloths show similar styles, mainly in tapestry, embroidery, and weft-pattern weaves.

In all coastal cultures, toward the end of the Urbanist period, Inca influence became strong, as is especially seen in the manufacture of pottery vessels of typical and characteristic Inca shape, such as the pointed-base aryballus, in local styles of paste and decoration.

South of the Nazca region the rainfall, the rivers, and the inhabited areas are even smaller, and the culture of the aboriginal population was apparently lower. Not much is known of the archaeology of this region, but around Arequipa a type of pottery, apparently on a late horizon, is found which is believed to be

more closely connected with the people and the culture of the
Atacama region of Chile than with the Peruvian cultures to
the north (Plate 33).

The Urbanist period is far less well marked or well known in
the highlands than on the coast, as has been noted before. Since
the inhabited areas were not restricted to irrigated river valleys,
the populations were naturally not so dense or concentrated, and
capital cities would not be expected. Nevertheless the ruins of a
number of large ones exist. In the northern highlands few excavations of this period have been made and there are few if any
traditions. The pottery is not very distinctive, some of it being
painted with red and black designs on a white slip, some decorated with incised, punched, or appliqué designs. The period
here is known as Late Huamachuco. No large cities are reported.
In the southern highlands and Bolivia this seems to have been
the period when the high masonry *chullpas*, burial towers made
of admirable masonry, were built (Plate 16B). This culture,
known as Colla, was one of the first to be conquered by the Inca,
which may explain the apparent lack of Urbanist remains. Both
here and in the northern highlands all trace of Wari-Tiahuanaco
influence seems to have disappeared by this time.

Toward the end of this period the highland peoples came into
the ascendancy with the rise of the Inca in the central highlands.
The history of the next short period, the Imperialist – really no
more than a subdivision of the Urbanist – is the history of the
Inca.

While the historical accounts of the chroniclers recount the
early history of the Inca, such as might be considered as falling
in the Urbanist period, these are obviously largely mythological and unreliable, and differ greatly. Archaeologically almost
nothing is known of the origin and early history of the Inca, or
of the central highlands in the days preceding the inception of the
Inca empire by the emperor Pachacuti about the year 1445.

That there were large cities in the central highlands before the
Inca period is indicated by some ruins such as that of the large
unique city of Pikillacta, not far from Cuzco. Evidently not
built by Inca, the nature of the city is still unknown, but it covers
a great area with terraces with retaining walls, streets, and the

walls of countless houses. Strangely, these seem to have been made without either doors or windows and were probably entered through the roofs, now gone. All the walls are built of natural field stones. Evidence of occupation is apparently absent.

A few sites that are ascribed to the Early Inca period have been excavated, and are presumed to cover the period A.D. 1200–1440. But the masonry, ceramics, and metallurgy are rather crude and bear slight resemblance to those of the Inca period.

The Urbanist period was not one of the longer ones, but nevertheless the estimates of the time-span vary greatly. Some good authorities grant it only 138 years (A.D. 1300–1438), instead of the 440 years (A.D. 1000–1440) allowed it here.

The Imperialist Period

A.D. 1440–1532

Historically, this is the Inca period, the only one known to the average reader. Like the Aztec in Mexico, the Inca were a small militaristic group that came to power late, conquered surrounding groups, and established one of the most extraordinary empires in the world.

Herein the Inca culture is treated in greater detail, both because data on it, derived from the accounts of the chroniclers of the time of the Spanish Conquest, afford more information than on any other people, and because their culture may be considered as typical of that of other peoples in Peru at this period.

Inca influence extended all over Peru as the various other culture groups were conquered – and possibly even a little before. In this period typically Inca objects are found in all regions, or blends of Inca and local styles.

The Inca is the third great horizon pottery style in Peru. Like the others, it appears suddenly in full vigour, as if it had developed elsewhere, but no developmental or proto-Inca types are known; it has all the marks of being in a late stage of ceramic evolution. Conservatism, and lack of imagination, invention, and initiative, are apparent; it is chaste and sedate. The shapes are simple and limited to rather few which are unmistakably Inca and restricted to this period. Foremost is the so-called aryballus for containing and carrying liquids – probably chicha; this has a pointed base and a knob around which, presumably, the carrying strap or rope was wound. The aryballus varies from a few inches to a yard in height. Other typical shapes are a plate with a handle of bird-head or hoof form, a cylindrical goblet, and kylix-footed vessels. The decoration is almost always painted, in small repeated geometric designs in panels, bands, or zones. Seldom are any life-forms used, and then they are small and highly conventionalized; the animals represented are themselves small, such as insects. The colours are few and sombre, mainly black, white, and red. Technically the ware is excellent, hard baked and highly polished (Plates 34, 35).

During the empire, Inca pottery was used throughout the land, either imported, locally manufactured in typical pattern, or adapted to local patterns. In the Ica region, many Late Ica II vessels of typical Inca shapes were decorated with Ica motifs. And in the Chimú area typical Inca shapes were made in the characteristic Chimú black-ware technique.

PART THREE

THE INCA

*

Chapter 7

HISTORY

As already noted, except for mnemonic devices such as the *quipu*, which served only as a reminder to the trained and informed recorder, Inca history was purely traditional until the Spanish chroniclers, soon after the Conquest, wrote down the legends. Like such 'history' everywhere, the earliest events are very largely mythological and entirely unreliable, while the latest ones are quite detailed and probably relatively authentic; the middle period is a mixture.

Peru is the one place in America where, as commonly in the Mediterranean region, history was recounted in terms of royal reigns. The Inca remembered the names of their divine emperors, and the traditional list is generally accepted as accurate:

1. Manco Capac (*c.* A.D. 1200)
2. Sinchi Roca
3. Lloque Yupanqui
4. Mayta Capac
5. Capac Yupanqui
6. Inca Roca
7. Yahuar Huacac
8. Viracocha Inca
9. Pachacuti Inca Yupanqui (1438–71)
10. Topa Inca Yupanqui (1471–93)
11. Huayana Capac (1493–1525)
12. Huascar (1525–32)
13. Atahuallpa (1532–3)

Of the above thirteen emperors, the first five belonged to the Lower Cuzco moiety (see page 177), the others to the Upper division. The first eight were local and of slight importance, with few reliable historical records. The first, Manco Capac, was a quasi-mythological character who may be dated about A.D. 1200. Inca history really begins with the accession of the great emperor Pachacuti, the ninth in succession, whose installation has been calculated, probably fairly accurately, as A.D. 1438. It was with Pachacuti that the great expansion of the Inca empire began.

The Legendary Empire

Manco Capac was a demigod who was considered the founder of the Inca dynasty. He was turned to stone, but the dried bodies or mummies of the next ten emperors – or at least bodies that were claimed and believed to be theirs – were preserved in Cuzco until the time of Pizarro.

The Spanish chroniclers recount several different and mutually contradictory legends of Manco Capac and of the origins of the Inca dynasty and empire, all of them containing supernatural elements. The best known of these is somewhat as follows:

About 18 miles south-east of Cuzco, at a place called Paccari Tampu ('Dawn Tavern'), is a hill known as Tampu-Tocco ('Tavern Hole'), in which there were three openings.[1] From these openings emerged the founders of the empire, the ancestors of some of the Inca *ayllus* ('clans'; see page 174) from the side holes, Manco Capac and his brothers and sisters from the central or 'Splendid Opening'. His three brothers were named Ayar Auca, Ayar Cachi, and Ayar Uchu; the four sisters Mama Ocllo, Mama Huaco, Mama Cora, and Mama Raua; Manco Capac himself was then known as Ayar Manco.

The eight assumed leadership of the ten ayllus that had come out of the side holes, and led them towards the valley of Cuzco.

1. The word *tocco* is translated 'window' by some, 'cave mouth' by others. Three 'windows' in a wall at Machu Picchu are identified by Bingham as the traditional site; others consider the reference to be to natural small caves in a hill.

The exodus occupied a number of years, for the migrants paused for a year or two in several villages on the way, in one of which Sinchi Roca, the second emperor, was born to Manco Capac and his eldest sister, Mama Ocllo. Also *en route* Manco succeeded in getting rid of his three brothers. Cachi was a husky fellow and the others feared him. He climbed to the top of the hill of Huanacauri (which Inca boys also had to climb in their puberty tests), and from there threw sling-stones with such force that he created new ravines. So they sent him back to the origin hole to fetch the sacred llama, and another man went back to help him and to wall him up in the hole – where he is yet. Uchu remained at Huanacauri where he turned to stone, the *huaca*[1] of the shrine there. Auca went on to Cuzco where he became the stone field-guardian huaca of the city. That left only Manco.

Manco and his sisters continued on to the valley of Cuzco where they tested the ground with a golden staff. Finding the soil a little to the east of modern Cuzco to be fertile, they decided to settle there. The valley, of course, was inhabited, but the Inca were the chosen people of the Sun, and wanted their land of corn and llamas. The several small tribes or ayllus in the region were attacked and driven out. The amazonian Mama Huaco killed one man with a bola stone, cut out his lungs and inflated them, which horrid sight frightened the rest away. Then Manco and his four sisters built their first houses on the site of the later Coricancha, and Temple of the Sun.

Naturally several versions of the origin myth, differing considerably in details, were recorded by the Spanish. Garcilaso gives a rather different story in which Manco Capac and his sister were created by the Sun on an island in Lake Titicaca. Manco was a culture hero rather than a conqueror, and he and Mama Ocllo taught the people industries and arts and gathered them together to found Cuzco.

Manco Capac may have been a purely mythological character, invented in later years to give paternity and supernatural origin to the real quasi-historical founder of the Inca empire, Sinchi Roca.

1. Sacred object or place. See page 209. Pronounced 'waca', which phonetic but non-standard form will be used herein.

Garcilaso de la Vega is one of the most famous of the many Spanish chroniclers who wrote down the Inca legends, and his version was followed by many of his successors and accepted by many modern writers (see 'Sources', page 273). Thus Means[1] adopts the Garcilassan accounts. According to this, the Emperor Sinchi Roca began the expansion of the Inca empire, Lloque Yupanqui extended it to Lake Titicaca, Mayta Capac reached Tiahuanaco and the headwaters of the coastal rivers, and Capac Yupanqui conquered some of the coastal peoples.

Garcilaso's account is not supported by most of the earlier chroniclers, and the modern opinion is against its acceptance and inclined to believe that it was not until the reign of Yahuar Huacac that the expansion of the empire began. Even regarding this time the various accounts are rather contradictory.

If the account of Garcilaso is to be credited, the predecessors of Pachacuti had already conquered and incorporated in the Inca empire a large part of Peru and Bolivia, and yet we find, in the time of Viracocha Inca, the Inca waging a life-and-death struggle with their rivals for ascendancy, the Chanca, Lupaca, and Colla, Cuzco besieged, and Emperor Pachacuti beginning his great conquests in the close vicinity of Cuzco. Garcilaso's accounts seem to be hardly compatible with these facts, and it appears more likely that the pre-Pachacuti wars were local ones, without permanent subjugation by the Inca of any enemy people.

The historical accounts of Pedro Sarmiento de Gamboa and of the Jesuit Father Bernabé Cobo seem to be more logical and reliable, and are supported by a number of the other chroniclers. They are accepted in general by the modern authority Rowe[2] instead of the Garcilaso-Means version, and are here adopted, with the understanding that they are not presented with any claim to exactitude or finality.

According to the versions here accepted, during the reigns of the first eight Inca emperors, Manco Capac to Viracocha Inca, the Inca did not extend their sway or political influence beyond the immediate region of Cuzco. There were many independent small groups in this area, probably physically identical with the Inca, speaking slightly variant dialects or varieties of the same

1. Means, 1931.   2. Rowe, 1946.

language, and enjoying very much the same culture, economic and non-material. That is to say, at this time the Inca were but one of a number of equally unimportant groups in their habitat. They were constantly in competition and often at war with their neighbours, but no group had any thought of establishing permanent hegemony over the others; the imperial concept had not yet developed. The victor in inter-tribal or inter-city wars looted the vanquished and possibly imposed a tribute on them, and then let them alone until, possibly, they again acquired enough power to become a menace. The traditions of the Inca record no defeats suffered, but such set-backs are readily forgotten; only victories are remembered. All of the great empires of antiquity had a similar rise from unimportance among the obscure. Possibly the Inca custom of hereditary succession for their leaders had something to do with their later rise; it is not known whether the neighbouring groups followed a similar pattern or not.

Sinchi Roca, second emperor and son of Manco Capac and his sister Mama Ocllo, was probably an historical character, but the legends say little about him. He was not warlike and made no military campaigns, adding nothing to the Inca dominions. He succeeded Manco Capac by his father's nomination. There is disagreement among the chroniclers as to whether or not he followed his father's example of marrying his sister. His son, Lloque Yupanqui, succeeded him; Lloque is said to mean 'left-handed'. Lloque Yupanqui had an elder brother; why in this case Manco Capac's rule of primogeniture was not followed is a question. Like his father he did nothing of historical importance and performed no military exploits. According to the legend, he had no children in spite of his advanced age. Like the early biblical patriarchs, they lived to a really ripe old age in that period; Sarmiento has all the early emperors living to an age of over one hundred! So they got old Lloque Yupanqui another wife – not his sister, it seems – and by her he had a son, Mayta Capac.

Mayta Capac was a strong character like his great-grandfather, Manco Capac, and so fabulous myths grew up about him, as in the case of Manco Capac. A vigorous three-month baby, he was born with a full set of teeth. At the age of one year he was as big as an average eight-year-old, and at two years he was fighting with big lads. When only a few years older he got into a quarrel with some boys of the Alcahuiza group, the nearest neighbours of the Inca, which developed into a full-scale battle and finally into a war in which, of course, the Inca were victorious. Still in early childhood, Mayta Capac gave a good account of himself in these battles, and so went through the maturity rites at that tender age. Like most kindly fathers, Lloque Yupanqui could not understand his belligerent brat and chided him, fearing that he would involve his family and people in disaster. However, the Inca were quite ready for a fight at any time and gave Mayta Capac enthusiastic support, especially after Lloque Yupanqui died and Mayta became emperor. Garcilaso makes him the first great conqueror, who subdued the country from Lake Titicaca to the headwaters of the coastal rivers, but later historical events, as well as the testimony of earlier and more reliable chroniclers, do not support this claim, and it is more probable that the wars under Mayta Capac did not extend more than a few miles beyond Cuzco and had few results beyond the taking of booty, the imposition of tribute, and the cultivation of hostility.

The chroniclers are in even greater disagreement than usual regarding the identity of Mayta Capac's *coya* or principal wife, no less than five different women being named; only one writer states that he married his sister. He followed the precedent of his father in making an inspection tour of his entire realm immediately after his inauguration, which custom was followed by all his successors. He also, according to one of the chroniclers, legitimized the great body of soothsayers, medicine men, and the like who had hitherto been accustomed to practise clandestinely their age-old professions.

The fifth emperor, Capac Yupanqui, was appointed by his father Mayta Capac just before his death. He also, apparently, was not the eldest son, but was selected because his older brother was ugly. Though his annals are short and simple, he is reported to have been the first emperor who made conquests beyond the valley of Cuzco, though these were only a dozen miles away.

Inca Roca, his son, also waged war with neighbouring peoples and subjugated some groups within twenty miles south of Cuzco.

For the greater part, however, he preferred the flesh-pots of Cuzco and idleness therein.

Inca Roca begat a number of legitimate – or, let us say, royal – sons, among whom Titu Cusi Hualpa and Vicaquirao left their marks on Peruvian history. The former succeeded to the throne under a new name, Yahuar Huacac, 'He Who Weeps Blood', for the origin of which name a legend – doubtless apocryphal except, possibly, in skeleton – was told.

Titu Cusi Hualpa's mother, Mama Micay, was a beautiful Huayllaca woman who, it was said, had first been promised to the chief of a neighbouring group, the Ayamarca. As this promise was broken, the Ayamarca went to war with the Huayllaca and were besting them. As the price of peace the Huayllaca agreed to deliver Mama Micay's child to the Ayamarca. Inducing Inca Roca to send the boy, then about eight years old, to a neighbouring town, he was seized and taken to the chief of the Ayamarca, the rejected suitor of his mother. With indignation beyond his years Titu Cusi Hualpa wept tears of blood and threatened a curse upon his captors if he were injured. It was several years before he was returned to his father, Inca Roca, the Inca 'emperor', which illustrates the slight power of the Inca in those days.

That Yahuar Huacac was chosen emperor is strange, for he seems to have been quite unsuited for the post, unenterprising and even cowardly. His brother (cousin, according to some accounts) Vicaquirao apparently was much more capable, as well as likeable. He led some campaigns against the groups south and east of Cuzco, and probably for the first time consolidated and organized these near-by regions as integral parts of the Inca empire. Another brother or cousin, Apo Mayta, is mentioned as a successful general; according to other accounts, Apu Mayta was merely another name for Vicaquirao.

Most of the chroniclers agree – for the first time – regarding the name and identity of the *coya* or queen of Yahuar Huacac; she was not his sister, indicating that at that time sister marriage was at least not a rule.

Hatun Tupac Inca, the eighth emperor, more commonly known by his later name of Viracocha Inca, was the most famous of the sons of Yahuar Huacac; on accession to the throne he assumed his new name in honour of Viracocha, the Creator, his reputed divine ancestor, who had appeared to him in a vision in his youth.

Viracocha was apparently the first true imperialist, the first emperor who planned permanent rule over foreign non-Inca peoples. Up until his time neighbouring groups had been conquered, but no garrisons had been placed among them, no Inca officials put over them; they were left alone, and eventually were again attacked and defeated. Viracocha began making them integral parts of his realm. With his experienced and efficient generals Vicaquirao and Apo Mayta he began a series of systematic conquests. He had passed his prime, however, before he had extended the empire more than some twenty-five miles around Cuzco. The larger expansion, more aptly compared with an explosion, began toward the end of his reign, and was animated by his even more capable and imperialistically minded son, Pachacuti.

Peru had by this time reached the economic and cultural stage when it was ripe for imperialism; it was in the air and in the cards. The Inca were but one of three or four rival strong groups in the Andean region, each about equally ready to progress towards imperialism and to gain ascendancy over the others. It was one of those times when the course of history depended on the outcome of a battle or two, and the latter largely upon the quality of leadership. The Inca under Pachacuti and Viracocha's generals had the experience and were the victors.

First it might be well to introduce some of the *dramatis personae*. Aged Emperor Viracocha's favourite child was the natural son Urco, or Urcon, whom he nominated as his successor, much to the disgust of the eldest royal son Inca Roca and the generals. The latter preferred the virile third royal son Cusi Inca Yupanqui, later known to Peruvian history as the great conqueror emperor Pachacuti.

Two Aymara-speaking groups of the Lake Titicaca region far to the south-east of Cuzco were then, with the Inca, the strong nations of the area. These were the Lupaca and the Colla. With that fatuous short-sightedness that has ever induced a people to solicit the aid of a more foreign and potentially more dangerous group in order to overcome a more closely related rival, each hoped for Inca aid to subdue the other. So did the Tlaxcaltec join with Cortés to crush the Aztec; so do today (1966) Chinese Nationalists seek Western aid to overcome the Communists; so would almost any nation today ally with beings from Mars to defeat its pet terrestrial enemy. Anyway, Emperor Viracocha formed an alliance with the Lupaca. The Colla, however, learning of this, attacked the Lupaca before Viracocha could send aid, but were defeated in a great battle at Paucarcolla; that eliminated them from the race for hegemony.

Immediately to the west of Cuzco were the Quechua, and to the west of the latter the Chanca, in the province of Andahuaylas. The Quechua, as the name suggests, were of the same blood, language, and culture as the Inca, and enjoyed friendly relations with the latter; the Chanca were a rather different people, and old enemies of the Quechua-Inca. In the early part of Viracocha's reign the Chanca had overcome the Quechua and established suzerainty over them, so that the Inca and Chanca territories were contiguous; they could not long remain so without conflict. Emperor Viracocha had strengthened his position by cultivating friendship with the Quechua and by taking his queen from that region.

Finally, towards the end of Viracocha's reign, the Chanca felt strong enough to attack, hoping that Inca leadership would be weak. They advanced on Cuzco with such a large army that many of the leaders, including Viracocha himself and his son and heir-apparent Urcon, believed the cause to be lost, and barricaded themselves in a fortress in Caquia-Xaquixahuana, which they believed could be defended better than the city. However, the two royal sons, Roca and Cusi Yupanqui, refused to yield and, together with the old generals Vicaquirao and Apo Mayta and a band of other last-ditchers, planned a desperate defence of Cuzco; Cusi Yupanqui was the leader. The Chanca attack was finally repulsed by resistance so heroic that the defenders believed that the stones of the battlefield must have turned into men to aid them; Cusi Inca Yupanqui had some of them taken and placed in the city's shrines as sacred *wacas*. After their repulse from the city, the Chanca were defeated in several other battles and disappeared as rivals to Inca power.

About this time, apparently, Viracocha died and was succeeded by his son, Inca Urcon, half-brother of Cusi Inca Yupanqui. His reign was short, however, for Cusi Yupanqui refused to recognize him, had himself enthroned in his place, and ordered Urcon's name removed from the official list of emperors. Cusi Yupanqui took the new name of Pachacuti, by which he is known to history, the first of the really great Inca emperors.

There are, of course, several different versions of the story of the accession of Pachacuti. According to Sarmiento he twice journeyed to Xaquixahuana to offer the spoils of the Chanca war to Emperor Viracocha, but his father kept insisting that his favourite son and nominee Urcon should receive them. Pachacuti finally, on the generals' urging, took the throne, without his father's consent or approval. The latter never again resided in Cuzco, which he had deserted.

The death of Viracocha Inca marks the close of the Middle period and of the legendary era of Inca history. Up until this time the many chroniclers have been in great disagreement, few details can be given as incontrovertible, and in most cases the truth is beyond assurance. With the advent of the next emperor, Pachacuti, all the major and more reliable authorities are in virtual agreement.

The Historical Empire

In addition to being a conqueror, Pachacuti was evidently a great civic planner. So many great works are ascribed to him that he seems to have been a minor culture hero, getting credit for many things done about this time. It is said that he made the city plan of Cuzco and erected many of the important public buildings there, especially enriching the Temple of the Sun, in which he placed the bodies of his seven imperial predecessors. To increase the size of the city and to give its inhabitants more land he obliterated all the villages for about a six-mile radius, and sent their populations to occupy other more distant areas.

The cyclopean agricultural terraces in the Cuzco region are ascribed to his initiative and direction, as well as the gnomon towers erected on the Cuzco skyline to determine the solstices, or at least to indicate the times for agricultural activities. Some of these accomplishments he probably completed before setting out for his conquests, or in his rest periods between campaigns; most of them he probably planned and left to be carried out by subordinates during his absences.

The great British South Americanist, Sir Clements Markham, has called Pachacuti 'the greatest man that the aboriginal race of America has produced', to which encomium the great American Peruvianist, Philip Means, gives his enthusiastic approval. He demonstrated his stature not only in accomplishments but in intellect.

The great and sudden expansion of the Inca empire is one of the marvels of history. It effectually began with the inauguration of Emperor Pachacuti, generally dated at 1438, was almost at its maximum at the time of the death of his son, Topa Inca, in 1493, and ended in 1532 with the conquest by Pizarro, just a little less than a century after its beginning. In little more than fifty years father and son extended Inca domination from northern Ecuador to central Chile, a coastal distance of close to 3000 miles, and an area of about 350,000 square miles. Possibly one must look to Philip and Alexander for analogous careers. Though some of the tribes offered vigorous resistance that delayed their conquest, nowhere did the Inca armies meet any nation that was able to compete with them; even the strong Chimu 'kingdom' of the north Peru coast was no match for them. Pachacuti and Topa Inca rank with Alexander, Genghis Khan, and Napoleon as among the world's great conquerors. It was apparently the conqueror's thirst for aggrandizement and power that provoked the Inca conquests; no enemy threatened them, neither did they need additional territory for economic reasons.

Apparently, Pachacuti assembled the Inca forces with intent to bring all neighbouring peoples under his control. Those that did not submit at once and pay homage to him were attacked. The first victims were groups within about twenty miles of Cuzco. These old hereditary enemies were apparently not treated with the leniency that attended later conquests at greater distances; it seems that there were old scores to be settled. According to Sarmiento, all except children and old women were killed. The first groups thus to feel the weight of the new Inca power were the Ayamarca, the Cuyo, and the towns of Ollantaytambo, Cugma, Huata, Huancara, and Toguaro.

The next campaigns took Pachacuti to the lower Urubamba Valley and Vilcapampa to the north; then he turned west to Vilcas and Soras, beyond the Quechua and Chanca country. Next came the near-by provinces to the south, Aymara, Omasayo, Cotapampa, and Chilque, and soon almost all the mountain provinces for a considerable area surrounding Cuzco had been subjugated. Pachacuti then turned his interests towards the more distant north, and sent general Capac Yupanqui, his brother, to conduct a campaign through Angara, Huanca, and Tarma, which were added to the realm. As was a frequent Inca custom, the general bore the same name as a former emperor, which practice must have been the cause for much of the disagreement among the Spanish chroniclers, and for the confusion among their commentators.

The Inca armies consisted largely of troops recruited or drafted from conquered tribes or nations; the Inca themselves were too few to supply the great forces required. The allies generally fought well, though not so desperately as the Inca themselves. A large body of Chanca warriors, recently subjugated by the Inca, therefore formed a part of Capac Yupanqui's army. These were under the command of their former chief who had been for some time a prisoner or hostage in Cuzco, for it was the imperial policy to put the foreign troops under the command of one of their own people. The Chanca so distinguished themselves in their first battle that invidious comparisons were made between them and the Inca. According to Sarmiento, when Pachacuti heard of this he feared that the Chanca might become intransigent, and so ordered Capac Yupanqui to have their leaders killed. Anco Ayllo, the Chanca leader, was secretly informed of this command and deserted and fled with all his followers to the forested jungles of the eastern Andes. Capac Yupanqui followed but was unable to overtake them.

Capac Yupanqui had been given strict orders by his brother Pachacuti not to march beyond Yanamayo but to establish there the boundary markers of the empire. But in pursuit of the Chanca he progressed beyond the limit, to the province of Cajamarca. Finding it populous and wealthy he completed its conquest and brought back to Cuzco a great booty and the sons of the vanquished rulers. Pachacuti had him executed there, ostensibly for disobedience to orders and for letting the Chanca escape. Capac Yupanqui, however, had apparently been boastful and had bragged that his conquests were greater than his brother's; the latter was jealous and also fearful that Capac Yupanqui would aspire to the throne and would start a rebellion, supported by his great army.

The practice of *mitima* was probably adopted about this time. To forestall rebellion in conquered regions the inhabitants were transferred *en masse* to other parts of the empire, their places being taken by peasants who had been longer under Inca rule, their spirit of independence broken.

Pachacuti next turned his attention to the region of Lake Titicaca where the Inca's old rivals, the Lupaca, were fomenting trouble and had induced some towns to revolt. The emperor soon quelled the rebellious villages and then continued on to crush the Lupaca nation on the south-western shore of Lake Titicaca; he also proceeded a little way around the south end of the lake. His next campaign was against the Chumpivilca, not far south of Cuzco, who had somehow until then escaped in the conquest of the rest of this near-by region.

Pachacuti was by this time getting along in years and had begun more and more to rely on his equally capable son Topa Inca, and to permit the young man to lead some expeditions, which the latter handled most creditably. Between them they carried the Inca empire practically to its maximum extent, and in a space of about thirty years, *c.* 1463 to 1493, increased its area by about a thousand per cent.

According to Sarmiento, Topa Inca Yupanqui had two brothers, considerably older, who had conducted successful campaigns against the Colla, a strong Aymara-speaking group of the Titicaca highlands who were frequently in revolt. In fact, the boy was born while Pachacuti and his two elder sons were engaged in quelling one of these revolts. For some reason, Pachacuti immediately decided to make him his successor. The boy was kept rather secluded until he was about fifteen years old, when the old emperor officially announced him as the next ruler. The two elder sons continued the subjugation of the Colla while Pachacuti devoted his attention more to the building of magnificent palaces and other edifices in the environs of Cuzco, and to the celebration of religious ceremonies.

The first great campaign of Prince Topa Inca was far to the north. He marched through the northern mountain provinces of Peru, consolidating those conquered by his father Pachacuti and continuing to the borders of Ecuador. No nations of any great importance or strength then existed in northern highland Peru, but in Ecuador were several of relatively high culture, approaching that of the Inca themselves, as evidenced both by historical traditions and by more recent archaeological studies. Most important were the Quitu, who occupied the region surrounding the city of Quito, the capital of modern Ecuador.

Several other groups of relatively high culture but of less political importance lay between Quito and northern Peru. First to be met by the Inca armies, advancing from the south, were the Cañari. Finally conquered, after valiant resistance, the Cañari became and remained a loyal portion of the Inca empire. As in all conquered territory, the country was reorganized on the Inca pattern, and temples, forts, palaces, and roads were built. Topa Inca took a great liking to Ecuador – with which preference future emperors concurred, probably because of the less arid countryside – and it is reported that he especially favoured this region with many edifices and other constructions of the best quality. He also organized a personal bodyguard of Cañari warriors.

After the reorganization and consolidation of the Cañari region, and the assembling of a large army, the campaign was pushed farther northward to the borders of the land of the Panzaleo, through areas of somewhat lower cultural scale. Then the customary conciliatory messages were sent to the chief of Quito, inviting him to join the pan-Andean co-prosperity sphere, which meant, of course, to yield to Inca arms and domination – or else.

The Quiteños were a proud people, accustomed to dominance, not subservience, and the 'king' returned the indicated answer. The war was long and bitter, but Quito finally fell.

During the course of the war with Quito, Topa Inca made an expedition to the coast in the region of Manta and Huancavilca. Here he was told of some islands, well populated and rich in gold, far off the coast, to which traders sailed in large rafts with masts and sails. Curious and covetous, he is reported to have prepared a great expedition with a flotilla of rafts and many men, sailed to the islands, and taken possession of them, bringing back some 'Indian prisoners, black in colour, much gold and silver, a seat of brass, and the hides of animals like horses', according to Father Cabello. One's imagination immediately recurs to the Galápagos Islands, and Sarmiento de Gamboa specifically identifies the legendary islands with the Galápagos, which he 'discovered' in 1567. There is no evidence of the former existence of peoples of any high culture on these islands, and until the present it has always been believed that they had never been seen by men until Spanish days. However, in January 1953, Thor Heyerdahl found potsherds in James Bay and in two valleys on Santiago Island, and on Black Beach on Floreana Island. The pottery was mainly plain except for some pieces with toads in relief. It could not be identified with any well-known ware, but showed some resemblance to pottery from the Chimú region or the Ecuador coast. The carved stone statue that Mr Heyerdahl went to investigate turned out to be very recent.

The fall of Quito left but one important independent nation in Peru and Ecuador, that of the old highly cultured Chimú on the north coast of Peru (page 100). Like most old civilizations, their vigour had apparently been sapped by years of peace and comfort, and they were ill-prepared to cope with the virility of the conquering Inca hordes. The frontiers of Chimú territory towards Cuzco had been fortified by such works as the great fortress of Paramonga, but the Inca advanced from the north, taking the Chimú on the flank. The struggle, probably about the year 1470, was short and uneven; the Chimú ruler wished to fight on to death, but his counsellors realized the hopelessness of the cause and induced him to surrender before many had been slain.

After subjugating the Chimú, Topa Inca Yupanqui continued down the coast, imposing Inca rule on all the coastal valleys, probably then independent states, to about the latitude of present Lima. The sons of the Chimú and other rulers were sent to Cuzco to be indoctrinated with Inca ideology and to serve as hostages for their fathers' good behaviour; the government was reorganized according to Inca pattern, but otherwise the life of the conquered people was altered little if any. In a second campaign, the coastal valleys as far south as Nazca were incorporated into the empire.

Of the history of these coastal peoples – at any rate of those to the south of the Chimú – we know historically nothing; they are known only by their archaeological remains. They may have spoken a dialect of Inca – or a language closely related to the Inca – or some quite unknown language; Inca Quechua had apparently replaced the earlier language by the time of the Spanish conquest.

Pachacuti had now been emperor for thirty-three years and was getting old (Sarmiento says one hundred and twenty-five!). For some years he had left the military aggrandizement of the Empire to his virile son, and had devoted his attention to internal affairs. In 1471 he abdicated in favour of his son Topa Inca Yupanqui, and a few years later he died.

The Indians of the tropical forests on the eastern slope of the mountains were a mild threat to the peace of the empire. Not that they offered any great danger, but they undoubtedly frequently provoked border troubles. Topa Inca decided to put them under control, or at least to teach them the fear of Inca might. One may suspect that the campaigns somewhat resembled those of British regimental commanders against Indians in the American colonies. Anyway, Topa Inca conducted such campaigns in the upper Madre de Dios River by way of Paucartambo. The legends speak of a great army descending the river in an immense flotilla of canoes.

Apparently, before the forest campaign was finished, or the wild tribes completely subdued – possibly a Sisyphean task – a revolt broke out in the region of Lake Titicaca. The Colla and Lupaca, Aymara-speaking groups that had formerly been rivals of the Inca for hegemony, were again restive under Inca rule, and awaiting an opportunity to regain their independence. The absence of the emperor and his armies in the deep forests seemed to present this opportunity, especially since a deserter reported to them that the Inca army had met defeat, the emperor killed. The Pacasa and Omasuyu, other Aymara-speaking nations, joined the Lupaca and Colla, but the revolt was not a pan-Aymara one, since some Aymara groups, not yet brought under Inca rule, did not partake, and some others, already conquered, remained loyal.

There could hardly be a better illustration of the extraordinary organization of the empire than the fact that the Inca armies were able and prepared to transfer operations quickly from the tropical forests, close to sea-level, to heights of 12,000 ft, and to wage a successful campaign there. Overcoming a stubborn resistance, they captured the hill of Pucara, which had been fortified, and then proceeded to invest the entire province of the Colla. Another battle was fought with the Pacasa and Lupaca at the Desaguadero River, south of Lake Titicaca, in which the Inca armies were again victorious, and the rebellion was quelled.

By this time the lust for power had apparently taken full possession of the Inca, and Topa Inca Yupanqui longed to have every region known to him under his sway. His next campaign was eastward into Bolivia, and the highlands of this region were soon added to the empire. Northern Chile came next, and in a series of campaigns this country was subjugated as far as the Maule River where, at the modern town of Constitución, Topa Yupanqui decided to place the southernmost limit of the empire; it was never extended farther.

Doubtless the practical difficulties of conducting a campaign at such a great distance from the base were very great; the problems of administration would have been equally difficult if the conquests had been carried farther southward. Moreover, the forested region could have had little appeal to the Inca. Primarily, however, it was almost certainly the fierce resistance of the indomitable Araucanian Indians that stopped the Inca advance. Physically and temperamentally they much resemble the Indians of the Great Plains of the United States, especially in their zeal for independence. They fought the Spanish with equal vigour, both in early days and in subsequent frequent revolts, and they were not completely pacified until 1883. Today they still occupy a large part of their former region, a fine, upstanding, vigorous people.

The Araucanians in the northern part of their territory were pushed southward and their lands were taken over by the Inca, but as the density of the people increased, their resistance strengthened until at last the Inca ceased their offensive, consolidated their gains, and set their boundary.

After one more small expedition into the eastern forests Topa Inca Yupanqui ended his military career, one that ranks with those of the greatest of conquerors. He, too, was now getting old, and he retired to Cuzco to oversee the organization and consolidation of his realm, and to enjoy the comforts of the imperial court, not the least welcome of which was, of course, his large seraglio.

One of Topa Inca Yupanqui's great accomplishments, apart from his conquests, seems to have been the building of the great fortress of Sacsahuamán protecting Cuzco, or, at least, the great enlargement of the immense work (see page 163 and Plates 15A and B). In his declining years he had a palace built for himself on the plain of Chita, to which he retired, gravely ill. Soon after naming his son Titu Cusi Hualpa or Huayna Capac as his successor he died about the year 1493 – the year after the landfall of Columbus – after a reign of some twenty-two years.

The introduction of several other customs or regulations of the later days of the empire are ascribed to Topa Inca Yupanqui. Apparently he was the first to have a census made of the entire empire, and to set up the pyramidal decimal system of administrative officials through which the population statistics were kept accurate and current. To do this he deposed all the old hereditary chiefs and replaced them by the appointed *curacas* (page 178). The introduction of the tripartite division of land and labour is also credited to him, as well as that of the 'Chosen Women'. He apparently also inaugurated the *yanacona* class of servants (page 184). All these are explained later.

Practically all the chroniclers agree that Topa Inca Yupanqui's queen was his own sister, Mama Ocllo. This practice must have been a permitted custom for some time, and it has been ascribed by some of the chroniclers to some earlier emperors, but this was apparently the first unquestionable case, and set the pattern for later emperors. Sarmiento says that Topa Inca Yupanqui was eighty-five years old at the time of his death, also that he left two royal sons, sixty natural ones, and thirty daughters. Of his royal sons he chose Titu Cusi Hualpa, better known by his official later title of Huayna Capac, as his successor.

Although the reign of Huayna Capac was a long and successful one, and though he brought the empire to its maximum extent, the apogee of Inca greatness probably passed with the death of Topa Inca Yupanqui. Considerable unrest filled the reign of his son. With the slow means of communication and transportation then available, the empire was too great to be successfully administered from one centre by one man, a quasi-divine being without whose sanction hardly anything could be done.

Early in the reign of Huayna Capac began those dynastic troubles of succession that were to become so acute with his sons. He was very young at the time of accession, as was evidenced by the title that he assumed then, meaning 'The Young Chief Rich in Virtues'. One of his half-brothers, son of one of his father's concubines, made a claim to the throne on the grounds that it had originally been promised to him. There seems to have been some justification for this pretension, which was supported by the large body of Capac Huari's relatives and friends. Apparently, however, the dispute never developed into open strife; the majority of the court, officials, and people supported the royal son and the choice of Topa Inca Yupanqui, and the pretender's mother, who had engineered his claim, was put to death as a traitress. A somewhat similar event took place shortly after Huayna Capac's accession. As he was then very young, a regent was appointed who schemed to seize the throne. The plot was thwarted by the Governor of Chinchaysuyu, who executed the culprit and assumed his post, which he thereafter administered with honesty and efficiency.

Huayna Capac was not the great conqueror that his father was;

possibly he could have been, but there were few more worlds for him to conquer. The empire had reached almost its maximum possible extent; to the south were the indomitable Araucanians, to the east the wild tribes of the tropical forests, both of them in regions strange and uninviting to the Inca. Only to the north were peoples of rather similar culture that could be assimilated, with habitats of relatively similar nature.

After the usual several years of travels of inspection through his realm to become somewhat familiar with it and its problems of administration, a custom that had been followed by several of his predecessors, Huayna Capac set out on his first military expedition to subdue the rebellious Chachapoyas; without great difficulty he pacified these, as well as subjugating some other hitherto unconquered neighbouring tribes. He thus enlarged the empire in the provinces of Chachapoyas and Moyopampa on the edge of the tropical forests in north-eastern Peru. After returning to Cuzco, celebrating the victory, and enjoying a little rest, he made another tour of the empire, journeying to its limits in present Bolivia and Chile. Dismissing incompetent officials and promoting efficient ones, and ordering the construction of engineering works, he saw to the welfare of his people and their land.

Reports then came to him of revolts in Quito and other provinces in Ecuador. He assembled the usual great army and started northward on a campaign of pacification and conquest, taking with him two of his natural sons, one of them Atahuallpa, his favourite, who later became the emperor captured and executed by Pizarro. Huayna Capac first proceeded against the Pasto, one of the northernmost groups. In the first encounter the Inca army was routed by the Pasto through a crafty stratagem. Most of the able warriors retired before the Inca advance, leaving the women and children and a few men. Pleased at the easy occupation, the Inca armies were celebrating it when the Pasto warriors fell on them, driving the advance-guard back on the main army with great slaughter. Of course, in the end the Pasto victory was of no advantage, for their land was soon savagely ravished.

The rest of northern Ecuador was conquered with considerable difficulty, as the inhabitants fought bravely. The most obstinate resistance was offered by the Cayambi, apparently a Cara tribe in north-eastern Ecuador. They defended several fortresses desperately and valiantly, and drove the Inca forces back several times with great losses. One of Huayna Capac's brothers, leading one attack, was killed and the emperor himself was knocked down and barely rescued. The stronghold was taken at last by a cunning manœuvre. The emperor sent a large part of his force to make a long detour of several days while he attacked openly. Giving his encircling general time to reach the rear of the fort, and at a prearranged time, he then feigned repulsion and flight; pursued by the entire garrison, the fortress was then easily taken by the army approaching from the rear. The Cayambi, now in the open, were soon annihilated by the Inca forces.

Huayna Capac set up the boundary stones indicating the northern limit of his empire at the Ancasmayo River in the land of the Pasto. It was never extended farther in that direction, and still remains the boundary between Ecuador and Colombia.

After pacifying and reorganizing highland Ecuador, the Inca turned towards the coast, where, around the Gulf of Guayaquil, were some yet unconquered tribes. These were subjugated without great difficulty, and considerable booty of emeralds, turquoise, and mother-of-pearl was taken. With this, the campaigns of conquest of Huayna Capac and of the Inca emperors came to an end. The empire had reached its maximum extent, approximately 380,000 square miles, about equal in extent to France, Belgium, Holland, Luxemburg, Switzerland, and Italy combined, or to the Atlantic Coast states of the United States. From north to south it stretched over 2500 miles (4000 km.). (See map, p. 40.)

Just before the death of Huayna Capac, about the year 1523, two interesting things happened. The empire was attacked by a foreign enemy, and the Inca had their first sight of a white man, who accompanied the invaders. The story of this Spaniard who saw Peruvians about a decade before Pizarro is not generally known to history.[1] Alejo García by name, he travelled with a band of Chiriguaná Indians from Paraguay to the eastern foot-hills of the Andes in Bolivia; he and a few companions, who probably accompanied him on the long journey, had been ship-

1. Nordenskiöld, 1917; Means, 1918b.

wrecked a few years before on the coast of Brazil. He was killed on his return to Paraguay before, unfortunately, he was able to write or recount his memoirs.

The Chiriguaná were a tribe of Guaraní-speaking Indians who made a practice, from time to time, of crossing the Paraguayan Gran Chaco to raid the eastern frontier Inca settlements of the province of Charcas in Bolivia in order to obtain bronze implements and gold and silver ornaments. Eventually they conquered some of the more primitive tribes of the eastern foothills and displaced them. While by no means threatening the existence of the great empire, they did cause some border troubles, and the Inca built several fortresses on their eastern frontier to control them. The Chiriguaná captured at least one of these, but were defeated in battle by Huayna Capac's general, Yasca.

In the year of his death, probably 1525, rumours began to reach Huayna Capac of the white men at Panama and of exploring expeditions down the coast.

With the death of Huayna Capac a schism rent the empire for the first time. He felt great affection for the region of Quito, Ecuador, and spent the final years of his life there in poor health; probably the climate, with its greater rainfall, appealed to him more than Cuzco. He had two prominent sons: Huascar, son of the queen, his sister, the legal heir; and Atahuallpa, his favourite, son of a secondary wife. Atahuallpa resided with him in Quito, Huascar in Cuzco. Huayna Capac had had as his queen an elder sister but she had borne no children and so was supplanted or supplemented by a younger sister, Ataua Ocllo, mother of Tupac Cusi Hualpa, later known as Huascar. The chroniclers differ as to the identity of Atahuallpa's mother.

According to one account, before his death Huayna Capac proposed to divide the empire, separating the 'kingdom' of Quito from the rest, and establishing Atahuallpa as its ruler; Huascar is said to have agreed to this. Sarmiento has it that a great pestilence, probably smallpox or measles, introduced by the Spanish, was then raging the country. Huayna Capac, dying of it, was asked to name his successor; he named his sons Ninan Cuyoche and Huascar, but the omens for both proved inauspicious. Before he could name another, Huayna Capac died.

The High Priest then set out to give the imperial fringe to Ninan Cuyoche, but found that he also had died. Huascar was then chosen. Sarmiento does not mention Atahuallpa in this connexion. At any rate, Huascar was installed as emperor by the High Priest in Cuzco while Atahuallpa was supported by the army and people in Ecuador.

It would almost seem that, as the Spanish believed, it was the divine plan that the great empire should be rent for the first time by civil war while the foreign invaders were planning its conquest. Had they come a decade earlier or later, the few men under Pizarro could hardly have accomplished their miraculous exploit.

It is not certain whether Atahuallpa originally intended to rebel and either to separate Ecuador from the empire or to claim the Inca throne. At first, whether sincerely or not, he seems to have given allegiance to Huascar. But the latter suspected him and maltreated the envoys that Atahuallpa sent to him, executing some of them, which act caused considerable ill feeling against him in Cuzco where the men had influential relatives. Both half-brothers then began assembling armies for the coming test of strength. Meanwhile the people of the province of Huancavilca deemed the time propitious for a revolt, but this was promptly quelled by Atahuallpa.

Huascar marched north with his army and met that of Atahuallpa at Riobamba. Like so many great battles of history better known to scholars, thousands of men died for the personal glory of their leaders. Sarmiento says that in his day the plain was still covered with their bones.

> But things like that, you know, must be
> At every famous victory.

Atahuallpa was the victor.

Huascar had another small force which caught the army of Atahuallpa resting and unwatchful after the battle, and caused it much loss, but Atahuallpa again attacked and was again victorious. Several other engagements were fought, terminating in battles at Cajamarca and Yanamarca; in all, it appears, the forces of Atahuallpa prevailed.

Atahuallpa's continued successes may probably be ascribed to the fact that he had in Ecuador his father's experienced army, as well as the best generals in the empire, Quisquis and Challcuchima. Whatever his first intentions, as soon as his armies began to register victories he gave up any thought of separating Ecuador from the rest of the empire or of offering any allegiance to Huascar, and determined to supplant him. The schism was not a national rebellion on the part of Ecuador so much as merely the following of an admired leader.

Atahuallpa journeyed south in the wake of his victorious armies, making his headquarters at Cajamarca. He was acclaimed emperor by the people through whose lands he passed, and assumed the imperial fringe of sovereignty. Success went to his head, and he apparently became very autocratic, self-conceited, vain, and cruel. Sarmiento tells a story that about this time he consulted an oracle which predicted that he would come to a violent end. Furious, he personally cut off the head of the old priest who had interpreted the prophecy, and demolished and utterly effaced the oracle and the *waca*.

Huascar set out from Cuzco with his remaining force for a last defence against the advancing enemy; he had made the most solemn sacrifices and consulted the greatest soothsayers, but most of their replies were unpropitious. The armies met at Cotabamba on the Apurimac River not far from Cuzco. Huascar's forces prevailed on the first day and he felt confident of victory when Atahuallpa's generals, Challcuchima and Quisquis, withdrew to recuperate. However, the following day his men were ambushed in a ravine, one division after another, and annihilated or captured. Challcuchima himself seized Huascar, pulling him out of his litter. Huascar's men lost heart at learning of the capture of their emperor and fled, hotly pursued by the victors, who established their new headquarters – and Huascar's prison – on the outskirts of Cuzco. Challcuchima contributed much to the flight by the crafty stratagem of having himself carried back in Huascar's litter, thus deceiving the latter's soldiers into thinking that he was their emperor, returning victorious with prisoners.

The people of Cuzco naturally feared that the city would be looted and the inhabitants slaughtered, but Atahuallpa's generals were wise administrators as well as capable warriors. They sent word that, the civil war being over, they were all one people again; there would be no reprisals. The Cuzqueños therefore came out and pledged allegiance to their new emperor, Atahuallpa. Nevertheless, several of Huascar's five principals – three generals and two high priests – were executed, and the others chastised and compelled to pull out their eyelashes and eyebrows as offerings to the new emperor. Huascar's mother blamed him for his unwise actions and slapped his face.

Atahuallpa, however, according to Sarmiento, was not so magnanimous. When he heard of his victory, receiving word at Cajamarca from his conquering generals, he ordered the entire family of Huascar, wives, children, and babies, to be killed and fastened to poles along a highway leading out of Cuzco. Huascar was compelled to watch the executions, which apparently extended even to his brothers and sisters, therefore close relatives of Atahuallpa. More than eighty of his children were thus killed, as well as most of his chief friends and supporters. Those of his concubines who had not borne him children and were not pregnant were spared.

The Spanish Conquest

The news of his victory sent by his generals to Atahuallpa in his encampment near Cajamarca reached him at just about the same time as did that of the landing of Pizarro near Tumbez in 1532. The wellnigh incredible story of the conquest of the great Inca empire by a handful of one hundred and eighty audacious Spaniards has been told in detail by Prescott, Helps, and other historians. Prescott's great work is one of the classics of history, and has doubtless been read by most educated persons. It need only be summarized here.

Atahuallpa was on the point of leaving for Cuzco to assume his imperial throne. He presumed that the Spaniards were the creator god Viracocha and his demigods returning as had been prophesied by old legends, and decided to remain where he was until they left – as Pizarro had done several years before – came to meet him, or made some other move. They came to Cajamarca. Pizarro had by this time, of course, learned all about the schism in the empire and its outcome, and realized that this source of weakness could be cultivated to suit his purposes. He urged that Huascar be brought to Cajamarca; as a matter of fact Huascar was apparently already on his way there on Atahuallpa's orders, a prisoner. Before he arrived, however, Pizarro had performed his great coup and made Atahuallpa a prisoner also. The latter, fearing that Pizarro might depose him in favour of Huascar, sent orders to kill Huascar and the other prisoners with him; this was immediately done. Huascar was then about forty years old, and had had a hectic reign of less than seven years.

Atahuallpa offered to have his cell filled with gold objects higher than a man could reach, as the price of his ransom. The area of the cell floor, according to three of the conquerors, was 25 by 15, 22 by 17, and 35 by 17 ft. The offer accepted, he dispatched messengers to all parts of the empire commanding that gold be brought to Cajamarca; soon it began to arrive, hundreds of llama loads. A large part of it, of course, came from the Temple of the Sun in Cuzco. Fabulous and wellnigh incredible though this immense quantity of gold is, apparently the room was filled to the stipulated height. Pizarro had a document drawn up to the effect that the ransom had been satisfied and paid – and there is no evidence that this callous man showed any mercy on any other occasion.

However, though officially declared free, Pizarro announced that, for the welfare of the country, Atahuallpa would remain under guard with the Spanish. His presence there became an impediment to the plans of the Spanish, and many of them began clamouring for his death. Pizarro at last consented, and the emperor was brought to trial on as many charges as could be trumped up: usurpation, the murder of Huascar, planning an uprising against the Spanish, idolatry, adultery, incest, polygamy, embezzlement, and several others. He was convicted and sentenced to be burned alive that very night in the public square of Cajamarca. A few souls were brave enough to sign a formal protest against the judgement. As the wood was about to be ignited, Atahuallpa was told that his sentence could be changed to strangulation (at that time both a Spanish and an Inca method of execution) if he would accept Christianity. He did, was baptized, and then garroted. Thus, on 29 August 1533, died the last Inca emperor.

The great heap of gold ornaments, fashioned laboriously by artistic Inca craftsmen, was melted down into bars. It is reported that it took the Indian goldsmiths a full month thus to undo their former labour, and that nine forges were employed in the process. Of the many other Peruvian gold ornaments that were sent intact to Spain not a piece is known to survive; all were melted down to bullion.

One is naturally inclined to dismiss the reports of the value of this fabulous loot as greatly exaggerated, but it must be remembered that the Crown claimed its fifth part of all such treasure, and took the indicated precautions to see that it was received; a royal treasurer accompanied expeditions to see – or try to see – that the Crown was not cheated. Moreover, we have the records of the amount of the royal fifth received in Spain. It is obvious then that the admitted value would not have been exaggerated. On the other hand there is considerable evidence – as might be expected – that the treasure was somewhat greater than reported, that some of the ransom was hidden and not reported. This was stated by some soldiers who complained that they did not get their full share of the loot, and the native *quipu* records, studied shortly after the conquest, indicate that about four per cent of the ransom was not reported or properly divided.

Various estimates of the amount of this ransom in terms of modern money have been made. In probably the most careful and reliable study, S. K. Lothrop[1] estimates that, at a valuation of $35.02 an ounce, the officially reported ransom amounted to $8,344,307.00; the purchasing value today would be many times greater. Moreover, this treasure was only one, though the most spectacular one, of a number of captures of gold and silver by the Spanish conquerors. Lothrop calculates that the loot later taken from Cuzco after the arrival of the expedition there was even greater than Atahuallpa's ransom, being worth $8,545,798.57. Also large sums were taken at Coaque, Pachacamac, and other places, which would certainly increase the total 'take' to over twenty million dollars.

1. Lothrop, 1938.

THE ANCIENT CIVILIZATIONS OF PERU

Furthermore, legends in Peru recount the credible fact that, ignorant of the exact amount required to fill Atahuallpa's cell, many more llama loads of gold ornaments were on their way to Cajamarca when word of his execution reached the native porters, whereupon they buried or otherwise hid the loads in the nearest available places. Also, on receipt of the same tragic news, the gold ornaments still remaining in temples and palaces all over the land were hidden. Much of the latter was soon found by the Spanish by judicious use of torture and other coercion, but traditions of buried and hidden treasure still abound in Peru, and labour to the amount of more than its value has been expended in the usually fruitless search for it.

The quarrels of the conquerors, abortive uprisings of the natives, and other events of Colonial Peruvian political history need not concern us here. Within a few years all the important leaders in the conquest had met violent ends by war, execution, or assassination. For forty years the Inca nobility with a few followers kept up a desultory resistance, but the last pretender to the Inca throne, Tupac Amaru, was beheaded in 1572.

The population of the Inca empire at the time of its apogee is a question on which estimates vary greatly. Means[1] estimates sixteen to thirty-two millions, with the lower number more probable, making the population double that of today. He bases this estimate on an average of five to ten persons to the family, probably much too large a number. Steward,[2] the most recent authority, estimates three and a half millions, excluding Ecuador, Colombia, and Chile.

The conquest of such an immense area by a handful of adventurers is one of the most extraordinary events of history, though it must be remembered that they were accompanied by a large army of native auxiliaries – recently conquered tribesmen and disaffected rebels. The reason, of course, was that the empire was so well organized and regimented, with all authority centred in the emperor, that, on his removal and replacement by a Spaniard, the well-geared machinery continued to function just as before. The top officials took their orders from a new man, but below the uppermost rank the *curacas* continued to

1. Means, 1931, p. 296. 2. Steward, 1949, p. 663.

138

execute their superiors' orders and to forward reports just as formerly. The common people farmed and lived as they always had, and, with slight change, continue to do today.

Slowly, of course, the imperial socialistic régime was altered to accord with European – and especially Spanish – sixteenth-century ideologies, though some of the old elements remain even today. The economic life was somewhat changed also, with the introduction of European cereals and other food plants, and domestic animals.

At first, the country was divided up into *encomiendas* or immense estates, and awarded – with their inhabitants – to important Spaniards as rewards for services during the conquest or later. Most of the surplus products that formerly belonged to state and church then went to the *encomendero*, whose demands constantly increased. The *yanacona* service was greatly increased to provide servants for the Spanish landlords, and quantities of Indians were drafted for very unhealthy labour in the mines. A large part of the population fled to regions then beyond Spanish control, and this, combined with the many deaths from unaccustomed diseases introduced by the Spanish, reduced the population very greatly.

The economic life of the people has bettered but slightly in the last century or two. Though no longer virtual slaves, many are in effect serfs or peons, living on the great estates of landed proprietors. Centuries of exploitation, degradation, and neglect have reduced them to a stolid, poverty-stricken people. Despite their greater freedom from regimentation and regulation, their lot is possibly less desirable than in Inca days. Since almost any change would be for the better, and since their ancient societal pattern is somewhat communal, they may present fertile ground for modern communistic ideology. Fortunately there are now national movements in the right direction.

Chapter 8

ECONOMIC LIFE

The Food Quest

BY the time of the empire, wild animals, the main support of
more primitive Indians, had become extremely scarce and,
except for the coastal fisheries, did not figure at all in native
economy. In fact, as in much of medieval Europe, private hunting was prohibited. The wild animals, however, were not kept
for the sport of the nobility, but were considered state property;
at intervals great public hunts were held, doubtless much enjoyed by emperor and commoner. At one of the last ones held,
after the Conquest, ten thousand natives are reported to have
participated, forming a ring thirty to sixty miles in circumference, and driving all the game towards the centre. Eleven thousand animals are said to have been killed and, with usual Peruvian
foresight, many more, including all the females, were released to
increase and perpetuate. The meat was dried for consumption
and most of it distributed to the people. Each province is reported to have been divided into four areas, each of which was
thus communally hunted over every fourth year.

The principal animals taken in such a hunt were deer and the
wild cameloids, the guanaco and vicuña; the latter were shorn for
their fine wool and then released. All predatory animals such as
bears, pumas, and foxes were killed. Another method of communal hunting was to build fences and drive the animals into an
area from which they could not escape. Nets and snares were
used for smaller animals such as the vizcacha, a large rodent, and,
in individual hunting, slings, bolas, and clubs were employed.

Wild plant food was equally unimportant. A few native plants
and fruits, unknown outside of Peru, were gathered and eaten,
raw or cooked, but wild plant products were useful primarily for
purposes other than food, such as *ichu* grass for thatching roofs
and making cordage.

As in every arid and well-populated country, fuel for cooking was a great problem; of course none could be wasted for warmth in the chilly altitudes. Centuries before Inca days the highland plateaux had been practically denuded of the few trees they contained. The farmers of the Inca period gathered all the brush and dead bushes and branches, and dried llama dung must have been the principal fuel in many regions; strange to say, this is said to burn with little odour or smoke. Naturally wooded valleys were protected by Inca laws; these areas and the tropical eastern forests produced the timber needed in house-building.

Ancient Peruvian economy was based mainly on agriculture, with considerable dependence on the herding of llamas and alpacas, especially in the southern highlands. The diet was almost exclusively vegetarian. Peru was one of the world's great centres of plant domestication, and modern agricultural economy has been tremendously enriched by Peruvian vegetables, unknown in Europe until after the Spanish Conquest. From a world point of view the most important of these was the white or 'Irish' potato. This, as well as coca, was peculiar to the Andean region. Then there were the plants that were known also in Mexico: maize or Indian corn, chilli, squash, several varieties of beans, sweet potato, tomato, peanuts, avocado, and manioc, as well as cotton and gourds, known also in the Old World (Plate 52).

On the high plateaux, up to 14,000 ft, only potatoes, together with a few other plants little known outside of Peru, quinoa, oca, ullucu, añu, mashua, lupin, and cañigua, could be grown; these were the main foods of the inhabitants of the higher altitudes. Maize, which here grows up to 11,000 ft, was the staple food for the middle heights, and the other plants mentioned above were cultivated mainly in the lower and warmer regions.

The punas, the high grassed tablelands, were – and are – naturally unsuited to agriculture but used for grazing. The cultivated fields are in the better-watered and more protected valleys. These tend to be narrow and steep, so that there is a relatively small amount of level land, and the steeper slopes were terraced with retaining walls of stone. Some valleys were so completely terraced as to be comparable with the rice-terrace valleys of Malaya; those preserved in the Urubamba Valley and at Yucay,

Pisac, and Ollantaytambo are typical. They served also to control the rapid run-off in the rainy season with its consequent damaging erosion. These great works must have been planned by engineers and built by great concentrations of manpower in a relatively short time; this suggests that it was done by *mita* labour in the later days of the empire. They were made with steps and irrigation channels. The steep terraces made irrigation easy, and this was generally practised; sometimes the nicely graded and stone-walled irrigation channels brought water for several miles (Plate 21).

Since the llama was never used – and is doubtless unsuited – as a draught animal, agricultural tools were naturally manual one-man implements; the plough was unknown. The principal tool was a strong wooden spade, *taclla*, generally called a foot-plough; breaking up the ground was hard man's work. The clods were broken up with a club consisting of a heavy stone ring on the end of a thick stick. A short hoe with a bronze blade completed the list of farming implements; the latter two were largely used by the women.

This aboriginal agricultural pattern still obtains, slightly altered, among the Quechua and Aymara of the Peruvian and Bolivian highlands. Barley, wheat, and broad beans have been added, but the potato still remains the staple crop and food. Most families own some sheep, pigs, and chickens, but oxen and horses – and consequently ploughs – are relatively rare and the mark of the well-to-do in most regions. The wooden spade and the hoe, now with iron blades, are still the principal farming tools. Some simple irrigation is practised, and some of the ancient terraces are utilized, but to nowhere near the former extent.

As in most tropical countries, the seasons are distinguished more by rainfall than by temperature. Being in the southern hemisphere, they are naturally the reverse of ours: summer, the rainy season, from December to March; the winter dry season from April to November. Ground-breaking began in the middle of the dry season, August, when the earliest corn was planted. Potatoes were put in later, just before the onset of the rainy season. A great festival preceded the first ground-breaking in the special fields devoted to the support of religion, and the labour was done to the accompaniment of singing. Husband and wife worked in pairs, each family having a long strip assigned to it. Chicha beer was provided for the workers. In Cuzco a public festival was held with sacrifices and merry-making, and the Priests of the Sun fasted from the time of planting until the appearance of the first sprouts.

The onset of the rainy season was awaited with the greatest anxiety, and if it was delayed everything possible had to be done to induce the gods, and especially the Thunder God, to send the needed rain. The people dressed in mourning and marched, weeping, through the towns. They tied up black llamas and dogs so that these would cry from hunger and thirst, and sprinkled chicha beer around them, hoping thus to appeal to the sympathies of the deities.

Throughout the rainy season the fields were tended, culti- vated, weeded, and watched to keep predatory birds and animals away. If the fields could not be seen from the family house, a small hut was built from which constant watch was kept; the farmer's wife often relieved her husband at night. Despite the strict laws, human as well as animal thieves had to be guarded against.

Harvest was naturally the joyous season. The earliest maize was harvested in January, potatoes in June. The corn was picked, husked, and stored in the houses to the accompaniment of festive songs and dances and public ceremonies. Unusual ears of corn were saved and used for divination.

The symbiotic pattern of Old World agriculture – live stock, manure fertilizer, and food plants – was not so fundamental in Peru, as the llamas were too few, and much of the dung was burned as fuel. However, as today, some pulverized dried llama dung was used as fertilizer. The natives on the coast had access to the great accumulations of bird guano on the islands, and made good use of it; they also used fish heads.

Like boating, fishing was of importance only on the coast and in Lake Titicaca; in the small rivers and lakes elsewhere the fish are too few and small to play a prominent role in the native economy. Doubtless in early days, as today, some groups of

Aymara and Uru on Lake Titicaca lived mainly by fishing. Here nets of a number of different types are used, as well as the fish spear, but no hooks and lines, weirs, traps, or poisons. On the coast, naturally, fishing was very important, and provided, together with the gathering of shell-fish and the pursuit of other marine life, a large part of the native dietary. Probably almost all common types of fishing apparatus were known there.

The Peruvians were more fortunate than the rest of the aboriginal Americans in that their highland region produced large animals capable of relatively easy domestication, the American cameloids. These are of four species: the llama, alpaca, vicuña, and guanaco. The former two are relatively large and were domesticated, the latter pair smaller and wild. Even the llama and alpaca, however, are much smaller than the Old World camels, lack the hump, and have shorter necks. They have, however, the same obstinate disposition and the same habit of spitting when angry. The vicuña was hunted for its fine wool, being generally caught, sheared, and then released; the guanaco was hunted for its meat.

The llama is a little the larger, with shorter and coarser hair, generally light-coloured, sometimes black, often spotted; the alpaca has longer wool, and is generally dark brown or black. Llamas were used primarily as beasts of burden, rarely killed for their flesh, and shorn for their wool only after death; this was then used for coarse fabrics. Alpacas were raised primarily for their long and finer wool, and were shorn frequently. In general, these distinctions obtain today among the modern Quechua and Aymara.

Because of their sure-footedness, endurance, and ability to go without water, llamas make very satisfactory pack-animals; moreover they graze on the upland plateaux or punas, which are unsuited to agriculture. They will not carry a load of much over one hundred pounds, however, and are seldom ridden, as they tire and balk quickly under a man's weight. They never travel swiftly, like a horse or mule, and are almost always driven in pack-trains, covering a distance of only about nine to twelve miles (15 to 20 km.) a day. In Inca days, when most of the llamas and alpacas were the property of the state, they were driven in large trains of several hundred, and about eight drivers were needed for every hundred animals. The life-usefulness of a llama, commencing at about the age of three years, is less than ten years. Inca law made the unauthorized killing of female llamas a crime.

Besides the useful llama and alpaca, the Inca had other domesticated animals: the dog, guinea-pig, and ducks. The latter two were native animals that had been domesticated in Peru; the ancestors of the dog had probably been brought to Peru in early days, and had, of course, become specialized in type by inbreeding. It was of medium size with a pointed nose, thick body and short legs, short hair, and a curling tail. The dog was a pet and a scavenger, but was eaten by a few Andean peoples, though the custom was abhorred by the Inca.

Since few llamas and alpacas were personal property in Inca days and almost all the wild animals had been killed off, practically the only meat the average commoner got to eat was that of guinea-pigs, and every family raised them. They breed quickly, eat refuse scraps and serve as scavengers, are cleanly and harmless, and the meat is palatable. The duck was a domesticated wild variety of which little is accurately known.

The preparation of food naturally differed very greatly from coast to highland according to the staple foods of these regions. When necessary, fire was made with the wooden firedrill which, apparently, was no improvement on that used by naked savages in the Amazonian forests; the drill was twirled in the hands. Most of the culinary apparatus was equally primitive. Most food was boiled in pottery vessels directly over the fire, or roasted; soup and stew were therefore the usual results. A porridge made of quinoa or oca was one of the staple dishes. Maize corn was not boiled and then ground to a dough as in Mexico, but the dry kernels were ground to flour, as with ourselves. Among the Inca this was done in a stone mill which consisted of a thin, more or less semicircular, large and heavy stone which was rocked over the grains scattered on a flat stone. The cornmeal was cooked in various ways. Corn, however, was often or generally eaten in the ear, boiled or roasted. Leavening was unknown, as it was throughout aboriginal America, so there was no staple food resembling our bread. Salt was generally licked, not added to the food.

In the cold highlands where potatoes were the staple food these were preserved by allowing them to freeze and thaw, squeezing out the water and letting them dry. The product was (and is) called *chuñu*. Meat was kept by cutting it into thin strips, allowing it to dry, and pounding it. This dried meat was called in Quechua-Spanish *charqui*, whence comes our term 'jerked' meat. Fish and other watery foods were also dried for storage. Corn and similar relatively anhydrous products were stored either in the house or in special granaries outside.

Cooking was generally done out of doors, weather permitting, but many houses had stoves of stone or clay, much like our kitchen ranges. Two meals per day, morning and evening, were the custom.

Most serving and eating vessels, like the culinary ones, were probably of pottery, though vessels of gourd, wood, and other materials were used also, and the Inca nobility employed gold and silver.

Throughout the Andean area and from earliest times to the present the chewing of coca[1] (*Erythroxlyon coca*) has been a universal male habit. The plant is native to this area and contains the principle that is the basis of the cocaine of today. It is chewed together with lime, which liberates the alkaloid in the leaves. The latter are picked, dried, and carried in a bag. The lime is obtained from calcined shells or burnt stems of certain plants, is carried in a gourd, and applied with a spatula. The technique is very similar to the use of betel-nut in Malaya, and there may be an historical relationship (see page 23). The drug allays weariness, hunger, and thirst, and therefore has a suitable place in the life of a hard-working people. Apparently it was not greatly abused in Inca imperial days – at least not by the commoners, since its use was prohibited to them except on special occasions; we may suspect that it was a government monopoly, or else the prohibition could hardly have been effective. With the cessation of this ban, coca-chewing became the problem vice of the area, and doubtless it contributes greatly to the decadence of

1. Mortimer, 1901.

the modern Andean peoples. To a large extent, however, its use – or abuse – is a result of habitual malnutrition; it is partly a substitute for food. Better economic and social conditions would doubtless reduce its use. Naturally it was and is considered a divine plant, used in shamanism, divination, and sacrifice.

Chicha, the native beer, also has been from earliest times to the present the intoxicating beverage of much of tropical and highland South America. Since it can be made from many different vegetal materials, its use is much more widespread than that of coca. In the Andean region it is generally made of maize corn, though on the highest punas quinoa and oca are substituted. In many regions the fermenting substance is saliva, the corn being chewed, generally by women; this seems to have been the practice in the Peruvian empire. Great quantities of chicha were consumed when the ceremonial occasion called for it, and intoxication to the point of insensibility was expected of the celebrants. Unfortunately the same custom prevails to the present; the ceremonial aspect remains, in that large communal gatherings, as for fiestas, are accompanied by heavy drinking, but the attitude is more hedonistic, without so much official sanction as in earlier days.

Tobacco was rather unimportant, but used to a small extent medicinally – generally as snuff, or ritually, but never as self-indulgence. Datura was also used to a slight extent in shamanism and ritual; the seeds were ground. A snuff, *villca*, was made of ground seeds of trees of the genus *piptadenia*. It was sometimes inhaled, sometimes mixed with chicha, and gave a mild intoxicating effect.

Costume

The costume of the Inca may be taken as typical of that of all the Andean and coastal peoples; at any rate it is the only one on which we have rather full information, and in imperial days it was enforced on the conquered populations. Grave finds, and modelled and painted figures on Moche pottery vessels, give us some data on coastal garb, and we may be sure that each group and each period had its peculiarities of dress. Naturally, more and warmer clothing was worn in the highlands than on the coast. In the earliest periods the inhabitants of the former region had only wool, the latter only cotton, but at a very early time trade made both materials available everywhere. These textile fibres, wool from the highlands and cotton from the coast – especially the former – were practically state monopolies and were regularly distributed to the people. Clothing everywhere consisted of woven or knitted textiles, and these were always worn whole, never cut or tailored; they were held together by large metal pins. The garments of the common people were of rather coarse textiles.

The ubiquitous breechcloth was the man's indispensable garment, and while at work in hot weather he often wore nothing else. The strip of cloth passed between the legs, the two ends passed over and hanging from the belt to front and back. Ordinarily a sleeveless tunic, generally made of a broad piece of cloth doubled and sewn together along the edges, the bottom being left open, was also worn. This made a shirt of inverted sack shape in the fold of which a slit was made for the neck, and incomplete sewing left two holes for the arms; it reached almost to the knees. A large cloak, worn over the shoulders with two corners tied in front, completed the man's attire; sometimes this passed under one arm to leave the latter free for activity. Breechcloth, tunic, and cloak were all of cloth woven with coloured ornamentation, the latter of course varying in quality according to the man's social position. Inca sandals were of untanned llama hide, but sandals of other materials such as braided fibre are known archaeologically from some regions (Plate 57). Every man wore between his cloak and tunic a small bag in which he carried his coca leaves, amulets, and other such small personal effects; the bag filled the role of the modern man's pockets.

Hair styles varied greatly from tribe to tribe, but Inca men cut their hair, leaving it short in front, medium long behind, and confined it with either the utilitarian sling or with a narrow ornamented woven band. The Aymara Indians of the coldest *punas* wore knitted woollen caps, as do most of the highlanders today.

Women wore a one-piece dress that combined skirt and

blouse, reaching to the ankles and bound at the waist by a long, wide, woven, and ornamented sash. At the top, it reached to the neck, the upper edges fastened together over the shoulders by long pins and passing under the arms at the sides. Like all garments, this dress was a large rectangular piece of woven cloth, merely wound around the body. The analogue of the man's cloak was a large mantle, worn over the shoulders and fastened at the front with a large straight metal pin known as *topo*. These pins, of copper, silver, or gold, have large heads of various types, sometimes in the form of animal or human figures, but most commonly ending in a large, thin, circular, or semicircular disk, the sharp edges of which could be used as a knife. The women wore sandals and head-bands similar to the men's, and also a large piece of folded cloth on the head. They did not cut their hair but parted it in the middle and wore it hanging down the back; it was cut, however, as a sign of mourning.

Deformation of the head was a very common practice in ancient Peru, but, like most such customs, it varied not only from region to region but from period to period, so that it may sometimes be used as an archaeological criterion. It apparently was not the Inca fashion in imperial days, but was practised by the Aymara who preferred long heads, and by some of the earlier coastal peoples.

'War paint' was used by the Inca, and other methods of face-painting were used at other times, but apparently only on special and ceremonial occasions. Black was the mourning colour, but red and purple were used at other times. The practice was probably a universal one throughout the Andean area, but naturally little information concerning it is available. Tattooing was practised at certain times and places on the coast but there are no records of it in the highlands.

Following nature's pattern, it was the Peruvian male who decorated himself; Inca women wore only necklaces and shawl-pins. Probably all men wore earplugs of some type, but the nobility, 'Inca' by birth or privilege, wore such great plugs in orifices in the ear-lobes that this class was generally referred to by the chroniclers as *Orejones*, 'Big Ears'. These insignia were up to two inches (5 cm.) in diameter, and made of various materials, those of men of higher rank being of course of gold or silver (Plate 61). Men also wore metal bracelets, the metal disks that were awarded as medals for military bravery, and necklaces made of the teeth of slain enemies. On ceremonial and festive occasions, of course, they also donned gaudy head-dresses, collars of feathers, and similar regalia.

Chapter 9

THE CYCLE OF LIFE

As among practically all peoples until recently, both birth and death rates were doubtless high in Peru; infant mortality was great. The average family was apparently about five. Babies were frequent, and always welcomed; birth control was unknown and infanticide rare. The mother performed her household duties until just before childbirth, and recommenced them very soon afterwards. The pregnant woman, for religious reasons, was not allowed to walk in the fields. She confessed her sins, prayed for a successful delivery and, together with her husband, fasted for a brief period. Experienced neighbours, especially those who had borne twins, helped her; there were no professional midwives. Immediately after delivery the mother washed both the child and herself in a near-by stream. The umbilical cord was preserved.

Until the child was old enough to walk it was kept bound in a four-legged cradle from which it was never removed. This was made so that it could equally well be rested on the ground or carried on the mother's back whenever she left the house. Two looped sticks protected the child's head so that it could be wrapped in a blanket without danger of suffocation. The mother's shawl, tied across her chest, bound the baby-carrier to her back.

The time of weaning was an important family event and marked a new stage in the child's life; a feast was held by all relatives, with drinking, dancing, and hilarity. The eldest uncle cut the baby's nails and hair, preserving them carefully, and then bestowed a name upon it, the first name it had had and which it would bear only until maturity. The relatives gave the child presents and prayed to the sun that its life might be long and lucky.

For the child of the commoner there were no schools, no formal education. There being no system of writing there was little to learn that could not be imparted by the parents in

151

ordinary conversation, and this education by precept and example was all that the average child got. The sons of the aristocracy and of hostages of high rank resident in Cuzco, however, received some formal instruction, as did the 'Chosen Women' (page 185). As soon as they could walk, the peasant children began helping their parents and thus learning to take their places in the community.

The next important crisis in the child's life was, of course, puberty, and, as in most societies, this was an occasion for important ceremonies. Those for girls and peasant boys were relatively simple, but boys of noble birth underwent an elaborate ceremony that lasted for several weeks. The rites for boys and girls differed in that the latter were individual or familial, while those for the boys were communal and of national scope.

At the onset of first menstruation the girl's relatives were called for the usual family feast. Preceding this she fasted for three days, remaining in the house; on the third day she was permitted to eat a little raw maize. The next day her mother washed her and dressed her neatly in new clothes and white sandals to greet and wait on the relatives assembled outside. Her most important uncle then gave her the name that she would bear throughout life, and all the other relatives gave her presents.

Once a year a communal ceremony was held for all the boys who had reached puberty during the past year. They were given breechcloths and new names during rites which were doubtless simpler forms of those recorded in greater detail for sons of the royal family (page 187).

As among practically all primitive peoples – and in England until long after the Norman Conquest – there were no surnames in ancient Peru. A child was given any name that appealed to the parents, generally descriptive of some quality, or referring to animals, places, or other natural phenomena. As we have seen, a person bore several different names in various stages of his life. A child might be given the same name as that of some relative, but there was no rule. Nicknames were also sometimes applied. Among the commonest names for men were 'Strong, Happy, Liberal, Tobacco, Crystal, Hawk, Condor, Jaguar'; for women: 'Pure, Star, Gold, Egg, Coca'. Those of noble blood

SESTA CALLE
CORO·TASQVE

feedad de doze años

mnan asupyalacumoridco   *enesta*

Figure 3. *Twelve-year-old girl fetching firewood, spinning
as she goes, and driving llamas*

153

often had several names, some of them being honorific and titles of rank.

In most primitive school-less societies marriage takes place and the individual is considered an adult at an early age, soon after puberty; such would be expected in ancient Peru. The chroniclers who mention this point are not in agreement, but it is difficult to credit the statement of Garcilaso that the men were twenty-four or more years old before they married, the girls eighteen to twenty. Cobo makes the ages much earlier, which seems more likely. At any rate, a person was not considered a full-fledged adult until he married, started a new household, and became subject to the laws regarding public labour. Since, as in most societies, especially martial ones, the adult male death-rate was higher, with a consequent surplus of women, polygyny was permitted or even favoured, but this was a privilege mainly of the aristocracy and the wealthy; the commoner had to be content with one wife. Even if marriage had not been practically required by Inca regulations, the economic pattern was such that there was no place for bachelors or spinsters; everyone was – or had been – married. Unlike most primitive societies, the state took cognizance of the marriage and sanctioned it; legal divorce was unknown, so far as the first or real wife was concerned.

The formal engagement was a function of the state. At intervals all the marriageable boys and girls were assembled and placed in two rows in the presence of the Governor. The betrothals had certainly been arranged beforehand with the approval of parents and children. Each lad chose his lassie. Only in case of rivalry for a girl's hand did the official adjudicate and decide; then the loser made a second choice. When all were paired, the Governor presented each boy with his bride-to-be, in the name of the emperor. Since travel was not permitted, marriage was of necessity within the local community.

The families of the bride and groom thereupon made preparations for the wedding which was celebrated with the feasting, drinking, dancing, and merriment which throughout the world accompany these joyous occasions. In some regions the young groom was expected to bring wood and straw and otherwise serve his parents-in-law-to-be for several days before the ceremony. There are also frequent but indefinite references by the chroniclers to a period of trial marriage, in some places at least, but it is difficult to see how this was arranged, unless it was practised before the formal betrothal.

In the Cuzco region the boy and his family went to the bride's home where her family formally presented her to him. He put a woollen sandal on her right foot if she were a virgin, one of grass if not. Then they all returned to the house of the groom where the girl gave him a tunic of fine wool, a man's head-band, and a metal ornament of a certain type, all of which he donned. After the usual Petronius-like precepts and admonitions, ubiquitous on such occasions, the customary presents to the couple, and the final feast, they were considered man and wife. There was no religious sanction for the marriage; no priest participated. According to some authorities, the state presented to each of the parties two complete sets of clothing, one for ordinary use, one for festive occasions. The boy retained the *topo* of land that had been assigned to his father for him; the girl's half-*topo* reverted to the common lands.

Incest restrictions were not so great as among ourselves. They were few for men of top rank; the last several emperors married their full sisters, and nobles were allowed to wed their half-sisters. Among the commoners, marriage was permitted with a first cousin, but prohibited for closer relationships.

Polygyny was, as before noted, permitted or even encouraged, and a man's wealth and prestige, in the absence of money, was largely indicated by the number of his wives. But in the nature of things this could be a perquisite of only a few men, who were, naturally, the aristocracy. The emperor bestowed concubines on his favourites and his victorious generals. He himself had, of course, the largest seraglio. Some of the emperors may even have out-Solomoned Solomon, for Cieza de Leon says that none of them had less than seven hundred. However, the usual exaggeration may be suspected here.

Peruvian polygyny, however, differed from most other types in that there was only one real wife, always the first one. She received state sanction, was officially betrothed, ruled over the other subsidiary wives or concubines, and could not be divorced.

If she died, the man might take another primary wife, but might not elevate one of the secondary ones to that rank. On the other hand a widow might not remarry except to her husband's brother – the old practice of the levirate, common to a number of peoples. Widows received state support.

Subsidiary wives were acquired in a number of ways besides as gifts from the emperor. In addition to inheriting the wives of his dead brother, a man inherited his father's wives who had borne no children. He also usually took over his nurses and his foster-mother; the latter might be dismissed after it was agreed that his obligations to her had been satisfied. Women captured in war would also come into this category. There was no marriage ceremony when a subsidiary wife was taken, and she could be divorced without any formality.

From marriage to death little interfered with the monotonous routine of the Peruvian commoner. The man tilled his fields and those of the church and the state, possibly did a tour of duty in the army or the mines, enjoyed his more or less regular trips to market, and the less regular celebrations on the occasion of one of the events in the lives of the children of the family, when he was probably allowed to get gloriously drunk with chicha beer. The woman was even more constantly busy with the care of the children, with preparing the meals, and with weaving the family clothing. Spinning and weaving occupied all the time not devoted to the other duties. Of course the regular religious ceremonies in which the entire population joined provided frequent occasions for public amusement.

The chroniclers give little data on the question of games. There were probably few organized athletic sports. We may be sure that adults gambled, for this is practically universal, and objects that are probably dice occur in archaeological collections, as well as 'boards' with regular depressions that were probably employed in some game requiring more skill. Few obvious toys have been found except, of course, dolls for little girls.

Ancestor-worship and the cult of the dead were of great importance in ancient highland Peru, and so mortuary customs were rather extensive. The practice held related groups together and prevented migration. The bodies of ancestors, dried and

PRIMERA CALLE
AVACOCVARMI

de edad de treynta y tres años

muger de tributo

Figure 4. *Thirty-three-year-old woman weaving*

wrapped in cloths, were carefully preserved and worshipped. Naturally the funerary rites of the nobility were much more extensive than those of the commoners, as were the number of preserved bodies and the recollection of genealogies. Such was the reverence for an ancestor that, if a malicious person got possession of an adored body, he could practically dictate to the descendants.

As with us, black was the mourning colour and, at the death of a close relation, all donned black clothes for a considerable period; the nobility are said to have mourned thus for a year. Women cut their hair and covered their heads with shawls. At the funeral, food and drink were served to all who came. After a slow dance was performed to lugubrious music some of the possessions of the dead man were burned, the rest buried with the wrapped body. During the funeral no fires were made in the house.

Some of a great man's subsidiary wives and servants might be sacrificed and buried with him. The funerary ceremonies continued for eight days of processions and eulogies, and for some time after the funeral the relatives would visit the tomb and leave gifts of food, chicha, and clothing.

Burial rites were also extensive at the death of the real wife of a noble, but much less so for a concubine, or the wife of a commoner. A man continued to wear black for a year after the death of his wife and might not remarry during that time. Strangely, it is reported that a poorer man, who needed more the household help of a woman, often was not given a new wife for two years.

'Entomb' describes the Inca method of disposal of the dead much better than 'burial', for the body was usually placed in a beehive-shaped tomb above ground, generally in a rock shelter or cave, rather than interred. These tombs were made of rude stone masonry and clay or mud. The body, wrapped in textiles or skins, was placed inside in natal posture, seated knees to chin. The small doorway was securely blocked with stones (Plate 9B). In the arid highland atmosphere the bodies dried without decomposition. Food and chicha in baskets, pottery vessels or gourds, and some of the personal ornaments and implements of the dead man were placed with him.

Some of these tombs were apparently family vaults, opened from time to time for new burials. Interments are rare but not unknown, especially in the rainier eastern canyons, as at Machu Picchu. Babies were apparently sometimes buried in large pottery urns. One of the more unreliable chroniclers mentions cremation and the voluntary immolation of widows (Indian *suttee*), but no corroboratory evidence of these has been found. On the coast, the dead were at all times disposed of by interment in deep graves in the dry desert sands. Everywhere in Peru cemeteries were made in places unsuited to agriculture.

Chapter 10

PUBLIC WORKS

Architecture

PERU presents such a complex of climatic and ecological conditions that the types of architecture and habitations varied – and vary today – tremendously. The warm dry coast needed a very different type of structure than the chilly highlands, and the hot humid eastern slopes of the mountains a different type again. In the latter region wood for timber was plentiful, but it was deficient both in the highlands and on the coast; also, suitable stone was uncommon on the coast, plentiful in the highlands. Naturally, therefore, adobe was the preferred building material on the coast, stone in the highlands, wood in the eastern lowland provinces. However, houses of adobe were also common in the highlands, especially for dwellings of the farmers.

The typical house, whether of adobe or stone, was rectangular, generally of one room, and with a thatched, gabled roof, differing little from that of the countryfolk today. The masonry was generally rude, of uncut stone set in and chinked with mud. The exterior walls were – at least in houses of the better type – covered with a facing of fine mud that filled the interstices. Round buildings were very rare, but may have been much more common or usual in earlier days.

The houses were generally windowless and had no chimney, the smoke from the fire escaping through the thatch, and the single door was low and small. The occupants slept on hides or mats laid on the floor, in their daily clothes, with a blanket wrapped around them. The furniture was likewise scanty, without tables or chairs, probably nothing but a stone-and-mud stove; owing to scarcity of firewood, the fire was always small. In the room walls were niches in which implements and the household fetishes were kept. Sometimes the large room was divided into smaller ones by partitions. The doorway was generally

(A) The Castillo, Chavin de Huántar, showing tenon heads

(B) The Huaca del Sol, Moche, nea Trujillo

I

(A) Eroded face of the Huaca del Sol

(B) Huaca Dragón, Chanchan, near Trujillo

2

Air view of Chanchan, the Chimú capital, near Trujillo

Arabesques in the mud walls at Chanchan

4

(A) Air view of hilltop fortress in the Casma Valley

(B) The great adobe fortress of Paramonga (Parmunca) at Pativilca

Air view of the fortress of Paramonga

The ruins of Cajamarquilla, Rimac Valley, not far from Lima

(A) Tambo Colorado, Pisco Valley

(B) The remarkably preserved Nazca site of La Estaqueria.
The posts probably supported a thatched arbour

8

(A) Remarkable and puzzling lines and figures on the stone-covered pampa at Ingenio, Nazca region

(B) A restored *chullpa*, or charnel house, near Huaraz

9

(A) Tiahuanaco, Bolivia

(B) Monolithic gateway at Tiahuanaco

Great monolithic figure found (by Wendell C.
Bennett) at Tiahuanaco

(A) The Callejón de Loreto, Cuzco, with Inca high stone walls of coursed masonry on both sides

(B) The Colcompata, Cuzco. Probably built by Emperor Pachacuti, c. 1450

The Church of Santo Domingo, Cuzco, built on the foundations of
the Coricancha, the Inca Temple of the Sun, the curving wall of which
may be seen at the base

(A) Inca wall of coursed masonry, Cuzco

(B) The famous 'Stone of Twelve Angles' in a wall in Cuzco

(A) Air view of the great fort of Sacsahuamán, overlooking Cuzco

(B) The face of Sacsahuamán. Probably built by Emperor Pachacuti
c. 1450

(A) Wall of great Inca temple of *Viracocha* at Cacha (Racche)

(B) *Chullpas* (burial towers) in Bolivia

Ollantaytambo, a great Inca fortress or place of refuge on the Urubamba River

(A) Machu Picchu

(B) Carved stone monument, Pucara

Machu Picchu, a late Inca hillside town above the Urubamba River

(A) Tambo Machay, near Cuzco

(B) The gate of Rumicolca, near Pikillacta

(A) Ancient agricultural terraces still in use at Pisac

(B) Agricultural terraces at Pisac

Large sailing balsa, Puno, Lake Titicaca

Stirrup-spout pottery vessel, Cupisnique

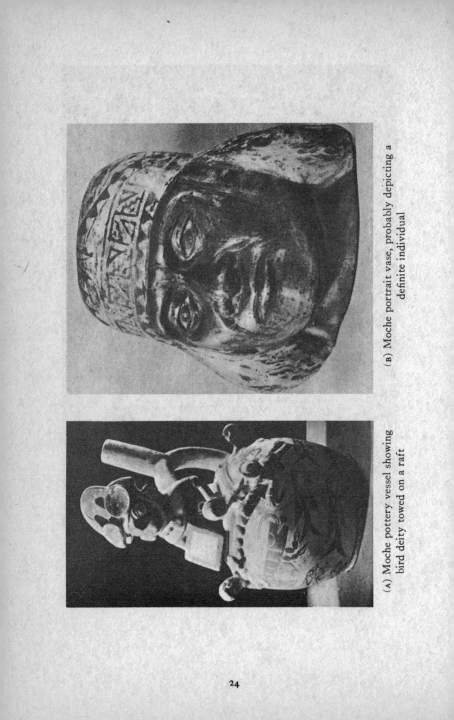

(A) Moche pottery vessel showing bird deity towed on a raft

(B) Moche portrait vase, probably depicting a definite individual

Group of Moche stirrup-spout pottery vessels

(A) Group of black-ware pottery vessels. The one at upper left is Moche, all the others Chimú

(B) Late Chimú black-ware pottery vessels

Pottery goblet of Tiahuanaco period and art

Nazca polychrome pottery; various periods

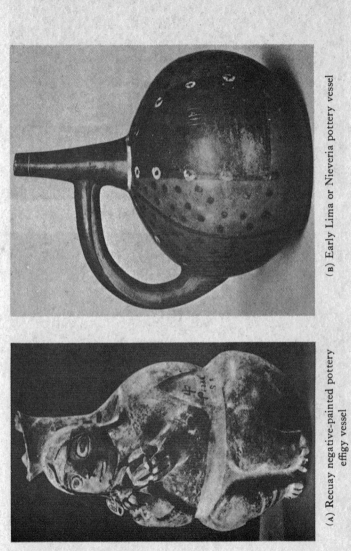

(A) Recuay negative-painted pottery
effigy vessel

(B) Early Lima or Nieveria pottery vessel

(A) Pottery vessels of the Ica period

(B) Pottery vessels of the Tiahuanaco period from the
Lake Titicaca region

(A) Tiahuanaco period pottery vessels from the central coast region

(B) Vessels of black-white-red ware, excavated at Pachacamac

Chancay black-on-white pottery vessels, mainly from Quintay

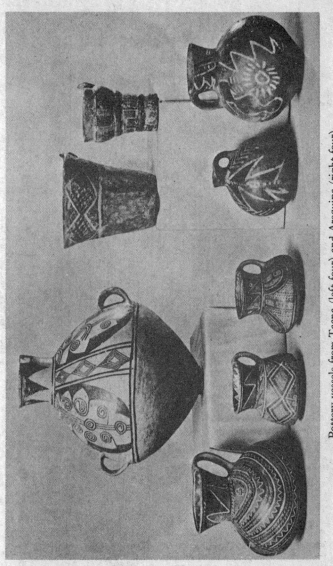

Pottery vessels from Tacna (left four) and Arequipa (right four)

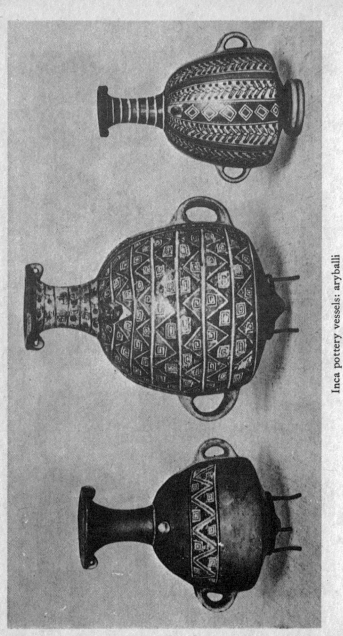

Inca pottery vessels: aryballi

Pottery vessels of Inca type and period

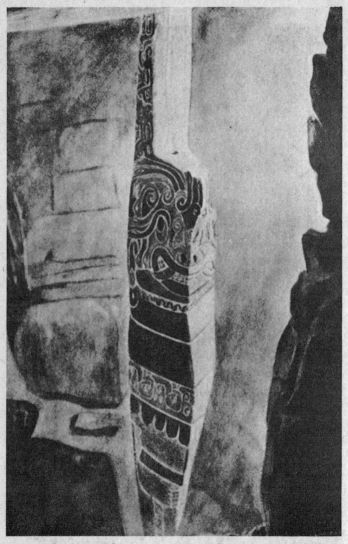

The Lanzón in the Castillo, Chavin de Huántar

(A) Stone puma, Chavin art style

(B) Inca stone bowl

Small stone containers in form of alpacas. Inca period

Wooden goblets or *queros*. Inca and Colonial periods

Wooden *quero* or *kero*

Bimetallic knife. Copper blade with gold bird on handle

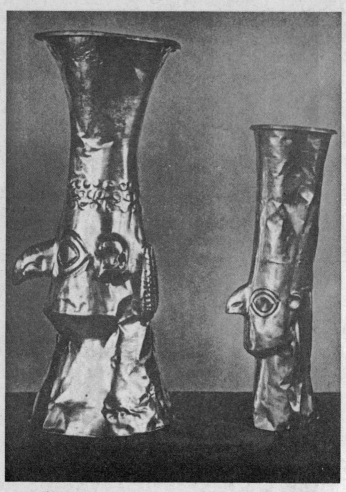

Chimú metal vases, the larger of silver, the smaller of gold

Chimú face mask of thin beaten gold

Inca silver figurine, front view

44

The same figurine, rear view

(A) Bone handle of spearthrower, showing man playing panpipes. Southern coast

(B) Lace-like cloth. Quintay

Painted cloth. Casma

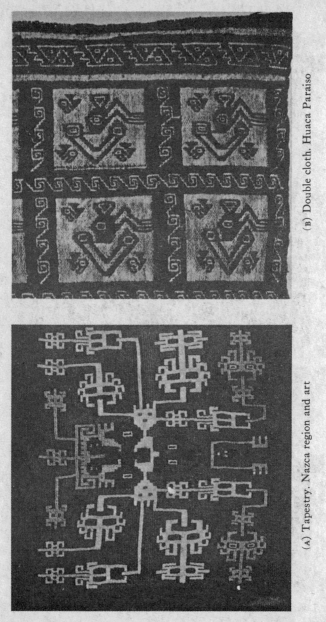

(B) Double cloth. Huaca Paraiso

(A) Tapestry. Nazca region and art

Embroidered Paracas mantle

(A) Hair-net. Pachacamac

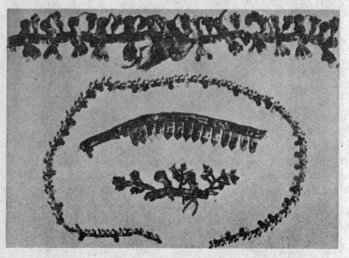

(B) Three-dimensional needle-knitted borders. Nazca region

A mummy excavated at Pachacamac

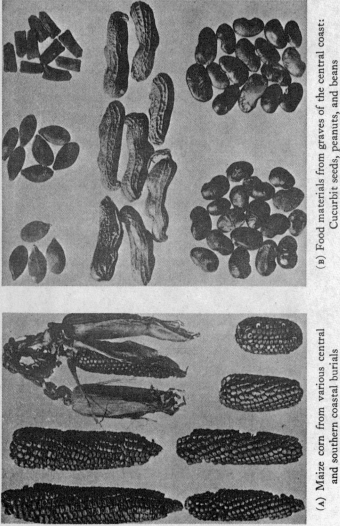

(A) Maize corn from various central and southern coastal burials

(B) Food materials from graves of the central coast: Cucurbit seeds, peanuts, and beans

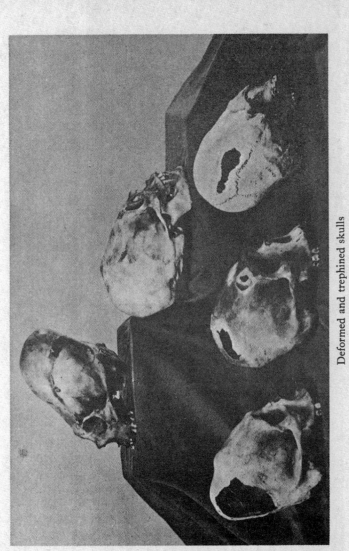

Deformed and trephined skulls

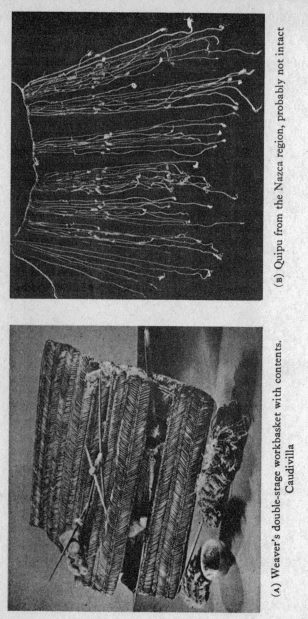

(A) Weaver's double-stage workbasket with contents. Caudivilla

(B) Quipu from the Nazca region, probably not intact

54

Pottery figurines from various sites of the northern and central coast

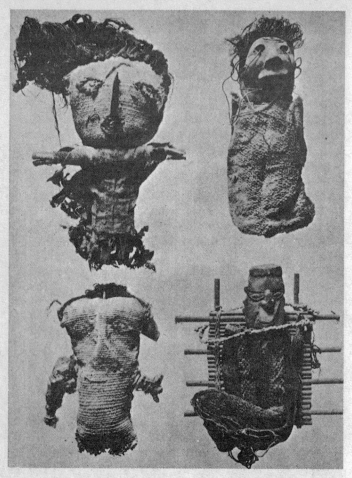

Dolls or dressed figures, from central coast sites

Ornaments, combs, and sandals, from central and southern
coastal sites

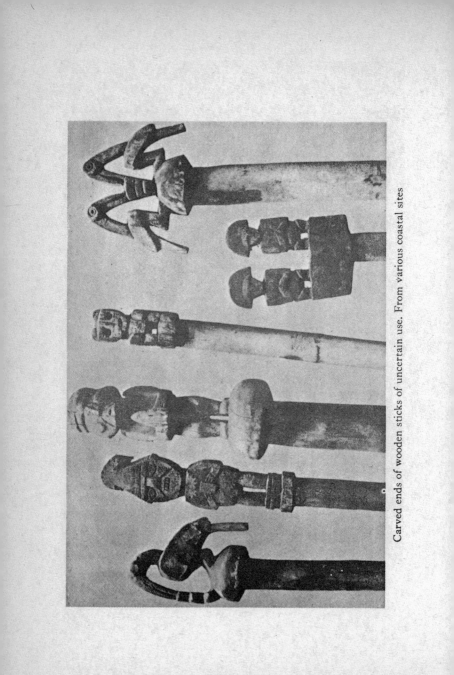

Carved ends of wooden sticks of uncertain use. From various coastal sites

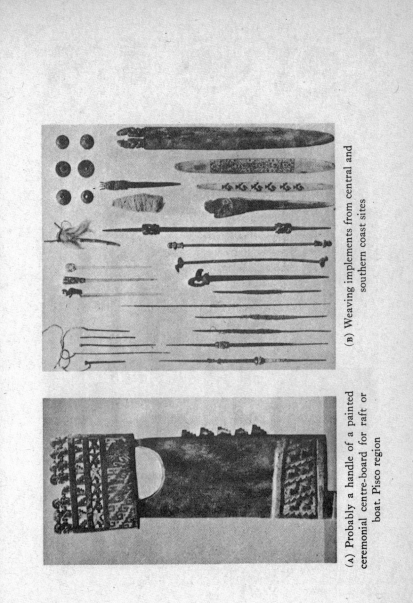

(A) Probably a handle of a painted ceremonial centre-board for raft or boat. Pisco region

(B) Weaving implements from central and southern coast sites

Small objects of carved wood

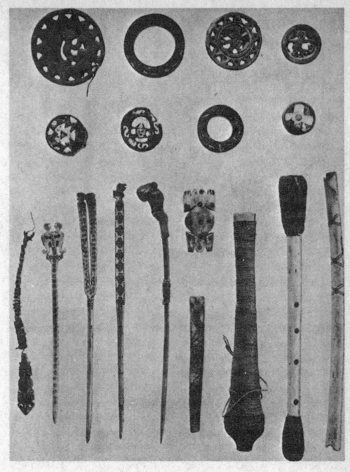

Ear ornaments, and objects of bone

Implements of copper and bronze

Implements and ornaments of copper and silver

(A) False heads of mummy bundles. Pachacamac

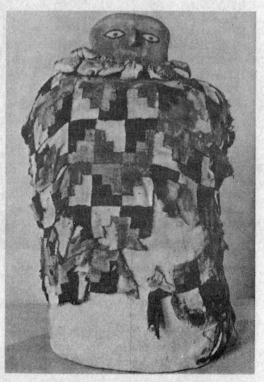

(B) Mummy bundle. Pachacamac

covered by a mat or hide, probably never by a permanent swinging door. The room was devoid of all ornamentation and decoration, for the occupants, especially the men, spent almost all their daylight hours out of doors. Pegs in the walls held clothing and implements, and on the earthen floor lay the household equipment, storage jars, pots, baskets, cooking utensils, gourds, grindstone or mortar, mats, hides – and of course vermin. However squalid, nevertheless, it was probably not much less comfortable than the house of the average European peasant of the same period.

Generally an extended family – the families of children and parents – occupied several such houses arranged rectangularly around a central court or patio in which were also some storehouses and other similar constructions. Such a compound was surrounded by a wall, generally also rectangular and with a single entrance; the wall might be of stone or adobe, but often was of sod. A number of such compounds, clustered irregularly, composed a village.

The public buildings, especially those in Cuzco and of the later periods, were of course of superior construction, with good stone masonry and little use of adobe. Even the best buildings, however, were generally roofed with grass thatch. But some of the latest Inca public buildings in the Lake Titicaca and northern highland region were covered with corbelled slabs of stone, and some of them were made with windows; this architecture is unknown in the Cuzco district.

The temple-crowned stepped or terraced pyramid with external staircases was not the characteristic feature of religious architecture in the Andean region that it was in the Mexican area. It is missing in Inca architecture, but a few are found in earlier periods in the northern highlands. On the coast, however, as noted before, in the early periods, and especially on the northern coast in the Moche period, immense pyramids of adobe were built, a single great pyramid with its summit temple thus composing a ceremonial site. The great 'Temple of the Sun' at Moche has already been described (page 77). The great Pyramid of the Sun at the famous ceremonial site of Pachacamac covers about twelve acres in area and rises to a height of about 75 ft. The architectural features of the coastal pyramids, however, differ greatly.

In the later periods the ceremonial sites were no longer isolated from the centre of population but consisted of edifices and groups of buildings within the cities. Every important Inca town had its temple and priests; the great Inca ceremonial centre was the Coricancha in Cuzco, on the principal square. Now levelled, and with the monastery of Santo Domingo built upon its lower walls, the original plan and dimensions are difficult to determine, and the figures given by various chroniclers differ greatly. It consisted of one great room, the Hall of the Sun, and other smaller edifices. Rowe[1] calculates from present evidence that the main hall measured 93 by 47 ft, or 28 by 14 metres (Plate 13).

Although almost all Peruvian edifices are of one storey only, buildings of two and even three storeys are known. These are not terraced like the pueblos of the south-western United States, but the second storey is directly over the first. Stone slabs formed the ceiling of the lower room and the floor of the upper. Buildings of more than one storey were more common in pre-Inca periods in the north highlands; here subterranean houses were also found. These have walls of upright stone slabs and roofs of very large flat slabs. Some of them have rather complex plans, and subterranean houses of two floors are known.

The better built, large, and more impressive buildings and those that are best preserved today are, of course, the Inca public edifices, built by government labour and, presumably, planned by state architects. These and the master masons were full-time professionals, state-supported; the common labour was drafted. The architects, lacking paper, worked from models made of clay or stone.

Little is known of engineering instruments. The plumb-bob was certainly known and used, and probably there were instruments for obtaining levels and angles and for measuring distances. Most of the stone-working tools, hammers and axes, were of stone, but bronze chisels were also available. Most of the stone-cutting was done by stone hammers, sand abrasives, time, and

1. Rowe, 1944

'elbow grease'. Wooden and bronze crowbars were employed in moving and placing stones.

It was formerly believed that the megalithic masonry, employing immense stones of irregular size and shape, was pre-Inca in age and related to the Tiahuanaco period, while masonry of stone blocks of relatively uniform size, laid in courses, was typical of the Inca. But it is now generally agreed that both types were built by the Inca, and that almost all the great masonry edifices and structures in the Cuzco region, including Sacsahuamán, Ollantaytambo, Machu Picchu, and Cuzco itself, are of the late Inca period (Plates 12–20). These include the most stupendous megalithic masonry as well as the finest regular coursed walls, and others of uncut field stones set in clay; the latter type is known as *pirca* masonry. Cuzco itself contains examples of masonry of all these types, all built after 1440 by Pachacuti and some of his successors.

The Inca stonemasons used mainly three kinds of stone, and cut and laid them differently according to the desired purpose. Yucay limestone was used for foundations and for terrace and retaining walls; the great walls of Sacsahuaman were built of it. It was always cut into polygonal blocks. Green Sacsahuamán diorite porphyry was also employed for retaining walls where unusual solidity was desired; it also was used in polygonal form. For regular rectangular masonry, often of uniform size and laid in regular courses, the Inca used black andesite. The most important structures in Cuzco are of this stone; the nearest known quarries are nine and twenty-one miles (15 and 35 km.) distant from Cuzco.

Certainly no other archaeological structure in the two Americas gives the visitor the awesome impression of stupendousness that Sacsahuamán does. Forewarned as one may be, the sight still exceeds expectations (Plate 15).

It is now believed that Sacsahuamán was not so much a fort built to protect Cuzco as a safe place of refuge for the inhabitants of the city in case of attack. Stretching for a distance of over 1800 ft (540 m.), more than a third of a mile, the three terrace walls reach a total height of about 60 ft (18 m.). Each wall is a saw-tooth line of angles, salient and retiring. The lower wall, fronting on a flat plaza, is the highest and most impressive, with the most enormous monolithic blocks. The largest of these is reported to be 5·2 m. (17·3 ft) high, 3 m. (10 ft) broad, 2·7 m. (9 ft) thick, with well over 100 tons weight. The task of quarrying, shaping, transporting, and placing such a behemoth staggers the imagination, but it was done somehow. This great wall is pierced in three places by easily defendable entrances. On the broad highest terrace were buildings, towers, and reservoirs for the beleaguered population, but all except the foundation stones were removed by the Spanish for building their houses in Cuzco.

For the transportation of these great blocks of stone few resources except unlimited manpower were available. Fibre ropes of any desirable strength could be made, and the principle of the lever was understood, possibly even that of the windlass. Massive blocks were dragged on wooden sleds, and earthen ramps, subsequently removed, were doubtless made to assist in placing them in position. Protuberances were left on the blocks, or indentations made in them to assist in their movement.

However it was done, the fitting is so exact that, as has often been remarked, a thin blade can seldom be inserted in the crack between adjacent blocks, and there was no necessity for the use of any mortar. This does not apply, of course, to the ruder masonry made of uncut natural stones. The edges of the blocks were generally bevelled, for artistic effect.

Bonding in masonry was not regular, but corners were more carefully bonded, and some attention seems to have been given to avoidance of long weak joints. In adobe construction regular bonding, with alternate rows of headers and stretchers, was more carefully observed. The true arch was unknown, and the corbel vault was used only to roof small chambers. Stone lintels were used over doorways and windows in masonry, but a bundle of poles bound with grass rope and covered with mud plaster was used in adobe buildings.

The adobe masses used in construction varied greatly according to period and region, and are sometimes used as criteria for temporal eras. Those of the earlier periods were generally hand modelled; the later, and particularly the Inca adobes, were moulded in forms to rectangular shapes. At various periods on the coast adobes were modelled in conical, hemispherical, cobble, cube, and sugar-loaf shapes, each characteristic of a certain time and region. Inca rectangular adobe bricks average about 32 by 8 by 8 inches (80 by 20 by 20 cm.).

In masonry construction, and especially in retaining walls, only the face was carefully finished, the rear left irregular. Free-standing walls generally had rubble fill in the centre. Walls were usually battered, and doors, niches, and other openings of Inca buildings were trapezoidal, narrower at the top. Corners were especially well made, and frequently the masonry was strengthened by a tenon or some other projecting feature that locked with the adjacent stone block.

Engineering: Roads, Bridges, Irrigation

Roads, paved or unpaved, were probably an ancient element in the Andean culture pattern, but few pre-Inca roads have been archaeologically verified, and it was the Inca who brought them to a high stage of development. In this respect the Inca bore a close resemblance to the Romans; both needed roads for the rapid transport of supplies for their conquering armies and for the quick conveyance of information and orders, and both built roads to the limits of their conquered dominions. The main difference between them was that the Inca, possessing no wheeled vehicles, did not need such good paving, if any, nor such wide roads and strong bridges; also they could use steps on steep slopes. Without good roads it would have been practically impossible to conquer regions at such a great distance from the centre, Cuzco, and, following conquest, to administer them. The Spanish were strong in their admiration for the Inca roads, wrote full descriptions of them, and utilized them constantly in post-conquest days.

There were two main north-south roads, one along the coast and one through the highlands. Transverse roads connected these, and minor roads ran to every village in the empire. The coastal highway ran from Tumbez southward along the coast to Arequipa and possibly even as far as Chile, but the latter section was not well known or much used. The longer highland road began at the Ancasmayo River on the Colombian border and ran south to Cuzco and beyond to Ayavire where it bifurcated around Lake Titicaca, and then south-east to Tucuman in present north-west Argentina. From here a line extended to Coquimbo on the coast of Chile, and from there south to the present region of Santiago. Another branch ran from Tucuman to Mendoza in Argentina. A transverse road connected Tumbez with the highland road, and other highways linked Cuzco with Nazca and with Arequipa. Still other roads ran eastward to the edge of the forested regions.

The roads through the highlands were of course the greater feats of engineering because of the precipitousness of the terrain in many places. Though they followed a straight line whenever possible, as did the ideal Roman road, they zigsagged up steep slopes, where they were often replaced by steps. Of an average width of three feet (1 m.) and paved in many places, they were carried over marshy places on causeways, over streams on bridges, and occasionally through hills in tunnels; in some places they were lined with walls. The causeways were made of earth paved with stone slabs, and were sometimes fifteen or twenty feet (4·5 to 6 m) in width and three to six feet (1 to 2 m.) high.

On the coast the roads were straighter and wider, twelve to fifteen feet (3·5 to 4·5 m.). Through the sandy, trackless deserts they consisted of no more than twin lines of posts to mark the trail, but through the thickly populated irrigated valleys they were lined with walls that were often painted in designs, and with shade trees, irrigated by a stream. When crossing steep rocky terrain, of course, they were built like the highland roads.

The old Inca roads have recently been followed and recorded by an expedition under the leadership of Victor W. von Hagen.[1]

At regular intervals along these roads the Inca government built *tambos* or rest-houses. Since they were used exclusively for persons travelling on official business they can hardly be termed 'inns'. Ordinary ones were placed a day's journey apart, and larger and more elegant 'royal tambos' were built in the cities on the road. Each of these latter was equipped with the special and

1. Van Hagen, 1955.

elegant accoutrements used by the emperor, awaiting the day when he might journey that way. Each tambo was furnished with a storehouse containing food and equipment, and was under the charge of local officials. 'Milestones' were set up on many of the roads at each unit of distance, which was the *topo*, about four and one-half miles (7 km.). (The same name is applied to a measurement of area, and to a shawl pin, usages already noted.)

Streams were crossed by bridges of several types, to meet diverse conditions. The smaller ones were spanned by a series of logs or by great stone slabs, supported by masonry piers, and the largest rivers by pontoon bridges, resting on floating rafts or small boats. Such a pontoon bridge apparently crossed the Desaguadero River near Lake Titicaca. The most interesting bridge, however, was the suspension bridge, generally spanning deep narrow ravines. Five great cables were stretched across and anchored firmly to beams embedded in masonry piers at either end. These cables were of braided or twisted fibre, vines, or long thin pliable twigs, and were up to sixteen inches (40 cm.) in diameter. Three formed the floor, which was flattened with crosssticks and matting or mud, and the other two served as hand railings, with other vines laced between them and the floor. The bridges sagged, and swayed in the wind, as no guy ropes were used, but were safe enough for foot travellers and llamas. Apparently the idea of hanging a level footpath from the cables, the method of modern suspension bridges, never occurred to the Inca. These bridges were repaired every year, this and their upkeep being the labour tax for the neighbouring inhabitants. Cobo describes one that he crossed at Vilcas which was two hundred feet (60 m.) long.

Where traffic was slight, a kind of breeches buoy is reported to have been employed: a suspended basket was drawn along a single cable by ropes in the hands of the bridge-tenders. On very long water crossings the passengers were ferried across on boats.

As before noted, irrigation was of the greatest importance in Peru, especially in the coastal region. Irrigation flumes and ditches were among the most admirable and important engineering features, often many miles in length, with the optimum gradient, following the contours of the hills. Over low spots they were carried on causeways, one in the Moche Valley being over fifty feet (15 m.) high. According to the nature of the terrain they were mere ditches, or stone-lined. Water was thus sometimes led to the top of a series of hillside terraces and allowed to flow over these.

Irrigation had been practised in Peru from a very early period, since at least Early Moche times. But, as in other engineering feats, the channels of the Inca exceeded others in efficiency. Smaller sluices controlled and closed by stone slabs led from the main channel to the fields. The terraces themselves, in certain areas covering the hillsides and supported by long parallel stone retaining walls, compared favourably with those of the Malayan region (Plate 21).

In Cuzco, drainage and water-supply were very efficiently handled. The streams running through the city were confined between walls, and the beds of the smaller streams were paved with stone. Water was conducted into some of the buildings by stone-lined and stone-covered conduits. In good agricultural land, streams were frequently straightened and narrowed in order to increase and preserve the arable area.

In several places the Inca built stone baths supplied by permanent running water. Relief models of newly conquered territory as well as of engineering projects, terraces, buildings, and even of towns were made for the guidance of the Inca engineers.

Transportation and Trade

Wheeled vehicles being unknown in Peru, as everywhere in America, land transportation was on the backs of men or llamas. Carrying objects balanced on the head does not seem to have been a usual practice. Small loads were ordinarily carried by wrapping them up in the mantles or cloaks and carrying this on the back, with two mantle corners tied across the chest; other objects were similarly carried with the help of ropes. The tumpline, with a carrying band across the forehead, was used in some places.

Litter-like frames were doubtless used for carrying heavier

objects, but the principal employment of the litter was for the personal transportation of the higher nobility. These litters of course varied in quality as befitted the rank of the rider; the finer ones had canopies for shade. The floor was solid, the seats portable stools. Litters were made for one or two persons, the latter facing each other. The ends of the long carrying poles rested on the shoulders of the four bearers.

Cieza de León gives a vivid description of the use of the litter by the Inca emperor.[1]

'When the Incas visited the provinces of their empire in time of peace, they travelled in great majesty, seated in rich litters fitted with loose poles of excellent wood, long and enriched with gold and silver work (Figure 5). Over the litter there were two high arches of gold set with precious stones, and long mantles fell round all sides of the litter so as to cover it completely. If the inmate did not wish to be seen, the mantles remained down, but they were raised when he got in or came out. In order that he might see the road, and have fresh air, holes were made in the curtains. Over all parts of these mantles or curtains there was rich ornamentation. On some were embroidered the sun and the moon, on others great curving serpents, and what appeared to be sticks passing across them. These were borne as insignia or arms. The litters were raised on the shoulders of the greatest and most important lords of the kingdom, and he who was employed most frequently on this duty, was held to be most honoured and in highest favour.'

In imperial days llamas were used mainly in large trains for transporting state goods and military supplies, but doubtless in earlier times and in other parts llamas were, as at present, privately owned, like the modern farmer's horses and cattle. They were never used for field cultivation or for any other activity except transport of goods (Figure 3).

While the planning of roads and bridges is a phase of engineering and is properly discussed in that section, their employment is pertinent to transportation.

In addition to the use of the roads for ordinary travel by officials, armies, and llama pack-trains, the Inca state maintained

1. Part 2, chapter 20, pp. 61–2 of Markham's translation, 1883.

ANDAS DELINGA
QVISPIRANPA

topa ynga yupanqui

mama ollo coya

lleuan al ynga los yñs callaua
ya·espaio
apaziarse

pascase el ynga

como

Figure 5. *Inca Emperor and his wife carried in a litter*

a twenty-four-hour relay post service for the rapid transport of messages and light objects. Small shelters were built about a mile apart,[1] in pairs, one on either side of the road and each holding two young men; one of these was on constant watch, looking for an approaching runner. When one appeared, he sprang up, ran with the panting messenger a short distance while he learned the message – generally accompanied by a quipu – or received the package, and then ran on at top speed to deliver it to the man at the next post. The runner (*chasqui*) was immediately replaced by another man ready at the post. The young men had been especially trained for this service which was their labour tax or *mita;* they served for periods of fifteen days.

By this relay system a very high average speed could be maintained indefinitely. The system was continued after the conquest, and the chroniclers report that the run from Lima to Cuzco, about 420 miles over a bad road, required three days. This is about 140 miles (224 km.) per day, or an average speed of about six miles per hour; this was doubtless exceeded on better roads and in Inca days when they were carefully maintained. For instance, it is reliably reported that fresh fish was brought from the coast in two days to the emperor in Cuzco.

While considering the topic of communication, mention should be made of the smoke signals by means of which messages could be sent across the country much faster than by courier.

Transportation by water was of importance only on the coast and on large Lake Titicaca. In both regions small fishing-boats made of bundles of *totora* reeds were made. These are called 'balsas', generally translated as 'rafts', but they are boats rather than rafts; boats of probably identical type are used on Titicaca today (Plate 22). Mat sails made of parallel reeds are borne on masts. The boats on the coast were small and light, generally carrying, and capable of being carried by, one man; nevertheless the fishermen in groups took them far to sea. In southern coastal Peru they used inflated sealskins, and in northern Peru a number

1. The chroniclers differ very much in their estimates of the distance covered by each relay runner. They range from a quarter of a league to one and a half leagues. Probably the distance varied in accord with the nature of the terrain.

of empty gourds under a net; the sealskins could be kept inflated at sea by means of tubes. Dugout canoes were made in peripheral areas, when suitable timber was available, but they were apparently unknown in the highland heart of the empire.

In far northern Peru and in Ecuador, where increasing rainfall produced forests near or on the coast, much larger rafts were built of the very light balsa wood. These were apparently real rafts, made of a number – generally seven to nine – of great logs of graded length so that the prow was pointed, the stern square. The logs were bound together with rope and covered with a platform, and a mast for a sail was erected in the centre; oars were also used. Such a raft could accommodate fifty men and sail a great distance. In such a raft (page 125) Topa Inca made his legendary voyage of exploration, and the *Kon Tiki*,[1] which drifted from Peru to the Tuamotu Islands in 1947, was of similar type. Barring a typhoon, and following the favourable current and winds, there is no reason why a large raft of this type should not have reached Indonesia or even the Asiatic mainland, and there is some evidence that in earlier days long Pacific voyages were not infrequent (pages 21–25).

Since in the Inca empire there was no private business and no standard medium of exchange, there was little trade. Persons were not permitted to change their residences beyond their immediate vicinity nor to travel for pleasure far from home. Almost the only exchange of property possible was that of small handicraft, which could be traded or bartered at local markets or fairs which were held at frequent or regular intervals. Thus a provident and industrious man or family might specialize in the production of some household goods or utensils in universal demand, produce a surplus of them in spare time, and exchange these for desired objects of another nature produced by other craftsmen. Other materials available for barter were surplus goods received in the periodic public distributions. A family receiving goods not needed or desired might trade them to another family deficient in these. The inequalities caused by the rule-of-thumb distribution were thus remedied.

1. Heyerdahl, 1950.

Emperor Pachacuti is credited with having decreed three market days or holidays each month. This seems reasonable for small local markets, but there were probably also larger ones at longer intervals in the principal centres.

Chapter 11

SOCIAL ORGANIZATION

THE Inca names for family relationships suggest that theirs was not a clan system with exogamy (marriage outside the group) and descent reckoned in a single female line. As with us, the primary distinction was that of sex, though sometimes the sex of the speaker was a determining factor. The respective generations with regard to the speaker were also of considerable importance. Our own system is so ingrained in us that anything else seems unnatural and incomprehensible. Cousins called each other by the same term as that employed for 'brother' and 'sister', and there was no distinction between parallel and cross-cousins by their own generation, though they were distinguished by the former generation. A father had sons and daughters, but the mother had only children. The same terms were used for father and for father's brother (uncle), for mother and for mother's sister (aunt), but father's sister and mother's brother had independent terms. The terms for brother and for sister were different when used by a man and by a woman.

In Inca times, just as in Peru today, the basic social group of the people – apart from the immediate family – was the *ayllu*. This group, already frequently mentioned, was an enlarged or extended family, a sub-tribe; all the members of an ayllu considered themselves related – and probably normally were. The ayllu, moreover, was a community; as before noted, it owned a definite territory.

The ayllu therefore had many of the aspects of the classic 'clan', and until quite recently most writers on Inca social organization have taken it for granted that it *was* a typical clan, with all the characteristics of such, including totemism, descent in the female lines, and exogamy. Where the modern Quechua or Aymara clans differ from this pattern it was assumed that they had changed since Conquest days. A careful study of the accounts of the early chroniclers, however, indicates that the Inca ayllu lacked any totem, that descent was reckoned in the male line, and that endogamy – marriage within the group – was the common practice. With these important differences in mind, the ayllu may well be considered a clan.

It is true that some of the ayllus traced descent from animals, but others ascribed their origins to mythical persons and places; the animal ancestor was not considered taboo for diet, and no ayllu bore an animal name, although each had a name, generally that of a place or person.

The ayllu was undoubtedly the fundamental social and political group of Peru, and was of very great age, far antedating the Inca empire. Kinship was its basis and bond. Probably residence was always patrilocal; the son brought his wife to live with or near his parents. The pattern of commoner agricultural labour for the support of the chief or *sinchi* must also have been a very ancient one. The chief had considerable authority, responsibility for the acts of his clansmen, and for the avenging of wrongs done to them. Each ayllu had its communal agricultural lands, pasture-lands, and woodlands, and functioned as a unit in external relations. Each recognized a founder, a common ancestor of all members, kept his body or mummy sacred, and built a ceremonial cult around his reverence. In the four years between 1615 and 1619, a century after the Conquest, the Spanish collected 1365 mummified bodies of adored ancestors.

In imperial days non-kinship institutions were superimposed on kinship ones or developed from them; the fundamental features were retained or slightly modified and the ayllu became the smallest social unit in the Inca system. More stress was laid on community of residence than on that of kinship. With the establishment of a class of nobility and its caste marriages, strict endogamy became impossible; probably it was still enforced for commoners, but apparently it was one of the first features to disappear with the Spanish conquest.

The Inca empire replaced allegiance to a familiar local chief by reverence to a distant foreign ruler, and drafted men for distant wars in which they had no patriotic interest. This naturally had quite an effect on the attitude of the commoner. New ayllus were frequently formed, especially as a result of the resettlement programme; some were formed for the descendants of prominent and distinguished men. Each emperor began a new royal ayllu consisting of all his male descendants except his eldest royal son who would, normally and in the natural course of events, establish his own royal ayllu. There were eleven of these royal ayllus at the time of the Spanish conquest, one for each of the historically recognized emperors; five of these belonged to the Lower moiety, six to the Upper (see page 177).

Some writers have claimed that the ayllu was standardized in empire days into the *pachaca*, the 100-household unit (see page 178), and the excess population periodically siphoned off for *yanacona* and similar distant services in order to keep the number at the standard decimal figure, but there seems to be no historical basis for this claim. Furthermore, it was apparently unnecessary, since the division of the population into decimally calculated groups was for administrative purposes only, and in that respect it mattered little whether the number of persons in the group was slightly above or below standard.

Bram[1] has well summarized the salient features of the Peruvian ayllu, and the changes brought about in it by its incorporation in the Inca imperial pattern:

Previous to the conquest and incorporation of an ayllu or a group of ayllus into the empire, the Indians lived in a small and circumscribed political, social, economic, linguistic, and religious world.

(a) Politically, the native owed allegiance to a sinchi or a curaca whom, in most cases, he knew personally and who was not a stranger to his group. When his settlement was in danger and he had to defend it, the nature of such a war was obvious to him. He fought in a familiar environment and for his own cause.

(b) Social relationships within an ayllu were those of an almost unstratified community with collective landownership. The curaca and his family formed the only nobility, while the mass of commoners were all equals. The possibilities of economic and social advancement were practically non-existent, and this must have insured a considerable degree of stability in inter-personal relations.

(c) Economically, a village community was a self-supporting

1. Bram, 1941, pp. 41–44.

176

unit, which engaged in a moderate amount of barter with neighbours. The curaca was exempt from labour in the fields, but it must have been relatively simple for a middle-sized community to support him and his family.

(d) The multiplicity of linguistic stocks in the Andean area limited the native to associations with related groups or tribes.

(e) This was even more the case in their religion. Most ayllus limited their cult to their own tutelary and totemic (*sic*) supernatural beings, and only occasionally displayed some interest in the cult of the neighbouring ayllus.

These five observations concerning the Andean ayllu-communities are literally true only of those that lived isolated and were not members of any alliances, confederacies, or feudal states. Such a state of isolation and of complete independence was not prevalent in this area. It is useful, however, for the purposes of analysis to understand first the above *simplified typical case*. Numerous changes occurred under Inca rule.

Bram then points out the great changes which incorporation in the Inca empire produced in the life of the ayllu and of the individual. They became relatively unimportant elements in a great organization instead of prominent entities in their provincial sphere. They were forced to take part in enterprises in which they had no interest, to contribute produce and labour to the support of distant projects and persons. Individuals from the village were taken to Cuzco or other distant places to be hostages, soldiers, craftsmen, servants, sacrifices, or concubines. Those that returned had broadened horizons through the experiences of travel, and introduced new points of view to the community.

The ayllus of pre-Inca Peru may have originally been grouped into two divisions or moieties, a rather common custom in primitive societies, but this dual division did not always fit into the imperial pattern and, in very populous regions, three groups were sometimes made. In general, however, there were two moieties, known as the Upper and the Lower; each ayllu belonged to one or the other. Those of the Upper moiety were given precedence over those of the Lower, and the two were rivals. They also showed a tendency toward endogamy.

The ayllus of a region, at any rate, were grouped into two – sometimes three – *saya*, or sections, and these formed a province (*guamán*). In the case of conquered peoples – the greater part of the empire – the province corresponded to a former tribe or native state; the provinces therefore differed considerably in size and number of population. Each province had its capital city, the centre for political and religious administration, and the inhabitants of each province wore some distinctive standard feature in their head-dresses.

The provinces were further grouped into one of the four quarters (*suyu*) into which the great empire was divided. Cuzco, the Inca capital, was the centre, geographically as well as politically, of all, for the division lines ran roughly north and south, east and west. The north-western quarter, Chinchasuyu, included Ecuador and northern and central Peru; the south-western, Cuntisuyu, consisted of southern Peru; to the north-east was Antisuyu, consisting largely of the eastern foothills and forests; Collasuyu to the south-east comprised the great highlands of the Aymara, the basin of Lake Titicaca, most of Bolivia, north-western highland Argentina, and northern Chile; this was the largest of the four quarters. The whole empire was appropriately called the 'Land of the Four Quarters', Tahuantinsuyu.

An Inca noble was the resident administrative official in each provincial capital, and the governors of the four quarters formed the great council of state in Cuzco; these also were Inca nobles of high rank, generally close relatives of the emperor, but their posts were not hereditary. The council reported its suggestions and opinions to the emperor for his decision and action.

Below the provincial governor were the *curacas* of four ranks, according to the number of men – or taxpayers – over whom they had charge; the latter were enumerated according to the decimal system. The curaca of lowest rank was the chief of one hundred men; he of highest rank, of ten thousand. The post of curaca was hereditary, subject to imperial approval. Over smaller groups of men, fifty and ten, were foremen of two ranks; these were commoners appointed by their curacas, and their offices were not hereditary. The two classes of leaders may cogently be compared with those in an army: corporals and sergeants over small groups, commissioned officers over progressively larger numbers. The official Inca titles of these officers of eight ranks below the emperor, listed by the chroniclers and by most other commentators, need not concern us here.

Some of the chroniclers state or imply that this system of decimal representation was a rigid one, and this has also been accepted by many writers on the Inca. But in the nature of things it would have been unworkable; the constant alteration in the numerical content of families and ayllus by births and deaths would have necessitated continual reshufflings and reclassifications. A man was presumably made the leader of a certain group, an ayllu or a saya, and given the rank called for according to the approximate number of families that his group proved to contain.

These numbers of taxpayers were determined by exact records constantly kept up to date by reports of births and deaths made by the foremen and forwarded to their superiors. The totals for major areas were recorded decimally on *quipus* and sent annually to the census office in Cuzco so that the authorities there had, at any time, an approximately correct record of population statistics for the entire empire. In these records, each individual was classified in one of a number of age-grade categories according to his physical status, from dependent babyhood to dependent senility. The chroniclers differ greatly in their reports on these groups, giving from six to twelve classes. The latter, that most generally quoted, seems unreasonable, since it makes four classes below eight years of age, years certainly of slight importance to the empire. Possibly the categories differed in different regions. The great important class, of course, was that of the *puric*, the able-bodied adult man, aged from about twenty-five to fifty years and capable of doing a hard day's work in the fields, the army, or the mines. He was the unit in the social system and represented his household. The classification applied only to male commoners, but there were probably other census records for women.

Chapter 12

POLITICAL ORGANIZATION
AND GOVERNMENT

THE Inca state was a queer blend of theocracy, monarchy, socialism, and communism, its categorization in one system or another depending mainly on definition. It has often been termed a socialistic empire,[1] for it was an aristocratic and autocratic socialism, not a democratic one. Land was the property of the state, and much of it was communally worked. Most of the llama herds were also state property, as also were the mines. These were almost the only 'means of production'. The state insured the people against hunger, exploitation, undue hardship, and all kinds of want, but regimented them rigorously and left them no choice, independence, or initiative. There were neither 'booms' nor depressions. It was the welfare state *par excellence*, toward which our modern democracies now seem to be (1966) tending. It, however, was at least efficiently administered; malfeasance, misfeasance, and nonfeasance on the part of officials were equally severely punished – or claimed to have been.

However, the Inca empire differed from the modern ideal of a socialistic welfare state in that there was a large class of nobles and priests, supported by the masses. Heavy tribute in the form of labour was demanded of the peasants, who profited very little from it.

All arable land was divided into three categories, though not into three equal parts, although fields of the three classes were necessarily close together. The produce of those of one class was for the government, of the second for the gods and religion, and of the third for the people. Although the first two were given primary consideration, their size depended on the population, for each family was first allotted just enough land to keep them

1. Baudin, 1927a, 1928; Karsten, 1949a.

180

comfortably fed without hunger; the balance was divided between state and church. Each year the land was reallotted by the local official – at least the communal land – and each family was given according to its current needs, the same as, or more or less than, the preceding year, according as the number of persons in the household may have increased or decreased.

The system might be termed agrarian collectivism rather than communism. Although in late days the land was considered the property of the state, i.e. of the emperor, it was controlled by the ayllu, the local clan group, communally; ayllu ownership doubt-less long preceded imperial days. Probably also the pattern of lands communally cultivated for the state (formerly for the local chiefs) and for the church (formerly the local priests) was an ancient Andean one, adopted and enlarged in imperial times. Probably the greater amount of land allocated to church and state was offset, if not more than made up for, by the agricultural land produced by state enterprise, making formerly sterile acres arable by irrigation and terracing. In the periodical allocation of family fields it is reported that one *topo* (page 234) of land was assigned to each married couple, an extra strip for every son, and half a strip for each daughter.

The boundaries of the fields, especially those separating communal, state, and church properties, were well marked, and their removal was a great and almost unheard-of-crime.

On the whole, the state lands seem to have been a little larger than the others, for reasons that we will see later. State overseers constantly supervised the non-communal lands, and the common people respected their sanctity and inviolability so much that they never crossed them without repeating ritual prayers for this special purpose.

The non-communal lands were cultivated by the people *en masse* and before their own fields, those of the gods first. When time for sowing or harvesting came, the commoners were called by the officials to work the sacred fields. At the inception everyone laboured, commoners, officials, nobility, and even the emperor himself. The latter offered only a token of work, and the nobles soon followed suit, those of lowest rank labouring the longest, and soon only the peasants remaining. The emperor, or the highest official on the spot, inaugurated the work with a golden implement.

The fields were divided up by lines, a section to each family, so that the man with the most household assistance finished his job first. Like all co-operative labour, it must have been a jovial and not an onerous occasion, with plenty of chicha beer, singing, and bantering. The songs, perhaps in honour of the gods when working the church lands, or in praise of the emperor while engaged in the state fields, were appropriate to the occasion. As soon as the fields of the gods were finished, the work was repeated on the government lands, and then the people were free to cultivate their own fields. There was a communal spirit of helpfulness, and if a man was called away on state business such as military service his neighbours quietly attended to his agricultural needs.

The harvests from the state and religious fields were gathered into separate storehouses of which the government maintained two sets in each district. Other, and probably more and greater, storehouses were built at the provincial capitals and at Cuzco. For fire protection, each set consisted of a number of small buildings sufficiently separated.

The food from the religious storehouses served to support the numerous priesthood, and for sacrificial and ceremonial purposes. The government's store was drawn on for the support of the nobility and all state officials, artisan craftsmen, the army, and all other non-religious non-producers. In the latter category were the aged, infirm, and widows. The state storehouses also served as insurance against unforeseen calamities and 'acts of God' – earthquake, storms, and other causes of crop failure. The curacas were authorized to draw upon these stores in the event of such disasters and famines. In seasons of plenty, when the storehouses were too full to hold the new crop, the emperor ordered a stock dividend, distributing the food to the people so that they might eat more heartily and be more contented. In such circumstances, food from one region was sent to another where it was not grown, so that the people might enjoy a change of diet. Potatoes were never destroyed because of over-production; the gods would have been angered and would have withheld the next harvest.

In the highland grazing regions, the same triple division was applied to the herds of llamas and alpacas, as well as to the pasture-lands; both were divided into three groups for church, state, and people. In this case, because most of the wool was distributed by the government and few animals were killed except for sacrifice, the allotments to the church and state were much greater than those to the populace. Ten animals was the limit for any commoner; nobles were allowed more. The majority of the stock belonged to the government, which gathered the wool into storehouses and distributed it to the families in proportion to their size, enough to clothe all the members. In this distribution no deduction was made for the privately owned animals; the man who owned many received as much as he who owned one.

Each family made its own clothing from the wool distributed by the government, as well as making all other household equipment and tools. These, together with house, stable-storehouse, and small domestic animals, were practically the only private property.

In addition to agricultural service on state and church lands each commoner was required to perform a certain amount of other public work each year. This obligation was known as *mita*. These men provided recruits for the army, labour on the roads and bridges and in the mines, runners on the post roads, personal service for the nobles, and other public work. The number of men needed was determined, and a definite percentage of these was selected from each district. Tradition reports that thirty thousand men were thus employed in building the great fortress of Sacsahuaman. It is also said that unnecessary work was often made just for the purpose of keeping these selective-service recruits busy. Like every good army sergeant, the officials knew well that 'Satan finds some evil still for idle hands to do', and that the busy man has no time to complain or foment revolt.

There were certain districts that were exempt from this *mita* service because they provided special materials or services. Thus the Chicha made carved logs of a resinous wood to be used for sacrificial fires, the Rucana supplied the litter-bearers, and the Chumpivilca the trained dancers for the court.

Craftsmen and other skilled labourers whose work required long practice and experience were especially provided for, and were relieved from agricultural, pastoral, or the *mita* service. They were government servants, supported at public expense. Actually they were court artificers, as their handiwork was for the emperor, who distributed it as favours to the nobility. Goldsmiths, potters, woodcarvers, sculptors, and similar artisans fell into this class, as well as the *quipucamayoc* who kept accounts. These positions were generally hereditary, since the father trained his sons in his craft. But often a boy who showed special ability was chosen from the peasant class. These were the only craftsmen; otherwise there was no division of labour.

Another important group exempt from the usual labour-tax service consisted of men known as *yanacona*. These were selected in youth, removed from their ayllus with which they lost all connexion, and taken for service in other parts. In fact, some authorities believe that the craftsmen were included in the yanacona category. The status of both was hereditary. Like the 'Chosen Women' next to be mentioned, boys were selected and placed at the disposal of the emperor, who employed them in state service as pages, servants, temple attendants, supervisors, and similar offices, or gave them as rewards for faithful and efficient service to favoured nobles and warriors. Though the latter apparently often used their yanacona labour for ordinary agricultural work, nevertheless the boys were certainly selected for unusual intelligence, ability, or promise, and most of them used their positions to rise to posts of considerable importance. Many of them were sons of curacas. Their status is a little difficult to define; they can hardly be considered as slaves, but in effect they were. However, the close relationship between them and their masters gave them great opportunities to receive favours and to be placed in positions of responsibility. Some of them rose to be curacas themselves.

The Spanish conquerors took full advantage of the yanacona relationship and enlarged it greatly, drafting great numbers of young men as servants on their estates, agricultural labourers and miners; these, of course, were practically slaves with no prospects for advancement or economic improvement.

Regimentation also extended to the women. Of course almost all of them became wives and mothers of commoners and participated in their husbands' agricultural activities as well as having their own domestic ones. These, however, were the less attractive and less talented women and were known as the 'left-out girls', *hauasipascuna*, since the choice maidens were selected for public service.

A government official visited each village at intervals and classified all the girls at about the age of ten. The most beautiful and physically perfect were chosen and sent to be educated in 'convents' in the provincial capitals where they spent about four years learning 'domestic science', religion, weaving, cooking, chicha-manufacture, and similar duties. They were known as *acllacuna*, 'Chosen Women'. A few were also chosen to be sacrificed on solemn occasions; these were especially honoured and particularly proud and happy at their selection, since it assured them of an after-life of happiness and leisure.

After completing their educations, the girls were again classified. Many were given by the emperor to nobles as secondary wives. He doubtless kept the *crème de la crème* for himself. The others were consecrated to the service and homage to the Sun and became the 'Virgins of the Sun', *mamacuna*, sworn to permanent chastity. Some were attached to each shrine or 'Sun Temple', where they wove the fine textiles used in ceremonies and worn by the priests, and prepared the chicha for festivals. They had considerable resemblance to the nuns of a religious order, and were headed by a high priestess who was of the noblest birth and was considered the wife of the Sun. The 'convent' in Cuzco was of course the largest and most important, but others, presided over by a priestess of noble birth, were connected with the temple in each provincial centre.

The Emperor and the Nobility

The Inca emperor was an absolute despot but distinctly not a tyrant, using these words in their proper senses, nowadays so often confused. That is, his power was limited only by custom, but it *was* thus limited. To his subjects he was an omnipotent tribal god, merciless to their enemies, firm but just to his subjects and worshippers. The comfort and peace of his people was his primary and constant concern. He could hardly be said to have been a legal ruler, since he was above the law – his word *was* the law – but, so strong was the force of custom and precedent that he probably never violated them to satisfy personal spite.

The Inca emperor was the supreme ruler of the state and could with better reason have echoed – or anticipated – Louis XIV's claim to *be* the state. As a lineal descendant of the Sun he ruled by divine right and was worshipped and implicitly obeyed as being himself divine. He was believed to be intimately associated with the Sun, and his health affected that of the latter.

In the earlier years of the empire the emperor married the daughter of a neighbouring ruler, as among recent European royalty, but in the last three or four generations before the Conquest his person had become so exalted that none but his own sister could be considered a fit consort. Here was the *ne plus ultra* of the idea of aristocracy, of blue blood; none but a replica could be an equal. The same sentiment and ideal were in vogue among another great people of antiquity, the Egyptians; for generations the Pharaohs married their sisters. Contrary to popular folklore, in both cases this – to us – incestuous marriage seems to have produced capable, vigorous rulers. All the historic Peruvian emperors were men of unusual energy and capacity. Close inbreeding among animals has long been practised to produce superior stock, and there is no reason why the same should not be true of humans, if there is no weakness or defect in the heredity.

Like many Oriental potentates, the emperor was also allowed a large seraglio of secondary wives, generally taken from the 'Chosen Women'. These concubines were not, as is often stated, the 'Virgins of the Sun', another group of 'Chosen Women' vowed to permanent chastity. The secondary wives prepared the emperor's food, made his attire, and performed the usual domestic duties.

Naturally the emperor had a large number of offspring who belonged to the nobility and were accorded special privileges.

The descendants of each emperor in the male line formed a special royal ayllu whose duty it was to attend to the upkeep of his palace and the maintenance of his cult. For each emperor built himself a new palace which was later used as his shrine and mausoleum. At the time of the Conquest these descendants of the emperors amounted to about five hundred. This large body of aristocratic men formed a valuable court around the current living emperor, and from them he chose most of the higher officials.

There seems to have been no very definite rule for succession to the 'throne'. The emperor named his successor, always his son, and generally the most capable of his sons by the *coya*, his principal wife. The boy probably had no formal education – for who could instruct a living deity? – but was trained for his future exalted position by his parents, and learned by court example.

When the heir apparent reached puberty he was by no means exempted, as any European princeling would have been, from the fatiguing trials of the manhood ceremonies that were held annually for all the boys of the noble class who had reached that physical stage during the past year. These rites were meant to test the physical and psychological fitness of the youths for the positions of authority that they were to hold, and the Peruvians had the proper idea that the higher the rank, the greater the required capability. So the young Inca prince was given no leniency and was even treated with more than usual severity; he was expected to outdo the others in physical effort and the endurance of hardships.

When the time came for the new ruler's inauguration or installation, he fasted for three days in a house built especially for the occasion and was then invested with the royal fringe in a great public ceremony at which each noble swore allegiance. This was followed by a feast lasting for several days.

Upon his death the members of his ayllu took charge of the elaborate funerary ceremonies which were observed throughout the empire. The body was preserved in his palace by the primitive means of mummification in vogue. The entrails were removed and preserved in a special container, and the body was dried and carefully wrapped in the finest textiles. The mummy was thereafter waited upon as during life, even, it is reported, having women constantly standing at its side with fans to keep the flies away! During the greatest public ceremonies the bodies of the emperors were brought out into the sacred square of Cuzco under the care of their descendants. The mummies of all the Inca emperors were seen as late as 1559.

It was expected that the deceased emperor's favourite wives and servants would volunteer to accompany him in death, and probably each of these did his or her duty as he saw it, confident of his reward in the after-world. They were intoxicated, probably with chicha beer, during a great dance, and then strangled.

The august emperor's presence could be approached by few, and with the greatest humility by these few. Usually, in interviews, he was invisible behind a screen; a face-to-face reception was an honour accorded to only the greatest or the most favoured. No one, however, no matter what his rank or blood, could enter the chamber without removing his sandals and placing a small burden on his back to indicate his humble position. When travelling, the emperor was carried on a litter by men from the province of Rucanas who wore a special livery. His retinue on such a journey amounted to several hundred men, to clear the road and relieve the bearers. Both on account of this large number and the slow pace that his dignity required, a day's journey averaged only about twelve miles.

Other servants of the imperial court also were recruited from particular villages and regions. Garcilaso's[1] remarks upon this subject are pertinent:

The attendants for the service of the palace, such as sweepers, water-carriers, and wood-cutters, as well as cooks for the table of the courtiers (for that of the Inca himself was served by his concubines), porters, keepers of the wardrobe, warders of the treasure, gardeners, huntsmen, and all other servants holding similar positions to those in the houses of the kings and emperors, were not persons chosen by chance. But each office was filled by natives of particular villages, whose duty it was to supply faithful and efficient men in sufficient number. They were changed at

1. Garcilaso de la Vega, Part 1, Book 6, chapter 3; Vol. 2, pp. 107–8 of Markham's translation (1869–71).

certain intervals, and this was the form that the tribute took in those villages. Any negligence or inefficiency on the part of these servants was looked upon as an offence committed by their village, and for one man's fault all the inhabitants were chastised more or less severely according to the offence. If the offence was committed against the royal majesty, the village was levelled with the ground. It must not be understood that the wood-cutters went to the forest for fuel, but that they found it provided in the palace, being brought there by the vassals, as well as all other things for the royal service. And these employments were much prized among the Indians, as they enabled them to be nearer the royal person, which was an honour they most esteemed.

The villages which furnished these servants were those within six or seven leagues of the city of Cuzco, and were the first which the Inca Manco Capac ordered to be formed by the savages whom he reduced to subjection. The inhabitants of them, by his special grace and bounty, he called Incas, and they received the insignia and dress of the royal person. . . .

The emperor's clothing was of the same pattern as that of all men, but was of the finest materials, specially woven or made for him by the women of his household. His most characteristic ornament was a wide fringe, the royal insignia with which he was invested upon assuming rule. This, about four inches wide, was composed of small gold tubes from which hung red tassels. The head-dress itself was rather simple, a braid (*llautu*) wound several times around the head. He wore very large ear-plugs. The higher members of the nobility were also allowed to wear ear-plugs, head-bands, and fringes, but always of other colours and smaller or of less fine materials. The emperor wore his hair rather short.

The royal throne was a low stool of red wood, only about eight inches high and covered with a rich cloth; this was placed on a raised platform. A small, square, stiff, painted cloth pennant was the royal standard, but the emperor personally carried a war-club or mace with a star head of gold. Two similar ones on long poles were carried to flank the royal standard.

Like the simplest of his subjects, the ruler slept on the floor, on a large cotton quilt covered with woollen blankets; he ate from the most ornate containers of gold, silver, or pottery. No one else might aspire to enjoy his superior goods, so all his discards and left-overs, clothing, food, or whatnot, were carefully saved and ceremonially burnt once a year by an official. On the latter point, however, as on many others, the chroniclers differ. Garcilaso[1] says that the emperor gave his once-used clothing to another member of his family. Garcilaso's description, while probably not entirely reliable as to details, gives a good impression of certain phases of the emperor's life.

The Inca usually sat on a stool of solid gold called *tiana* . . . without arms or back, and with a concave surface for the seat. It was placed on a great square board of gold. All the cups for the whole service of the house, as well for the table as for the kitchen, were, large and small, of gold and silver; and some were placed in each depot for the use of the king when travelling. This was done to avoid the necessity of carrying them about with him, and thus every royal lodging, whether on the roads or in the provinces, was fully supplied with all he required when he marched with his armies, or visited his people. . . .

There was also great store of new clothing, both for wearing and for the bed, for the Inca never put on the same dress twice, but gave it to one of his relations. All his bed clothes were woollen, woven from the wool of the vicuñas, which is so fine that, among other things belonging to that land, it has been brought over for the bed of the king, Don Philip II. These blankets were placed both under and over. They did not use mattresses, because they did not want them, for when they saw those used by the Spaniards they would not have them in their houses. They seemed to be too great a luxury, and too artificial to be in conformity with the natural life that they profess to lead.

They did not have tapestry for the walls, because they were covered with gold and silver. The dinners were very plentiful, as they were prepared for all the Inca's relations who might come to dine with the king, as well as for all the servants of the household, who were numerous. The hour for the principal meal, both for the Inca and for the people, was eight or nine in the morning. They supped before the light of day was gone, and these were their only meals. They were generally bad eaters; that is to say, they ate little. But they were not so abstemious in drinking. They

1. Garcilaso de la Vega, Part I, Book 6, chapter 1; Vol. 2, pp. 100–1 of Markham's translation (1869–71).

did not drink during the meal, but they made up for it afterwards, and their potations were continued until night. This was the custom of the rich, for the poor had only sufficient of all things, though no scarcity. They went to bed early, and got up very early to do the business of the day.

In a period of only about thirty years the Inca empire expanded from a relatively small, homogeneous state to an immense empire containing dozens of alien peoples with different languages and diverse governmental patterns. To keep these dissident elements in subjection and peace required a tremendous increase in the number of reliable administrative officials. Up until that time the Inca pattern had been to select officials from the more capable members of the royalty, blood relatives or descendants of the emperors, but now there were too few of these, and every official who showed any administrative ability was quickly advanced to a responsible position and placed among an alien group to enforce the will of the emperor. It was just as at the beginning of our recent World Wars, when a capable Navy warrant officer soon found himself a commissioned lieutenant, or a regular army sergeant a captain, drilling a company of raw recruits. It is not certain, however, whether an ordinary commoner could ever rise to the nobility.

When a former ruler or leader of one of the conquered peoples was willing to accept the new régime, he was confirmed in his position and his children were taken to Cuzco as hostages. There they were educated and indoctrinated in Inca ideology in what seems to have been the only formal school in the empire. Probably the sons of Inca nobles also attended the school, or certain classes of it. It is reported to have been, as in most modern colleges, a four-year course, the first year spent in learning the Inca language, the second in Inca religion, the third in the intricacies of the *quipu* (the knot-records) (see pages 230–31), and the fourth in Inca history. The teachers were firm believers in the pedagogical qualities of the rod, but the caning was applied to the soles of the feet. However, this phase of instruction was, by custom, limited to one application of ten blows per day.

On the father's death a son succeeded him. An able son of a former low-rank official now enjoying a high position of authority among an alien group was likewise appointed to his father's position, and in every way the Inca strove to follow their pattern of an hereditary aristocracy. The noble class was thus greatly augmented and fell into two classes, the higher and the lower aristocracy, possibly better distinguished as the royalty and the nobility.

The higher aristocracy was termed the 'Inca class' by the Spanish chroniclers; its nucleus consisted of the real old royalty, Incas by blood, descendants of the emperors in the male line. Since these were not sufficient to provide the necessary officials, the Emperor Pachacuti extended the privileges of Inca nobility to all the inhabitants of certain districts, all of whom spoke Inca as their native language and practised Inca customs; many of these were sent as officials to newly conquered distant territories. They were all given the privilege of wearing large ear-plugs, and all the other perquisites of the Inca royalty.

The lower class of nobility or aristocracy was known as the 'Curaca class' and consisted of the former independent conquered leaders who had been confirmed in their positions, and all other administrators down to those over one hundred persons.

Both the royalty and the nobility were allowed many privileges such as the use of litters, parasols, and attire somewhat resembling the emperor's, secondary wives, luxury articles, and *yanacona* servants. They were exempt from taxation and were supported by the government. Llamas and land were also awarded them for efficient service, but, in accord with the basic Inca (and usual pan-American) principle regarding land, the latter was considered as the property of the group and not of the individual. The noble might enjoy its usufruct but could not dispose of it; at his death it was similarly used by his progeny. While the nobility composed a relatively large group numerically, they formed only a tiny fraction of the entire population.

Although in Incaic Peru there was a large body of non-producers, slavery of the type of the ancient Old World despotisms was unknown; the entire class of commoner peasantry contributed equally to the support of the officials, priests, and aristocracy. There being no money, no capitalists, no private property except for the simplest and most elemental possessions, all taxation was in the form of labour service. This was accomplished by stringent rules or laws, enforced by officials, each responsible to another in a higher category until the last was the emperor himself. The laws of the emperor, moreover, were accepted by both officials and commoners as those of divinity itself and therefore just and inexorable. Disobedience and infractions were exceedingly rare, and sternly punished.

Though, theoretically, all commoners were of the same economic status, as in every society a few seem to have secured more than their share of goods, especially in the possession of llamas. There were also very poor ones who had somehow lost their ayllu affiliations and drifted to the large cities. The women of this class were probably the prostitutes, of which there was a large group in Cuzco.

In another respect also there was some economic inequality. The commoner with many children, especially boys, to help him with labour on his farm and his tax labour, was deemed richer than the man with few – or female – children.

War and Conquest

Among most American Indian peoples of relatively low cultural status, inter-group hostility and combat can hardly be dignified by the name of war. Hostility was felt towards all neighbouring groups, culminating in small semi-private war parties. It assumed a more national character with the larger sedentary groups in more thickly populated regions, and with the Inca it became the primary instrument of national policy. Warfare in Peru doubtless went through these sequential stages. In the earliest days the villages were probably constantly at enmity, the hostilities of small scope; later, the growing states, especially those on the coast such as the Chimú, probably had organized armies, but Inca warfare was of a grade that surpassed everything else in pre-Columbian America. The causes were complex, but war became a most important feature of Inca culture. While based on the primitive Andean pattern of warfare it naturally evolved practices suited to large-scale operations with immense armies.

Though some of the earlier wars, both of the Inca and of other Peruvian peoples, may have had an economic basis, economy was certainly not the primary cause of war, and it was lacking entirely in the later days of the empire. Then it was a desire for aggrandizement and increased power on the part of the emperor and the policy-makers, and an ambition to excel and to achieve glory and the advancement, perquisites, and favours that fell to the brave and victorious warrior on the part of the subordinate leaders; the common soldier was the traditional 'cannon-fodder'. Each new Inca emperor aspired to outdo his predecessor. Unlike the Aztec, annual tribute was not demanded of the conquered, though some looted spoils of victory were taken at the time of the conquest. Indeed, some conquered regions were so economically ill-favoured that their acquisition was more a liability than an asset. The nobility were already so well off that they could use little more. Neither was there the urge for captives for sacrifice that animated much of Aztec war, and the subjugated peoples were not enslaved or made to work any harder than the victors. Nevertheless, war was, on the whole, advantageous to the Inca – and probably also to the conquered peoples. The life of the people was so regimented and channelled that war presented practically the only opportunity for competition and manifestation of superiority. Moreover, in later days at least, the large organization needed by the immense forces almost required that the army be a standing one, permanently in action, and the rulers knew well that, unless busy with foreign wars, the generals might well plot revolution. Some of the wars were obviously planned to prevent peripheral enemies from stirring into revolt their recently conquered neighbours.

Doubtless among all Peruvian groups every able-bodied man was a potential warrior and had received some training in warfare since boyhood; to be incapable or inefficient was a disgrace. In the days of the Inca empire every ordinary man in the proper age-class was liable to military service, and practically all of them certainly served their terms. It is obvious that, with the size and extent of the army and the empire, most of the troops came from recently conquered peoples with little interest in subjugating others; the actual Quechua Inca of the Cuzco region were so relatively few that they served only as higher officers. The only force of 'regulars', professional soldiers, was the bodyguard of the emperor. These, of course, were a picked group; Atahuallpa executed those who broke ranks when naturally frightened by their first sight of a rearing horse. The army was subdivided according to the same decimal system that was employed with the civilian population, with the same pyramidal ranking of officers.

As with the Mediterranean, the Aztec, and most early conquering nations with large armies, Inca warfare was based on close in-fighting with hand weapons. The bow and arrow, the usual American Indian weapon in fighting as in hunting, was not employed by the mountain tribes, though of course it was known and was used by forest Indians in the Inca armies. It was little used on the coast also; in both regions suitable wood was scarce. Nor were javelins and throwing spears employed in Inca times, though they had been in earlier days. Their use lasted until the Conquest among the natives of the coast, who cast them with the help of spear-throwers; archaeologically the spear-thrower is very old in America (Plate 46A). The spears were of hard wood with fire-hardened points.

Inca battles, however, generally opened at a slight distance with the use of slings and bolas, the missile arms; these are more adapted to the open country of the Peruvian highlands. The sling was not the forked-stick-and-rubber-band weapon of the modern boy, but rather of David's Goliath-killing type. Generally of braided wool or fibre, it was up to six feet (2 m.) in length, with a wider cradle for the stone in the centre. Doubled, with both ends held in one hand, it was whirled around the head to give momentum, and then one end released, thus hurling the stone with great force and – with practice – great accuracy. The sling, constantly carried to kill or frighten away small animals or to drive domestic ones, was as ubiquitous as a modern Mexican's *machete*, and was often worn as a fillet to keep the hair back.

The bolas consisted of several stones, each fastened to the end of a cord, or thong, and the latter tied together at the other ends.

Thrown, they whirled by centrifugal force and covered a considerable area, wrapping around the victim's body or legs; this also was primarily a hunting weapon.

After the first stone-hurling, the Inca warriors closed in for hand-to-hand combat. The main arm of the common soldier was the club, generally with a doughnut-shaped stone on the end; this was often modified to a star shape with a number of points, especially in club-heads made of copper or bronze. A double-edged sword of hard wood which has given its Quechua name *macana* to this weapon was another arm; this was a heavy two-handed sword, and the wielder carried no shield. There were also various types of battle-axes and poleaxes, with blades of stone or copper. The long wooden spears had fire-hardened ends, or tips of copper or bronze.

Armour had been considerably developed among the Inca troops. Quilted cotton shirts or lengths of cloth wrapped around the body were worn. These were so efficient against native arms that the Spanish adopted the custom in preference to their heavier and hotter steel armour. Helmets of wood or plaited cane protected the head, and shields of wooden slats were worn on the back. Smaller round or rectangular shields were carried in the hand; these were generally covered with hide and decorated with some painted design or feather mosaic. Like the Roman *testudo*, a great strong cloth that could cover many men was sometimes used in siege operations.

Except for these protective devices the Inca soldier wore the usual man's costume without the cloak. Almost all wore round metal plaques which were a sort of military decoration, probably awarded by the commanding officer for valour – copper for the lowest rank, gold for the highest. There was probably no military band *per se*, but martial music was produced by small drums, trumpets, and flutes, and the fighting was accompanied by a din of shouts and curses, and possibly concerted singing of insulting songs. Each company carried a small square stiff pennant which bore the insignia of the group; this was fastened to the end of a spear.

Compared with their enemies, the Inca armies were strong and efficient, mainly because of their size and the excellently organized commissariat. Of course they were no match for fire-arms and cavalry.

Excellent discipline was observed in the Inca armies until the ranks were broken for hand-to-hand combat, from which time on there was no direction or organization. On the march, how-ever, the troops were under strict control; no deviation from the ranks was tolerated, and any foraging or molestation of non-combatants was severely punished.

Though most military operations were pitched battles in the open, the art of fortification was rather well developed. Tem-porary breastworks and trenches were apparently never used, but most important towns had hill-top forts to which the people re-tired in case of attack, and the large centres, such as Cuzco, were provided with great fortresses. These were often constructed with considerable military engineering skill, with walled terraces on the hillside, bastions, and salients. The great fortress of Sacsahuamán (Plate 15) (see page 163) overlooking Cuzco is the most noteworthy example, but many others, both in the high-lands and on the coast, remain to attest to the quality and nature of these works.

Capable and experienced generals had many military man-œuvres, strategies, and ruses up their sleeves, and the history of the Inca contains many of these. Grass was fired to demoralize an enemy army; it was led into an ambush in a ravine and over-whelmed with boulders. Retreating, apparently defeated from a battle, the Inca force would return and surprise the confident and unwary 'victors' the following dawn. The army was fre-quently divided and a large part of it kept in reserve for a surprise attack.

The great success of the Inca armies was in large measure due to the recognition of the truth of the aphorism that an army travels on its stomach. The commissariat was efficiently planned and operated. In the organized parts of the empire supplies were available in government storehouses; beyond its limits they were brought by trains of pack llamas. The storehouses were so frequent along the high-roads that the marching troops could always make their night camp at one.

Few captives, and these mainly the leaders, were brought back as prisoners of war. The emperor trod upon the conquered chiefs as a symbol of their subjection to him; they were sometimes marched through the streets of Cuzco in a triumphant victory parade. A few of the prisoners might be sacrificed, and a few of the culpable or dangerous leaders tortured, flayed, killed, or imprisoned. Heads were frequently taken as trophies, and the skull often made into a drinking-cup from which the victor drank chicha. War drums were sometimes made of the skin – and even, it is reported, of the entire body – of important defeated enemies as a particular not-to-be-forgotten insult. Necklaces were often made of the teeth of slain enemies, and flutes of their shinbones. The absence of the frequent South American custom of cannibalism is noteworthy.

The main incentive of the warrior, however, especially of the leaders of whatever rank, was glory, honours, rewards, and advancement. The emperor was lavish in his gifts to nobles who had served him well; they were given secondary wives, fine clothing and other handicraft made by the state-supported artificers, promotion, and special privileges such as sitting on a special stool. Even for the humble common soldier there were commendatory metal plaques, gifts of clothing, and similar awards.

Pre-combat negotiation or diplomacy was a unique feature of Inca imperial militarism. Envoys invited neighbouring groups to join the empire, pointing out the advantages of alliance, the terrors of refusal. The efficient socialistic economic system was doubtless advantageous to the ordinary native, and the local rulers were generally permitted to retain their positions under the new régime. Most small groups and tribes realized the hopelessness of resistance and therefore submitted peacefully; the stronger ones generally preferred to fight against odds for their independence, almost always ineffectually.

Church and state were one in the Inca empire, and their motives, policies, and practices were practically identical with those of many other triumphant nations of the past. They firmly believed that they were the superior and master race – for hadn't they proved it both in culture and by force of arms? Like all imperialistic nations, they doubtless – and properly – felt that they could utilize the land to better advantage. Moreover, they brought the blessings of the true religion – that of the Sun – to their benighted heathen neighbours, without, however, interfering with the religious practices of these subjugated peoples.

As among most peoples before the recent atheistic ideology, the gods were importuned to lend aid, since the war was fought largely for their glory, and final victory was ascribed to divine help. In addition to ceremonies, sacrifices, fasts, and other rites to increase the sympathy and favour of their gods, an incantation was performed before the opening of hostilities to weaken the power of the enemy gods and supernatural spirits. To the accompaniment of some magical rites, such as the burning of wild birds on a fire of thorny wood, the priests prayed that the power of the enemy's supernatural aids might be weakened. Holding stones on which figures of various dangerous, noxious, and fierce animals had been painted, they marched around the fire, chanting and praying. Some black llamas which had been starved for some time were then sacrificed with the prayer that the bodies and spirit of the enemy might likewise be weakened. Black dogs were also sacrificed, and certain persons compelled to eat the meat. During these rites the participants ate only at night.

Divination, of course, played a large part in all military actions, and nothing was begun until the auguries proved auspicious. The oracles were frequently consulted, and inherently lucky days, such as that of the new moon, were always chosen. In the above-mentioned ceremony of the sacrifice of the starved black llamas, the hearts were inspected to see whether some flesh near the heart had been absorbed during the deprivation from food; the prognostication was bad if it had not.

Each fighting group carried into battle some of its portable idols, fetishes, or wacas, which served not only as moral sustainers and rallying points, like modern flags and pennons, but also lent their supernatural aid. The allies naturally carried those of their own regions and deities. As the major idols of the army, the Inca carried images or wacas representing ancestors, especially former emperors; the stones representing Manco Capac and Huanacauri were particular favourites.

The surprising success of the Inca in unifying and controlling with such relatively little belligerent unrest such a great empire, composed of many previously hostile elements, was due almost entirely to their wise policies with regard to newly conquered regions. The important elements of this programme were re-settlement or colonization, and administrative reorganization.

As soon as armed resistance had ceased, a careful survey was made of the region and a census taken of its population. The survey took into account all geographical features, village sites, arable land, water supply, etc., and was recorded in clay relief models; the census noted the inhabitants by the age-grade Inca system; these were registered on *quipus*. Such data as the number of llamas were doubtless included. All these records were then forwarded to Cuzco where they were studied carefully by the emperor and his advisers who then drew up a programme. A provincial capital was chosen and official buildings erected there, and the people were moved from their protected towns and hill-top fortresses and made to settle on or near their arable fields.

Cieza de León[1] gives a vivid description of Inca resettlement practices, of which he rather approved:

Having established a governor, with garrisons of soldiers, the army then advanced, and if the new province were large, it was presently ordered that a temple of the Sun should be built, and women collected for its service, and that a palace should be erected for the lord. Tribute was collected, care being taken that too much was not exacted, and that no injustice was done in any-thing; but that the new subjects were made acquainted with the imperial policy, and with the art of building, of clothing them-selves, and of living together in towns. And if they needed any-thing, care was taken to supply it, and to teach them how to sow and cultivate their lands. So thoroughly was this policy carried into effect, that we know of many places where there were no flocks originally, but where there has been abundance since they were subjugated by the Incas; and others where formerly there was no maize, but where now they have large crops. In many provinces they went about like savages, badly clothed, and bare-footed, until they came under the sway of the Incas; and from

1. Cieza de León, Part II, chapter 17; pp. 49–50 of Markham's translation (1883).

that time they have worn shirts and mantles, both men and women, so that they always hold the change in their memories.

The Inca programme of resettlement and colonization was an element of the greatest importance not only for the peace of the empire, but for administrative problems in colonial days, for modern Peru, and for studies on the anthropology of Peru. For the shuffling of populations was carried to such an extent that the empire became a great melting-pot and was rapidly on its way to becoming, as was the intent of the policy, a unified homogeneous nation. Although the system had been in effect for less than a century before the time of the Conquest, by that time many of the tribes in Andean and coastal Peru had lost their identity, their language,[1] and many of their peculiar customs. The Inca language was made the official speech everywhere and quickly supplanted the native languages. This general medium of communication was a great boon to the Spanish, who quickly adopted it as a second official language, and its use has continued to spread ever since.

The extent of the resettlement programme naturally depended on the bellicosity and intransigence of the population. In some provinces the major part of the inhabitants were deported and replaced by colonists. The new settlers were brought from provinces that had been under Inca domination long enough to have lost their desire for independence and to have become rather thoroughly indoctrinated with Inca ideology and familiar with the imperial pattern of government. They were always taken from regions with similar climatic and ecological conditions. Native-born Quechuas from the Cuzco region were, of course the most desirable colonists. The new colonists were naturally scattered in villages among the newly conquered natives, and the recalcitrant elements of the latter took their places, sprinkled among the pacified population of the earlier conquered region.

These colonists were termed *mitimaes*. While under the same provincial authority as the natives, they formed favoured groups, receiving special gifts and privileges. They formed Inca garrisons whose responsibility it was to set an example to the benighted, to

1. See Mason, 1950.

convert the heathen to the true faith, and to teach the superior Quechua language to the barbarians!

Garcilaso[1] gives a good description of the Inca *mitima* practice and attitude towards it – or at least his interpretation thereof:

The Incas transplanted Indians from one province to another for special reasons, some for the good of their vassals, and others for their own purposes and to secure their dominions from insurrections. In the course of their conquests the Incas found some provinces to be naturally fertile, but thinly populated. To these districts they sent Indians who were natives of other provinces with a similar climate. This precaution was taken that no injury might befall the settlers. On other occasions, when the inhabitants of a locality multiplied rapidly, so that their province was not large enough to hold them, they removed a certain proportion of the people to some other district. They also removed Indians from barren and sterile tracts to such as were fertile and prolific, with a view to the benefit both of those that remained and of those that went; because, being relations, they would help each other with their harvests.

As has been stated or intimated in some previous pages, Inca policy was to leave administrative matters *in statu quo ante* as much as possible, and to adapt the new régime to fit pre-existing conditions. All amenable chiefs were confirmed in their positions, made curacas and considered as nobility, their sons taken to Cuzco to serve as hostages and to be indoctrinated in Inca ideology, eventually to succeed to their fathers' positions. However, the Governor was always an Inca noble. The Inca tripartite system of land division and labour service was introduced, storehouses built, Quechua established as the official language and Sun-worship as the official religion, though no coercion was practised on the native population to compel them to abandon their old language and religion. If the people were in distress as a result of the late war, food and other supplies were brought from government storehouses in neighbouring pacified regions.

The principal portable idols or wacas of the conquered people

1. Garcilaso de la Vega, Part I, Book 7, chapter I; Volume 2, pp. 213 215 of Markham's translation (1869–71).

were also taken to Cuzco to be held as hostages, where they might be worshipped by visiting delegations; the sacred objects were generally accompanied to Cuzco by some of their native priests. This practice gave the native peoples a feeling of community with Cuzco as their capital instead of merely that of foreign invaders. For some reason, however, Inca costume was enforced on the conquered people, though they were allowed to retain their former head-dress, or required to adopt some other distinctive one, as an identifying symbol.

Rather similar in their melting-pot result, but in a slightly different category from the mitimaes, were some colonies of Aymara on the coast and on the warm slopes of the eastern mountains. The Aymara inhabited – and inhabit – the highest, chilliest, and most inhospitable parts of the plateau, and to permit them access to tropical or semi-tropical fruits and other desired products – as well as, probably, to enjoy occasional warmth – the Inca permitted them to establish colonies in these places. These were homogeneous enclaves, under the authority of their highland home officials. We may suspect that these Aymara were not true permanent colonists but vacationers, frequently changing residence between highland and lowland.

Law and Crime

In referring to Inca law – or, for that matter, to all Peruvian and to all pre-Colombian American law – it must be remembered that it was exclusively 'common' law, uncodified, *lex non scripta*; in the absence of any system of writing it could not have been otherwise. Since there was no private ownership of real estate, little personal property, and no private business, law was practically limited to crime and punishment. The authorities remembered the custom and precedent for punishments, and the common people also knew the sanctions. Though it can hardly be said that the emperor's wish was law, at least the laws represented his will, and their transgression was construed as disobedience to him rather than as an offence against the state or against any individual. Therefore some acts that would be considered by us as misdemeanours or even as merely sins were severely punished.

Treason and disobedience to the emperor were considered the greatest crimes.

All offences against the state, treason, theft from imperial or church fields or storehouses, burning bridges, breaking into convents, and similar crimes were punishable with death, as was murder. Capital punishment, however, could be decreed only by the highest authorities, a governor or the emperor himself, and a curaca who put any subject to death without higher official sanction was severely punished himself, even receiving the death penalty for a second offence. Capital punishment was inflicted by several methods: generally the culprit's head was bashed in with a club, but he might be thrown off a cliff, stoned to death, or hung up by the feet. Probably the choice was so that the punishment might more or less fit the crime. Imprisonment was unknown except for one delicate variety reserved for the most egregious traitor; he was placed in an underground dungeon filled with snakes and other venomous, noxious, and dangerous animals. His incarceration was necessarily a brief one. Lesser punishments were public rebuke, removal from office, banishment, torture, flogging, and the *hihuaya*, which consisted in dropping a heavy stone from a height of about three feet (1 m.) on the malefactor's back; this was often equivalent to a capital sentence.

Following their usual pattern, the Inca made openly the distinction between noble and commoner that is often made in practice in modern days. It was felt that a reprimand and loss of his emperor's approbation were worse punishment for a noble than physical castigation to a peasant. In this they probably were good judges of human nature, and anyway it was necessary to uphold the prestige of the aristocracy. On the other hand, transgressions of *noblesse oblige* were more severely punished than a similar sin by a commoner; thus, adultery with a noblewoman was a capital offence for both; the common or garden variety was punished by torture.

Extenuating circumstances were always allowed for. Killing in self-defence or slitting the throat of a wife caught *in flagrante delicto* was not murder. Intentional injuries were more severely punished than accidental ones. A lazy or improvident man might be rebuked for theft; a covetous one would be banished.

Accused persons were held under guard until their trials, which were, of course, not before a jury of their peers, but before state officials, the regular administrative officers, such as the curacas. Minor offences were judged by minor officials, important ones by higher officers; these heard testimony and the defence of the accused, called witnesses, and pronounced judgement from which there was no appeal to higher authorities. There were no lawyers, solicitors, or advocates, no fees to be paid. The only peculiarly judicial officers were the full-time governmental inspectors who regularly investigated the affairs of state officials and pressed charges against dishonest ones. On the whole, crime was rare; the static nature of the society did not provoke it, and the rigid enforcement of the laws tended to prevent it.

The government inspectors were usually of imperial blood and were considered the direct and personal representatives of the emperor, taking upon themselves one of his functions. Periodically – probably at irregular and unannounced occasions – and incognito they visited every corner of the empire.

The greatest crimes, such as treason, and all crimes committed by the royalty, were judged by the emperor in person, generally with the advice of his privy council. The penalties were severe, but the purpose was the prevention of crime rather than its punishment. A father was held equally responsible for the crime of a minor child. If a robber could prove that want drove him to the crime, the official who permitted such an abnormal and illegal situation to come to pass was also severely punished.

The guilt of an individual was often determined by divination or ordeal, such as torture. Judgement was given within a few days, five at the most. Fines, of course, were unknown. The entire village or ayllu of a great criminal was held guilty with him, and in the most heinous crimes the village was destroyed and the entire population put to death.

Chapter 13

RELIGION

PROBABLY the ancient religions of all parts of Andean Peru conformed to one general pattern but differed greatly in details and in the names of the deities. The following digest, like those of our other sections on the life of old Peru, refers particularly to the Inca or Quechua of the Cuzco district, the only region on which the data are extensive.

In empire times the religion was state-established and supported; this seems to have been the only instance in aboriginal America of an established church. But in essence it was doubtless the age-old beliefs of the Cuzco-region Quechua. There was a principal god, other gods and goddesses of greater or lesser importance, local animistic spirits or objects, and unembodied and disembodied spirits. In its later years under the empire the religion had evolved an organization in which rich ritual and ceremonialism were important. Its chief purposes were the increase or maintenance of the food-supply and the cure of the sick; spirituality, mysticism, and non-pragmatic ethics had little place in it. However, concepts of sin, confession, penance, and purification were important. Divination was one of the principal duties of the priesthood, and sacrifice to the gods was a vital element of almost every rite.

The supreme deity was the Creator. He is generally known as Viracocha, but this name was merely one of his many titles. He is said to have had no true name, but, like the great god of some other peoples, his name may have been too sacred to be spoken, and thus was unknown to the chroniclers. His form was that of man, and he was thus represented in images in temples. He was eternal and created everything, including the other deities; he was the supernatural analogue of the Inca emperor. Garcilaso was probably in error when he identified Viracocha with Pachacamac, a deity of the inhabitants of the central coast where he had a shrine, famous over all Peru, dedicated to him. Viracocha was also a culture hero who taught his people how to live. After the creation he interfered little in human destinies, remaining a benign divinity in the heavens. He was therefore little worshipped, at least by the common people; the emperor and the nobles appealed to him more frequently – in time of trouble.

The Creator god was apparently a very old and fundamental deity in Peru; Means believes that he was the god worshipped at Tiahuanaco, possibly under some other non-Quechua name. Viracocha in many respects resembles the Mexican god Quetzalcoatl who was also a culture hero. According to Inca mythology, after travelling through the country instructing his people, Viracocha set off across the Pacific from the shores of Ecuador, walking on the waves. Pizarro and his men were therefore identified with the returning god, just as was Cortés in Mexico, and the white men were – and in some places are to this day – called Viracocha. In these days, when anthropologists are giving more credence than formerly to the probability of pre-Columbian trans-Pacific influences and voyages, these old American traditions of culture heroes might well be accorded new appraisals. In later years the term Viracocha seems to have been equivalent to 'Lord'; the semantic analogy with both uses of the English term is obvious.

The worship of Viracocha was apparently mainly, if not exclusively, a function of the upper classes, a philosophical rather than an animistic religion. Emperor Viracocha ascribed the defeat of the Chanca and the preservation of the Inca hegemony to his namesake god, and reanimated and encouraged his worship. He built two temples to Viracocha, the only two in Peru, one in Cuzco and another at Cacha. The latter (Plate 16A), judging by the ruins that survive, was one of the great triumphs of Peruvian architecture. The median wall, still standing in good condition, was over three hundred feet (90 m.) long and over fifty feet (15 m.) high. The lower eight feet are of excellent masonry, supporting over forty feet of adobe wall. The walls are five to six feet thick, and the building consisted of three storeys.

More important in mundane affairs than Viracocha were the sky deities – the gods and goddesses of the sun, moon, stars, and thunder, and the terraqueous goddesses, those of the earth and the sea; these were all servants of the Creator. The cult of the Earth Mother was probably the oldest, most fundamental, and most popular of all; she was the one most supplicated by the common farmer.

The Inca were sun-worshippers; the Sun, Inti, was the great deity and the progenitor of the royal dynasty. Although the priests and the Chosen Women served all the gods, the Sun was so pre-eminent that the chroniclers always referred to the women as the 'Virgins of the Sun', and to the shrines as 'Sun Temples'. The sun and the rain, together controlling the crops, tend to be the primary interest of almost every agricultural people. Though apparently generally conceived of as a man, the Sun was generally represented – as often today – by a round human face with surrounding rays. Naturally, the disk was almost always of gold, and the one in the Coricancha, the great 'Temple of the Sun' in Cuzco, was immense. One of the best-remembered tales of the Spanish Conquest is that of the Spanish soldier Sierra de Leguízano who, having received the great disk as his share of the booty, gambled it away that very night; popular tradition has it that this was the origin of the Spanish saying 'jugar el sol antes que amanezca', 'to gamble away the sun before it rises'. Sad to say, iconoclastic historical research indicates that the sun disk had then been removed, and Sierra de Leguízano's gold piece, though a great prize, was a more utilitarian object. Doubtless also Hispanic folklorists have found another origin for the proverb.

Naturally the Thunder or Weather God was the divinity of next importance; he was importuned to send the rain. The name, Illapa, connotes both thunder and lightning. He was envisaged as a man dressed in shining apparel and carrying a sling and a war club. According to one myth, his sister kept the rain in a jug which Illapa broke with his sling-shot when he yielded to earthlings' pleas for rain. As he threw, the crack of the sling was the thunderclap, the stone the thunderbolt, and the lightning was the refulgence of his glistening garments. The rain water came from the heavenly river, the Milky Way. Illapa was identified with a constellation.

The Moon, Mamaquilla, was a goddess and wife of the Sun. She was little worshipped but her functions were chiefly with reference to the calendar and the festivals and work connected therewith. The beliefs regarding eclipses of the moon paralleled others current in many places throughout the world: a serpent or puma was trying to eat the Moon Goddess, and was scared away by threats and din.

Inca star lore was extensive and, although there seems to have been no true zodiac, many of the stars and constellations were given names and apparently were considered as deities that watched over terrestrial beings and certain activities. The Morning Star, Venus, was an important figure in mythology. The Pleiades took care of seeds, and another constellation the herds; the latter was seen as a speckled llama. Other kinds of wild animals each had its star protector.

The Earth and the Sea Goddesses, Pacamama and Mamacocha, were of importance in the highlands and on the coast respectively. Their functions dealt with agriculture and fishing.

The word 'waca' (*huaca, guaca*) was and is of great importance in Peru. It originally meant 'sacred shrine' and is so used by the Indians today. Among the Spanish and the mestizos, however, it applies to one of the great coastal pyramids of adobe, or to any archaeological Indian grave, and the native scoundrel who makes a business of excavating aboriginal graves and selling their contents – the main source of most Peruvian collections in museums – is today known as a *huaquero*; the masculine form *huaco* is now applied to a pottery vessel from such a grave.

In ancient as in modern Peru there were thousands of wacas, ranging from great temples to hills, springs, and piles of stones. Each was believed to be – or to harbour – a spirit which might be malevolent and which should be gratified or placated by some gift or sacrifice whenever it was neared. Each native knew only those in his vicinity. One of the chroniclers lists three hundred and fifty within twenty miles of Cuzco. Springs and stones were the most numerous wacas, but hills, caves, roots, quarries, forts, bridges, palaces, prisons, houses, meeting-places, battlefields, stone field boundary-markers and field guardians, calendar markers, and other similar objects are included in the category, as well as temples, tombs, and historical or mythological sites.

Mountains and hills were especially likely to be considered

sacred and, generally speaking, the higher they were, the more important; all snow-capped peaks were reverenced or worshipped, and several hills around Cuzco were especially sacred, were supposed to represent deceased emperors or other persons, and played important parts in certain ceremonies.

Especially sacred was a stone on Huanacauri hill near Cuzco which was supposed to represent one of the brothers of the great Emperor Manco Capac, and which therefore was a protector of the dynasty. The city of Cuzco itself was probably considered a waca.

The wacas of the Cuzco region were thought of as lying on lines radiating from the Temple of the Sun. Three of the quarters each had nine such radiating lines; the fourth, Contisuyu, had fifteen. In the first three, the nine lines were arranged in three groups of three each, and there were from four to fifteen wacas on each line. Naturally, the lines were not perfectly straight.

Only two ceremonial directions, east and west, were recognized by the Inca; these were of course important because of the rising and setting of the sun. The wacas in the neighbourhood of Cuzco were classed according to their location in one of the four quarters into which the region was divided. These in turn corresponded to the four quarters of the empire, the two north quarters being considered as Upper Cuzco, the southern pair as Lower Cuzco. They were under the care of the royal ayllus living in those quarters.

Another type of waca called *apachita* was a sort of cairn at a dangerous or important place on a road where the traveller paused to pray for safety and strength; here he would add a stone to the pile or leave something of trivial value, such as a piece of worn-out clothing, a quid of coca, or even a handful of straw. This custom is still practised.

Almost anything strange or unusual was considered sacred and a waca: twins, persons with supernumerary digits, plants of peculiar forms. Corpses, of course. Then there were portable wacas, amulets and talismans; these might be pseudomorphs – natural stones in the shape of some object, crystals, bezoars, or any article that seemed queer.

Household fetishes, the Andean analogues of the Roman

Lares and Penates, were the guardians of the family; they were kept in niches and were inherited. Every person also had an individual fetish, the abode of his guardian spirit who was considered his twin brother or *huauqui*. Bezoars were common household fetishes; those most prized came from the vicuña, deer, guanaco, and llama, in this order.

This animistic belief in spirits of inanimate objects is widespread and wellnigh universal among primitive peoples and must have been very ancient, far pre-empire, and fundamental in the Andean area.

There were both unembodied and disembodied spirits in addition to the stationary spirits of the wacas. The minor spirits were malevolent and greatly feared. As is the situation with many societies of more logical persons, there seems to have been a confusion of belief regarding the disembodied spirits, the dead, without any realization of incompatibility. The spirits of the dead went to 'heaven' or 'hell', but nevertheless they – or some of them – might also hang around their old homes to annoy – though with a helpful purpose – the living. The dead liked to have their 'mummies' brought out to enjoy fiestas, and they expected to be given food and chicha beer now and then. The cult of the dead was very important.

'Heaven' was with the Sun, where the good enjoyed life much as on earth with a plethora of food and drink, while evil-doers went to a subterranean hell where it was always cold and there were only stones to eat. The nobility, however, were *ipso facto* guiltless; all went direct to heaven.

Properly speaking, there were no churches in ancient Peru, for almost all ceremonies were performed out of doors, and only the priests and high officials entered the temples. The great national ceremonies were enacted in one of the squares in Cuzco, to which the sacred objects were brought from the temples. The most important of these plazas was, of course, the Great Square adjacent to the imposing Temple of the Sun. This, the most sacred shrine in Peru, was a magnificent building, or group of buildings around a courtyard, and was lavishly furnished. Known as the Coricancha (Plate 13), parts of it are still preserved but so much altered by rebuilding in the upper parts that its former shape and nature are difficult to visualize. According to accounts of the time of the Conquest it consisted mainly of one great room. The roof was gabled and covered with thatch. There was only one exterior doorway. However, it served mainly as a repository for sacred objects, an altar, idols of the principal deities, and the bodies of deceased emperors. Many great religious objects of solid gold hung on the walls. Adjacent to this great room were smaller 'chapels' and shrines, and even some small independent buildings for priestly residences. The circumference of the ensemble was about twelve hundred feet.

Similar smaller Sun temples were located in all the main centres of population, especially in the provincial capitals. The more important shrines or wacas also had houses or 'temples' for the attendant priests.

The priesthood was graded into ranks very much like the secular population. At the apex was the High Priest or Pontifex Maximus, the *Villac Umu*, resident in Cuzco. He was always a brother, uncle, or other close relative of the emperor, and one of the officials of highest rank in the state. He held office for life, and presided over a council of nine other priests of high rank, each in charge of a large area. He led an exemplary life, hedged about by restrictions and taboos.

The other priests of higher rank were also of royal blood, all from the Tarpuntary ayllu, and were elected by a council of other priests, apparently for a definite term of office. The clergy of the lowest ranks were commoners and not state-supported. These lowest offices were hereditary; many of them, presumably, were local patriarchs, too old for active agricultural labour, who tended a waca.

The larger temples sheltered a considerable body of clergy, diviners, sacrificers, and servants, in addition to 'Chosen Women', and 'monks', while smaller shrines might have had only one attendant, and probably the smallest outdoor wacas had none. The principal priest at the large provincial Sun temples belonged to the imperial caste. Like the secular government, a corps of church inspectors visited the religious institutions frequently, and reported instances of malfeasance to the higher authorities.

The duties of the priests, in addition to caring for the sacred paraphernalia and participating in the regular ceremonies, were to hear confessions, make divinations, interpret oracles, make sacrifices, pray for suppliants, and cure the ill. In major temples, where there was a large group of priests, probably all specialized in one or another of these functions.

Connected with each Sun temple was a building that housed the female associates. These were not inappropriately considered by the Spanish as nuns, their quarters as a convent; it had many of the functions of one. The nature of these women and their method of selection have been mentioned before (page 185). They were of two main classes, the 'Chosen Women', *acllacuna*, and the so-called 'Virgins of the Sun', *mamacuna*. The latter formed a permanent staff and had taken vows of perpetual chastity; the 'Chosen Women' were more or less transient and were eligible to be given as secondary wives to nobles at the emperor's pleasure – or taken for himself.

No man was supposed to enter a convent, though some of the chroniclers speak of eunuchs who acted as servants and door-keepers, and also as confessors to the Virgins; this is not unlikely. These men were called monks by the chroniclers, but it is not clear whether all 'monks' were eunuchs and vice versa, or whether some non-eunuch monks had other duties.

The chroniclers differ greatly in their explanations of the roles of these women, and some certainly confused the two classes, but the true situation was probably that given above. Naturally some historians state that the Virgins of the Sun were no more than the emperor's private seraglio, and many recent writers have assumed the same. The emperor, however deified by his people, was human – and above the law. Father Cobo[1] says that, every now and then, the 'monk' (eunuch?) in charge of the convent gate would approach the emperor in the great square where he might be making a sacrifice to the Sun, would gently tug at the imperial mantle and whisper in his ear, 'Inca, on such and such a night you stole into the Sun's mansion and lay with one of his wives'. Whereat the emperor, also *sotto voce*, would answer, 'I sinned', and the guard would know that he was thereby

1. Cobo, 1890–5, Book 13, chapter 37.

absolved from neglect of duty. Any transgressor of lower rank, however, was paid the proverbial wages of sin; he was strangled and his paramour buried alive.

In the convents the women cared for the necessities of the priests, prepared their food, and wove their garments. Those in the great convent connected with the Sun Temple in Cuzco wove the imperial garments, probably the finest cloths made in Peru, which is to say about the finest in the world; it is reported that some of these textiles required a year of work to manufacture. One of the chroniclers states that the inmates of the great convent attached to the Cuzco Coricancha numbered three thousand.

As among ourselves, Inca prayers were of two kinds: personal and private, or congregational and ritualistic. The private prayers were naturally appeals for personal welfare such as health or good crops, and might be addressed to a spring, for instance, while the congregational prayers were traditional, fixed, and on a rather high aesthetic plane. Several of these prayers were preserved and recorded by some of the chroniclers. One of the most famous of these is:[1]

Viracocha, Lord of the Universe!
Whether male or female,
at any rate commander of heat and reproduction,
being one who, even with His spittle, can work sorcery.
Where art Thou?
Would that Thou wert not hidden from this son of Thine!
He may be above; He may be below;
or, perchance, abroad in space.
Where is His mighty judgement-seat?
Hear me!
He may be spread abroad among the upper waters;
or among the lower waters and their sands
He may be dwelling.
Creator of the world, Creator of man,
great among my ancestors,
before Thee my eyes fail me,
though I long to see Thee;
for, seeing Thee, knowing Thee,
learning from Thee, understanding Thee,

1. Means, 1931, p. 437, 438.

I shall be seen by Thee, and Thou wilt know me.
The Sun – the Moon; the Day – the Night; Summer – Winter;
not in vain, in orderly succession,
do they march to their destined place, to their goal.
They arrive wherever Thy royal staff Thou bearest.
Oh! Harken to me, listen to me,
let it not befall that I grow weary
and die.

Some prayers were recited, others given silently; a suppliant might ask his relatives and friends to pray for him, or might pay a priest to do so.

Fasting was an accompaniment of many religious observances. As among ourselves, it might be slight or strict, ranging from abstinence from salt and pepper to the prohibition of meat, chicha beer, and sex relations.

Confession of sin also played a prominent role in Inca religion, since sin made the gods angry and impelled them to punish the sinner by bad luck in this life and condemnation to the under-world in the next. It must be remembered that concepts and de-finitions of sin differ greatly according to the morals of various peoples, and Inca morals by no means paralleled ours. Offences against neighbours, such as murder and theft, were naturally condemned, but disobedience to the emperor's wishes and ne-glect of festivals and worship were also sinful. All misfortune, even such as congenital natal malformation, was deemed to be a punishment for sin. The sinner was disqualified from taking part in religious observances until he had confessed and purged him-self. It was not necessary to confess sinful thoughts, however. An illness of the divine emperor presented quite a philosophical and theological problem; he was sickened by the sins of his sub-jects who cured him by their confessions and purification.

Confessions were made to the priests, generally the minor priests of either sex, in charge of local wacas. The confessor heard all the members of his ayllu; the confession was generally heard by the side of a stream. More serious sins had to be taken to priests of higher rank; the confessions were in secret, and were not to be divulged. The emperor, the royal family, and the High

Priest confessed in secret to the Sun, whose intercession they asked with Viracocha, the Creator.

Incomplete confession of sin was considered a great sin in itself, and the priest-confessor took measures, including interrogation, physical coercion, and divination, to make sure that the confession was full. When thus assured, he fixed a penance, usually a period of fasting and praying, or both. Often, it is said, the expiation was in opposite ratio to the priest's fee. After such penance, the sinner washed in a stream so that the sin might be borne away. Or he might spit into a handful of straw and throw that into the river.

The Spanish clergy of colonial days were naturally astounded at the many close analogies to their religion, which resemblance they ascribed to the machinations of the Great Deceiver, Satan.

As with most religions, sacrifice was also a most important feature among the Inca, the concept undoubtedly being that of *quid pro quo*, a gift to the god or gods in return for favours bestowed or solicited. Sacrifices had a great range, from a handful of straw left at a wayside *apachita* to human sacrifices by the High Priest in a great public ceremony in Cuzco.

Food and drink, the latter in the form of chicha beer, were regular offerings to the wacas, and to preserved bodies, especially those of the emperors. The food was burned, the chicha libation poured on the ground. Coca was, of course, a frequent offering; this was burned, either as dried leaves or as quid after chewing. Other frequent sacrificial materials were corn flour, wool, and llama fat. Sea-shells were offered to springs, generally after sowing time. If a worshipper had nothing else, he offered a few eyelashes or eyebrow hairs. Wealthier men sacrificed fine clothing, which was burned, and little gold or silver figurines, or even lumps of these metals; these were buried or hung in the temples.

However, domestic animals, llamas and guinea-pigs, were the most common sacrifices; wild animals were not ordinarily used. Llamas, being valuable animals, were rarely sacrificed by individuals – and then only by wealthy ones, but were generally from the governmental herds, offered in public ceremonies to the image of one of the deities. The priest led the llama around the figure and made it face it, recited the proper prayer, and cut the animal's throat. White llamas and alpacas were sacrificed to the Sun, brown llamas to Viracocha, and mottled ones to Thunder.

Human sacrifice was rare in Peru, at least in Inca days, in contrast to the hecatombs that Cortés encountered in Mexico. To the gods it was the most precious and most welcome offering, given on only the most sacred or most ominous occasions, such as the installation of an emperor, his illness or departure for war, or military defeat, famine, or plague. Human beings were offered to only the most important deities or shrines by priests at great communal ceremonies.

Boys and girls about ten years old were the principals – the word 'victim' is not quite appropriate – in these sacrifices. The girls were selected from the 'Chosen Women' being educated in the 'convents' (page 213); some at least of the boys were offered by their parents who were in great need. The children had to be physically perfect, and fine examples of youth. They were feasted and sometimes made drunk before the sacrifice so that they might appear before the deity contented and happy. Less often, adults were immolated. These were from a newly conquered province, brought to Cuzco to be sacrificed to the Sun in celebration of the victory. Like the children, they were outstanding physical examples.

After marching several times around the image or waca, the victims were strangled and their throats slit or, as in Mexico, the heart cut out. The priest then marked or smeared the venerated object with some of the blood, and sometimes a libation of blood was poured on the ground.

Sometimes, when a very ill man had been told by a diviner that he would certainly die, he would sacrifice one of his sons to the Sun, or to Viracocha, in the hope that thus his own life would be spared.

Most of the sacrifices were made to wacas, and at set ceremonial occasions in connexion with the seasonal calendar. For these the sacrificed objects – mainly llamas – were taken from the flocks and fields devoted to religion, some of which were allocated to every waca and from which also the attendant priests derived their support. Part of the sacrifice of an individual was also devoted to the upkeep of the personnel of the waca.

State sacrifices to Viracocha were made in the name of the wacas of the country rather than in that of the emperor.

Cuzco was of course the great centre for sacrifices as for all Inca religious ceremonies. Every morning, as it rose, the Sun was greeted with a sacrifice of some food that had been specially prepared, the rest of which served for the priests' breakfast. A fire of specially carved wood had been laid; this was kindled at sunrise and the food thrown in, while a priest recited, 'Eat this, Lord Sun, and acknowledge thy children'. Later in the day a dark-red llama was sacrificed to the Sun, together with some coca. The fragrant carved wood for the fire was supplied by the Chicha people. Another fire of this same material was kept constantly burning in a stone brazier near the Temple of the Sun, and from this all sacrificial fires had to be kindled.

On the first day of each month a preparatory ceremony was held in the presence of the emperor and his court assembled in the Great Square. One hundred selected llamas were brought in and divided among some thirty attendants, three or four to each. Every attendant had one day of the month allotted to him, and on this day he brought his animals and sacrificed them. Before the division, all the llamas had been ceremonially made to circle the images of the gods four times and had been dedicated by the High Priest to Viracocha in the name of the Sun. These animals were cut into quarters and completely burned in a large fire made of the same carved scented wood, into which coca, white corn, and ground chilli peppers were also thrown. The bones that remained were ground to a fine powder, and the priests blew a little of this into the air while they recited a short ritual. The remaining powder was stored in a neighbouring building called the 'Puma's tail'.

Calendrical Ceremonies

The major Inca public religious ceremonies were performed in the Great Square in Cuzco, and the majority of these were recurrent annual church holidays (holy-days). Most of them also were associated with agricultural events, such as with planting-time and harvest. The cult objects, such as images of the gods and bodies of deceased emperors, were brought out and venerated by the assembled populace. The current emperor and his court always attended. The ceremonies, accompanied by sacrifices, dancing, singing, recitations, and the consumption of quantities of chicha beer, were elaborate and impressive. The effect must have been, in general, very similar to a church fiesta in Peru or other parts of Latin America today, and the transition from pagan to Christian must have been effected with little change in attitude on the part of the people.

In each month at least one important annual ceremony was held, generally associated with the current agricultural activity. The chroniclers of the time of the Conquest recorded these in considerable detail. In describing these monthly ceremonies the Spanish chroniclers correlate the Inca lunar months with ours, giving one of our names to each. Such correlation is only approximate and applicable for only a short time (see pages 228–9); nevertheless it must be adopted for descriptive purposes.

December was a most important month, for then the puberty ceremonies for boys of noble rank were held; these filled not only the entire month but a part of the next one. Athletic tests and competitions took place, as well as a sham battle. Many of the other monthly ceremonies occupied many days.

Sacrifices of llamas by various methods and with details appropriate to the occasion were an important part of almost every ceremony, and on rare occasions children were sacrificed. A sacred white – probably albino – llama, which was carefully tended until he died a natural death, played an important role in some rites. Fasting and feasting, the drinking of quantities of chicha beer, and community dancing accompanied most of the more joyful ceremonies, and offerings and auguries played a large part in many. Some were followed by ceremonial baths to cleanse the partakers from evil and illness. The ceremony for the month of June was second only to that of December and was centred about the adoration of the Sun. An important feature of the solemn occasion was the making of new fire – also a vital element of Aztec ceremonialism.

Divination and Omens

Unlike the Mexicans, the Inca apparently did not recognize good and bad, lucky and unlucky days, or at any rate these were not of such transcendent importance. Their priests, instead of determining these days, made divinations to predict the future – as of course did the Mesoamericans, also – and the success or misfortune of any project. The results of these divinations and consultations of oracles were, of course, supposed to represent the will of the gods, whose wishes should be consulted before any undertaking. Divination was practised to determine any doubtful question, future or past; also unsolicited omens were constantly looked for.

For the most serious problems, such as identifying traitors, the solemn divination by fire was practised. The emperor himself often partook in this, after a fast of several days, and it was generally accompanied by the sacrifice of most valuable objects, sometimes including children. By means of this fire, communication with spirits was established. The chief practitioners, known as *yacarca*, who came from the town of Huaro near Cuzco, were most respected and feared.

This method of fire divination required considerable preparation. Fire was built in two braziers placed end to end, wood soaked in fat being used. Food and drink in dishes were placed around the fire, which was intensified by blowing through a tube with copper and silver ends. The Chief Priest, taking a quid of coca in his mouth, begged the spirits to come to the banquet in the presence of Fire, Sun, and Earth. Either the spirits of living or dead persons might be thus invoked with chanting and weeping. The flames from the holes in the braziers were considered the voices of the spirits, and the diviners heard and interpreted them, answering questions put to them. Sometimes a different spirit appeared in each brazier.

Divination by means of a llama's viscera was a more common practice and has been mentioned before. With its head held to the east by four priests, another cut open the left side and extracted the heart, lungs, and gullet, entire, connected and uncut.

If the lungs were still breathing when they were drawn out it was considered a most propitious omen. If this and other signs failed, a second and even a third trial was given, and if all proved calamitous there was great foreboding of ill luck. Another method was to inflate the lungs by blowing and to interpret the augury by the vein pattern. Important yes-or-no questions were thus decided; for ones of less importance a guinea-pig or even a bird might be used.

There were also many simpler and more easily practised methods of divination. One, like our 'she loves me . . not' daisy-petal method, involved the counting of objects for odd or even total. Pebbles, beans, corn kernels, and pellets of llama dung were among the most usual materials employed; the pebbles were generally wacas to which a magical origin had been ascribed. Llama fat and coca leaves were burned and the fire watched. Or the diviner spat into his hand and watched the spittle run down his two fingers; if the flow was equal, the augury was good, otherwise it was bad.

The movements of confined animals, particularly snakes and spiders, were watched as an augury; spider divination was especially practised in the Chinchasuyu quarter of central and northern Peru. The spider was kept in a jar, and if, on first observation, any of its legs was bent, the prognosis was bad.

While almost every waca would serve as an oracle to be consulted by divinatory practices, there were several oracles that were peculiarly such, and that were consulted on important questions by many pilgrims from all over the empire. Two of them gave their names to the rivers on which they were situated: Apo-rimac on the Apurimac River near Cuzco, and Rimac (meaning 'oracle') on the Rimac River near Lima. Probably most important, however, was the great shrine of Pachacamac, on the coast south of Lima; Huari in the Jauja Valley was another. The Apurimac oracle was a tree-trunk in a house; it was dressed in female apparel, with breasts of gold and a sash. A row of smaller figures was placed to either side. This oracle was in the charge of a priestess who may have hidden in or behind the trunk, for a Spanish prisoner heard it reply to a question put to it by Manco

Inca in 1534. The oracles seen by the Spanish were generally thickly smeared with sacrificial blood.

The soothsayers were supposed to talk directly with the spirits; they wore special garb and hair-dress, and spoke with the spirits in the dark in words that could be heard but not understood. Some of them drank chicha beer mixed with the juice of an intoxicating berry, and gave their answers after they had recovered. Diviners found missing articles, predicted future or described distant events, diagnosed diseases, determined the truth of statements, and settled all dubious questions.

Unsolicited omens were numerous and constantly watched for. A rainbow was generally an evil omen, and comets, eclipses, and meteors were especially bad, the latter foretelling the death of the emperor. The word for comet meant 'ill-luck star'; Atahuallpa gave up hope immediately when one appeared during his imprisonment by Pizarro. The sight of noxious animals, such as snakes, spiders, lizards, toads, worms, moths, or foxes, especially in the house, was a bad omen. The howling of a dog or the hooting of an owl presaged the death of a relative, and the singing of other birds foretold a quarrel. The ill luck occasioned by encountering a snake could be avoided by killing and urinating on it, and stepping on it with the left foot. Birds were made offerings of coca and told to take their ill luck to the man's enemies. Somewhat like our 'burning ears', a twitching in any part of the body, a humming sound in the ears, or a stumbling indicated that one was about to hear some news, good if the manifestation was on the person's right side, bad if on the left. If the fire flared or gave off sparks it was angry and had to be appeased by an offering of a little chicha or maize corn.

Dreams, as usual, had their standard interpretations; they were regarded as supernatural experiences and very important omens. Deities and spirits sometimes appeared to important persons in dreams. To dream of fire predicted illness; the sun, moon, a river, or a bridge foretold the death of a parent, and killing a llama meant the death of a father or brother.

When praying or otherwise addressing a deity or the emperor, a standard attitude or gesture of reverence was observed. With arms outstretched to the front, the suppliant bowed low from the hips; the arms were parallel and high, the hands open with palms outward. He next made a kissing sound and then kissed his finger-tips. A switch was held in the hands when addressing the highest deities.

Slight value was attached to ceremonial or sacred numbers. Three and four seem to have had some value, and quipus found on the coast appear to stress the importance of the number seven.

A little chicha beer was always sprinkled towards the sun, and also to the ground and to the fire, whenever natives were indulging in that drink.

Travellers always took a drink of the water when passing a spring or crossing a stream, meanwhile breathing a prayer for a safe passage.

Disease and Healing: Sorcery

Among many if not most pre-scientific peoples, as has been remarked before, no misfortune, accident, or illness just happens; it is always a result. Illness, disease, and death in particular are always caused by the ill-will of someone, by sorcery or otherwise; someone wanted it to happen. The ancient Peruvians had progressed somewhat beyond this stage, and the magic of hired sorcerers was only one of the causes of illness. A more important and more frequent cause was the supernatural ill-will of deities angered by sin or by neglect of worship, or accidental contact with inherently malevolent spirits found especially in winds and springs. Illness might also be caused by winds, and by loss of soul which could be frightened out of the body. The Inca still retained the belief, wellnigh universal in aboriginal America, that the proximate cause of illness was generally the presence in the body of some foreign object, placed there by sorcery.

Just as personal illness was considered punishment for individual sin, so public calamity was thought to be the punishment for mass or public sin.

All illness thus having a supernatural cause, it had to be treated by magical and religious means. Even when herbs and other medicines of genuine therapeutic value were employed, their effect was presumed to be magical, and there was no appreciation of their chemical nature and reactions. As outlined in preceding pages, sacrifice, prayer, penance, fasting, confession, bathing, and other similar rites were as important healing measures as pharmacy and therapeutics.

The relationship between publicly supported and recognized priests of the state religion, and curers, medicine-men, and diviners is not quite clear. Diagnosis and curing were certainly among the important functions of the priesthood, and probably priests of high rank performed these duties for the emperor and the royal family. Ordinary curers were doubtless priests of low rank, and probably many of them were laymen not supported by the church; secret sorcerers were certainly not members of the priesthood. The offices of diviner or diagnostician and curer were almost always combined.

Like the medicine-men of more uncultured peoples, the curer generally acquired his power in a vision or dream; a man who had recovered quickly from a severe illness also had unusual capabilities as a physician. In the usual vision a human spirit appeared and gave the man his power, instruments, and instructions. A sacrifice was generally made to this vision by the curer before commencing the treatment.

Different treatments were indicated according to the cause of the illness as diagnosed by the curer by divination. If the cause was a foreign object in the body, the doctor proceeded like the usual American Indian medicine-man: he sucked at the seat of the pain and produced some small object which he claimed – and probably himself believed – to have extracted. If he decided that the viscera had been displaced, he oiled the body with guinea-pig fat, massaged it, and thus restored the organs to their proper places.

If the illness was the result of neglect of worship, the doctor made a powder of corn-flour of various colours and pulverized sea-shells, and placed it in the patient's hand. The latter blew it in the direction of a waca while reciting a prayer for forgiveness. To the Sun he offered some coca, and for Viracocha he might put some bits of gold and silver on the ground. If it was the man's ancestors that were offended, he offered them some food and chicha, placing it on the tomb if possible. Then the invalid was purified by washing. This was done by the curer if the man was bedridden; if he was able to walk he went to a stream or, better, to the junction of two rivers, and washed himself with water and flour made from white corn.

Broken bones or dislocations were caused by the malevolence of the local spirit of the place where the injury occurred, and were cured by appeasing the spirit, mainly by sacrifices at the spot.

If the diagnosis indicated that a man was bewitched, that his illness was caused by sorcery and black magic, the cure, of course, had to be of the same nature, and a sorcerer was called in to counteract the evil. His treatment was akin to that used to cause the illness.

There was probably no class of professional midwives – women who did nothing or little else, though there is some disagreement on this point. However, in every neighbourhood there were doubtless women who made this an avocation. They qualified through having a vision like the male doctor, by bearing twins, or by performing a long series of rites and ceremonies; they could produce abortions. However, many women delivered unassisted.

The pharmacopoeia of ancient Peru was most extensive and probably every plant was thought to have some magical property for good or evil. Many, of course, have actual therapeutic value in the complaints for which they were used, and some have been adopted by modern medicine; many others could have had no value.

Strangely, and contrary to general belief, cinchona, from which quinine is derived, Peru's most valuable gift to the medical world, apparently was not used to any extent, if at all, in ancient Peru. The *quina-quina*, from which the name was derived, was a different tree, Peruvian balm. This queer fact is understandable when it is realized that malaria, against which cinchona is a specific, was apparently unknown in pre-conquest America, and was one of the plagues introduced from Europe.

Animal products and mineral substances were also used as *materia medica*: fresh meat, ointments from animal fats, blood, urine, bezoar stones, and ointments containing mercury, sulphur, or arsenic. Blood-letting, purges, emetics, and enemas, baths, and control of diet were also prescribed. Tobacco in the form of snuff was used for medical purposes. Embalming was rudimentary and consisted mainly in the removal of the viscera, after which the body was allowed to dry in an arid place.

Even today Bolivian native doctors known as *collahuaya* travel over a large part of South America and are everywhere welcomed by the Indians and reverenced for their medical knowledge. They carry chests of medicines.[1]

A great paleopathologist, R. L. Moodie, thus[2] characterizes ancient Peruvian surgery:

I believe it to be correct to state that no primitive or ancient race of people anywhere in the world had developed such a field of surgical knowledge as had the pre-Columbian Peruvians. Their surgical attempts are truly amazing and include amputations, excisions, trephining, bandaging, bone transplants(?), cauterizations and other less evident procedures.

The information on Peruvian surgery is mainly based on the examination of skeletal remains rather than on the statements of the chroniclers, and is pan-Peruvian in extent. In fact, in some respects the earlier peoples of the coast seem to have been superior surgeons to the Incas. Moche pottery vessels frequently depict the results of surgical operations, or even the operation itself. Probably coca was used as an anaesthetic. Forceps were employed and probably also the tourniquet. Bandaging with gauze and cotton was a frequent practice.

Some skulls show the result of operation on the frontal sinus, but the most striking – and apparently one of the most frequent – ancient Peruvian operation was that of trephination or trepanning. The percentage of trephined crania among those known is the highest anywhere in the world; the proportion seems to be greatest among the skulls from Paracas Cavernas (see page 66) (Plate 53). One skull shows five such operations. It is not definitely determined whether trephination was performed to relieve compressions – the result of fractures – or to release demons,

1. Wrigley, 1917.   2. Moodie, 1927, p. 278.

but obviously cranial fractures must have been very frequent among a warlike people who fought mainly with cast stones and clubs. The incisions might be round or rectangular, and were performed by scraping, sawing, or cutting with sharp obsidian, copper, or bronze instruments.

In all serious operations the patients were first made insensible, possibly with coca, possibly intoxicated with chicha, possibly by hypnotism. The operating-room was first cleaned and purified by the sprinkling and burning of maize corn-flour, first black, and finally white.

Malpractitioners who dealt in sorcery and black magic existed in Peru as almost everywhere and were, of course, beyond the law. When convicted of murder, not only the sorcerer but all his family were put to death. They were naturally feared and hated, but doubtless the suspects far outnumbered the few practitioners. Poison and magic were the two methods by which they worked. Poisoning needs no explanation; the practice of magic follows the same general pattern as throughout the world, that of sympathy and contagion.

A figure might be made to represent the victim, dressed in bits of his cast-off clothing or containing something belonging to him, especially some of his exuviae such as nail parings or hair; the image was then maltreated and possibly finally burned, the suffering being similarly felt by the human prototype. Or the sorcerer would take a toad, skewer the eyes and mouth shut with thorns, tie up the feet, and bury it where the victim would come into contact with it. A noose might be made of black and white wool, spun in the opposite-to-ordinary direction, and placed where the victim would catch his foot in it. By burning fat, thorns, ears of maize, and some of the enemy's hair in his corn-field the harvest could be ruined. Other tools of black magic were the ubiquitous witches'-cauldron ingredients: hairy spiders, animal heads, dried animals, roots, herbs, ointments, shells, figurines, and amulets.

Of course sorcerers could also supply love philtres and charms – all at the proper price. The ingredients, except for feathers, differed little from the above list. The charm was to be hidden in the bed or the clothes of the uncomplaisant loved one.

Chapter 14

INTELLECTUAL LIFE

Astronomy and the Calendar

IT is often asserted that the astronomical knowledge of the Peruvians was much less than that of the ancient Mexicans, and they were certainly much less astronomically and calendrically minded than the Maya. But all cultured peoples of antiquity took great interest in the celestial bodies and their recurrent periods, especially as they bore on the stages of the agricultural year. Though proof is lacking, the Inca probably knew the length of the year and that of the lunar month, and possibly also the period of Venus, with considerable accuracy.

The complexities and accuracies of the Maya calendar have been worked out mainly through studies on the surviving codices. These are entirely lacking in Peru, and the chroniclers have given us insufficient information on the Inca calendar; the Spanish immediately put their own calendar into operation, the two were fused, and the Conquest chronicles represent some of this fusion – and confusion.

The Inca were not particularly interested in dates and calendars. The basic calendar was apparently a lunar one, counted from new moon to new moon. Such a lunar calendar is all that the majority of aboriginal peoples in America had, and probably all that the Peruvian commoner ever had. They seem to have reckoned roughly, like most peoples, twelve lunar months to a year, but the twelve lunations are short of the solar year by about 10·9 days, so that in a little less than three years they were a lunar month behind. Since the ceremonies of the month were integrated with the agricultural activities pertinent to that period, and each month had a name appropriate to the activities or the festivities, it is likely that they interpolated a nameless month – or repeated the last one – when the ceremonies got too much out of step with the season. The chroniclers are silent on this point; apparently they did not realize the problem.

Some more modern writers also have not realized the difficulty and have made inconsistent and irreconcilable statements. Thus Means makes each month run from about the 22nd to the 22nd (obviously based on the solstices and equinoxes), but has the full moon occur regularly on the 15th of January.[1] Others have presumed that there were twelve thirty-day months and that some months had – as with us – an extra day, or that five days were added at the end of the year, as with the Mexican-Maya calendar. This would, of course, have been entirely incompatible with a sequence of lunar periods as divisions of the solar year. In practice the lunar months and the solar year were probably not correlated exactly; the high priest and the emperor doubtless knew the discrepancy pretty accurately, and when something had to be done about it they issued an order.

The months probably began at conjunction, or, more likely, at visible new moon. It is not fully agreed which was the first month of the Inca year; it was either the one containing the June solstice or the December one. The best opinion favours the latter since it marked the beginning of the welcome rainy season.

According to one tradition, the ancient people originally timed their planting season by the blooming of a certain variety of cactus – a natural way for primitive peoples. Then the Emperor Viracocha established the twelve-month (lunation) 'annual' calendar. Finding, in a very few years, that the months and the seasons and festivals were all out of their proper relation, the Emperor Pachacuti had some towers built on the skyline by which the progress of the seasons could be accurately observed and allowed for. It is difficult to believe, however, that the discrepancy between the twelve lunar periods and the solar year was not known to all from time immemorial.

It is certain that four small masonry towers were built in rows on the skylines east and west of Cuzco, and that from a seat in the centre of the Great Square of that city the rising of the sun could be observed with relation to these towers. While a few of

1. Means, 1931, p. 382.

the chroniclers state that the solstices, and even the equinoxes, were thus observed, the evidence is against this, and apparently the sun positions thus observed merely indicated the proper times for planting.

Record-keeping: the Quipu

In spite of the Peruvians' high accomplishments in almost every phase of material culture, they never developed any system of writing – pictographic, ideographic, hieroglyphic, or alphabetic. The statement of one chronicler, Montesinos,[1] that a system of writing on leaves had once been in vogue among the Inca but had been forbidden and forgotten, is given no credence by modern scholars. However, at least one, possibly two, mnemonic devices were in use.

As before noted (page 80), many Moche pottery vessels picture runners carrying bags, together with kidney-shaped objects, generally identified as beans, that are painted with lines, dots, and similar devices. Other scenes depict persons apparently examining these objects. Larco Hoyle[2] claims that these are ideographic symbols, denoting standardized concepts; he also believes that they show close analogies with Maya glyphs. The evidence is purely archaeological, without historical verification, and conservative Peruvianists, while intrigued at the interesting suggestion, are not yet convinced of its proof.

The Inca had a highly developed mnemonic device known by the native name of *quipu*. Probably in simple form it had a long and widespread history in this region, but, like many other devices, had been perfected by the Inca for their special needs. All the extant examples of the quipu are from the dry coastal graves, but most if not all are of the Inca period (Plate 54B). As it was in constant use among the Inca, many of the chroniclers have left us descriptions and explanations of it.

The quipu consists basically of a series of strings in which knots are tied. The great variation possible in the colour and posi-

1. Montesinos, 1920, pp. 33, 62, 64; Bingham, 1922, pp. 308–10, *id.*, 1930, pp. 226–7.
2. Larco Hoyle, 1942, 1943.

tion of the strings, and the nature, number, and position of the knots permits its use for numerical records and mnemonic purposes. All known quipus are different and vary greatly in size and complexity; relatively few of those extant are complete, a necessity for the correct interpretation of any mathematical record.

The main cord, which was held in a horizontal position, is generally of larger size, from a few inches or centimetres to over a yard or metre in length. To this are attached from one to over one hundred pendent strings, of various colours, twists, and other modifications. They may be fastened to the main cord in groups, and subsidiary strings may be attached to them. Knots of various types and positions were tied in these pendent cords. The knots certainly have numerical values; the colours and other qualities of the strings probably signify the nature of the objects thus counted. Several of the chroniclers give interpretations for some of the colours, but the disagreement is so great that no deductions can be drawn.

Studies of quipus by several specialists[1] in this field have demonstrated clearly that the numerical records are given in a decimal arithmetical system very much like our own, with place-value. This was to be expected, since the Quechua numeral system was and is decimal, and the social system was organized on a decimal basis. A simple knot represents 'one'; digits from two to nine are denoted by longer knots in which the cord was wound or looped a given number of times before it was pulled tight. The concept of zero was understood but required no symbol; the absence of any knot in the expected position denoted zero. Place-value was indicated by distance from the main cord; the unit digits were at the farther or lower end of the string, the higher multiples – tens, hundreds, and thousands – closer to the main cord. In the known extant quipus calculations in thousands are rare, and apparently only one instance of ten thousand is known. Generally the long knots of many loops were employed only for the unit digits; multiples of the higher orders were represented by the proper number of single knots close together.

The quipu was a recording and mnemonic, not a calculating device. Its principal purpose was doubtless that of statistical

1. Locke, 1912, 1923, 1938; Nordenskiöld, 1925a, 1925b.

record; this is obvious from the statements of the chroniclers who saw them in use. Probably the majority were censuses of the population by age-classes in given districts, as well as records of domestic animals, quantities of agricultural products, and such statistics. Probably the figures could be read by any Inca *quipucamayoc* or professional quipu-interpreter, who doubtless also knew the meaning – or various meanings – of the string colours, but certainly in many or most instances some verbal information of interpretative value had to accompany a quipu (Figure 6).

However, the quipu could be, and certainly was, employed as a mnemonic device for the recitation of traditional material such as historical ballads and genealogical records. Thus, according to some of the chroniclers, the life and activities of each emperor were recorded on a quipu. Such quipus could, of course, be interpreted only by the maker or by someone fully familiar with the data.

As a result of his study of many quipus found in graves on the coast – the only extant ones – Nordenskiöld[1] comes to the conclusion that these at least were not statistical records but were used in divination and possibly for the determination of lucky and unlucky days. He argues, from his wide experience with American aborigines, that it would be absolutely contrary to American Indian psychology to place with the dead any information regarding the living, since this would give the former some control over the latter. His point is doubtless well taken, and we may be rather confident that these quipus were not current censuses. Nordenskiöld finds in these quipus an unexpected frequency of occurrence of the number seven and concludes that this must have been a sacred number. Also he derives sums and totals, many of which seem to agree, more or less closely, with the rotation periods of celestial bodies; therefore he believes these quipus to be calendrical and astronomical in nature and used in magic and divination. Although Nordenskiöld was one of the greatest Americanists, his conclusions on this point are not generally accepted by modern authorities, mainly because there are many discrepancies in his calculations that need to be explained away, and because the Inca apparently had little interest

1. Nordenskiöld, 1925a, 1925b.

Figure 6. *Quipucamayoc with quipu and counting apparatus*

233

in lucky and unlucky days, which were so important among the Mesoamericans. It must be kept in mind, however, that we have no historic information regarding the peoples of the coast where these quipus were buried.

It is rather certain that an abacus[1] was employed in making the calculations that were later recorded on the quipus. No example has yet been discovered archaeologically, but some chroniclers have described its use[2] and even given a picture of one (Figure 6). This seems to have been a rectangular block with twenty (5 by 4) compartments in which from one to five kernels of corn or other small objects were placed and manipulated.

Standards

Inca standards of measurement were quite accurate and exact, and in the case of at least one of them – the 'fathom', used in the measurement of land – a measure of this standard length is reported to have been kept as a criterion and official check. Small measures of length up to the fathom, about 64 inches (162 cm.), the height of an average man, were based on parts of the human body. Larger measurements of distance were based on the pace, and the unit for long distances was the *topo*, about $4\frac{1}{2}$ miles (7·25 km.). Areas were also figured by the *topo*, but the areal *topo* was only an acre or so.

Standard measures for weight and volume were of much less importance, and the Inca are said to have had none for weight or for liquid volume, but dry materials, such as grain, were measured by a standard that amounted to about twenty-seven quarts (29 litres).

The weighing balance-beam was known, and possibly even the steelyard.

Music, Art, Literature

Peruvian music would probably have sounded very dissonant and cacaphonic to our ears. Probably the music of the modern Quechua and Aymara resembles it greatly, and detailed studies

1. Wassén, 1931, 1940.　　2. Acosta, 1880 (1590).

have been made upon this.[1] The nature of the ancient music is deduced from the musical instruments that have been preserved. These are of two kinds, wind and percussion, for stringed instruments were practically unknown everywhere in America. Among the monotonic instruments were drums, rattles, whistles, bells, and trumpets. Flutes with finger-holes produced several tones, but of especial interest and importance is the syrinx or pan-pipe, closely resembling those of ancient China (Plate 46A). Musical instruments were made of wood, reeds, pottery, bone, shell, or metal.

The art of the Inca period was that of a pragmatic people and the last stage of a long history: it was technically excellent, under perfect control, but uninspired, aesthetically the poorest of the several major art traditions developed in Peru.

Stone sculpture was entirely missing, architectural decoration extremely rare, so that art was expressed almost exclusively in the form and embellishment of small manufactured objects, mainly in pottery, weaving, and metal-work, with minor attention to feather mosaics, woodcarving, and work in bone, shell, gourds, and other such materials.

Pottery forms were limited and of simple silhouettes, with little relief ornamentation. Colours were few and sombre, the designs almost exclusively geometric, generally repetitions of small simple figures (Plate 35). But in the decades just preceding the Spanish Conquest, some realistic painting appeared in the form of small animals, birds, and insects. There was no realistic modelling. Most of the ceramic forms, especially goblets, plates, and a pointed-base liquid-container now called an aryballus (Plate 34), were characteristic of the period.

Much the same can be said of the textiles, which are largely geometric in ornamentation with over-all designs and many small panels. Very characteristic of the period are the wooden goblets, painted in thick mastic, and called *quero*; these show scenes of human activity (Plates 39, 40). Many of them date from the Colonial period. The small figures in stone and metal are natural but lifeless and generally standardized to a few characteristic forms, such as llamas and plain human figures.

1. Harcourt and Harcourt, 1925.

Despite the fact that it was unwritten, the Inca had a considerable body of literature of high quality. For greater ease in memorizing, this traditional material was cast in metrical, poetic form. History and mythology were thus preserved in quasi-epics and sagas. Also there were religious prayers and hymns and secular poems, songs, and dramas. An example of a prayer has been given on page 214.

Very little indeed of this literature has been preserved for us, and most of that little was recorded in Spanish translation, generally much abbreviated. Most of it contained ancient religious ideology and so, together with the more purely religious literature, it was condemned or repressed by the Spanish clergy. The few preserved examples indicate lofty sentiment and beauty of expression, with many allusions to natural phenomena.

The folk literature consisted largely of love poetry and songs, and apparently differed slightly from similar material found today in the Andean region, the content and spirit of which are strongly aboriginal.

There was probably no true drama in pre-Conquest days, but merely dramatic parts of native dances with solos and choruses. The Spaniards, however, soon wrote morality plays in the Inca language, and later true dramas were composed which embodied old legends and songs. The most famous of these, which has been recorded in several old versions, is a play called 'Ollanta'. Its earliest recorded form, however, does not antedate the eighteenth century.

Presumably almost every Peruvian group had its legendary tradition of the creation of the world and of the origins of local features and institutions, and these of course differed greatly in detail if not in essence. That of the Inca is the only one preserved for us, and this doubtless existed in a number of versions with minor details. The best known of these is as follows:

The Creator, Viracocha, made the world, but it was a dark, sunless one. Then he created a population of giants by carving figures of stone and giving them life. But they displeased him, so he turned some of them back to stone – the great stone figures found at Tiahuanaco and other archaeological sites – and drowned all but two of the rest in a great flood. Before creating other beings of this same human shape he produced light by causing the sun and the moon to rise from Titicaca Island. At first the moon was the brighter, but the envious sun threw ashes in the moon's face, thus reducing its radiance. Viracocha then, at Tiahuanaco, made clay figures of all the animals and men of different nations, and decorated the latter with their assigned and traditional costumes. Putting life into them, he instructed them in their various and characteristic languages, customs, and even their ceremonies and songs, and sent them underground to emerge in the districts that they were to occupy.

Viracocha himself, with his two assistants, journeyed north to observe the results of his orders and the extent of their obedience; he travelled up the cordillera, one assistant went along the coast, and the other up the edge of the eastern forests. Since he travelled in the disguise of an old man, few of the people recognized him, and in some places greeted him with stones, an almost universal method of treating foreigners – and therefore *ipso facto* enemies – in pre-internationalistic days. At Cacha, in Canas province, he was so angered at his reception that he caused a rocky hill to ignite, which began to burn up the country. Terrified, the people beseeched his pardon and aid, whereat he extinguished the fires with a blow of his staff. On the burned hill, a volcanic cone, the Canas erected a shrine, and the Inca later built a great temple.

The Creator then proceeded to Urcos, near Cuzco, where he commanded the future population to emerge from a mountain, on which a shrine dedicated to him was later made. He visited Cuzco, and then continued north to Ecuador where, in the coastal province of Manta, he took leave of his people and, walking on the waves, disappeared across the ocean.

A NOTE ON THE NAME 'INCA'

The best terminology to employ for the people of Peru in the imperial period, for their emperor and their language, presents a difficult problem and a point on which there has been little agreement and much cause for confusion.

The native word 'Inca' designated originally a member of a

group of related families at Cuzco which became the focus of imperial expansion. Later, by imperial edict, the term was extended to include any other native speaker of the same language, Inca by privilege; the Spanish further extended the term to include any native subject of the Inca empire. However, they also applied the term specifically to the Inca *par excellence*, the emperor, just as the chief of a Scottish clan is *the* Campbell, for instance. In a language that can distinguish between *el Inca* and *los Incas* there is little room for confusion, but not so with English *the Inca*, especially with the modern tendency – advisable on the whole – of using only the singular forms of rare native proper names, such as 'the Maya', 'the Bagobo'. Some writers avoid the equivocation by calling the people 'Peruvians', surely an inadmissible term in a work such as this. Herein the people are termed 'the Inca'; the emperor is designated by that latter term.

Today the Peruvian Indians and their language – both but slightly changed from aboriginal days – are known as 'Quechua', a usage begun only a century ago. Although now standard, it is an unsuitable term, since the Quechua, being native to the region of Abancay, were originally only one of many small groups speaking the language of the Inca. Herein we refer to the pre-Spanish idiom as 'the Inca language'.

PART FOUR

ARTS AND CRAFTS

*

THE ancient Peruvians erected no Parthenons or Colosseums, they carved no Venus di Milo, they painted no masterpiece. Their architecture was characterized by massiveness rather than by beauty, remarkable for its stupendous masonry rather than for its art. Stone sculptures are rare on the coast, ponderous and severe in the highlands. It was on the smaller objects, the pottery vessels, the textiles and the metal-work, that the Peruvian artist lavished his skill and his creative art. Art was a constant element of his daily life, not an interest apart from it. However, it was as a craftsman – or craftswoman – rather than as an artist, that the Peruvian was pre-eminent. As weavers, potters, and goldsmiths they could hold their heads proudly among their peers anywhere in the world. And in the textile industry the Peruvian woman is considered by many technical experts to have been the foremost weaver of all time.

Chapter 15

TEXTILES

I T is difficult to write of Peruvian weaving in any but fulsome phrases or to avoid suspicion of exaggeration and bias. Textile experts – not merely enthusiastic archaeologists – state that the ancient Peruvians employed practically every method of textile weaving or decoration now known, with the exception of roller and block printing and several very special techniques of recent invention, and made finer products than are made today. Certain of the finer fabrics have never been equalled from a point of view of skill. Among the textiles one finds twining, twilling, braid, gingham, repp, plain weave, warp-face and weft-face or bobbin-pattern weave, warp and weft interlocking, brocade, tapestry, tubular weave, pile knot, gauze, double cloth, triple cloth, embroidery, needle-knitting, painted and resist-dye decoration, and several other special processes peculiar to Peru, probably impossible to produce by mechanical means.

In its aridity, coastal Peru much resembles Egypt. In both countries burials were made deep in places where rain is almost unknown, with consequent remarkable preservation of objects made of organic materials, such as wood and fibre. Superficially, some Peruvian fabrics resemble Coptic. Peruvian 'mummies' (Plates 51, 64), like Egyptian embalmed ones, were wrapped in quantities of cloth, probably made specifically for mortuary purposes and of especially fine quality, and were buried, often at great depths, in the barren deserts that flank the cultivated river valleys. The rare but occasional rains have damaged most of the cloths, especially in the northern coastal region, and the quantities now preserved in museums must be but a small fraction of those originally interred. Most of the textiles in collections, like most of the pottery and other grave furniture, were dug by *huaqueros*, mercenary natives who make a business of such excavation. Recent laws, making the practice illegal, have not entirely stopped this vandalism. Practically all the known Peruvian fabrics come from these coastal graves. Judging from the examples of cloths obviously woven in the highlands that have been found in these graves, it is certain that the highlanders of Peru and Bolivia wove as excellent textiles as the coastal peoples, and this may also have been true of Ecuador and Colombia.

There are three reasons why the textile art was of such importance in Peru, and therefore attained such a high degree of excellence. The cool climate of the high plateau required warm clothing, and even on the coast it was welcome protection from the chill fogs. The Peruvians had the advantage over all other American Indians in possessing wool, from the cameloid animals; thus, of the four important natural textile fibres, cotton, wool, bast, and silk, they lacked only the last. The most important bast fibre, flax, was also absent. And last, owing to their developed agricultural economy, there was plenty of leisure time between harvest and planting, leisure to be devoted to technical and artistic progress. In Peru, under the Inca empire at least, certain persons, especially some of the 'Chosen Women', spent practically their entire time at spindle and loom.

Probably throughout Peruvian history as in the later Inca period, and as generally among primitive peoples throughout the world, the women were the weavers; presumably as today they spent much of their time at the loom, and constantly spun as they walked. In addition to weaving new garments they mended old ones, re-weaving worn and torn places, much like a modern 'invisible mender', instead of darning them. Weaving new cloths for mortuary purposes consumed not a little of the time. Frequently found in Peruvian graves, probably always those of women, are work-baskets made of rushes, oblong with lids. These always contain a number of spindles, balls of cotton and wool yarn or thread, and other such small weaving implements and materials (Plate 54A).

Practically all the woven cloths were of course used for personal apparel, but some are so immense that they must have been employed as wall hangings in temples.

The development of textile techniques in Peru seems to have been a native evolutionary one, from simple beginnings. Among the earliest known Peruvian fabrics are those that were found in the excavations at Huaca Prieta (see page 34), a very early pre-ceramic site.[1] While the Huaca Prieta cloths are by no means primitive, they are much ruder than those of later periods, and made by a few simple methods.

Twining and netting are very ancient techniques the world over, possibly having developed from basket, bag, and net making, and preceding the invention of the loom. Tapestry weaving and embroidery are also very old textile arts of world-wide extent, and we would expect them to have been the next developments in Peru. Tapestry weaving requires only a rudi-mentary loom, hardly more than a frame, necessitating neither lease rods nor heddle, while embroidery might be expected to develop early from the practice of attaching objects to the surface of plain cloth. Tapestry, as expected, is very early, on the Chavín-Cupisnique horizon, in some instances combined with gauze. Embroidery, however, does not appear until the Paracas period and, if our chronological sequences are correct, was preceded at Supe by more complicated techniques such as brocade, pattern weaves, and gauze.

While twining and weaving were contemporary throughout the pre-ceramic period at Huaca Prieta, it is curious that weaving remained subordinate to twining for so long. It has been sug-gested that this implies the lack of any effective heddling device.

However, it is on the south coast that the greatest amount of material is available for study of textile art and development. In this almost perfectly arid region the state of preservation of the fabrics is remarkable. The known quantity is very great, the technical and artistic quality extraordinary. The most prolific source of fine textiles is the Paracas Necropolis, but the Nazca cemeteries have also yielded their quota.

According to radiocarbon datings, about a thousand years elapsed between the time of the last potteryless fishermen-farmers of Huaca Prieta and that of the men who deposited the burials in the Paracas Necropolis, and technology had made tremendous advances in this period. From then up to the time of Pizarro no great technical advancement was made in the textile industry. The tools used by the 'Chosen Women' who made

1. Bird, 1948a, 1948b.

Atahuallpa's vestments were practically the same as those used by the women who made the Paracas mantles: simple spindles, loom, bobbin, and weaving sword. There was no shuttle that was thrown through the warp sheds; the bobbin was passed through by hand. Probably the spindle itself often served as bobbin also.

The earliest known weavers of the southern coast, those of the Paracas period, as well as those of the later Nazca Valley, practised every important fundamental technique known in the latest periods.

There is considerable difference between the weaves and materials at Paracas Cavernas, Paracas Necropolis, and Nazca. Plain weaves are common everywhere, and plaiting common at Necropolis. Twill is missing in the early period and very rare in the middle and late ones. Tubular weaves are extremely rare but several very early ones are found. Tie-dye is missing in the early period, and pile-knotting absent entirely. Pattern weaves, brocade, and double-cloth are rare and brocade is missing at the Necropolis site. Paracas painted fabrics are the earliest known.

Wool is found in the earliest periods in this southern region, indicating regular trade with the highlands even at this time. Wool was always used for embroidery and for tapestry weft, as it was over most of Peru in all periods.

From Nazca-Paracas times on, almost all techniques were found in all regions, varying in proportion according to the prevailing fashions. In the middle periods embroidery became relatively rare, the emphasis being on tapestries, generally large and complex. From the north coast few fabrics from this period are preserved. Coast Tiahuanaco textiles are noted for their tapestries, though brocade, double cloth, and other techniques are found. The designs are of highland origin. The finest tapestries were made in this period, especially those of the Tiahuanaco horizon found at the central coast sites of Ancón and Pachacamac.

In the late periods embroidery again became prominent, but not an over-all veneer as Paracas embroidery tended to be. Double cloth, painted cloth, and resist-dye processes were in vogue also. Fabrics from the Chimú period on the north coast are now preserved, tapestry and embroidery being favoured over other techniques, these, with weft patterns, being the most common decorative weaves in the late periods on the south coast.

Much of our knowledge of Peruvian textile industry is derived from Colonial accounts of Inca weaving, though few fabrics from this period have been preserved, except on the coast. Tapestry, repp, and warp patterns were the favourite weaves, but all techniques were known. Three types of loom were used, one no wider than the span of a woman's arms, a horizontal loom mainly for blankets, and a vertical one for tapestry weaving. The first one, the backstrap loom (Figure 4, p. 157), was the one on which most textiles were woven. One loom bar was attached to a pole or tree, the other to a belt which went around the woman's waist, and supplied the needed tension. After about half of the cloth had been woven, it seems that the loom was reversed and weaving begun from the other end. As the gap between lessened. the wooden weaving tools had to be removed and the picking done by hand, the last interstice finished with a needle.

Three types of cloth were also distinguished, a coarse grade for blankets, a medium grade for ordinary apparel, and the finest fabrics. The latter was certainly tapestry, of the finest alpaca or vicuña wool; the medium class for ordinary clothing was a warp-faced cloth, with the pattern in the warp, probably made of alpaca wool. Probably llama wool was employed for the utilitarian blankets. While tapestry weave is still practised today, especially in Bolivia, warp-patterns are now almost universal; the manu-facture of fine tapestries ceased soon after the Conquest.

The amount of time required to plan and weave a patterned textile is far greater than ordinarily realized. The entire ensemble has to be conceived and planned beforehand, and the order of the picking of the warps carefully calculated. Primitive craftsmen often seem to have an almost incredible ability to visualize the design that they are working on, and to calculate and memorize the steps to be followed in producing it, and it is quite possible that the Peruvian weaver had no material visual aid whatever, and certainly no very detailed or complete one. It is also possible, however, that some model, possibly painted on wood, a small woven sampler, or some other mnemonic aid was used. In a well-known painted Moche vase, showing a group of weavers, some of them seem to have by them an object showing the pattern to be reproduced in the fabric.

Fibres

Nothing is known of the beginnings of the textile industry in the Peruvian highlands, but on the coast cotton was the earliest fibre, with bast definitely of secondary importance. In early Ancón and Supe only a trace of wool was found, and on the south coast and in northern Chile the older fabrics show a much higher percentage of cotton than the later ones. Cotton, however, continued in use in all periods and regions.

Cotton occurs naturally in Peru in a slight colour range from white to reddish-brown and grey. Today the natives are said to apply different terms to cotton of six naturally different hues. These were – and still are – employed in weaving to provide contrasting colours, just as the dyed cotton was.

Linen and silk were unknown in Peru, but bast, the fibres of various plants, was used in all periods and places. It was seldom if ever employed for cloth, however, but generally for special products, such as fine hair-nets, and especially for cordage.

Wool appears early on the coast and was in constant use thereafter, especially in the highlands. The source was the native highland cameloids, the domesticated llama and alpaca, and the wild vicuña. Llama wool is coarse and generally a yellow-brown; it was employed for only the coarsest fabrics. The garments of the average person, in the highlands at least, were probably made of alpaca wool, which is finer than llama wool and white, black, or brown in colour. Most highly prized was the fine wool of the wild vicuña, which was caught in communal drives. This is very soft and long, generally of a dark-yellow colour, and in Inca times it is reported that its use was confined to the nobility. However, the finest selected alpaca wool is as fine as vicuña, and apparently in every case where a very fine textile has been closely examined by an expert, the wool has turned out to be alpaca.

The oft-quoted statement that the Peruvians spun bat wool is given no credence by modern authorities; the hair (maximum length 5 mm.) is much too short to spin into yarn. Human hair was occasionally employed for certain purposes, and probably also the wool of the viscacha, a chinchilla-like rodent. In northern Chile, textiles made of the wool of the guanaco, the small wild cameloid of the pampa, are said to have been found, but guanaco wool is probably too short for efficient use.

Dyes

The use of colouring materials certainly long preceded the manufacture of textiles, and their application to cloth was a natural extension of an age-old practice of painting. Most of the dyes were probably of vegetal origin, such as indigo (*Indigofera suffruticosa*) for blue, and a madder (*Relbunium*) for red, but products of the animal world were known, and possibly mineral colours also. The red insect cochineal (*Coccus cacti*) was cultivated for this purpose, and probably a purple colour was obtained from *Purpura* molluscs, as it was by natives of Central America. A related shellfish produced the famed Tyrian purple of classic Mediterranean days. Pigments were mixed to obtain a great variety of tones; O'Neill distinguished one hundred and ninety hues in the textiles from Paracas Necropolis, though doubtless many of these may be ascribed to differential fading. In addition, of course, there were the natural variations in the tones of cotton, white to brown, and those of llama, alpaca, and vicuña wool.

Cotton was sometimes dyed raw before the removal of the seeds; this is probably the explanation for the statement made by some observers that a blue cotton was grown. Wool was more often dyed as yarn, since dyeing tends to tangle the fibres. The dyeing of woven cloth does not seem to have been a common practice, though it must have been done at times, and was necessary in the *plangue* type of tie-dye process of decoration.

Little is known about the use of mordants to fix the colours and to make them permanent. Generally no trace of them remains today to respond to any chemical test, and it is possible that often no fixative was employed. Some tests indicate the validity of one colonial statement to the effect that alum was used; urine is a more common reagent in aboriginal South America.

Spinning

The twisting of the raw fibres into yarn or thread is the first technical process in weaving; this is termed spinning. It must be preceded, however, by some preparation of the fibres. In the case of cotton the lint has to be separated from the seeds in the boll. Whatever the fibre, it must first be cleaned and the strands placed in parallel alignment so that they will combine evenly; the latter process is known as carding.

In Peru the cotton seeds were probably torn from the lint by hand – just as they were everywhere until the invention of the cotton gin – and bits of foreign material were picked out. Wool was presumably washed to remove the dirt. Carding, for which process most peoples use some special brush- or comb-like implement, was apparently done by hand, though it has been suggested that possibly some of the one-row combs that are frequently found in graves were used for this purpose. Thus loose fluffy balls of cotton or wool with the fibres roughly parallel were obtained.

The threads and yarns spun by the pre-Columbian Peruvian women with simple hand spindles have awakened the admiration of expert authorities in this industry. 'The perfect thread is not to seek', says one.[1] 'It has been made.' 'The yarns are the best ever produced. . . . No machine yarns, however excellent, can approach their perfection.'[2] Primarily these praises refer to the fineness, though the evenness is also at least equal to that of modern machine-made yarns.

Aboriginal Peruvian cotton was not of the fine quality of modern cotton, and finer cotton threads have been hand-spun in Dacca, India (500 count), and occasionally made by machine in Manchester (420), but, considering their material, the old Peruvians made by hand extraordinarily fine cotton yarns with a count up to 250; the finest yarns made today of Peruvian cotton do not go higher than 70.

Wool cannot be spun as fine as cotton, but in the alpaca and

1. Murphy, 1912, Volume 3, p. 83.
2. Crawford, 1915, p. 77.

vicuña the Peruvians had exceptionally fine wool, and they utilized it to the full; their wool yarns were the finest and most perfect ever made. The finest worsteds made today have a count, on the industry's cotton scale, of 70 to 90; the best old Peruvian wool yarns are almost three times as fine, between 180 and 200. The finest wool tapestry weaves frequently have over two hundred weft strands to the inch, and three hundred is not very rare.

Such extremely fine threads and yarns were of course the product of years of care, experience, practice, emulation, and competition. The yarns in the oldest known textiles, those found in the Chicama Valley, are relatively coarse and uneven, evidently an early stage in the art. But progress was fast, and the fabrics in the very early Paracas period were already approaching the perfection achieved in the latest periods. In fact, some of the finest thread was made in the early periods.

The implements employed in the manufacture of these extraordinarily fine and even threads and yarns were of the simplest, a forked stick for a distaff to hold the fluffed fibre, and a plain hand spindle. In these, as in the loom, there seems to have been little improvement throughout the long history of Peruvian weaving, although in the very earliest period, as for instance in the Chicama Valley, no identifiable spindles or whorls have been found, and it is possible that plain sticks were used. However, the simple hand spindle, a straight stick with a whorl or disk on it to give momentum, was the universal spinning implement almost everywhere in the world until relatively recently, for the spinning wheel was only a few centuries old when it went the way of the whale-oil lamp. The spindle was given a whirl with the fingers, which twisted into thread or yarn the cotton or wool fibres as they were pulled out from the loose ball of fibre on the distaff. While it was twirling, the spinner's fingers teased out over-large knots of fibre to make the thread of even thickness.

Today the Peruvian Indian woman is constantly spinning as she walks when away from home, letting the spindle fall and thus providing the needed tension. The drop spindle is used today only with wool yarn; cotton is spun while seated, the spindle whirling in a gourd or bowl. The drop spindles are larger, with larger whorls, and the yarn produced is probably coarser than the cotton threads. Presumably the customs were the same in early days (Figure 3). Many of the spindles found archaeologically, of thorn or hard wood, are so small with such tiny whorls that it has been doubted whether they really served this purpose. They were probably used in spinning the finest threads and yarns, revolving in a cup and thus reducing strain and vibration.

The direction of the twist varied in different times and places. In the Inca period it was generally clockwise. However, in doubling, to produce a two-ply yarn, the direction was always opposite to that used in making the single-ply yarn, so the spinner had to be equally adept in both directions.

Single-element Techniques

True knitting and crocheting are claimed to have been unknown in ancient Peru, but somewhat similar results were obtained by other processes. Netting was of the greatest importance since earliest days, and probably long preceded loom weaving; it was a common technique at Huaca Prieta. Several other knotted and looped techniques were known. The products range from large, coarse fishing-nets and sacks to small bags and hair-nets. Lace-work falls in this category. Knotting reached its highest development in the creation of closely knotted fabrics, usually caps or hats, frequently including decorative feathers or pile. Single-element fabrics are found in all horizons, but are more common in the early ones.

Lace is often mentioned casually in articles and books on Peruvian fabrics, but no definite study of Peruvian laces seems to have been made. The delicate gauzes have a very lace-like appearance and doubtless have often been mistaken for lace. The term lace covers a number of different techniques, some single-, some multi-element, and even drawn-work. Doubtless many non-woven products of the early Peruvians, such as some hairnets, will be found to match some of these techniques (Plates 46B, 50A).

PLAITING AND BRAIDING

Naturally the technique of making objects by twisting together three or more similar elements was not unknown to or ignored by the ancient Peruvians. The process is somewhat related to twining, except that all three elements are parallel. It was employed to some extent in almost all periods and regions, naturally mainly in the manufacture of long narrow objects such as slings, ropes, and cords, and to a lesser extent in flat bands. Even in these utilitarian objects, however, the Peruvian talent and artistic sense manifested themselves, for every possible method of decoration was applied to them, and every conceivable variation of manufacture employed. Since a long cultural history, antedating loom weaving, would be expected, it is surprising that no examples of braiding or plaiting were found at Huaca Prieta.

PILE KNOT

Several processes for giving a raised effect to fabrics were known in Peru. Loom-woven cloth was varied by pulling out weft strands to form loops like a Turkish towel, and fibre was caught in the weave in a quasi-pile technique (see page 257). But the most interesting and most attractive pile-knot technique, and the one that gives an effect most approaching that of Oriental rugs, was apparently peculiar to Peru. The piles was not woven into the fabric, but the technique was related rather to the single-element one of netting. That is, the bunches of fibre were caught in the loops of a single yarn. The pile was later trimmed off to give an even, regular surface.

Bright colours forming designs and patterns were used in these bunches of wool fibre, and the technique was employed principally on hats, head-bands, and bags. A variation of the process produced long cords of unknown purpose; the looped yarn enmeshing the pile tufts was wound around long fibre cords. The pile technique was apparently a rather late invention, and was particularly favoured in the Tiahuanaco period, in which it first appeared.

Weaving

The admirable fineness and quality of Peruvian fabrics were due to the patience, care, knowledge, and skill of the weaver, not to the quality of her apparatus, for this was of the simplest. The primitive back-strap loom was used in all periods and underwent little development from earliest to latest time; it was the implement on which the finest textiles were woven. One end was fastened to a post or tree, the other to a band round the weaver's back, by which means the desired tension was maintained. The heddle was lifted and fixed in position by hand; there was no treadle. Apparently several other types of loom were known at different times and places, for different products, but the small, one-woman, arm-span loom was the standard everywhere at all times, as it is today (Figure 4).

Apparently the weaver's only other tool was a weave sword or batten for separating the sheds more widely and for beating down the weft (Plate 59B). As the weaving proceeded, the finished cloth was wound up on the lower loom bar while the warps were unwound from the upper bar. It is believed that after about half of the cloth had been woven, the loom was reversed and weaving begun from the other end. As the gap between lessened, the wooden weaving tools had to be removed and the picking of the warps done by hand, the last interstice finished with a needle.

TWINING

Twining is the simplest, and probably the oldest method of fabric-making, and was possibly adopted from the certainly earlier processes of basket- and mat-making. While made by crossings of warp and weft, a true loom is not required, a simple frame sufficing. The intertwining of warp and weft is done by hand, a pair of weft strands being twisted around a warp element; the twisting is continuous.

Twining is certainly the oldest fabric technique in Peru. Excavations in the pre-ceramic sites of the northern Peru coast indicate that 78 per cent of the fabrics were twined, most of the remainder being single-element netted objects. The twining, however, was highly developed, the crossings being varied to produce pleasing patterns and effects.

Soon, with much greater dependence on woven textiles, twining became unimportant and disappeared from the picture almost completely.

GAUZE

Delicate lace-like gauzes in a great number of patterns were very popular in the early periods on the coast, especially at Paracas Cavernas, though they continued to be made in all periods. Pairs or more of warps are crossed or intertwined in various patterns and then fixed in position by the weft. Though the manipulation may be done with the fingers, the work is simplified by the use of a heddle. Almost all Peruvian gauzes are fancy, or combinations of plain and fancy techniques, elaborate and skilful. They are also decorated with other techniques, such as embroidery. Almost all are of cotton, a very few of wool. Developed at a very early period, gauzes are among the loveliest, most interesting, and most varied of many admirable Peruvian weaves. They somewhat resemble lace and are sometimes mistaken for it.

TAPESTRY

Tapestry is generally visualized as a large, loosely woven fabric used as a wall covering or other hanging. None of these characterizations applies to Peruvian tapestries, which are very tightly woven, of moderate size, and used for garments, pouches, and similar purposes. For, to the textile expert, tapestry is a technique, not a product, and tapestry technique is basically the same in the small exquisite Peruvian fabrics and in the great Gobelin wall hangings.

Tapestry weaving has been defined as darning or embroidery on bare warps. Though generally woven on a loom with a heddle, only a frame is needed since there is no division into warp sheds, and the weft is ordinarily not carried across the full width of the warps. The pattern is always formed by the weft. More colours can be employed than in loom pattern weaves; there is no limit to the number of colours that can be used in a fabric. Each coloured yarn is carried on a separate bobbin, and the weaver builds up the pattern bit by bit, passing the bobbin over and under the warps until the pattern calls for a new colour, then letting the old colour bobbin hang, and taking up the new one. Two methods of procedure are possible. The weaver may finish one line of weft at a time, dropping one colour bobbin and taking up the next as the design changes, or she may build up one complete coloured design before proceeding to the next. In the latter case it requires much skill to keep the weft lines even and the cloth unpuckered. Nevertheless, this seems to have been the usual technique of the Peruvian weaver when making slit 'kelim' and 'eccentric' tapestry; in the more usual interlocked weave the weft lines were carried straight across.

Gobelin tapestries portray life scenes; Peruvian ones are not pictorial but have regular patterns, generally rectilinear and frequently geometric, though more often stylized and conventionalized biomorphic. Gobelin tapestries have the backs unfinished, with loose-hanging yarn ends, but Peruvian tapestries are mostly two-faced, the two sides identical and equally well finished; the ends of the yarn are carefully tucked in and hidden between the warps so that they are never seen and never come loose. The pattern with the same colour on both sides of the cloth is the identifying criterion of tapestry; in loom pattern weaving in two colours the two are different to front and back.

Tapestry weaving is simpler than loom pattern weaving and presumably older, preceding the adoption of the heddle. It is the weave used in much primitive weaving, at least in America; Navaho blankets or rugs, Mexican serapes, and most other examples of aboriginal American weaving are done in this technique.

Tapestry seems to have been the favourite – or at least the most highly prized – Peruvian technique, especially in the Middle and the Inca periods. It was at its apogee in the Coastal Tiahuanaco or Epigonal period. The most perfect, the finest, and the loveliest

Peruvian fabrics are the tapestries; they are among the world's triumphs in the textile art (Plate 48A).

Peruvian tapestry is always made with warp of cotton and weft of wool, generally fine alpaca or vicuña wool, and the weaving is the finest and daintiest. The weft is always battened down hard so that it completely covers the warp. Gobelin tapestries are coarse, with an average of twenty wefts per inch, and the finest European tapestries seldom exceed eight-five. In Peru two hundred per inch is not uncommon, and Bird records[1] one extraordinary piece with an average of 327 and running up to 500 in some closely packed parts of the design. This is presumably of two-ply vicuña wool. The warp is of three-ply cotton, sixty-seven to the inch.

In almost every type of weaving, the Peruvians experimented and produced variations which are unknown elsewhere. One such has been termed 'sheer tapestry'. Though made by tapestry technique it has the appearance of voile, being loosely woven of singly-ply cotton crape, interlocked. A very rare variation of this is the Swedish or two-way interlock, in which the weft-locks produce a ridge on the rear side of the cloth.

In tapestry weaving, rectilinear patterns present no problem when they are diagonal, but it is obvious that vertical straight lines leave a slit between the design elements unless both wefts encircle the same dividing warp, which makes closely battened weaving impossible. Frequently the slits, especially if short, were left open – a technique known as kelim. To close them, and to eliminate this element of weakness, any one of several tricks might be employed. In the Nazca area subsidiary wefts of hard-spun, single-ply cotton, so fine that they were hidden between the wool weft, were often inserted; the term 'reinforced kelim' has been suggested for this. Another method was to interlock half or less of the weft loops across the slit. Or a vertical weft might be wound round an intervening warp strand, occasionally looping to the sides to blind in the adjacent warps. This independent weft is often of a black colour, and gives a dainty dark outline to the coloured pattern; the same black yarn is sometimes employed to outline all rectilinear design areas.

1. Bennett and Bird, 1949, p. 277.

TEXTILES

SCAFFOLDING TECHNIQUES

The Peruvian weaver, as has been intimated before herein, was no routine labourer; she took the old-fashioned guildsman's pride in her work. Every piece was somewhat different from any other; her loom was an instrument for art expression, not merely a machine. And just as she gave thought to the intended design, and calculated the number of picks required to produce it, so she experimented with all possible manipulations of warp and weft. Often combinations of several techniques are found on one fabric. It is natural, therefore, that complicated textile processes were invented that have been found nowhere else in the world, that must be described in detail to be understood, that cannot be duplicated by mechanical means, and for which a new nomenclature must be developed. It is unnecessary to go into such detail here.

Several such techniques were performed on skeleton yarns or cords which were removed after the cloth was woven, and the fabric later strengthened and locked by the insertion of other new and additional strands.

This technique has been called 'weft scaffolding' or 'patchwork', and is found in a number of variations. One of these gave rise to the term 'patchwork'. In this the cloth was woven in solid-colour squares, but the vertical weft loops were not interlocked. When the horizontal yarns over which the warps were looped were removed, the cloth fell apart into small rectangles. These were then decorated with tie-dye designs and, since the edge loops to top and bottom were open, the fabric was pieced together again by the insertion of the horizontal yarns, doubtless with the aid of a needle.

PATTERN WEAVES

Both warp-faced and weft-faced or bobbin patterns were made by the ancient Peruvians, and the results were up to their usual high standard, but these processes were never so popular as tapestry, embroidery, and brocade; brocades are much more common than bobbin-weaves. The best examples of warp-faced textile are found in the later periods on the southern coast, and the technique continues important in Peruvian native weaving today.

The warps were always of cotton, the weft of wool or cotton. While one or two heddles may have been used, the design was probably most often made by hand-picking the warps.

One variety of warp-faced plain cloth known as repp was very common and is often considered a characteristic feature of ancient Peruvian weaving. The fewer and heavier weft strands give a ribbed appearance to the fabric.

DOUBLE CLOTH

Double cloth was a favourite weave, though a rather intricate one. Two sets of warps and wefts, each pair of the same colour, are employed, producing two layers of cloth of contrasting colours, the design being made by interlocking the cloths so that the motif appears on the reverse face in the opposite colour. This weave was popular in earlier days in the United States for home-made bedspreads.

In Peru, double cloth was employed principally for pouches where light weight and durability were essential; the pieces are never large. The weave is not very fine, never more than forty-eight to the inch, the warp and weft count always equal. Almost all are of cotton yarn, and brown and white are the colours most frequently employed. The setting up of the loom is of course rather complex, and for rapid work four heddles would be required. It is doubtful if these were employed in Peru; in this, as in all simple weaving, heddles can be dispensed with if the weaver takes the time to count the warps and pick them by hand. Rare examples of three- and even of four-layered cloths, each of a different colour, have been found in Peru (Plate 48B).

The earliest example of double cloth is from Paracas Cavernas, but the high quality of the work indicates a long developmental period somewhere; the technique became quite common in later periods in practically all areas.

Decoration of Fabrics

On the question of cloth decoration, there is a gradual variation from pure weaving to the attachment of objects, a gradation that makes it difficult to separate the techniques into categories. At one extreme there is the drawing out of weft strands into loops like a Turkish towel, a process very different in technique from, but producing much the same effect as, the insertion of pile fibres during weaving. Another process of decoration during weaving is brocade; embroidery gives much the same effect but is applied after weaving. The tie-dye technique may be used either before or after weaving.

The Turkish-towel effect is found on some cotton shirts where a loop an inch long is left between the warps on certain weft strands, producing horizontal lines of loops at regular spaced intervals. Probably the wefts thus manipulated were passed over a gauge or rod that was later withdrawn. The purpose was probably warmth rather than decoration, which can certainly be said of some shirts and shawls from northern Chile of a later period. Here ten-inch tufts of alpaca wool were wrapped around certain warps during the process of weaving; the result is coarse, heavy, and utilitarian but definitely not beautiful. Both of these processes were probably rare and of very limited temporal and geographical distribution.

BROCADE

Though brocade resembles embroidery so closely that they are sometimes difficult to distinguish, the methods of manufacture are entirely different. Both are decorative overlays on cloth, but embroidery is added with a needle-like implement after the cloth is woven, while brocade is applied during the weaving process by means of supplementary wefts which are brought to the surface when needed to form the pattern, and hidden under the utilitarian weft when not. Brocade must therefore always follow the weft line, while embroidery may be sewn at any angle. One criterion for distinction is that embroidery is always carried through the cloth and appears equally plainly on the reverse side, while brocade is hidden in the cloth when not desired in the design. Brocade wefts are thicker and less hard-spun than the real weft so as to cover the latter in patterns; they are also inserted more loosely.

The earliest brocade is found at Supe; it is also common at Paracas Cavernas.

Both brocade and embroidery were very popular in Peru, and the former is much more common than bobbin weave, probably largely because more colours could be used.

EMBROIDERY

The fundamental technique of embroidery has been discussed in the preceding section on brocade. Embroidery was both very popular and extraordinarily well made in Peru, especially in some of the early periods. It was done with a needle-like implement in cotton or wool yarn, and generally on a loosely woven cotton fabric. Unknown at Huaca Prieta, no examples have been found at Supe, and the earliest known pieces are from Paracas Cavernas. Later it declined in popularity as in quality, and late embroideries are distinguishable from brocades only on careful examination, since the stitch always follows the weft line. In fact in all periods, free embroidery, with stitches at any angle, is virtually unknown; it was not in accord with the aesthetic sense. The exquisite embroidered Paracas mantles (Plate 49) have been described earlier.

'Needleknitting'

Some of the daintiest and loveliest Peruvian sewing is done in a technique now generally termed 'needleknitting', although other names have been applied to it, for its exact nature was long not understood. It has the superficial appearance of knitting, but is actually an embroidery technique, and probably was done with a needle. The stitch used is that known as 'buttonhole' in embroidery. While it is also employed in edge and seam bindings, and even to decorate rather large fabrics, its highest and most spectacular and admirable development is in small three-dimensional figures which, as one writer has aptly remarked, must be seen to be believed. These are tiny realistic figures, generally of birds and flowers but occasionally of other objects, that were made independently as a border or fringe, and sewn to the edges of Nazca fabrics. They give the impression of the most delicate and even knitting but are actually embroidered on a foundation of yarn or tape, completely veneering it. The work is always done in two-ply wool yarn, with an average of twenty loops to the inch, and in five or six bright colours. This technique is found in all periods in the southern and central Peruvian coast but not on the north coast; it was most common and brought to highest perfection in the early periods at Paracas and Nazca (Plate 50B).

Shaped Fabrics

Tailored clothing – that is to say, garments made of cloth, cut to desired shape and sewn together – is a relatively recent concept in the world and one mainly due to European influence. Most native peoples wear – and wore – their textiles uncut and just as woven; this was probably universally true in aboriginal America. With their highly developed textile industry, however, it is natural that the Peruvians should have experimented with the manufacture of fabrics woven in non-rectangular shapes, a process today practically limited to knitting. The techniques involved, however, are rather simple, as were the results. Most of the shaping was achieved by making one edge of the cloth – generally the upper edge – wider or narrower than the opposite one.

Tubular Weaving

Weaving seamless tubular belts, ribbons, and straps was one of the interesting accomplishments of the Peruvians; such objects are much more easily and frequently produced – today at least –

by knitting. No technical study of these has been made, but presumably the warps were strung on rings serving as loom bars, the weft forming a continuous spiral. They are generally decorated in warp-faced technique. Sometimes they are perfectly tubular, of circular cross-section, but more often the two sides are combined to make a thick, flat fabric with rounded hollow edges in a sort of double-cloth fashion; these were used especially for the handle bands of cloth pouches. The historical development of tubular weaving has not yet been worked out, but, as might be expected, it apparently is not found in the early periods but became common and popular in the later ones.

Tie-and-Dye Techniques

The decoration of cloth – and of other objects – by processes that involve the covering of certain parts so that these remain unaffected when the object is dyed is one of widespread distribution, especially in south-eastern Asia. The best known of these is the batik technique, by which a design is painted in wax on the cloth which is then dyed and the wax removed, leaving the design in white, the background in colour. This process was and is unknown in America on cloth, though on pottery, known as negative painting, it was sporadically widespread. The pre-Columbian American resist-dye processes on cloth are those known as tie-dye, in which the parts of the cloth or fibre to remain undyed were bound with cord or some other similar relatively impermeable material. Two varieties of the technique were practised: *plangue*, in which the finished cloth was treated and dyed, and *ikat*, in which the yarn was tied and dyed before being woven into cloth.

The designs that can be made on cloth by the plangue process are necessarily simple, and the cloth is generally a loosely woven fabric that can easily be thoroughly soaked. The most common technique was to gather up and tie small puckers of the cloth in regular lines. This resulted in lines of small, light-coloured, rude squares or circles with a dark dot in the centre, on a dark background. Sometimes this was done twice with different colours.

This tie-dye process was often used in connexion with 'patch-work' weaving (see page 255).

The ikat tie-dye process was much more intricate, for the entire pattern had to be planned and calculated in advance so that the warps would be dyed in such a manner that they would form a design when woven into cloth; wefts were never dyed in this fashion. The warps were counted, grouped, and tied with impermeable cord before dyeing; they were often retouched with paint later. Relatively few examples are known, and all are limited to the late Tiahuanaco horizon of the Chimú area; however, the process is well known today in the Andean highlands and in Guatemala. It apparently appeared later than the plangue technique. Both processes are still very popular in Indonesia.

Borders and Fringes

By far the majority of Peruvian fabrics were made to be worn as garments and therefore their aesthetic effect was of maximum importance. Very rarely were edges left plain, and generally the last few inches of the cloth adjoining the border were decorated with a pattern different from the body of the textile; this was often also done in a different weaving technique. Very generally also tassels or fringes were made on the edges, either sewn on or, much more often, made during the weaving process.

Fringes were easily made from the warp loops where they encircled the loom cord or rod, and the wefts were often carried out to either side, possibly with the help of temporary warps; these warp and weft loops were either left open or treated in some decorative fashion. Another method of finishing the warp-end edges of cloth was to complete the weft weaving around the loops so that a tubular edge of very slight diameter was produced. To do this it was almost certainly necessary to remove the fabric from the loom and probably to complete the weave with the aid of a needle.

Painting and Appliqué

One of the simplest methods of decoration, whether of cloth or of any object, is by painting. Painted fabrics are found in various periods in Peru, but apparently none earlier than Paracas Necropolis. Probably most often made hastily in an emergency, they are not in keeping with the Peruvian perfectionist sense in textiles; they are common in no period. Naturally the cloths and the designs are rather large, the colours few (Plate 47). A few cloths decorated with designs made by stamps, presumably of carved wood, are known.

Fabrics covered with a mosaic of feathers are rather common and are exquisite, but the emphasis is on the overlay; they are feathers attached to a utilitarian background rather than decorated fabrics. Sometimes they are cemented to the cloth, but more often attached to cords and sewn on.

In the later periods cloth garments were decorated by the attachment of metal sequins, bangles, beads, and such extraneous ornaments.

Chapter 16

OTHER CRAFTS

Ceramics

POTTERY is the consuming interest of the archaeologist – at least of the archaeologist working in America. This interest, however, is in slight degree aesthetic; in fact, a bit of a broken plain un-painted vessel of unusual provenance is of more importance to him than an artistic creation from a better-known region. For the lowly potsherd is the archaeologist's principal diagnostic criterion of cultural phases, the standard by which he determines, distinguishes, and often describes major and minor temporal cultural developments and local differences. The possible varia-tions in form and in technique of manufacture are so great, those of ornamentation so limitless, that the archaeological expert can distinguish the ceramic product made in any region – often at any single site – at any given time, and sometimes even recognize the work of individual potters. Moreover, the potsherd is almost as imperishable as stone, and vessels carried in trade to distant regions afford clues to the contemporaneity of two cultures.

Thus, since pottery is the principal distinguishing criterion for a number of Peruvian culture phases of which we know nothing historically, the latter are often designated by the characteristics of their ceramics, as, for instance, the 'White-on-Red', 'Black-on-White', 'Black-Red-White', and 'Inter-locking' periods.

However, in America, ceramics achieved the status of a major art medium; it was a craft, not merely a trade. Practically every group with any claims to cultural advancement made excellent and artistic pottery, as did a number of otherwise quite primitive peoples. The vessels upon which the most artistic skill was lavished were of course those interred with the dead, and prob-ably made especially for that purpose; the burial of many pottery vessels with the dead seems to have been a rather frequent

American practice. Fortunately, of course, these are the best preserved; the plainer utilitarian pots were replaced only when broken, and the fragments thrown away with the household rubbish.

Ancient Peru can probably claim first rank in America both for the quantity and the quality of its ceramic products. The majority of these come from the graves of the coastal cemeteries. The latter, made in the arid deserts on the edges of the cultivated and populous valleys, contain quantities of graves from which native treasure-hunters – and in recent years professional archaeologists – have excavated great numbers of pottery vessels, many in 'mint' condition. The Peruvian pottery vessels in the world's museums must amount to several tens of thousands. Some graveyards have been discovered relatively recently, and probably others, with types of pottery unknown today, will later be found. For instance, the beautiful Nazca pottery, of which almost every large archaeological museum now owns a large collection, was known by only a few examples until Dr Max Uhle discovered the cemeteries in 1902.

The ceramics from the Peruvian highlands, while good, especially from a technical point of view, are neither so common nor so artistic, admirable, or interesting as those from the coast. The cemeteries were smaller and more widely scattered, and also probably the production was less.

Deposits of clay suitable for pottery-making were accessible to most population centres in Peru, but naturally they ranged from excellent to poor, and this had its effect on the quality of the result. Few of the clays, however, could be used just as found, and the addition of a tempering material to prevent cracking in the baking process and to make the clay more malleable was generally necessary. This was generally pulverized rock, mica, sand, shell, or potsherds; each region and era had its favourite material, one of the criteria for ceramic determination.

One of the great differences between pottery-making in the New and Old Worlds is that in the former the potter's wheel was unknown; vessels were shaped by hand or cast in hand-modelled moulds. Generally they were made by the process most common and widespread in America, that of coiling. The clay was puddled to the proper consistency and mixed with the tempering material. After modelling the base the potter then rolled out a 'snake' of clay, varying in thickness according to that of the desired vessel, and coiled this round and round, gradually building up the side of the vessel to the desired shape. As the height increased he smoothed the vessel outside and inside and obliterated the depressions between the coils with his hands, aided by a smooth stone or a piece of cloth. The 'paddle and anvil' method, of striking the exterior of the vessel against a stone held inside it, was probably also used. Vessels and other objects were also made from large lumps of clay by simple modelling without the use of coils. Contrary to the usual American Indian usage, men and not women seem to have been the potters in Peru; at least they are at present.

Smaller pottery objects were often made in clay moulds, and on the northern coast this technique was used even for vessels of fair size. Few of these moulds have survived, and apparently none for the large vessels, but the finished products betray their method of manufacture. Human figurines or dolls were the principal mould-made product. Moulds were of two separable parts so that quantity production was possible, but – in the case of the larger vessels at least – known duplicates are rather rare. The small solid figurines were made in one piece, the large hollow vessels in two, later luted together, the seams smoothed, and relief parts, such as spouts, handles, and ornamentation, applied later. Some vessels in the form of fruits, vegetables, and such small objects are so perfect that it is obvious that the mould was made from the natural original. Probably grease from animal fat was used to prevent the object thus cast and the resultant product from sticking to the mould (Plate 55).

After modelling or moulding, the exterior of the vessel or object was smoothed and sometimes polished. Generally, especially if painting was to be applied, a wash of thin clay called a 'slip' was applied to the surface. Vessels were decorated by relief ornamentation, by incision, engraving, or carving, by stamping with relief stamps, or by painting. This was usually done before baking; paint applied after firing is not permanent.

The ancient Peruvian techniques of baking pottery are imperfectly known, but as the results were excellent we may be sure that they were good and well controlled. Baking was probably done in the open, but in some places and periods kilns or pits may have been used. The temperature achieved was quite high, though of course nothing like that required for modern vitreous ware. The two principal types of firing were understood and controlled, the oxidizing and the reducing. In the former a fast fire, sometimes fed by forced draught, produced hard, light-coloured wares of red, yellow, or creamy paste. In the reducing atmosphere the supply of oxygen was restricted, as in charcoal-burning, the heat kept lower, and much smoke produced. This resulted in a black *bucchero* ware which took a high polish. Glazed pottery was unknown.

In addition to painting designs with coloured pigments, incising them with some tool, and applying relief ornamentation, vessels were decorated with stamps cut in a pattern, and the background was sometimes cut away, leaving the design in relief. The incised or impressed design might be made by a sharp or blunt instrument, a finger-nail, a notched shell, decorated dies or paddles, and other methods.

Direct painting in one or many colours was the most common painting process, but in a few places and in certain periods an interesting resist-dye process known as negative painting (formerly called 'lost colour') was practised. Most often, apparently, the decoration was painted on the surface with some wax-like substance, after which a solid colour was applied, or the entire vessel dipped in a dye, thus colouring the background. The wax was then burned or melted off, leaving the design in negative. This process is found sporadically over America from Peru to Ohio, and probably has some historical relationship with dye-resistant textile processes such as batik and ikat. Sometimes parts of the vessel were then painted with a second colour. Pieces of soft clay or other removable substances might be used in place of the wax.

A very large number of pottery shapes are found in Peruvian ceramics, although, naturally, any given cultural phase utilized only a few of these. Bowls, plates, goblets, pitchers, vases, and jars, with their many possible variations, are all common. Typical of Peru are the vessels with double vertical spouts connected by a solid bridge, and especially the stirrup-spouted ones, in which two upward-curving tubes unite in one vertical tube. The double whistling vessel is common in Peru. This consists of two bottle-shaped jars connected at the bottom. One of them has an open neck, while that of the other contains a whistle, generally combined with a naturalistic figure. When tilted so that the liquid flows from one chamber to the other, air is forced out of the whistle orifice.

In Peru, as indicated by the excavations at Huaca Prieta, the art of weaving preceded that of pottery-making. However, the earliest known Peruvian ceramic is already of good quality and must have had a long period of development behind it, possibly in some other area, near by or far away. The sequence of technical ceramic development still remains to be worked out for Peru. However, there seems to have been no important technological improvement from earliest to latest times; the Inca potter used essentially the same processes as his Guañape predecessor.

Metallurgy

Because of the technical difficulties of producing and working metals they always appear late in the histories of cultures and are marks of considerable advancement. In the Old World, copper and bronze appeared late in human history, iron even later, and all were used mainly for utilitarian objects.

Aboriginal America never achieved an iron age. Iron in a free state is almost never found except in meteorites, and the melting temperature is very difficult to attain by primitive methods. Native copper was worked by prehistoric Indians in the region of Lake Superior, and in Mexico gold and a very little copper and silver appear on a late horizon, but the Andean region was the great, and probably the earliest, centre of metallurgy in America. Gold, silver, copper, and even platinum were worked, and tin was alloyed with copper to form bronze. Very rarely lead and mercury were utilized. Most of the products, however, were ornamental rather than utilitarian.

Historically, gold was doubtless the first metal to be worked

It is easily secured in pure condition by placer mining, and can easily be fashioned into lovely untarnishable ornaments. The first gold objects in America were probably made either in Colombia or on the coast of Peru. The earliest technique was apparently that of repoussé; the gold was beaten into thin plates and tooled or hammered over forms into designs.

In the Chavín period goldsmithing had already reached a high technical and artistic plane. The next gold ornaments appear in the Salinar period on the Peruvian northern coast and the Nazca-Paracas period on the southern coast; the latter are not uncommon and of a high quality of art and technique. In these early times there seems to have been no copper or silver used, and no casting in gold.

The development of metallurgy is not of sufficient importance – nor indeed are the evolutionary details well enough known – to warrant detailed exposition here. Suffice it to say that through the centuries the casting of metal objects was developed, copper was melted and cast and mixed with tin to form bronze, and silver was also melted, beaten, and cast.

Goldsmithing was widespread, and both the quantity and the quality of the work in Ecuador, Colombia, and Panama were equal to that in Peru. Silver and bronze are not found in the northern countries, and platinum was worked only in southern Colombia and Ecuador.

The discovery of ornaments of platinum on the coast of Ecuador has astounded and intrigued modern metallurgists, for its melting point (about 1770° C. or 3218° F.) is beyond the capabilities of primitive furnaces, and it was unknown in Europe until quite late. The tiny beads and other ornaments appear to be of pure platinum but actually consist of an alloy rich in platinum with some gold and a little silver. It was worked by the process known as sintering. Small grains of platinum were mixed with a little gold dust; the gold melted under heat and soldered or welded the grains together; it was then hammered into shape.[1]

Gold was apparently secured only by placer washing in streams. The nuggets and 'dust' sometimes contain a consider-

1. Bergsoe, 1937; Root, 1949b.

able quantity of silver. Silver, copper, and tin were mined from pure veins or lodes; it is questionable whether the Peruvians were ever able to smelt these metals from ores, but the evidence favours the smelting of copper and silver.

In their furnaces the Indians seem to have used charcoal, but they had not invented the bellows; draught was produced by blowing through tubes, and sometimes a large number of natives were thus employed on one furnace. Another method was to build the furnace on a hillside where there was a constant updraught.

Gold, silver, and copper were all hammered into thin sheets and embossed (Plates 42-5). They react differently to cold hammering and to tempering. Cold-hammering makes copper very hard, harder than cast bronze of low tin content; this is probably the true explanation of many legends of lost arts of tempering copper. Apparently all processes of hammering, annealing, and alloying were practised in Peru to give the most desirable results. Alloying lowers the melting point of metals, and bronze was probably produced primarily for greater ease in casting rather than for greater hardness.

Gold, silver, copper, and bronze objects, and especially gold ornaments, were made by casting. The process was that known as *cire perdue* or 'lost wax', a technique known also to Old World goldsmiths; it is an open question whether it was independently invented in America. The desired ornament was modelled in wax, either with or without a core of clay or of some similar substance. This was then covered with a thick envelope of clay through which an orifice was left. After the clay had hardened, the mass was heated and the melted wax allowed to run out through the hole. Molten metal was then poured in to replace it, duplicating in metal – sometimes with a pottery core – the wax figure. The outer envelope was broken to extract the ornament, so there was no duplication or quantity production. This was the method employed in Mexico, and almost certainly also in Peru and the regions between.

Probably pure gold was the first metal to be cast in the Moche period, then silver and copper, later various alloys, and finally bronze. An alloy of gold and copper known as *tumbaga* was much used in Colombia and the Isthmian region, but to no great extent in Peru; this and bronze were the most important alloys. All South American bronzes are of the so-called alpha type, with a tin content of less than twelve per cent; they are relatively soft unless cold-hammered.

The technique of annealing or tempering was probably discovered even before casting; some metals or alloys are hardened by this process, some softened. It is uncertain whether or not welding was known, but soldering was practised from the earliest periods. No mercury or amalgam was used, but powdered copper salt was mixed with a gum and applied to the surface with heat; this reduced the salt to metal and fused the surfaces together.

Several processes of gilding were known. One was true gilding, the application of thin gold – or silver – leaf to a surface. A mould was sometimes lined with gold before the molten copper was poured into it. Much more common, at least in Colombia and the Isthmian region, was a process which is known as *mise en couleur* and was known also to Old World goldsmiths. An object was cast of an alloy of gold and copper, and the surface then treated with the juice of an acid-bearing plant which dissolved the copper. The pure gold surface could then be burnished.

Tiny beads of exquisite and dainty workmanship were cast, especially in Ecuador, and larger objects were made of two different metals such as gold and copper, gold and silver, or of two different alloys of gold of different colours (Plate 41). Gold or silver inlays were also made in base metal or other materials.

Woodcarving

Carving in wood is a practically universal craft that must have been practised by almost every American group, past or present. Owing to rapid decay, however, only under exceptional conditions have wooden objects of past civilizations been preserved; such American archaeological objects are extremely rare everywhere except in Peru. Here, as in Egypt, very arid desert conditions on the coast have permitted their preservation almost in their original state. They occur mainly in graves on the coast, but many have also been found while excavating guano on the islands off the coast; these were probably lost there during similar visits for fertilizer in pre-Columbian days.

Spades, shovels, paddles, clubs, digging-sticks, batons, and similar objects are the larger things known; very often their use is problematical. Many are ornately decorated with carving and painting. Weaving tools such as loom sticks, weaving swords, spindles, and bobbins are the commonest objects found in graves, but there are also ear ornaments, figurines, spear-throwers, and dozens of other implements and ornaments (Plates 58-60).

One of the most characteristic types of wooden objects is the kero or *quero*, a tall, flaring wooden cup of thick, hard, dark wood. While the shape was most characteristic of the Tiahuanaco period, most of the known keros date from the last days of the Inca empire, or from early colonial times. They are usually painted with pictorial scenes featuring ornately dressed human figures, and frequently these wear Spanish costumes. The bright colours are in a sort of mastic lacquer, inlaid in a modified cloisonné technique. Most of those now known have probably been preserved in Peruvian houses since the day of their manu-facture (Plates 39, 40).

Miscellaneous Techniques

Feathers were favourite materials of the ancient Peruvians. Brilliant colours such as red, blue, and yellow were preferred, and feathers of the parrot and macaw probably supplied the bulk of the material; for small and delicate mosaics, humming-bird feathers were used. Naturally few of these fragile art pieces are preserved in a state approaching their pristine beauty. Feathers were applied to many things, but large mantles, collars, and the capes of head-dresses, with rich designs in feather mosaic of bright colours, are the most striking. The small feathers of uniform size were individually tied to a background fabric.

Colourful fine-grain stones taking a high polish were naturally carved into beads, pendants, and ornaments of many types. Most of these stones are extremely hard, but nevertheless the lapidary probably practised his art with little if any use of metal tools (he had only bronze at the best), but depended more on abrasives. Naturally the work was very slow. Beads tend to be small. Small stone bowls with llama effigy heads are very characteristic of the Inca period (Plate 38).

Similar objects were made of bone and shell, but each material has its specific properties; thus bone was used for awls, needles, weaving implements, and many long tools. The large spondylus shell was happily employed for roseate inlays and ornaments, while the triton and other large univalve shells were used as trumpets.

Basketry, an art in which many American Indian groups excelled, was of no artistic importance in Peru. Doubtless rather rude utilitarian basket containers were made for many purposes, but few of these have been preserved. The best known are small oblong rectangular baskets with attached lids, made of rushes or grass, which were used by women to hold their small weaving tools and balls of yarn, and which were buried with them (Plate 54A).

APPENDIX

*

Sources

IT must be constantly kept in mind that we have no first-hand sources of information on Peruvian history and customs until the Inca were overwhelmed by the Spanish in 1532. Before that time there was no system of writing; the only known records, the quipus – knotted strings – were mnemonic aids, accurate only arithmetically, the context known only to those cognizant of the subject in question. For the greater part of this pre-Columbian era our only data are those supplied by the trowel of the archaeologist and the spade of the native *huaquero* (treasure-hunter), data mainly on material culture and manufactures. Some deductions regarding social and religious life can be drawn from these – a good deal in the case of the life forms and paintings on Moche pottery – but no clues to such topics as history.

Immediately after the Spanish Conquest chroniclers began to record in Spanish their observations of Peruvian life and customs, and to interrogate informed natives regarding these and the historical traditions. These are our principal sources. They vary greatly, especially on such points as history. In appraising their value modern students take into account such factors as the circumstances under which they were written, the presumptive reliability of the native informants, the degree to which statements agree with the general picture of Peruvian life and national temperament and ideology, and especially whether several reliable chroniclers corroborate a given statement.

In English – and probably in any language – the most thorough study of Peruvian sources is *Biblioteca Andina*, by Philip Ainsworth Means,[1] one of the greatest of recent Peruvianists. Means gives full data on the lives of the many chroniclers, the circumstances of their writings, and appraisals of the value of their works. The latter, however, do not always agree with the opinions of Means' successors of to-day. In his evaluations he placed great

1. Means, 1928.

stress upon the attitudes of the writers, and contrasted two 'schools', the Toledan and the Garcilassan. The former consists of those who, like Francisco de Toledo,[1] Viceroy of Peru from 1569 to 1582, and his associate, Pedro Sarmiento de Gamboa,[2] were antagonistic to the Inca régime and who sought to prove that the Inca emperors were tyrannical usurpers who had no just claim to rule. The Garcilassan 'school' was typified by the 'Inca' Garcilaso de la Vega,[3] of royal Peruvian blood, whose point of view was naturally sympathetic towards his mother's people. Means concluded that the statements of the latter group would naturally be more reliable than those of the former, took Garcilaso as his most reliable source, and accepted his statements whenever they conflicted with those of other chroniclers assigned by Means to the Toledan school. Garcilaso's statements were also widely copied and plagiarized by later writers, and he has long enjoyed a reputation as the foremost authority. Many modern critics, however, consider Garcilaso unreliable, especially as regards pre-Conquest history and religion.[4] Garcilaso wrote his 'Royal Commentaries' long after he had returned to Spain, and based much of his historical accounts on the writings of the now discredited Jesuit Blas Valera.[5]

Both Means and Rowe, however, agree in their high opinion of Father Bernabé Cobo[6] who wrote his four-volume *Historia del Nuevo Mundo* about 1653, and, in spite of its relatively late date, this can probably be recommended as on the whole the most reliable account of Peruvian life and history. Pedro de Cieza de León's *Crónica del Perú*[7] is another of the best-known sources, and he is generally considered 'honest, conscientious, and thorough'. These above-named are the largest, most important, and best-known sources, but a large number of others were their contemporaries. Means and the great British Peruvianist, Sir Clements R. Markham, have translated a number of these sources into English.

1. Toledo, 1940; Levillier, Roberto, 1935.
2. Sarmiento de Gamboa, 1906, 1907; Ocampo, 1907.
3. Garcílaso de la Vega, 1722, 1723, 1869–71.
4. Rowe, 1945, 1946.
5. Valera, 1879.
6. Cobo, 1890–95.
7. Cieza de León, 1554, 1864, 1880, 1883, 1932.

APPENDIX

Spelling of Native Words

The spelling of native words of a language without written or printed literature always presents a most difficult problem. All languages have sounds that are missing in another language, and for which the latter has no character. Usually these are expressed, in non-technical writing, by their nearest equivalent, or by combinations of characters, though sometimes special characters are invented – a much preferable procedure, but requiring a key for the non-cognizant. Unfortunately, every modern language has its particular pattern of orthography. English, with its irregular and illogical orthography – indicating different vowels by doubling a following consonant or by suffixing a voiceless *e*, as *filing* and *filling*, *not* and *note*, is perfectly hopeless for recording unaccustomed words and exotic sounds.

Fortunately Spanish, with which we are at present concerned, is one of the best in this respect, though lacking characters for many rather common sounds, such as English *sh*, and employing a few double characters for simple sounds, as *qu* for *k*, *hu* for *w*. Immediately after the Conquest, the Spanish in Peru began writing the Inca language, now known as Quechua, made it a second official language, and developed a standard orthography for it, as they did with Aztec, Maya, and several Guatemalan languages. This differed little from the standard Spanish of the time, employing no new characters, but a few devices such as a doubled letter for a peculiar Inca consonant of *k* type.

Today many native Peruvian archaeologists and other writers are adopting a modified system of writing Quechua, at least as regards proper names, writing *k* and *w* in the English manner in place of Spanish *qu* and *hu*, and changing a few other sounds to give a closer approximation to the proper Quechua. Thus they are coming to write and print – in scientific publications at least – Keshwa for Quechua, Wira Kocha for Viracocha, Pisaj for Pisac, etc. Newly discovered or slightly known archaeological sites that have not become standardized in Spanish spelling are ordinarily known by only the more modern phonetic form, as Kenko, Wilka Wain, Kuntur Wasi.

Of course, linguistic studies of modern Quechua employ the phonetic alphabet of the linguists, which requires special characters in printing, but certain Peruvianists are using an orthography without special characters which gives a much closer approximation to the Quechua or Inca pronunciation. Logically it might have been better to employ this spelling in the native words used herein, but since the system is new and the words not standard, in general the traditional and standard Spanish spelling has been employed.

One such modified phonetic orthography was developed by Dr John H. Rowe and used in his classic article, 'Inca Culture at the Time of the Spanish Conquest'.[1] Further study of the Inca language at the time of the Conquest led him to modify this orthography somewhat, as explained in a later article.[2] He has graciously supplied revised phonetic forms for most of the Quechua-Inca words used in the Inca section of this book, which are given below.

Dr Rowe's modified phonetic form of Quechua orthography has met with almost universal approval. The Inter-American Indianist Congress of 1954 meeting in La Paz gave the system its formal recommendation, it is already widely used in Cuzco, and the Bolivian government is considering making it an official orthography.

ll represents a palatal *l* in both Colonial Spanish and Rowe's phoneticized orthography.

A glottal stop and glottalized stop consonants are frequent in Inca-Quechua. Ignored in standard orthography, they are represented phonetically by an apostrophe ('). All Inca-Quechua words apparently beginning with a vowel actually begin with a glottal stop.

Quechua has a velar (back throat) stop in addition to *k*. They were frequently undifferentiated in classic orthography, but *q* is used phonetically for the velar stop.

Stops (*p, t, k, q*) are found as both aspirated and unaspirated. In phonetic orthography the aspirated stops are represented by a following *h*, as *ph, th, kh, qh*. This applies also to the affricative *ch* and *chh*.

Glossary of Spanish and Quechua Words

(From Spanish)

Adobe	Sun-dried mud, generally as bricks
Altiplano	High plateau, specifically that of southern Peru and Bolivia, and the Lake Titicaca region
Balsa	Raft; in this region made of reeds
Cordillera	Major mountain range

1. Rowe, 1946.   2. Rowe, 1950.

Encomienda	Assignment of Indians to a landlord
Encomendero	Landlord of an *encomienda*
Hacienda	Plantation or landed estate
Hacendado	Owner of an *hacienda*
Llano	Plain, prairie
Maotaña	Forested foothills; specifically those at the eastern base of the Andes.
Páramo	High, wet grasslands
Sierra	Mountain range

(From Quechua)

Classic Form	Phoneticized	
Acllacuna	'akllakuna	'Chosen Women'
Alpaca	(Aymara word)	Domestic cameloid animal
Amauta	hamawt'a	Sage, wise man
Apachita	'apachita	Sacred offering, cairn
Aquilla	'akilla	Golden goblet
Ayllu	'ayllu	Social division, 'clan'
Çanca	zankhu	Sacred bread
Charqui	chharki	Dried, 'jerked' meat
Chasqui	chazki	Relay runner
Chicha	(not Quechua)	Fermented beverage, corn beer
Chullpa	ch'ullpa	Burial vault or tower
Chuñu	ch'uñu	Desiccated potatoes
Coca	kuka	Narcotic plant
Collahuaya	qollawaya	Class of native physicians
Coya	qoya	Queen
Curaca	kuraka	Subsidiary chief
Guaman	wamani	Province, political division
Guanaco	wanaku	Wild cameloid animal
Guano	wanu	Bird or bat excrement
Hauasipascuna	hawasipaskuna	'Left-out Girls'
Hihuaya	hiwaya	A form of punishment
Huaca	wak'a	Sacred place; archaeological site
Huaco	wako	(Sp.) Archaeological vessel
Huaquero	wakero	(Sp.) Native digger; treasure-hunter
Huauqui	wawqe	Supernatural Guardian; brother
Huayara	wayara	Fertility festival
Ichu	'ichhu	Coarse grass
Inca	Inka	Inca
Llama	llama	Domesticated cameloid animal

Classic Form	Phoneticized	
Llautu	llawt'u	Fillet, head-band
Macana	maqana	War club
Mamacuna	mamakuna	Mother Superior
Mita	mit'a	Tax-service
Mitima(es)	mitma	Compulsory colonist, settler
Napa	napa	White (albino) llama
Oca	oqa	Cultivated tuber (*oxalis*)
Pachaca	pachaka	Political unit of 100 families
Pampa	pampa	Low-level treeless or grassy plain
Pirca	pirqa	Masonry of undressed field stones
Pucara	pukara	Fortress
Puna	puna	High-level grassy plain
Puric	pureq	Able adult man, head of household
Quechua	K'ichuwa	Quechua
Quero	qeru	Wooden goblet
Quinua	kinuwa	Cultivated amaranth (*Chenopodium*)
Quipu	khipu	Knotted record
Quipucamayoc	khipu-kamayoq	Knot-record keeper
Saya	saya	Section of a province
Sinchi	zinchi	Chief, leader
Situa	Sithuwa	Curatice festival
Suyu	suyu	Quarter of empire
Taclla	taklla	Spade *or* foot-plough
Tambo	tampu	Inn, barracks
Tocco	t'oqo	Cave mouth, window
Topo	tupu	Shawl pin; standard of measurement
Totora	t'utura	Reed, rushes
Tumbaga	(not Quechua)	Gold-copper alloy
Vicuña	wik'uña	Fine-haired wild cameloid animal
Villac Umu	Willa-'uma	High Priest
Villca	willka	A narcotic (*Piptadenia*)
Yacarca	yaqarqa	Soothsayer, diviner
Yanacuna	yanakuna	Class of servants

DEITIES

Illapa	'Illap'a	Thunder
Inti	'Inti	Sun
Mamacocha	Mamaqocha	Mother Sea

APPENDIX

Classic Form	Phoneticized	
Mamaquilla	Mama Killa	Moon
Mama sara	Mama Zara	Mother Corn
Pachamama	Pachamama	Earth Mother
Viracocha	Wiraqocha	Creator

PERSONS

Ayar Auca	'Ayar 'Awqa	Brother of Manco Capac
Ayar Cachi	'Ayar Kachi	Brother of Manco Capac
Ayar Uchu	'Ayar 'Uchu	Brother of Manco Capac
Ayar Manco	'Ayar Manku	Manco Capac
Mama Ocllo	Mama 'Oqllu	Sister of Manco Capac
Mama Huaco	Mama Waqo ('jaw')	Sister of Manco Capac
Mama Cura	Mama Qora	Sister of Manco Capac
Mama Raua	Mama Rawa	Sister of Manco Capac
Manco Capac	Manku Qhapaq	Mythical founder of Inca empire
Sinchi Roca	Zinchi Roq'a	Son of Manco Capac

MONTHS

Capac Raimi	Qhapaq raymi	December
Camay	Kamay	January
Hatun Pucuy	Hatun poqoy	February
Paucar-Huara or Pacha-Pucuy	Pawqar waray or Pacha poqoy	March
Ayrihua	'Ayriwa	April
Hatun Cuzqui	'Aymuray or Hatun kuzki	May
Yntip Raimi	'Inti raymi	June
Chahuar Huarquiz	Chawawarkiz	July
Yapaquiz	Yapakiz	August
Coya Raimi	Sithuwa or Qoya raymi	September
Uma Raimi	K'antaray or 'Uma raymi	October
Ayamarca Raimi	'Ayamarka raymi	November

REGIONS AND PLACES

Chinchasuyu	Chinchay-suyu	North-east quarter of empire
Cuntisuyu	Kunti-suyu	West quarter of empire
Collasuyu	Qolla-suyu	Southern quarter of Empire
Antisuyu	'Anti-suyu	Eastern quarter of empire
Tahuantinsuyu	Tawantin-suyu	The Inca empire
Apurimac	'Apu-rimaq	Apurimac River

279

Classic Form	Phoneticized	
Rimac	Rimaq	Rimac River
Paccari Tampu	Paqari Tampu	'Origin *tambo*'
Tampu-Tocco	Tampu T'oqo	'Tambo Hole' (Mythical Inca place of origin)
Huanacauri		Sacred hill near Cuzco
Coricancha	Qori-kancha	Temple of Sun in Cuzco

KEY TO BIBLIOGRAPHY

*The titles, etc., of the books indicated in the following classification
can be found in the bibliography on pp. 287–324*

(A) *General*

BIBLIOGRAPHIES

Basadre 1938a; Dorsey; Espejo Núñez Horkheimer 1947, 1950;
Markham 1907; Means 1928; Medina; Richardson and Kidder;
Rivet and Créqui-Montfort; Schwab; Tello 1927.

GEOGRAPHY, ENVIRONMENT, AND ECOLOGY

Bowman 1916; Gilmore; Monge 1948; Ogilvie; Sauer 1950a; Sievers;
Troll.

PHYSICAL ANTHROPOLOGY

Boyd; Candela; Eaton 1916; Eickstedt; Gonzales; Hartweg; Hrdlička
1914; Imbelloni 1946b; MacCurdy; Monge; Newman; Quevedo;
Steggerda; Stewart; Stewart and Newman.

LINGUISTICS

Basadre 1938b; Carrera; González Holguín; Markham 1864; Mason
1950; Medina; Middendorf; Rivet 1952; Rivet and Créqui-Montfort;
Rowe 1950; Santo Tomás; Torres Rubio; Tschudi, 1853 1891.

CULTURE SEQUENCE

Bennett 1953b; Kidder 1956, Kidder *et al.* 1963, Lumbreras Means
1917b, 1918e; Steward 1948, 1949a, 1949d; Strong 1948; Willey
1953b.

ABSOLUTE AND RADIOCARBON DATING

Bird 1951; Johnson, Frederick; Johnson, Rainey, Collier, and Flint;
Kubler 1948; Libby; Rowe 1945, 1948b; Wauchope.

(B) *Pre-Inca Culture*

ANCIENT MAN IN AMERICA

Ameghino; Aveleyra Arroyo de Anda and Maldonado-Koerdell; Bird
1938, 1965; Créqui-Montfort and Rivet; Gamarra Dulanto; Hrdlička
1917; Hrdlička *et al.*; Lütken; Jennings and Norbeck; Krieger;
Lanning and Hammel; Macgowan; McCown 1950, 1952; Rivet 1908;
Sellards; Sullivan and Hellman; Ten Kate; Uhle 1928; Walter *et al.*
Wormington.

OLD-WORLD CONTACTS

Carter; Dixon; Ekholm 1965; Estrada and Meggers Gladwin; Heine-Geldern; Heyerdahl; Hutchinson, Silow, and Stephen; Imbelloni 1934; Meggers and Evans; Meggers, Evans and Estrada; Perry; Rivet 1926; Schmidt, Wilhelm; Smith; Sullivan and Hellman.

AGRICULTURAL AND PASTORAL ORIGINS

Cook 1937; Cutler, Kelley and Bonavia; Mangelsdorf; Mangelsdorf and Reeves; Mangelsdorf and Smith Means 1918c; Sauer 1936, 1950b, 1952; Stonor and Anderson; Towle; Yacovleff and Herrera.

TRAVEL AND EXPLORATION

Bingham 1913, 1922; Bollaert; Castelnau; Enock 1907, 1912; Humboldt; Hutchinson 1873; Johnson, George R.; Kosok, 1964; Langlois 1935–6; Mason 1926a, 1952; Means 1918a; Middendorf 1893–5; Nordenskiöld 1906; Orbigny; Raimondi 1874–1913; Seler 1912; Squier 1877; Tschudi 1847, 1869; Uhle 1906c, 1906d; Wiener; Rowe 1954.

PREHISTORIC CULTURE: GENERAL

Baessler 1906b; Bastian; Bennett 1946a, 1946b; Bennett and Bird; Bird 1962; Buse; Bushnell; Canals Frau; Fuhrmann; Hewett; Horkheimer 1950a, 1950b; Joyce 1912; Kidder 1964; Lothrop et al. 1961; Markham 1892; Mead 1924; Means 1919a, 1931; Nordenskiöld 1946; Rivero and Tschudi; Rowe 1958, 1963; Seler 1893; Steward 1949c; Steward (Editor); Tello 1921, 1929, 1942; Thompson; Trimborn 1936; Tschudi 1891; Uhle 1910, 1926, 1935, 1939; Urteaga 1909; Valcárcel 1943–9, 1953; Von Hagen 1965; Wiesse.

ARCHAEOLOGY, GENERAL

Bennett 1945, 1948a; Bennett (Editor); Coe; Hrdlička 1911; Hutchinson 1874; Kauffmann Doig 1963a, 1965; Kidder 1942, 1956; Kroeber 1926c, 1927, 1944, 1948; Newman 1948; Nordenskiöld 1931a; Strong 1943; Uhle 1906a, 1920b; Von Hagen 1949b; Willey 1945, 1948, 1951a.

NORTH COAST

Antze; Bennett 1939, 1950; Bird 1948a, 1948b; Brown; Carrera; Collier; Ford; Ford and Willey; Harcourt 1928a, 1928b; Harth-Terré; Holstein; Horkheimer 1944; Joyce 1913a, 1913b, 1921, 1922; Kelly; Kroeber 1925a, 1926a, 1930; Kroeber and Muelle; Kutscher; Larco Herrera; Larco Hoyle 1938–9, 1941, 1942, 1943, 1944, 1945a, 1945b, 1945c, 1945d, 1946, 1948, 1965; Lilien; Lothrop 1941, 1948, 1951a, 1954; Mason 1926b, 1930; Middendorf 1892; Muelle 1936; O'Neale 1946; Posnansky 1925; Raimondi 1903; Rowe 1942, 1948b, 1948c; Schaedel 1949, 1915b, 1951c; Strong and Evans; Tello 1938, 1956; Towle 1952a; Uhle 1913a, 1920a; Von Hagen 1965; Wardle 1940; Whitaker and Bird; Willey 1947, 1953a.

KEY TO BIBLIOGRAPHY

CENTRAL COAST

Gayton; Harcourt 1922; Jijón y Caamaño 1949; Kroeber 1925b, 1926b, 1954; Lanning 1963; Lothrop 1950; Lothrop and Mahler 1957a; Muelle 1935; Patterson and Lanning Reiss and Stübel; Strong 1925; Strong and Corbett; Strong and Willey; Strong, Willey, and Corbett; Stumer; Tabio 1965; Tello and Miranda; Uhle 1903, 1908a, 1913c; Víllar Córdova 1935; Wallace; Willey 1943a, 1943b; Willey and Corbett.

SOUTH COAST

Berthon; Cañas; Carrión Cachot 1931, 1949; Doering 1927; Donnan; Engel; Gayton and Kroeber; González de la Rosa 1908; Kosok and Reiche; Kroeber 1937, 1953; Kroeber and Strong; Larrabure and Unánue; Levillier, Jean; Lothrop and Mahler 1957b; Mason 1932; Menzel; O'Neale 1932, 1935, 1936, 1937, 1942; Putman; Reiche; Root 1949a; Sawyer; Seler 1923; Squier; Stafford; Strong 1957; Tello 1917, 1928, 1959, Uhle 1913b, 1917b, 1919a, 1919b, 1922, 1924a, 1924b, 1924c, 1924d; Wardle 1939; Wendt, Kroeber, 1956; Soldi; Volcarcel 1932; Wallace 1962; Yacovleff 1931; Yacovleff and Muelle.

NORTHERN HIGHLANDS

Bandelier 1907; Bennett 1942, 1943, 1944; Casdich; Casafranca, Engel 1956; Enock 1905; Espejo Núñez; Ishida et al.; Izami and Sohol; Kauffmann Doig 1963b; Kinzl; Kroeber 1953; Langlois; Lathrap; Markham 1910b; McCown 1945; Polo; Raimondi; Reichlen; Schaedel 1948b, 1948c; Tello 1923, 1930, 1943, 1961; Willey 1951b.

CENTRAL HIGHLANDS

Bennett 1953a; Bingham 1911, 1912a, 1912b, 1913, 1914, 1915a, 1915b, 1916, 1922, 1930, 1948; Bonavia; Bowman 1912; Collier 1962a; Fejos; Flores Espinoza Franco Inojosa; Franco Inojosa and González; Kubler 1952; Pardo; Rowe 1944; Rowe, Collier, and Willey; Saville 1926; Tschopik, Harry; Uhle 1920c; Valcárcel 1924, 1933, 1934–5, 1939; 1946; Víllar Córdova 1923; Von Hagen 1949a; 1952a.

SOUTHERN HIGHLANDS

Ballivián; Bandelier 1905, 1910, 1911; Bennett 1934, 1936, 1948b; Casanova; Créqui-Montfort; Fung de Lanning; González de la Rosa 1910; Kidder II; Lothrop 1937; Markham 1910b; Means 1918f; Menghin; Menghin and Schroeder; Nestler; Ponce Sanginés; Posnansky 1911a, 1911b, 1913, 1914, 1946; Rowe 1956; Rydén; Schaedel 1948a; Stübel and Uhle; Tschopik, Harry, 1950; Tschopik, Marion; Uhle 1898; Valcárcel 1935.

THE ANCIENT CIVILIZATIONS OF PERU

(c) *The Inca and Their Culture*

(See also 'Sources')

GENERAL

Bingham 1917; Brindage; Hanstein; Hewett; Joyce 1912; Karsten; Krickeberg; Markham 1856, 1873, 1910a; Mead 1924; Means 1931, 1938; Murdock; Nordenskiöld 1925–7; Rowe 1946, 1948a; Tello 1937; Urteaga 1931; Verger; Von Hagen 1957.

HISTORICAL

Buchwald; Helps; Imbelloni 1946a; Kubler 1946; Lothrop 1938; Markham 1871; Means 1918b; 1932; Michkin; Nordenskiöld 1917; Prescott; Rowe 1945; Uhle 1912.

ECONOMIC LIFE, FOOD-QUEST, COSTUME, LIFE CYCLE

Baudin 1927b, 1929, 1942, 1958; Carrión Cachot 1923, 1931; Cook 1938; Eaton 1925; Harshberger; Kosok 1940–3; Montell; Torres-Luna; Uhle 1907b; Weberbauer; Yacovleff and Herrera.

ARCHITECTURE, ENGINEERING, TRANSPORTATION

Bennett 1949a; Kosok 1942; Lothrop 1932; Means 1942; Oyague y Calderón; Regal; Von Hagen 1952b.

POLITICAL AND SOCIAL ORGANIZATION

Antonio; Baudin 1927a, 1928; Belaúnde; Castaing; Cosio; Cúneo Vidal; Cunow; Eguiguren; Falcón; Joyce 1913b; Kirchhoff; Latcham; Means 1925a; Minnaert; Saavedra; Trimborn 1923–4; Tudela y Varela; Valdez de la Torre; Zurkalowski.

CRIME AND SIN

Minnaert; Trimborn 1925, 1927; Urteaga.

WAR, CONQUEST, AND COLONIZATION; WEAPONS

Bram; García y Merino; Harcourt 1928b; Means 1919c; Uhle 1907a, 1909, 1917a.

RELIGION

Ávila; Jijón y Caamaño; Lehmann-Nitsche; Métraux; Mortimer; Polo de Ondegardo 1916a, 1917a.

MEDICAL PRACTICES, SURGERY, TREPHINING

Ackerknecht (large bibliography); Lastres *et al.*; Moodie; Muñiz and McGee; Nordenskiöld 1907; Quevedo 1943; Tello 1912; Wrigley.

RECORDING, QUIPU, STANDARDS

Altieri; Bennett 1949b, 1949c; Cipriani; Guimaraes; Kreichgauer; Larco Hoyle 1942, 1943; Locke; Nordenskiöld 1921b, 1925a, 1925b, 1930; Saville 1925; Uhle 1897, 1908b; Wassém 1931, 1940.

284

KEY TO BIBLIOGRAPHY

Basadre; Garcés Bedregal; Harcourt, Raoul and Marie 1925; Izi-kowitz; Mason 1932; Mead 1903; Middendorf 1891; Mitré.

(D) *Arts and Crafts*

ART

Baessler 1902–3, 1928; Bennett 1954; Bird 1962, 1963; Dusselhoff and Linne; Doering 1936, 1952; Greslebin; Hamy; Kelemen; Kroeber 1949; Kubler 1962; Larrea; Lehmann and Doering; Mason 1931; Mead 1906, 1909, 1916a, 1917; Means 1917a, 1918d, 1921a, 1921b; Muelle and Blas; Museum of Modern Art; Posnansky 1913; Rubin de la Borbolla; Sanyen, King; Schmidt, Max; Tello 1918, 1938; Uhle 1889; Yacovleff 1932.

TECHNOLOGY: GENERAL

Bailey; Bennett and Bird 1949; Uhle, 1889–90.

TEXTILES AND WEAVING

Barnett 1909, 1910; Benners; Bird 1947, 1961; Bird and Bellinger; Crawford; Fester; Frödin and Nordenskiöld; Harcourt 1934; Harcourt, Raoul and Marie 1924b; Holmes; Joyce 1921, 1922; King; Levillier, Jean; Mead 1906, 1916b, Means 1925b, 1927, 1930a, 1930b; O'Neale; O'Neale and Clark; O'Neale and Kroeber; Osborne; Schmidt, Max 1910, 1911; Singer; Stafford; Valette; Van Stan; Wardle 1936, 1939, 1944, 1949; Yacovleff and Muelle 1934; Zimmern.

CERAMICS

Bingham 1915b; Doering 1927; Gayton and Kroeber; Harcourt 1922; Harcourt, Raoul and Marie 1924a; Joyce 1913b; Kelly; Kroeber 1925a, 1925b, 1926a, 1926b; Kroeber and Muelle; Kroeber and Strong 1924b; Lastres *et al.*; Lilien; Linné; Mason 1926b, 1932; Menzel; Posnansky 1925; Putnam; Rowe 1942; Rowe and Dawson; Sawyer; Saville 1926; Seler 1923; Strong 1925; Strong and Corbett; Valcárcel 1935; Wardle 1940; Wassermann-San Blas; Willey 1943b, 1949.

METALLURGY

Antze; Baessler 1906a; Bergsøe; Caley and Easby; Easby; Farabee; Harcourt 1928a; Heine-Geldern; Joyce 1913a; Lothrop 1937, 1941, 1950, 1951a, 1951b, 1954; Mason 1930, 1933; Mathewson; Mead 1915; Nordenskiöld 1921a; Orchard; Rivet 1924; Rivet and Arsandaux; Root; Saville 1921; Valcárcel 1930.

WOOD, STONE, FEATHERS, AND MISCELLANEOUS

Lavachery; Mason 1935; Mead 1907; Nordenskiöld 1931b; Rowe 1961; Schaede 1951a; Tello 1918; Uhle 1898, 1906b; Wardle 1948; Yacovleff.

SOURCES

Acosta; Anonymous Conqueror; Arriaga; Avendaño; Ávila; Betanzos; Cabello de Balboa; Cabral; Calancha; Castro and Ortega Morejón; Cieza de León; Cobo; Estete; Garcilaso de la Vega; Gutiérrez de Santa Clara; Jiménez de la Espada; Las Casas; Levillier, Roberto; Markham 1872, 1873; Means 1928; Molina of Cuzco; Molina of Santiago; Montesinos; Morúa; Ocampo; Oviedo y Valdés; Pachacuti-Yamqui Salcamayhua; Pizarro, Hernando; Pizarro, Pedro; Polo de Ondegardo; Poma de Ayala; Quipucamayocs; Ramos Gavilán; Relaciones Geográficas; Román y Zamora; Sancho de la Hoz; Santillán; Sarmiento de Gamboa; Tello 1939; Tito Cusi Yupanqui; Toledo; Valera; Vargas Ugarte; Vega Toral; Xérez; Zarate.

BIBLIOGRAPHY

For subject classification see Key, pp. 281–6

ACKERKNECHT, Erwin H. (1949). 'Medical Practices'. *In* Steward (Editor) 1949, pp. 621–43.

ACOSTA, Father José de (1880). *The Natural and Moral History of the Indies.* Edited by Clements R. Markham. 2 vols, nos 60, 61, Hakluyt Society, London.

(1940). *Historia natural y moral de las Indias.* Mexico.

ALTIERI, Radamés A. (1941). 'Sobre 11 antiguos Kipu peruanos', *Revista del Instituto Antropológico de la Universidad Nacional de Tucumán,* 2, 8, pp. 177–211.

AMEGHINO, Florentino (1880). *La antigüedad del hombre en el Plata,* vol. 1. Paris.

Anonymous Conqueror (1929). *The Conquest of Peru as related by a Member of the Pizarro Expedition.* New York Public Library (facsimile reproduction of the edition of 1534).

ANTONIO, Fray (1920). *Discurso sobre la descendencia y gobierno de los Incas.* Colección de Libros y Documentos referentes a la historia del Perú, Ser. 2, vol. 3, pp. 1–53.

ANTZE, Gustav (1930). 'Metallarbeiten aud dem nördlichen Peru. Ein Beitrag zur Kenntnis ihrer Formen', *Mitteilungen aus dem Museum für Völkerkunde in Hamburg,* vol. 15, pp. 1–63. Hamburg.

ARRIAGA, Pablo José de (1920) (1621). *Extirpación de la idolatría del Perú.* Col. Libs. Docs. refs. hist. Perú. Lima.

AVELEYRA ARROYO DE ANDA, Luis, and Manuel MALDONADO-KOERDELL (1952). 'Asociación de artefactos con mamut en el pleistoceno superior de la cuenca de México', *Revista Mexicana de Estudios Antropológicos,* 13, 1, pp. 3–29. Mexico.

AVENDAÑO, Hernando de (1648). *Sermones de los misterios de nuestra Santa Fe Católica, en lengua Castellana, y la general del Inca.* Lima.

ÁVILA, Father Francisco de (1873). 'A Narrative of the Errors, False Gods, and other Superstitions and Diabolical Rites in which the Indians of Huarochiri lived in Ancient Times.' Translated and edited by Clements R. Markham in *Rites and Laws of the Yncas,* pp. 122–47. Hakluyt Society, London.

(1939). 'Dämonen und Zauber im Inkareich, aus dem Khetschua übersetzt und eingeleitet von Dr. Hermann Trimborn', *Quellen und Forschungen. Geschichte der Geographie und Völkerkunde,* vol. 4. Leipzig.

AYRES, F. D. (1961). 'Rubbings from Chavín de Huántar, Peru', *American Antiquity,* vol. 27, pp. 238–45.

BAESSLER, Arthur (1902–3). *Ancient Peruvian Art.* 4 vols, Berlin and New York.

(1906a). *Altperuanische Metallgeräte.* Berlin.

(1906b). *Peruanische Mumien*. Berlin.

(1928). *L'Art précolombien*. Paris.

BAILEY, Truman (n.d.). *The Manual Industries of Peru*. Museum of Modern Art, New York.

BALLIVIAN, Manuel Vicente (1910). *Monumentos prehistóricos de Tiahuanaco*. La Paz.

BANDELIER, Adolf Francis (1905). 'The Aboriginal Ruins of Sillustani, Peru', *American Anthropologist*, VII, pp. 49–68.

(1907). *The Indians and Aboriginal Ruins near Chachapoyas, Northern Peru*. New York.

(1910). *The Islands of Titicaca and Koati*. New York.

(1911). 'The Ruins at Tiahuanaco', *American Antiquarian Society Proceedings*, XXI, pp. 218–65.

BARNETT, Anna (1909). 'Étude technologique d'un tissu péruvien', *Journal de la Société des Américanistes*, VI, pp. 265–8.

(1910). 'Étude sur la mode de fabrication des frondes péruviennes antiques', *ibid.*, VII, pp. 117–20.

BASALRE, Jorge (1938a). *Bibliografía de la literatura quechua*. Biblioteca de Cultura Peruana, vol. 1. Paris.

(1938b). *Literatura inca (Selección de...)*. Biblioteca de Cultura Peruana, Primera Serie, no. 1. Paris.

BASTIAN, Adolf (1878–89). *Die Culturländer des alten America*. 3 vols., Berlin.

BAUDIN, Louis (1927a). 'Une Expérience socialiste: le Pérou des Inka', *Journal des Économistes*, LXXXVII, pp. 506–19. Paris.

(1927b). 'La Formation de l'élite et l'enseignement de l'histoire dans l'empire des Inka', *Rev. des Études Historiques*, 93rd year, pp. 107–114. Paris.

(1928). *L'Empire socialiste des Inka*. Institut d'Ethnologie, Travaux et Mémoires, vol. 5. Paris.

(1929). 'L'Organisation économique de l'empire des Incas', *Rev. de l'Amérique Latine*, XVII, pp. 385–93. Paris.

(1942). *La actualidad del sistema económico de los Incas*. Congreso Internacional de Americanistas, 27, Lima, vol. 2, pp. 175–87.

(1958). *La vida cotidiana en el tiempo do los últimos Incas*. Lima.

BELAÚNDE, Victor Andrés (1908). *El Perú antiguo y los modernos sociólogos*. Lima.

BENNERS, Ethel Ellis (1920). 'Ancient Peruvian Textiles', *Museum Journal*, University Museum, University of Pennsylvania, vol. 11, no. 3, pp. 140–7.

BENNETT, Wendell C. (1934). *Excavations at Tiahuanaco*, Anthropological Papers, American Museum of Natural History, vol. 34, pp. 359–494. New York.

(1936). *Excavations in Bolivia*, *ibid.*, vol. 35, pp. 329–507. New York.

(1939). *Archaeology of the North Coast of Peru*, *ibid.*, vol. 37, pp. 1–153. New York.

(1942). *Chavín Stone Carving*. Yale Anthropological Studies, vol. 3. New Haven, Connecticut.

(1943). 'The Position of Chavín in Andean Sequences', *Proceedings of the American Philosophical Society*, vol. 86, no. 2, pp. 323–7. Philadelphia.

(1944). *The North Highlands of Peru*, Anthropological Papers, American Museum of Natural History, vol. 39, pt 1. New York.

(1945). 'Interpretations of Andean Archeology', *Transactions of the New York Academy of Sciences*, Ser. 2, vol. 7, pp. 95–9. New York.

(1946a). 'The Andean Highlands: An Introduction'. *In* Steward (Editor) (1946), pp. 1–60.

(1946b). 'The Archeology of the Central Andes'. *Ibid.*, pp. 61–147.

(1948a). 'The Peruvian Co-tradition'. *In* Bennett (Editor) (1948), pp. 1–7.

(1948b). 'A Revised Sequence for the South Titicaca Basin'. *Ibid.*, pp. 90–2.

(1949a). 'Architecture and Engineering'. *In* Steward (Editor) (1949), p. 1–65.

(1949b). 'Numbers, Measures, Weights and Calendars'. *Ibid.*, pp. 601–10.

(1949c). 'Mnemonic and Recording Devices'. *Ibid.*, pp. 611–19.

(1950). *The Gallinazo Group, Virú Valley, Peru*. Yale University Publications in Anthropology, 43. New Haven.

(1953a). *Excavations at Wari, Ayacucho, Peru. Ibid.*, 49. New Haven.

(1953b). 'New World Culture History: South America'. In *Anthropology Today*, pp. 211–25. Chicago.

(1954). *Ancient Arts of the Andes*. Museum of Modern Art. New York.

BENNETT, Wendell C. (Editor) (1948). *A Reappraisal of Peruvian Archaeology*. Memoir 4, Society for American Archaeology. Menasha.

BENNETT, Wendel C., and Junius B. BIRD (1960 Revised edition). *Andean Culture History*. Handbook Series No. 15, American Museum of Natural History. New York.

BERGSØE, Paul (1937). *The Metallurgy and Technology of Gold and Platinum among the pre-Columbian Indians*. A, *Ingeniørvidenskabeliege Skrifter*, A, no. 44. Copenhagen.

(1938). *The Gilding Process and the Metallurgy of Copper and Lead among the pre-Columbian Indians. Ibid.*, no. 46. Copenhagen.

BERTHON, Paul (1911). *Étude sur le précolombien du Bas-Pérou*. Nouvelles archives des missions scientifiques, fascicule 4. Paris.

BETANZOS, Juan de (1880). *Suma y narración de los Incas*. Ed. Marcos Jiménez de la Espada. Biblioteca Hispano-Ultramarina, vol. 5. Madrid.

BINGHAM, Hiram (1911). 'The Ruins of Choqquequirau'. *American Anthropologist*, XII, pp. 505–25.

(1912a). 'Vitcos, the last Inca Capital', *American Antiquarian Society Proceedings*, XXII, pp. 135–96.

(1912b). 'The Discovery of Pre-historic Human Remains near Cuzco, Peru', *American Journal of Science*, XXXIII, pp. 297–305.

(1913). 'In the Wonderland of Peru', *National Geographic Magazine*, vol. 24, no. 4, pp. 387–573. Washington, D.C.

(1914). 'The Ruins of Espíritu Pampa, Peru', *American Anthropologist*, XVI, pp. 185–99.

(1915a). 'The Story of Machu Picchu', *National Geographic Magazine*, February 1915. Washington.

(1915b). 'Types of Machu Picchu Pottery', *American Anthropologist*, XVII, pp. 251–271.

(1916). 'Further Explorations in the Land of the Incas', *National Geographic Magazine*, May 1916. Washington.

(1917). *The Inca Peoples and their Culture*. International Congress of Americanists XIX, pp. 253–60. Washington.

(1922). *Inca Land*. Boston.

(1930). *Machu Picchu, a Citadel of the Inca*. New Haven.

(1948). *Lost City of the Incas*. New York.

BIRD, Junius B. (1938). 'Antiquity and Migrations of the Early Inhabitants of Patagonia', *Geographical Review*, 38, 2, pp. 250–75.

(1947). 'A Pre-Spanish Peruvian Ikat', *Bulletin, Needle and Bobbin Club*, vol. 31, nos. 1 & 2, pp. 73–7. New York.

(1948a). 'Preceramic Cultures in Chicama and Virú'. *In* Bennett (Editor) (1948), pp. 21–8.

(1948b). 'America's Oldest Farmers', *Natural History*, 57, 7, pp. 296–303, 334, 335. New York, 1948.

(1951). 'South American Radiocarbon Dates'. *In* Johnson (Editor) (1951), pp. 37–49.

(1961). 'Textile Designing and Samplers in Peru'. *In* Lothrop and others, pp. 299–316.

(1962). 'Art and Life in Ancient Peru', *Curator*, 2, pp. 145–209. New York.

(1963). 'Pre-ceramic Art from Huaca Prieta, Chicama Valley', *Nawpa Pacha* I, pp. 29–34. Berkeley.

(1965). 'The Concept of a "Pre-Projectile Point" Cultural Stage in Chile and Peru', *American Antiquity*, vol. 31, no. 2, pp. 262–70.

BIRD, Junius B., and Louisa BELLINGER (1954). *Paracas Fabrics and Nazca Needlework*. Washington.

BOLLAERT, William (1860). *Antiquarian, Ethnological, and Other Researches in New Granada, Ecuador, Peru, and Chili, with Observations on the Pre-Incarial, Incarial, and Other Monuments of Peruvian Nations*. London.

BONAVIA, Duccio (1964). *Investigaciones en la Ceja de Selva de Ayacucho*. Museo Nacional de Antropología y Arqueología. Lima.

BOWMAN, Isaiah (1912). 'A Buried Wall at Cuzco and its Relation to the Question of a Pre-Inca Race', *American Journal of Science*, XXXIV, pp. 497–509.

(1916). *The Andes of Southern Peru*. New York.

BOYD, William C. (1950). 'Blood Groups of South American Indians. *In* Steward (Editor) (1950), pp. 91–5.

BRAM, Joseph (1941). *An Analysis of Inca Militarism.* Monographs of the American Ethnological Society, No. 4. New York.

BROWN, C. Barrington (1926). 'On Stone Implements from North-West Peru', *Man*, vol. 26, pp. 97–101. London.

BRUNDAGE, Burr C. (1963). *Empire of the Inca.* Norman, Oklahoma.

BUCHWALD, Otto von (1919). 'Los primeros Incas', *Boletín de la Sociedad Ecuatoriana de Estudios Históricos Americanos*, VII, pp. 115–121.

BUSE, H. (1962). *Peru 10,000 Años.* Lima.

BUSHNELL, G. H. S. (1949). 'Ancient Peoples of the Andes', *Science News*, no. 13, pp. 58–86. Penguin Books, Harmondsworth.

(1956). *Peru.* London.

CABELLO DE BALBOA, Miguel (1840). 'Histoire du Pérou'. Translated and edited by H. Ternaux-Compans, in *Voyages, relations, et mémoires originaux pour servir a l'histoire de la découverte de l'Amérique.* Paris.

CABRAL, Jorge (1913). *Los cronistas é historiadores de Indias y el problema de las dinastías de la monarquía peruana.* Buenos Aires.

CALANCHA, Antonio de la (1638). *Corónica moralizada del orden de San Agustín en el Perú, con sucesos egemplares en esta monarquía.* Barcelona.

CALEY, Earle R., and Dudley T. EASBY, Jr. (1959). 'The Smelting of Sulfide Ores of Copper in Pre-Conquest Peru', *American Antiquity*, vol. 25, no. 1, pp. 59–65.

CANALS FRAU, Salvador (1950). *Prehistoria de América.* Buenos Aires.

CAÑAS, Francisco (1854). *Exploración de las islas de Chincha con tres planos.* Lima.

CANDELA, P. B. (1943). 'Blood Group Tests on Tissues of Paracas Mummies', *American Journal of Physical Anthropology*, vol. 1, pp. 65–7 Philadelphia.

CARDICH, M. Agusto (1959). 'Los yacimientos de Lauricocha, Perú', *Revista del Centro Argentino de Estudios Prehistóricos.* Buenos Aires.

(1960). 'Investigaciones prehistóricas en los Andes peruanos'. *In* Matos Mendieta (Editor), pp. 89–118.

(1964). 'Lauricocha. Fundamentos para una prehistoria de los Andes Centrales', *Studia Prehistórica* III. Centro Argentino de Estudios Prehistóricos. Buenos Aires.

CARRERA FERNANDO DE LA (1939). *Arte de la lengua yunga* (1644). Publicaciones Especiales del Instituto de Antropología de la Universidad Nacional de Tucumán, no. 3. Tucumán, Argentina.

CARRIÓN CACHOT, Rebeca (1923). 'La mujer y el niño en el antiguo Perú, *Inca*, I, pp. 329–54.

(1931). 'La indumentaria en la antigua cultura de Paracas', *Wira Kocha*, vol. 1, no. 1, pp. 37–86. Lima.

(1948). 'La Cultura Chavín', *Revista Museo Nacional de Antropología y Arqueología*, vol. 2, pp. 99–172. Lima.

(1949). *Paracas, Cultural Elements*. Corporación Nacional de Turismo. Lima, Perú.

CARTER, George F. (1950). 'Plant Evidence for Early Contacts with America', *Southwestern Journal of Anthropology*, 6, 2, 161–82. Albuquerque.

(1953). 'Plants across the Pacific'. *In* 'Asia and North America; Transpacific Contacts', Memoir 9, Society for American Archaeology, pp. 62–71.

CASAFRANCA, José (1960). 'Los nuevos sitios arqueológicos Chavinoides en el Departamento de Ayacucho'. *In* Matos Mendieta (Editor), pp. 325–33.

CASANOVA, Eduardo (1942). 'Los yacimientos arqueológicos en la península de Copacabana', *Anales del Museo Argentino de Ciencias Naturales 'Bernardino Rivadavia'*, vol. 40, pp. 333–99.

CASTAING, Alphonse (1884). *Le Communisme au Pérou*. Paris.

CASTELNAU, Francis de (1852). *Expédition dans les parties centrales de l'Amérique du Sud. Troisième partie: Antiquités des Incas et autres peuples anciens*. Paris.

CASTRO, Cristóbal de, and Diego Ortega MOREJÓN (1936). *Relación y declaración del modo que este valle de Chincha y sus comarcanos se governavan . . . etc.* (1558). 'Quellen zur Kulturgeschichte des präkolumbischen Amerika', *Studien zur Kulturkunde*, vol. 3. Stuttgart.

CIEZA DE LEÓN, Pedro de (1554). *Parte primera de la chrónica del Perú, que tracta de la demarcación . . . etc.* Antwerp.

(1864). *The travels of Pedro de Cieza de León. A.D. 1532–1550* (contained in the first part of his chronicle of Perú). Hakluyt Society, no. 33. London.

(1880). *Sefunda parte de la crónica del Perú, que trata del señorío de los Incas Yupanquis . . . etc.* Biblioteca Hispano-Ultramarina, vol. 5. Madrid.

(1883). *The Second Part of the Chronicle of Peru*. Translated and edited by Clements R. Markham. No. 68, Hakluyt Society, London.

(1932). *Parte primera de la crónica del Perú*. Edición Espasa-Calpe, Madrid. (Also many other editions.)

CIPRIANI, Lidio (1928). *Su due 'quipus' del Museo Nazionale di Antropologia e Etnologia di Firenze*. International Congress of Americanists, XXII, pt 1, pp. 471–80. Rome.

COBO, Bernabé (1890–5). *Historia del Nuevo Mundo*. Ed. Marcos Jiménez de la Espada. 4 vols, Sociedad de bibliófilos andaluces, Seville.

COE, Michael D. (1960). 'Archaeological Linkages with North and South America at La Victoria, Guatemala', *American Anthropologist*, vol. 62 pp. 363–93.

(1962). 'An Olmec Design on an Early Peruvian Vessel', *American Antiquity*, vol. 27, pp. 579–80.

COLLIER, Donald (1955). 'Cultural Chronology and Change as Reflected in the Ceramics of the Virú Valley, Peru'. *Fieldiana: Anthropology*, vol. 43. Chicago Natural History Museum, Chicago.

(1961). 'Agriculture and Civilization on the Coast of Peru'. *In The Evolution of Horticultural Systems in Native South America*, pp. 101–9. Sociedad de Ciencias Naturales La Salle, Caracas.

(1962a). 'The Central Andes', *Viking Fund Publications in Anthropology*, no. 32, pp. 165–76. New York.

(1962b). 'Archaeological Investigations in the Casma Valley', *Akten des 34 International Amerikanistenkongressen, Wien*, 1960, pp. 411–17, Vienna.

COOK, O. F. (1937). *El Perú como centro de domesticación de plantas y animales*. Imprenta del Museo Nacional, Lima.

(1938). *Campos de cultivo en andenería de los antiguos peruanos*. Translated by Federico Ponce de León. Cuzco.

COSIO, Felix (1916). *La propiedad colectiva del ayllu*. Cuzco.

CRAWFORD, M. D. C. (1915). *Peruvian Textiles*. Anthropological Papers of the American Museum of Natural History, 12, 3, pp. 52–104. New York.

(1916a). *Peruvian Fabrics. Ibid.*, 12, 4, pp. 105–91. New York.

(1916b). *The Cotton of Ancient Peru*. Boston.

(1916c). 'The Loom in the New World', American Museum of Natural History, *Journal*, XVI, pp. 381–6.

CRÉQUI-MONTFORT, Count G. de (1906a). *Fouilles de la mission scientifique française à Tiahuanaco*. International Congress of Americanists XIV, pt 2, pp. 531–51. Stuttgart.

(1906b). Fouilles dans la nécropole de Calama. *Ibid.*, pp. 551–67.

CRÉQUI-MONTFORT, Count G. de and Paul RIVET (1914a). 'L'Origine des aborigènes de Pérou et de la Bolivie', *Comptes-rendus des séances de l'Académie des Inscriptions et Belles-Lettres*, 1914, pp. 196–202. Paris.

(1914b). *L'Origine des aborigènes des hauts plateaux boliviens et péruviens*. Institut français d'anthropologie, II, p. 39.

CÚNEO VIDAL, Rómulo (1914). 'Del concepto del "Ayllu" ', *Boletín de la Sociedad Geográfica de Lima*, XXX, pp. 4–9.

CUNOW, Heinrich (1896). *Diesoziale Verfassung des Inkareichs*. Stuttgart.

(1898. *Die soziale Verfassung des Inkareichs*. Brunswick.

(1930). *El sistema de parentesco peruano y las communidades gentilicias de los Incas*. Translated by María Woitscheck. Paris.

CUTLER, Hugh C. (1946). 'Races of Maize in South America', *Botanical Museum Leaflets*, vol. 12, no. 8, pp. 257–91. Harvard University, Cambridge, Mass.

DISSELHOFF, H. D., and S. LINNE (1961). *The Art of Ancient America; Civilizations of Central and South America*. New York.

DIXON, Roland B. (1933). 'Contacts with America across the Southern Pacific'. *In* Diamond Jenness, *The American Aborigines; their Origin and Antiquity, pp.* 313–53. Toronto.

DOERING, Heinrich Ubbelohde (1926). 'Tonplastik aus Nazca', *Ipek*, vol. 3, pp. 167–76.

(1936). *Old Peruvian Art*. London.

(1952). *The Art of Ancient Peru*. New York.

(1959). 'Bericht über Archäologische Feldarbeiten in Peru, II', *Ethnos*, nos. 1–2. Stockholm.

DONNAN, Christopher B. (1964). 'An Early House from Chilca, Peru', *American Antiquity*, vol. 30, no. 2, pp. 137–44.

DORSEY, George A. (1898). *A Bibliography of the Anthropology of Peru*. Field Museum of Natural History, Anthropological Series, vol. 2, no. 2. Chicago.

EASBY, Dudley T., Jr. (1955a). 'Los vasos retratos de metal del Perú: Cómo fueron elaborados?', *Revista del Museo Nacional*, vol. 24, pp. 137–53. Lima.

(1955b). 'Sahagún y los orfebres precolombinos de México', *Abales del Instituto de Antropología y Historia*, vol. 9, pp. 85–177. Mexico.

(1956a) 'Ancient American Goldsmiths', *Natural History*, vol. 65, no. 8, pp. 401–9. New York.

(1956b). 'Orfebrería y orfebres precolombinos', *Anales del Instituto de Arte Americano*, vol. 9, pp. 9–26. Buenos Aires.

(1966). 'Early Metallurgy in the New World', *Scientific American*, vol. 214, no. 4, pp. 72–8, 81.

EATON, George F. (1916). *The Collection of Osteological Material from Machu Picchu*. Memoirs, Connecticut Academy of Arts and Sciences, vol. 5. New Haven.

(1925). *Food Animals of the Peruvian Highlands*. International Congress of Americanists, XXI, pr 2, pp. 61–6. Göteborg.

EGUIGUREN, Luís A. (1914). *El ayllu peruano y su condición legal*. Lima.

EICKSTEDT, Egon F. von (1934). *Rassenkunde und Rassengeschichte der Menschheit*. Stuttgart.

EKHOLM, Gordon F. (1950). 'Is American Indian Culture Asiatic?' *Natural History*, 59, 8, pp. 344–51, 382. New York.

(1965). 'Transpacific Contacts'. *In* Jennings and Norbeck, pp. 489–510.

ENGEL, Frederic (1956). 'Curayacu, A Chavinoid Site', *Archaeology*, vol. 9, pp. 98–105.

(1957). 'Early Sites on the Peruvian Coast,' *Southwestern Journal of Anthropology*, vol. 13, pp. 54–68.

(1957b). 'Sites et établissements sans céramique dans la côte péruvienne', *Journal de la Société des Américanistes*, vol. 46, pp. 67–155. Paris.

(1957c). 'Early Sites in the Pisco Valley of Peru – Tambo Colorado', *American Antiquity*, vol. 23, pp. 34–45.

(1958). 'Algunos datos con referencia a los sitios precerámicos de la costa peruana', *Arqueológicas*, vol. 1, no. 3. Lima.

(1960). 'Un groupe humain datant de 5000 ans a Paracas, Pérou', *Journal de la Société des Américanistes*, vol. 49, pp. 7–35. Paris.

BIBLIOGRAPHY

(1963a). 'A Preceramic Settlement on the Central Coast of Peru: Asia, Unit 1'. *Transactions*, vol. 53, no. 3. American Philosophical Society, Philadelphia.

(1963b). 'Notes relatives à des explorations archéologiques à Paracas', *Travaux de l'Institut Français d'Études Andines*, Tomo IX. Paris.

(1964). 'El precerámico sin algodón en la costa del Perú', *XXXV Congreso Internacional de Americanistas*, vol. 3, pp. 141–52. México.

ENOCK, C. Reginald (1905). 'The Ruins of "Huánuco Viejo" or Old Huánuco', *Journal of the Royal Geographical Society*, XXVI, pp. 153–79. London.

(1907). *The Andes and the Amazon*. London.

(1912). *Peru*. London (3rd ed., improved).

ESPEJO NUÑEZ, Julio. (1964). Bibliografía arqueológica de Chavín. Lima.

ESTETE, Miguel de (1872). *The Narrative of the Journey made by . . . Hernando Pizarro . . . from the city of Caxamalca to Parcama, and thence to Xauxa*. Translated and edited by Clements R. Markham, and inserted in pp. 74–94 of his edition of Xérez. Hakluyt Society, London.

(1924). *Noticia del Perú*. Edition H. H. Urteaga and C. A. Romero. Colección de Librosy Documentos referentes a la historia del Perú, Ser. 2, vol. 8, pp. 3–56. Lima.

ESTRADA, Emilio, and Betty J. MEGGERS (1961). 'A Complex of Traits of Probable Transpacific Origin on the Coast of Ecuador', *American Anthropologist*, vol. 63, pp. 913–39.

ESTRADA, Emilio, Betty J. MEGGERS, and Clifford EVANS (1962). 'Possible Transpacific Contact on the Coast of Ecuador', *Science*, vol. 135, no. 3501, pp. 371–2.

FALCÓN, Francisco (1918). *Relación sobre el gobierno de los Incas*. Edited by Drs Horacio H. Urteaga and Carlos A. Romero. Colección de Libros y Documentos referentes a la historia del Perú, Ser. 1, vol. 11, pp. 135–76. Lima.

FARABEE, William Curtis (1921). 'The Use of Metals in Prehistoric America', *Museum Journal*, vol. 12, no. 1. Philadelphia.

FEJOS, Paul (1944). *Archaeological Explorations in the Cordillera Vilcabamba, Southeastern Peru*. Viking Fund Publications in Anthropology, no. 3. New York.

FESTER, G. A. (1954). 'Some Dyes of the Ancient South American Civilizations', *Dyestuffs*, vol. 4, no. 9. Bulletin National Aniline Division, Allied Chemical and Dye Corporation, New York.

FLORES ESPINOSA, Isabel (1960). 'Wichqana: Sitio temprano en Ayacucho'. *In* Matos Mendieta (Editor), pp. 335–44.

FORD, James Alfred (1954). 'The History of a Peruvian Valley', *Scientific American*, vol. 191, no. 2 (August), pp. 28–34.

FORD, James Alfred, and Gordon R. WILLEY (1949). *Surface Survey of the Virú Valley, Peru*. Anthropological Papers of the American Museum of Natural History, 43, 1. New York.

FRANCO INOJOSA, José María (1935–7). 'Janan Kosko', *Revista del Museo Nacional de Lima*, vol. 4, pp. 209–33; vol. 6, pp. 201–31.

FRANCO INOJOSA, José María, and Alejandro GONZÁLEZ (1936). 'Exploraciones arqueológicas en al Perú', *Revista del Museo Nacional de Lima*, vol. 5, pp. 157–83.

FRÖDIN, Otto, and Erland NORDENSKIÖLD (1918). *Über Zwirnen und Spinnen bei den Indianern Südamerikas*. Göteborg.

FUHRMANN, Ernst (1922a). *Reich der Inka*. Hagen.

(1922b). *Peru ii*. Hagen.

FUNG DE LANNING, Rosa (1959). 'Informe preliminar de las excavaciones efectuades en el Abrigo Rocoso No. 1 de Tschopik'. In *Actas y Trabajos del II Congreso Nacional de Historia del Peru*, vol. 1, pp. 253–74. Lima.

GAMARRA DULANTO, Luís (1942). 'Apuntes sobre el guano del Peru y la antigüedad del hombre en América', International Congress of Americanists, *Proceedings*, Session 27 (Lima, 1939), vol. 1, pp. 123–127.

GARCÉS BEDREGAL, Miguel (1942). 'Evolución técnica de la música peruana, gama eptafónica', *Actas y Trabajos Científicos del xxvii Congreso Internacional de Americanistas de Lima* (1939), t. 11, pp. 25–32. Lima.

GARCIA Y MERINO, Manuel (1894). 'Proyectiles primitivos de los peruanos', *Boletín de la Sociedad Geográfica de Lima*, IV, pp. 210–217.

GARCILASO DE LA VEGA (El Inca) (1722). *Historia general del Perú*, 2nd edn. Madrid.

(1723). *Primera parte de los Commentarios reales que tratan, de el origin de los Incas, reies, qve fveron del Perú, de sv idolatría, lcies, y govierno, en paz, y en guerra: de svs vidas, y conquistas: y de todo lo que fue aquel imperio, y su república, antes que los Españoles pasaran á él*. 2nd edn. Madrid.

(1869–71). *The First Part of the Royal Commentaries of the Yncas*. Translated and edited by Clements R. Markham. 2 vols, nos 41, 45, Hakluyt Society, London.

GAYTON, A. H. (1927). *The Uhle Collections from Nievería*. University of California Publications in American Archaeology and Ethnology, vol. 21, pp. 305–29. Berkeley.

GAYTON, A. H., and A. L. KROEBER (1927). *The Uhle Pottery Collections from Nazca*. *Ibid.*, vol. 24. pp. 1–46. Berkeley.

GILMORE, RAYMOND M. (1950). 'Fauna and Ethnozoology of South America'. *In* Steward (Editor) (1950), pp. 345–464.

GLADWIN, Harold S. (1947). *Men out of Asia*. New York.

GONZÁLES, Alberto Rex (1961). 'Les squelettes des sites sans céramique de la Côte du Pérou', *Journal de la Société des Américanistes*, Tomo L. Paris.

GONZÁLEZ DE LA ROSA, Manuel (1908). 'Estudio de las antigüedades halladas bajo el huano', *Revista Histórica*, II, pp. 180–99. Lima.

(1910). *Les Deux Tiahuanaco, leurs problèmes et leur solution.* 16th International Congress of Americanists, pp. 405–28. Vienna.

GONZÁLEZ HOLGUIN, Diego (1901). *Arte y diccionario qquechua-español.* Lima.

GRESLEBIN, Hector (1926). *El arte prehistórico peruano. Anales de la Sociedad Argentina de Estudios Geográficos,* t. II, num, 2, pp. 1–44. Buenos Aires.

GUIMARAES, Enrique de (1907). 'Algo sobre el quipu. With a Note by Max Uhle', *Revista Histórica,* II, pp. 55–65. Lima.

GUTIÉRREZ DE SANTA CLARA, Pedro (1904–10). *Historia de las guerras civiles del Perú.* Col. libs. docs. refs. hist. América, vols 2, 3, 4, 10 Madrid.

HAMY, E. T. (1897). *Galerie américaine du Musée d'Ethnographie du Trocadéro.* Paris.

HANSTEIN, Otfrid von (1925). *The World of the Incas.* Translated by Anna Barwell. London and New York.

HARCOURT, Raoul d' (1922). 'La Céramique de Cajamarquilla-Nievería'. *Journal de la Société des Américanistes de Paris,* XIV, pp. 107–18.

(1928a). *La Fabrication de certains grelots métalliques chez les Yunka.* International Congress of Americanists, XXII, pt I, pp. 541–3. Rome.

(1928b) *Les Vêtements et les armes d'un guerrier Yunka d'après le décor d'un lécythe de la région de Trujillo. Ibid.,* pp. 545–8. Rome.

(1934). *Les Textiles anciens du Pérou et leurs techniques.* Paris.

HARCOURT, Raoul, and Marie d' (1924a). *La Céramique ancienne du Pérou.* Paris.

(1924b). *Les Tissus indiens du Vieux Pérou.* Paris.

(1925). *La Musique des Incas et ses survivances.* Paris.

HARSHBERGER, J. W. (1898). 'The Uses of Plants among the Ancient Peruvians', *Bulletin of the Free Museum of Science and Art,* vol. 1, no. 3. Philadelphia.

HARTH-TERRÉ, Emilio (1923). 'La fortaleza de Chuquimancu', *Revista arqueológica del Museo Larco-Herrera,* no. 2. Lima.

HARTWEG, Raul (1958). 'Les squelettes des sites sans céramique de la côte du Pérou', *Journal de la Société des Américanistes,* vol. 47, pp. 179–98.

HEINE-GELDERN, Robert von (1954). 'Die asiatische Herkunft der süd-amerikanischen Metalltechnik', *Paideuma,* vol. 5, pp. 347–423. Bamberg.

HELPS, Sir Arthur (1900). *The Spanish Conquest in America.* London and New York.

HEWETT, Edgar Lee (1939). *Ancient Andean Life.* New York.

HEYERDAHL, Thor (1950). *Kon-Tiki.* London.

(1952). *American Indians in the Pacific.* London.

HOLMES, William H. (1889). *Textile Fabrics of Ancient Peru.* Bureau of American Ethnology, Bulletin 7. Washington.

HOLSTEIN, Otto (1927). 'Chan-Chan: Capital of the Great Chimu', *Geographical Review*, vol. 27, pp. 36–61. New York.

HORKHEIMER, Hans (1944). *Vistas arqueológicas del Noroeste del Perú.* Trujillo.

(1947). 'Breve bibliografía sobre el Perú prehispánico', *Fénix*, no. 5, pp. 200–82. Lima.

(1950a) *El Perú prehispánico.* Lima.

(1950b). *Guía bibliográfica de los principales sítios arqueológicos del Perú.* Lima.

HRDLIČKA, Aleš (1911). *Some Results of Recent Anthropological Exploration in Peru.* Smithsonian Institution Miscellaneous Collections, vol. 56, no. 16. Washington.

(1914). *Anthropological Work in Peru in 1913, with Notes on the Pathology of the Ancient Peruvians. Ibid.*, vol. 61, no. 18. Washington.

(1917). *The Genesis of the American Indian.* 19th International Congress of Americanists, 1915, pp. 559–68. Washington.

HRDLIČKA, Aleš, W. H. HOLMES, B. WILLIS, F. E. WRIGHT, and C. N. FENNER (1912). *Early Man in South America.* Bulletin 52, Bureau of American Ethnology. Washington.

HUMBOLDT, Baron Alexander von (1810). *Vues des cordillères et monuments des peuples indigènes de l'Amérique.* Paris.

HUTCHINSON, J. B., R. A. SILOW, and S. G. STEPHEN (1947). *The Evolution of Gossypium and the Differentiation of the Cultivated Cottons.* London, New York, and Toronto.

HUTCHINSON, Thomas J. (1873). *Two Years in Peru, with Exploration of its Antiquities.* 2 vols. London.

(1874). 'Explorations amongst Ancient Burial Grounds (chiefly on the Sea-Coast Valleys) of Peru'. Royal Anthropological Institute of Great Britain and Ireland, *Journal*, vol. 3, pp. 311–26. London.

IMBELLONI, José (1934). 'Toki del Perú', *Actas y Trabajos Científicos del xxv Congreso Internacional de Americanistas de La Plata*, 1932, t. II, pp. 253–7. Buenos Aires.

(1946a). *Pachacuti ix* (*El Inkario Crítico*). Buenos Aires.

(1946b). 'Recientes estudios craniológicos sobre los antiguos peruanos', *Boletín bibliográfico de Antropología Americana*, vol. 7, pp. 85–99. Mexico.

ISHIDA, Eichiro, Taiji YAZAWA and others (1960). *Andes: The Report of the University of Tokyo Scientific Expedition to the Andes in 1958.* Tokyo.

IZIKOWITZ, Karl Gustav (1935). *Musical and Other Sound Instruments of the South American Indians: a Comparative Ethnographical Study.* Göteborg.

IZUMI, Seiichi, and SONO, Toshihiko (1963). *Andes 2: Excavations at Kotosh, Peru*, 1960.Tokyo.

JENNINGS, Jesse D., and NORBECK, Edward (Editors) (1964). *Prehistoric Man in the New World.* William March Rice University, Houston.

BIBLIOGRAPHY

JIJÓN Y CAAMAÑO, Jacinto (1919). *La religión del imperio de los Incas.* Quito.

(1949). *Maranga. Contribución al conocimiento de los aborígenes del valle del Rímac, Perú.* Quito.

JIMÉNEZ DE LA ESPADA, Marcos (1879). *Tres relaciones de antigüedades peruanas.* Madrid.

JOHNSON, Frederick (1951). 'Introduction to *Radiocarbon Dating*'. *In* Johnson (Editor) (1951), pp. 1–3.

JOHNSON, Frederick (Editor) (1951). *Radiocarbon Dating.* Memoirs of the Society of American Archaeology, 8. Salt Lake City.

JOHNSON, Frederick, Froelich G. RAINEY, Donald COLLIER, and Richard F. FLINT (1951). 'Radiocarbon Dating: A Summary'. *In* Johnson (Editor) (1951), pp. 58–62.

JOHNSON, GEORGE R. (1930). *Peru from the Air.* American Geographic Society, Special Publications No. 12. New York.

JOYCE, Thomas Athol (1912). *South American Archaeology.* London.

(1913a). 'Note on a Gold Beaker from Lambayeque', *Man*, XIII, pp. 65–6. London.

(1913b). 'The Clan-Ancestor in Animal Form as Depicted on the Ancient Pottery of the Peruvian Coast', *ibid.*, pp. 113–17.

(1921). 'The Peruvian Loom in the Proto-Chimu Period', *ibid.*, XXI, pp. 177–80.

(1922). 'Note on a Peruvian Loom of the Chimu Period', *ibid.*, XXII, pp. 1–2.

KARSTEN, Rafael (1949a). *A Totalitarian State of the Past: the Civilization of the Inca Empire in Ancient Peru.* Helsingfors Societas Scientarum Fennica Commentationes Humaniorum Litterarum, XVI, 1.

(1949b). *Das altperuanische Inkareich und seine Kultur.* Leipzig.

KAUFFMANN DOIG, Federico (1963a). *El Perú arquelógico.* Lima.

(1963b) *Tres étapas pre-Chavín.* Lima.

(1965). 'La cultura Chimú'. *Las grandes civilizaciones del antiguo Perú*, Tomo 4. Lima.

KELEMEN, Pál (1943). *Medieval American Art.* 2 vols. New York.

KELLEY, David H., and Duccio BONAVIA B. (1963). 'New Evidence for Pre-ceramic Maize on the Coast of Peru', *Nawpa Pacha* I, pp. 39–42. Berkeley.

KELLY, Isabel T. (1930). *Peruvian Cumbrous Bowls.* University of California Publications in American Archaeology and Ethnology, XXIV, pp. 325–41, Berkeley, California.

KIDDER II, Alfred (1942). 'Speculations on Andean Origins', *Proceedings, 8th Pan-American Scientific Congress*, vol. 2, p. 161. Washington.

(1943). *Some Early Sites in the Northern Lake Titicaca Basin.* Papers of the Peabody Museum of Archaeology and Ethnology, Harvard University, vol. 27, no. 1. Cambridge, Mass.

(1948). 'The Position of Pucara in Titicaca Basin Archaeology'. *In* Bennett (Editor) (1948), pp. 87–9.

(1956). 'Settlement Patterns, Peru'. *In Prehistoric Settlement Patterns in the New World*. Viking Fund Publications in Anthropology, no. 23, pp. 148–55. New York.

(1964). 'South American High Cultures'. *In* Jennings and Norbeck, 1964, pp. 451–86.

KIDDER II, Alfred, Luis G. LUMBRERAS S., and David B. SMITH (1963). 'Cultural Developments in the Central Andes – Peru and Bolivia'. *In Aboriginal Cultural Development in Latin America*. Smithsonian Miscellaneous Collections, vol. 146, no. 1, pp. 89–101. Washington.

KING, Mary Elizabeth (1965). *Ancient Peruvian Textiles from the Collection of the Textile Museum, Washington, D.C.* A Museum of Primitive Art Book. New York Graphic Society, Greenwich, Conn.

KINZL, Hans (1935). 'Altindianische Siedlungsspuren im Umkreis der Cordillera Blanca'. *In* Philipp Borchers, *Die Weisse Kordillere*, pp. 262–95. Berlin.

KIRCHHOFF, Paul (1949). 'The Social and Political Organization of the Andean Peoples'. *In* Steward (1949), pp. 293–311.

KOSOK, Paul (1940–3). *The Role of Irrigation in Ancient Peru*, 8th American Scientific Congress, vol 2. Washington.

(1942) 'Extensión de la irrigación en el antiguo Perú', *Boletín de la Sociedad Geográfica de la Paz*, no. 64, pp. 30–1. La Paz, Bolivia.

(1964). *Vida, Tierra, y Agua en el antiguo Perú*. Long Island University.

KOSOK, Paul, and María REICHE (1947). 'The Mysterious Markings of Nazca', *Natural History*, vol. 56, no. 5, pp. 200–7 and 237–8. New York.

(1949). 'Ancient Drawings on the Desert of Peru', *Archaeology*, vol. 2, pp. 206–15.

KREICHGAUER, P. D. (1926–8). 'Das Rätsel der Quipus', *Anthropos*, t. XXI, pp. 618–20; t. XXIII, pp. 322–4. Wien.

KRICKEBERG, Walter (1922). 'Die Völker Sudamerikas'. In *Illustrierte Völkerkunde*, G. Buschan (Editor). Stuttgart.

KREIGER, Alex D. (1964). 'Early Man in the New World'. *In* Jennings and Norbeck, pp. 23–81, 1864.

KROEBER, A. L. (1925a). *The Uhle Pottery Collections from Moche*. University of California Publications in American Archaeology and Ethnology, vol. 21, pp. 191–234. Berkeley.

(1925b). *The Uhle Pottery Collections from Supe. Ibid.*, pp. 235–64. Berkeley.

(1926a). *Archaeological Explorations in Peru. Pt i: Ancient Pottery from Trujillo*. Field Museum of Natural History, Anthropological Memoirs, vol. 2, no. 1, pp. 1–43. Chicago, Ill.

(1926b). *The Uhle Pottery Collections from Chancay*. University of California Publications in American Archaeology and Ethnology, vol. 21, pp. 265–304. Berkeley.

(1926c). 'Cultural Stratifications in Peru', *American Anthropologist*, vol. 28, pp. 331–51.

(1927). 'Coast and Highland in Prehistoric Peru', *ibid.*, vol. 29, pp. 625–53.

(1930). *Archaeological Explorations in Peru. Pt ii: The Northern Coast.* Field Museum of Natural History, Anthropological Memoirs, vol. 2, no. 2. Chicago, Ill.

(1937). *Archaeological Explorations in Peru. Pt iv: Cañete Valley. Ibid.*, vol. 2, no. 4. Chicago, Ill.

(1944). *Peruvian Archaeology in* 1942. Viking Fund Publications in Anthropology, no. 4. New York.

(1948). 'Summary and Interpretations'. *In* Bennett (Editor) (1948), pp. 113–21.

(1949). 'Art'. *In* Steward (Editor (1949), pp. 411–92.

(1953). *Paracas Cavernas and Chavín.* University of California Publications in American Archaeology and Ethnology, vol. 40, no. 8, pp. 313–48. Berkeley and Los Angeles.

(1954). 'Proto-Lima; A Middle Period Culture of Peru'. *Fieldiana: Anthropology*, vol. 44, no. 2. Chicago Museum of Natural History, Chicago.

(1956). 'Towards Definition of the Nazca Style'. *University of California Publications in American Archaeology and Ethnology*, vol. 43. Berkeley.

(1963). 'The Methods of Peruvian Archaeology', *Nawpa Pacha* I, pp. 61–71. Berkeley.

KROEBER, A. L., and J. C. MUELLE (1942). 'Cerámica paleteada de Lambayeque', *Revista del Museo Nacional*, vol. 11, pp. 1–24. Lima.

KROEBER, A. L., and W. D. STRONG (1924a). *The Uhle Collections from Chincha.* University of California Publications in American Archaeology and Ethnology, vol. 21, pp. 1–54. Berkeley.

(1924b). *The Uhle Pottery Collections from Ica. Ibid.*, pp. 95–133. Berkeley.

KUBLER, George (1946). 'The Quechua in the Colonial World'. *In* Steward (Editor) (1946), pp. 331–410.

(1948). 'Towards Absolute Time: Guano Archaeology'. *In* Bennett (Editor) (1948), pp. 29–50.

(1952). *Cuzco; Reconstruction of the Town, and Restoration of the Monuments.* UNESCO: Museums and Monuments, III. Paris.

(1962). *The Art and Architecture of Ancient America; The Mexican, Maya, and Andean Peoples.* Pelican History of Art series, z 21. Harmondsworth.

KUTSCHER, Gerdt (1950). *Chimu; eine altindianische Hochkultur.* Berlin.

LANGLOIS, Louis (1935–6). 'De ci de là à travers le Pérou précolombien', *La Géographie*, vol. 64. pp. 297–308; vol. 65, pp. 25–38, 203–11.

(1940). 'Utcubamba, investigaciones arqueológicas en el Departamento de Amazonas (conclusión)', *Revista del Museo Nacional*, vol. 9, pp. 191–228. Lima.

LANNING, Edward P. (1963a). 'A Pre-agricultural Occupation on the Central Coast of Peru', *American Antiquity*, vol. 28, pp. 360–71.

(1963b). 'An Early Ceramic Style from Ancón, Central Coast of Peru', *Nawpa Pacha* I, pp. 47–60. Berkeley.

(1965). 'Early Man in Peru', *Scientific American*, vol. 213, no. 4, pp. 68–76.

LANNING, Edward P., and Eugene A. HAMMEL (1961). 'Early Lithic Industries in Western South America', *American Antiquity*, vol. 27, pp. 139–54.

LARCO HERRERA, Rafael (1928). *La civiltà Yunga*. International Congress of Americanists, XXII, pt 1, pp. 565–81. Rome.

LARCO HOYLE, Rafael (1938–9). *Los Mochicas*. 2 vols. Lima.

(1941). *Los Cupisniques*. Lima.

(1942). 'La escritura mochica sobre pallares', *Revista Geogràfica Americana*, Año IX, vol. 18, 93–103. Buenos Aires.

(1943), 'La escritura peruana sobre pallares', *ibid.*, Año XI, vol. 20, pp. 1–36. Buenos Aires.

(1944). *Cultura Salinar*. 20 pp. Buenos Aires.

(1945a). *La cultura Virú*. 28 pp. Buenos Aires.

(1945b). *Los Cupisniques*. 25 pp. Buenos Aires.

(1945c). *Los Mochicas*. 42 pp. Buenos Aires.

(1945d). 'La cultura Salinar. Una civilización remota del Perú preincáico', *Revista Geográfica Americana*, vol. 23, no. 141, pp. 327–36. Buenos Aires.

(1946). 'A Culture Sequence for the North Coast of Peru'. *In* Steward (Editor) (1946), pp. 149–75.

(1948). *Cronología arqueológica del norte del Perú*. Trujillo, Peru, and Buenos Aires, Argentina.

(1965). *La cerámica Vicus*. Lima.

LARRABURE Y UNÁNUE, Eugenio (1874). *Cañete, apuntes geográficos y arqueológicos*. Lima.

LARREA, Juan (1935). *Arte peruano (Colección Juan Larrea)*. Madrid.

LAS CASAS, Bishop Friar Bartolomé de (1892). *De las antiguas gentes del Perú*. Edited by Don Marcos Jiménez de la Espada. Madrid.

LASTRES, Juan, Jorge MUELLE, J. M. B. FARFÁN, y Abraham GUILLÉN (1943). *Representaciones patológicas en la cerámica peruana*. Publicaciones del Museo Nacional. Lima, Imp. del Museo Nacional.

LATCHAM, R. E. (1923). *La existencia de la propiedad en el antiguo imperio de los Incas*. Santiago.

(1927a). 'El dominio de la tierra y el sistema tributario en el antiguo imperio de los Incas', *Revista Chilena de Historia y Geografía*, LII, pp. 201–57. Santiago de Chile.

(1927b). 'The Totemism of the Ancient Andean Peoples', *Journal of the Royal Anthropological Institute*, LVII, pp. 55–87.

(1927–8). 'Los Incas, sus orígenes y sus ayllus', *Revista de la Universidad de Chile*, v, pp. 1017–1154; VI, pp. 159–233.

LATHRAP, Donald W. (1958). 'The Cultural Sequence at Yarinacocha, Eastern Peru', *American Antiquity*, vol. 23, no. 4, pp. 379–88.

LAVACHERY, H. A. (1930). 'Neuf Sculptures péruviennes en bois',

BIBLIOGRAPHY

Bulletin de la Société des Américanistes de Belgique, pp. 20–5. Brussels.

LEHMANN, Walter, and Heinrich DOERING (1924). *The Art of Old Peru.* New York.

LEHMANN-NITSCHE, Robert (1928). 'Coricancha, el Templo del Sol en el Cuzco y las imágenes de su altar mayor', *Revista del Museo de La Plata*, XXXI, pp. 1–260. La Plata, Argentina.

LEVILLIER, Jean (1928). *Paracas, A Contribution to the Study of Pre-Incaic Textiles in Ancient Perú.* Paris.

LEVILLIER, Roberto (1935). *Don Francisco de Toledo, supremo organizador del Perú: su vida, su obra* (1515–1582), vol. 1. Madrid.

LIBBY, Willard F. (1952). *Radiocarbon Dating.* Chicago.

LILIEN, Rose (1950). 'Tripod Vessels from the Virú Valley', *American Antiquity*, vol. 15, no. 4, pp. 339–40. Menasha,, Wisconsin.

LINNÉ, Sigvald (1925). *The Technique of South American Ceramics.* Göteborgs Kungl Vetenskaps- och Vitterhets-Samhälles Handlingar, Fjärde följden, vol. 29, no. 5. Göteborg.

LOCKE, L. Leland (1912). 'The Ancient Quipu, a Peruvian Knot-Record', *American Anthropologist*, XIV, pp. 325–32.

(1923). *The Ancient Quipu, a Peruvian Knot-Record.* New York.

(1938). *Supplementary Notes on the Quipus in the American Museum of Natural History.* Anthropological Papers, American Museum of Natural History, vol. 30, pt 2, pp. 39–74. New York.

LOTHROP, Samuel Kirkland (1932). 'Aboriginal Navigation off the West Coast of South America', *Journal of the Royal Anthropological Institute*, 67, 229–56.

(1937). 'Gold and Silver from Southern Peru and Bolivia', *ibid.*, pp. 305–25. London.

(1938). *Inca Treasure as Depicted by Spanish Historians.* Frederick Webb Hodge Anniversary Publication Fund. Vol. 2. Los Angeles.

(1941). 'Gold Ornaments of Chavín Style from Chongoyape, Peru', *American Antiquity*, vol. 6, no. 3, pp. 250–62. Menasha, Wisconsin.

(1948). 'Pariñas-Chira Archaeology; A Preliminary Report'. *In* Bennett (Editor) (1948), pp. 53–65.

(1950). 'Metalworking Tools from the Central Coast of Peru', *American Antiquity*, vol. 16, pp. 160–4.

(1951a). 'Gold Artifacts of Chavín Style', *ibid.*, 226–40. Salt Lake City.

(1951b). 'Peruvian Metallurgy'. In *The Civilizations of Ancient America.* Selected Papers of the XXIXth International Congress of Americanists, pp. 219–23. Chicago.

(1954). 'A Peruvian Goldsmith's Grave', *Archaeology*, vol. 7, pp. 31–36.

LOTHROP, Samuel K., and MAHLER, Joy (1957a). *A Chancay Style Grave at Zapallan, Peru.* Papers of the Peabody Museum of Archaeology and Ethnology, Harvard University, vol. 50, no. 1. Cambridge.

(1957b). *Late Nazca Burials in Chavina, Peru. idem*, vol. 50, no. 2.

LOTHROP, Samuel K., and others (1961). *Essays in Pre-Columbian Art and Archaeology.* Cambridge, Mass.

LUMBRERAS, S. Luis G. (1960a). 'Espacio y cultural en los Andes', *Revista del Museo Nacional,* vol. 29, pp. 222–39. Lima.

(1960b). 'Algunos problemas de arqueología peruana'. *In* Matos Mendieta (Editor), pp. 129–48.

LÜTKEN, Chr. Fr. (1884). *Des crânes et des autres ossements humains de Minas Geráes dans le Brésil Central, découverts et déterrés par le feu. Professeur P. W. Lund.* Congrès International Américaniste (Copenhagen, 1883). Pp. 40–8.

McCOWN, Theodore D. (1945). *Pre-Incaic Huamachuco: Survey and Excavations in the Northern Sierra of Peru.* University of California Publications in American Archaeology and Ethnology, vol. 39, no. 4. Berkeley.

(1950). 'The Antiquity of Man in South America'. *In* Steward (Editor) (1950), pp. 1–9.

(1952). 'Ancient Man in South America'. In *Indian Tribes of Aboriginal America,* pp. 374–9. Selected Papers of the 29th International Congress of Americanists, Chicago.

MACCURDY, George Grant (1923). 'Human Skeletal Remains from the Highlands of Peru', *American Journal of Physical Anthropology,* vol. 6, no. 3, pp. 217–329. Philadelphia.

MACGOWAN, Kenneth (1950). *Early Man in the New World.* New York.

MANGELSDORF, Paul C. (1954). 'New Evidence on the Origin and Ancestry of Maize', *American Antiquity,* 19, 4, pp. 409–10.

MANGELSDORF, P. C., and R. G. REEVES (1939). *The Origin of Indian Corn and Its Relatives.* Texas Agricultural Experimental Station, Bulletin No. 574.

(1959). 'The Origin of Corn', *Botanical Museum Leaflets,* vol. 18, no. 7, pp. 329–56. Harvard University, Cambridge, Mass.

MANGELSDORF, P. C., and C. Earle SMITH, Jr. (1949). 'New Archaeological Evidence of Evolution in Maize', *Botanical Museum Leaflets,* vol. 13, no. 8, pp. 213–47. Harvard University, Cambridge, Mass.

MARKHAM, Sir Clements Robert (1856). *Cuzco: A Journey to the Ancient Capital of Peru; with an Account of the History, Language, Literature, and Antiquities of the Incas.* London.

(1864). *Contributions toward a Grammar and Dictionary of Quichua. the Language of the Yncas of Peru.* London.

(1871). 'On the Geographical Positions of the Tribes which Formed the Empire of the Yncas', *Journal of the Royal Geographical Society,* 41, pp. 281–338. London.

(1872). *Reports on the Discovery of Peru.* Hakluyt Society, no. 47. London.

(1873). *Rites and Laws of the Incas.* Hakluyt Society, no. 48. London.

(1892). *A History of Peru.* Chicago.

(1907). *Bibliography of Peru* (1526–1907). Hakluyt Collection, Ser. 2, vol. 22, pp. 267–358. Cambridge, England.

(1910a). *The Incas of Peru*. London and New York.

(1910b). *A Comparison of the Ancient Peruvian Carvings and the Stones of Tiahuanacu and Chavín*. International Congress of Americanists, XVI, pp. 389–95. Vienna.

MASON, J. Alden (1926a). 'Dr Farabee's Last Journey', *Museum Journal*, vol. 17, no. 2, pp. 128–65. Philadelphia.

(1926b). 'Additions to the American Section', *idem.*, vol. 17, no. 3, pp. 273–93. Philadelphia.

(1930). 'A Silver Vase from Peru', *University Museum Bulletin*, vol. 1, no. 2, pp. 23, 24, 26. Philadelphia.

(1931). 'A Peruvian Painting Set', *idem*, vol. 3, no. 1, pp. 10–12. Philadelphia.

(1932). 'Peruvian Pottery Whistles', *idem*, vol. 4, no. 1, pp. 20–22. Philadelphia.

(1933). 'Gold and Copper Ornaments from Peru', *idem*, vol. 4, no. 4, pp. 94–6. Philadelphia.

(1935). 'Three Inca Wooden Cups', *idem*, vol. 5, no. 5, pp. 53–5. Philadelphia.

(1950). 'The Languages of South American Indians'. *In* Steward (Editor) (1950), pp. 157–317.

(1952). 'Peruvian Panorama', *Archaeology*, vol. 5, pp. 220–7.

MATHEWSON, C. H. (1915). 'A Metallographic Description of Some Ancient Peruvian Bronzes from Machu Picchu', *American Journal of Science*, vol. 40, no. 240.

MATOS MENDIETA, Ramiro (Editor) (1960). *Antiguo Peru, Espacio y Tiempo*, Lima.

MEAD, Charles W. (1903). *The Musical Instruments of the Incas*. Guide Leaflet No. 11, American Museum of Natural History, New York.

(1906). *The Six-Unit Design in Ancient Peruvian Cloth*. Boas Anniversary Volume, pp. 193–5. New York.

(1907). *Technique of Some South American Feather-work*. Anthropological Papers of the American Museum of Natural History, New York, 1, pt 1.

(1909). *The Fish in Ancient Peruvian Art*. Putnam Anniversary Volume, pp. 126–36. New York.

(1915). *Prehistoric Bronze in South America*. Anthropological Papers, American Museum of Natural History, vol. 12, pp. 15–52. New York.

(1916a). *Conventionalized Figures in Ancient Peruvian Art. Idem.* vol. 12, pp. 193–217. New York.

(1916b). 'Ancient Peruvian Cloths', *American Museum of Natural History Journal*, XVI, pp. 389–93.

(1917). *Peruvian Art*. Guide Leaflet No. 46, American Museum of Natural History, New York.

(1924). *Old Civilizations of Inca Land*. American Museum of Natural History, Handbook Series, No. 11, New York.

MEANS, Philip Ainsworth (1917a). *A Survey of Ancient Peruvian Art.* Connecticut Academy of Arts and Sciences, *Transactions,* vol. 21, pp. 315–442. New Haven.

(1917b). *Culture Sequence in the Andean Area.* International Congress of Americanists, XIX, pp. 236–52. Washington.

(1918a). *A Glimpse of Northern Peru.* Bulletin, Pan American Union, no. 47, pp. 333–49. Washington.

(1918b). 'A Note on the Guarani Invasions of the Inca Empire', *Geographical Review,* American Geographical Society, IV, pp. 482–484.

(1918c). 'The Domestication of the Llama', *Science,* XLVII, pp. 268–9.

(1918d). 'Realism in the Art of Ancient Peru', *Art and Archaeology,* VI, pp. 235–46. Washington.

(1918e). 'Precolumbian Peruvian Chronology and Cultures', *Man,* XVIII, pp. 168–9.

(1918f). 'A Note on Two Stone Objects from Southern Bolivia', *American Anthropologist,* XX, pp. 245–6.

(1919a). 'La civilización precolombina de los Andes', *Boletín de la Sociedad Ecuatoriana de Estudios Históricos Americanos,* III, pp. 213–42. Quito

(1919b). *Una nota sobre la prehistoria peruana.* Lima.

(1919c). 'Distribution and Use of Slings in Pre-Columbian America, with Descriptive Catalogue of Ancient Peruvian Slings in the United States National Museum', *Proceedings of the U.S. National Museum,* vol. 55, pp. 317–49. Washington.

(1921a). 'Aspectos estético-cronológicos de las civilizaciones andinas', *Boletín de la Academia Nacional de Historia,* I, pp. 195–226.

(1921b). 'Ciertos aspectos estéticos del arte antiguo del Perú', *Mercurio Peruano,* VI, pp. 215–23. Lima.

(1925a). 'A Study of Ancient Andean Social Institutions', Connecticut Academy of Arts and Sciences, *Transactions,* vol. 27, pp. 407–469. New Haven.

(1925b). 'A Series of Ancient Andean Textiles', *Bulletin of the Needle and Bobbin Club,* IX, pp. 3–27. New York.

(1927). 'A Group of Ancient Peruvian Fabrics', *ibid.,* XI, pp. 10–25. New York.

(1928). 'Biblioteca Andina: Part One, the Chroniclers, or, the Writers of the Sixteenth and Seventeenth Centuries Who Treated of the Pre-Hispanic History and Culture of the Andean Countries', Connecticut Academy of Arts and Sciences, *Transactions,* vol. 29, pp. 271–525. New Haven.

(1930a). *Peruvian Textiles; Examples of the Pre-Incaic Period.* New York.

(1930b). *The Origin of Tapestry Technique in Pre-Spanish Peru.* Metropolitan Museum Series, III, pt 1, pp. 22–37.

(1931). *Ancient Civilizations of the Andes.* New York.

(1932). *Fall of the Inca Empire and the Spanish Rule in Peru*, 1530–1780. New York.

(1938). 'The Incas, Empire Builders of the Andes', *National Geographic Magazine*, 73, pp. 225–64.

(1942). 'Pre-Spanish Navigation off the Andean Coast', *American Neptune*, 2, 2, pp. 107–26. Salem, Mass.

MEDINA, José Toribio (1930). *Bibliografía de las lenguas quechua y aymará*. Contributions, vol. 7, no. 7, Museum of the American Indian, Heye Foundation. New York.

MEGGERS, Betty J., EVANS, Clifford, and ESTRADA, Emilio (1965). 'Early Formative Period of Coastal Ecuador: The Valdivia and Machalilla Phases'. *Smithsonian Contributions to Anthropology*, vol. 1. Washington.

MEGGERS, Betty J., and EVANS, Clifford (1966). 'A Transpacific Contact in 3000 B.C.', *Scientific American*, vol. 214, no. 1, pp. 28–35.

MENGHIN, Osvaldo, F. A. (1954). 'Cultures precerámicas en Bolivia', *Runa*, vol. 6. Buenos Aires.

(1957). 'Vorgeschichte Amerikas'. In Oldenbourg's *Abriss der Weltgeschichte*. Munich.

MENGHIN, Osvaldo F. A., and SCHROEDER, Gerhard (1957). 'Un yacimiento en Ichuña (Dept. Puno, Peru) y las industrias precerámicas de los Andes centrales y septentrionales', *Acta Praehistórica* I. Buenos Aires.

MENZEL, Dorothy (1959). 'The Inca Occupation on the South Coast of Peru', *Southwestern Journal of Anthropology*, vol. 15, no. 2, pp. 125–42.

MENZEL, Dorothy, ROWE, John H., and DAWSON, Lawrence E. (1964). 'The Paracas Pottery of Ica: A Study in Style and Time', *University of California Publications in American Archaeology and Ethnology*, Vol. 50. Berkeley.

MÉTRAUX, Alfred (1949). 'Religion and Shamanism'. *In* Steward (Editor) (1949), pp. 559–99.

MIDDENDORF, E. W. (1890–2). *Die einheimischen Sprachen Perus*. 6 vols. Leipzig.

(1890a). *Das Runa-Simi oder die Keshua-Sprache*. Leipzig.

(1890b). *Wörterbuch des Runa-Simi*. Leipzig.

(1891). *Dramatische und lyrische Dichtungen der Keshua-Sprache*. Leipzig.

(1892). *Das Muchik oder die Chimu-Sprache*. Leipzig.

(1893–5). *Peru*. 3 vols. Berlin.

(1960). *El Muchik o lengua de los Chimú*. Spanish version by Federico Kauffmann Doig. Lima.

MINNAERT, Paul (1925). *Les Institutions et le droit de l'empire des Incas*. Ostende.

MISHKIN, Bernard (1946). 'The Contemporary Quechua'. *In* Steward (Editor) (1946), pp. 411–76.

MITRÉ, Bartolomé (1881). *Ollantay: Estudio sobre el drama Quichua*. Buenos Aires.

MOLINA (of Cuzco), Cristóbal de (1873). 'The Fables and Rites of the Yncas'. Translated and edited by Clements R. Markham, in *Rites and Laws of the Yncas*, pp. 1–64. Hakluyt Society, London.

(1913), 'Relación de las fábulas y ritos de los Incas', *Revista Chilena de Historia y Geografíca*, 5, pp. 117–90. Santiago de Chile.

(1916). *Idem.* Colección de Libros y Documentos referentes a la historia del Perú, vol. 1. Lima.

MOLINA (of Santiago), Cristóbal de (1916). 'Relación de muchas cosas acaecidas en el Perú . . .', *idem*, vol. 1, pp. 105–90. Lima.

MONGE, Carlos (1948). *Acclimatization in the Andes*. Baltimore.

(1952). 'Physiological Anthropology of the Dwellers in America's High Plateaus'. In *Indian Tribes of Aboriginal America*, pp. 361–73. Selected Papers of the 29th International Congress of Americanists, Chicago.

(1953). 'Biological Basis of Human Behavior'. In *Anthropology Today* pp. 127–44. Chicago.

MONTELL, Gösta (1925). 'Le vrai poncho, son origine postcolombienne', *Journal de la Société des Américanistes de Paris*, vol. 17, pp. 173–83.

(1929). *Dress and Ornaments in Ancient Peru*. Göteborg.

MONTESINOS, Fernando (1882). *Memorias antiguas historiales y políticas del Perú*. Édition Marcos Jiménez de la Espada. Colección de libros españoles raros o curiosos, vol. 16, pp. 1–76. Madrid.

(1906). *Anales del Perú*. 2 vols. Madrid.

(1920). *Memorias antiguas historiales del Peru*. Translated and edited by P. A. Means. Hakluyt Society, Ser. 2, no. 48. London.

MOODIE, Roy L. (1926). 'Studies in Paleopathology, XIV: A Prehistoric Surgical Bandage from Peru'. *Annals of Medical History*, vol. 8, pp. 69–72.

(1927). 'Studies in Paleopathology, XXI: Injuries to the Head among the pre-Columbian Peruvians', *ibid.*, vol. 9, pp. 277–307.

(1928). 'Studies in Paleo-odontology, I: Materials for a Study of Prehistoric Dentistry in Peru', *Journal of the American Dental Association*, vol. 15, pp. 1826–50.

(1929). 'Studies in Paleopathology, XXII: Surgery in Pre-Columbian Peru', *Annals of Medical History*, N.S., vol. 1, pp. 698–728.

MORTIMER, W. Golden (1901). *Coca, the Divine Plant of the Incas*. New York.

MORÚA, Martín de (1922–5). *Historia del origen y genealogía real de los reyes Incas del Perú, de sus hechos, costumbres, trajes y manera de gobierno*. Edited by H. H. Urteaga and C. A. Romero. Colección de Libros y Documentos referentes a la historia del Perú, Lima, Peru.

MUELLE, Jorge C. (1935). 'Restos hallados en una tumba en Nievería', *Revista del Museo Nacional de Lima*, vol. 4, pp. 135–52.

(1936). *Los valles de Trujillo.* Lima.

MUELLE, Jorge C., and Camilo BLAS (1938). 'Muestrario de arte peruano precolombino', *Revista del Museo Nacional,* vol. 7, pp. 163–280. Lima.

MUÑIZ, Manuel Antonio, and W. J. McGEE (1895). *Primitive Trephining in Peru.* Annual Report, Bureau of American Ethnology, XVI, pp. 1–72.

MURDOCK, George Peter (1934). *Our Primitive Contemporaries.* New York.

MURPHY, William S. (1912). *The Textile Industries.* 8 vols. London.

MUSEUM OF MODERN ART (1955). *32 Masterworks of Andean Art.* New York.

NESTLER, Julius (1910). *Die Bedeutung der Ruinenstätte von Tiahuanaco nach den Publikationen von Dr. Max Uhle and Sir Clements Markham.* 16th International Congress of Americanists (1908), pp. 395–407. Vienna.

(1913). *Beiträge zur Kenntnis der Ruinenstätte von Tiahuanaco.* Vienna.

NEWMAN, MARSHALL T. (1943). 'A Metric Study of Undeformed Indian Crania from Peru', *American Journal of Physical Anthropology,* N.S., vol. 1, pp. 21–45. Philadelphia.

(1947). *Some Indian Skeletal Material from the Central Coast of Peru.* Papers of the Peabody Museum of Archaeology and Ethnology, Harvard University, vol. 28, no. 1.

(1948). 'A Summary of the Racial History of the Peruvian Area'. *In* Bennett (Editor) (1948), pp. 16–19.

NORDENSKIÖLD, Baron Erland (1906.. 'Ethnologische und archaeologische Forschungen im Grenzgebiet zwischen Peru und Bolivia', *Zeitschrift für Ethnologie,* XXXVIII, pp. 80–99. Berlin.

(1907). 'Recettes magiques et médicales du Pérou et de la Bolivie', *Journal de la Société des Américanistes,* t. IV, pp. 153–74. Paris.

(1917). 'The Guaraní Invasion of the Inca Empire in the Sixteenth Century', *Geographical Review,* IV, pp. 103–21. American Geographical Society, New York.

(1921a). *The Copper and Bronze Ages in South America.* Comparative Ethnographical Studies, vol. 4. Göteborg.

(1921b). 'Emploi de la balance romaine en Amérique du Sud avant la conquête', *Journal de la Société des Américanistes,* t. XIII, fasc. 2, pp. 169–71. Paris.

(1922a). *Deductions Suggested by the Geographical Distribution of Some Post-Columbian Words Used by the Indians of South America.* Comparative Ethnographical Studies, vol. 5. Göteborg.

(1922b). 'La Moustiquaire est-elle indigène en Amérique du Sud?' *Journal de la Société des Américanistes,* t. XIV, pp. 119–26. Paris.

(1925a). *The Secret of the Peruvian Quipus.* Comparative Ethnographical Studies. Gothenburg (Göteborg) Museum, vol. 6, part 1. Göteborg.

(1925b). *Calculations with Years and Months in the Peruvian Quipus. Idem*, vol. 6, pt 2. Göteborg.

(1925–7). 'Peru under the Incas and After', *Peru*, t. 11. London.

(1930). 'The Ancient Peruvian System of Weights', *Man*, t. xxx, pp. 215–21. London.

(1931a). *Origin of the Indian Civilizations in South America*. Comparative Ethnographical Studies, 9. Göteborg.

(1931b). *Ancient Inca Lacquer Work. Idem*, vol. 9, pt 2, pp. 95–100. Göteborg.

(1946). *Origen de las civilizaciones indígenas en la América del Sur*. Buenos Aires.

OCAMPO, Baltasar de (1907). *Account of the Province of Vilcapampa and a Narrative of the Execution of the Inca Tupac Amaru*. Hakluyt Society, Ser. 2, no. 22, pp. 203–47.

OGILVIE, Alan Grant (1922). *Geography of the Central Andes*. American Geographic Society, Map of Hispanic America. Publication no. 1.

O'NEALE, Lila M. (1932). 'Tejidos del período primitivo de Paracas', *Revista del Museo Nacional*, vol. 1, no. 2, pp. 60–80. Lima.

(1933a). 'A Peruvian Multicolored Patchwork', *American Anthropologist*, vol. 35, pp. 87–94.

(1933b). 'Peruvian "Needleknitting" ', *ibid.*, pp. 405–30.

(1935). 'Pequeñas prendas ceremoniales de Paracas', *Revista del Museo Nacional*, vol. 4, no. 2, pp. 245–66. Lima.

(1936). 'Wide-loom Fabrics of the Early Nazca Period'. In *Essays in Anthropology, presented to A. L. Kroeber*, pp. 215–28. Berkeley.

(1937). *Archaeological Explorations in Peru. Pt. iii: Textiles of the Early Nazca Period*. Field Museum of Natural History, Anthropological Memoirs, vol. 2, no. 3, pp. 119–218. Chicago, Ill.

(1942). *Textile Periods in Ancient Peru: ii, Paracas Caverns and the Grand Necropolis*. University of California Publications in American Archaeology and Ethnology, vol. 39, pp. 143–202. Berkeley.

(1946). 'Mochica (Early Chimu) and Other Peruvian Twill Fabrics', *Southwestern Journal of Anthropology*, vol. 2, no. 3, pp. 269–94. Albuquerque.

(1949). 'Weaving'. In Steward (Editor) (1949), pp. 97–138.

(1954). 'Textiles'. In Willey and Corbett.

O'NEALE, Lila M., and Bonnie Jean CLARK (1948). *Textile Periods in Ancient Peru. iii: The Gauze Weaves*. University of California Publications in American Archaeology and Ethnology, vol. 40, no. 4, pp. 143–222. Berkeley.

O'NEALE, Lila M., and A. L. KROEBER (1930). *Textile Periods in Ancient Peru. Idem*, vol. 39, pp. 143–202. Berkeley.

O'NEALE, Lila M., and others (1949). 'Chincha Plain-Weave Cloths', *Anthropological Records*, vol. 9, no. 2. University of California, Berkeley.

ORBIGNY, Alcide d' (1876). *Voyage dans les deux Amériques*. Paris.

ORCHARD, William C. (1930). 'Peruvian Gold and Gold Plating'. *Indian Notes*, Museum of the American Indian, Heye Foundation, VII, pp. 466–74. New York.

OSBORNE, Carolyn M. (1950). 'Shaped Breechcloths from Peru', *Anthropological Records*, vol. 13, no. 2. University of California, Berkeley.

OVIEDO Y VALDÉS, Gonzalo Fernández de (1851–5). *Historia general y natural de las Indias, islas y tierra-firme del mar océano*. Edition José Amador de los Rios, 4 vols, Madrid.

OYAGUE Y CALDERÓN, Carlos (1904). ˙Arquitectura incáica y construcción general', *Boletín de la Sociedad Geográfica de Lima*, XV, pp. 410–417.

PACHACUTI-YAMQUI SALCAMAYHUA, Juan de Santa Cruz (1873). *An Account of the Antiquities of Peru*. Translated and edited by Clements R. Markham in *Rites and Laws of the Yncas*, pp. 67–120. Hakluyt Society, London.

(1879). *Relación de antigüedades deste reyno del Pirú*. Edited by Marcos Jiménez de la Espada, *Tres relaciones de antigüedades peruanas*, pp. 229–328. Madrid.

PARDO, Lufs A. (1937). *Ruinas precolombinas del Cuzco*. Cuzco.

PATTERSON, Thomas C., and LANNING, Edward P. (1964). 'Changing Settlement Patterns on the Central Peruvian Coast'. *Nawpa Pacha*, No. 2, pp. 113–23. Berkeley.

PERRY, William James (1923). *The Children of the Sun*. London.

PIZARRO, Hernando (1872). 'Letter to the Royal Audience of Santo Domingo, November 1533'. In *Reports on the Discovery of Peru*, Hakluyt Society Publications, no. 47, pp. 11–127. London.

PIZARRO, Pedro (1844). *Relación del descubrimiento y conquista de los reinos del Perú, etc.* Colección de Documentos inéditos para la historia de España, vol. 5, pp. 201–388. Madrid.

(1921). *Relation of the Discovery and Conquest of the Kingdoms of Peru*. Cortes Society. Translated and edited by P. A. Means. 2 vols. New York.

POLO, José Toribio (1899). 'La piedra de Chavín', *Boletín de la Sociedad Geográfica de Lima*, IX, pp. 192–231, 262–90'

POLO DE ONDEGARDO, Juan (1873). Report by Polo de Ondegardo. 'The Rites and Laws of the Incas'. Translated and edited by Clements R. Markham. Hakluyt Society, pp. 151–71. London.

(1916a). *Los errores y supersticiones de los Indios, etc.* Colección de Libros y Documentos referentes a la historia del Perú, Ser. 1, vol. 3, pp. 1–43. Lima.

(1916b). *Relación de los fundamentos acerca del notable daño que resulta de no guardar a los Indios sus fueros. Idem*, pp. 45–188.

(1917a). *Relación de los adoratorios de los Indios en los cuatro caminos (zeques) que salían del Cuzco*. Edited by Drs Urteaga and Romero. Colección de Libros y Documentos referentes a la historia del Perú, IV, pp. 3–44. Lima.

(1917b). *Del linage de los Ingas y como conquistaron.* Edited by H. H. Urteaga. *Idem*, pp. 45–138. Lima.

(1940). 'Informe del Licenciado Juan Polo de Odegardo . . . sobre la perpetuidad de las encomiendas en el Perú'. *Revista Histórica*, vol. 13, pp. 125–96. Lima.

POMA DE AYALA, Felipe Guamán (1936). *Nueva corónica y buen gobierno (codex péruvien illustré).* Institute d'Ethnologie, Travaux et Mémoires, vol. 23. Paris.

PONCE SANGINÉS, Carlos (1961). *Informe de labores, octubre 1957 – febrero 1961. Centro de Investigaciones Arqueológicas en Tiwanaku*, Publicación no. 1. La Paz.

POSNANSKY, Arthur (1911a). *Tihuanacu y la civilización prehistórica en el altiplano andino.* La Paz.

(1911b). 'Razas y monumentos prehistóricos del altiplano andino', *Trabajos del iv Congreso Científico*, XI, pp. 2–142. Santiago

(1913). *El signo escalonado . . . con especial referencia a Tihuanacu.* Berlin

(1914). *Una metrópoli en la América del Sur.* Berlin

(1925). *Die erotischen Keramiken der Mochicas und deren Beziehungen zu occipital deformierten Schädeln.* Festschrift zur Feier des 25-jährigen Bestehens der Frankfurter Gesellschaft für Anthropologie und Urgeschichte, pp. 67–74.

(1946). *Tihuanacu. The Cradle of American Man.* 2 vols. New York.

PRESCOTT, William Hickling (1847). *History of the Conquest of Peru.* (Many later editions.)

PUTNAM, Edward K. (1914). 'The Davenport Collection of Nazca and other Peruvian Pottery', *Proceedings of the Davenport Academy of Science*, vol. 13, pp. 17–45. Davenport.

QUEVEDO A., A. SERGIO (1941–2). 'Ensayos de antropología física. Los antiguos pobladores del Cuzco (región de Calca)', *Revista del Museo Nacional*, vol. 10. pp. 282–309. Lima.

(1943). 'La trepanación incana en la región del Cusco', *Revista Universitaria.* Cusco, 2 sem. de 1943, pp. 1–197.

Quipucamayocs (1920). *Discurso sobre la descendencia y gobierno de los Incas.* Edited by Drs Horacio H. Urteaga and Carlos A. Romero. Colección de Libros y Documentos referentes a la historia del Perú.

RAIMONDI, Antonio (1874–1913). *El Perú.* 6 vols. Lima.

(1901). 'Ruinas de Huánuco Viejo', *Boletín de la Sociedad Geográfica de Lima*, XI, pp. 397–400.

(1903). 'Enumeración de los vestigios de la antigua civilización entre Pacasmayo y la Cordillera', *ibid.*, XIII, pp. 159–71.

RAMOS GAVILÁN, Alonso (1621). *Historia del célebre santuario de Nuestra Señora de Copacabana, y sus milagros, é invención de la cruz de Carabuco.* Lima.

REGAL, Alberto (1936). *Los caminos del Inca en el antiguo Perú.* Lima.

REICHE, María (1949). *Mystery on the Desert.* Lima.

REICHLEN, Henry et Paule (1949). 'Recherches archéologiques dans les

Andes de Cajamarca. Premier rapport de la Mission Ethnologique française au Peróu septentrional', *Journal de la Société des Américanistes*, t. XXXVIII, pp. 137–74. Paris.

(1950). 'Rescherches archéologiques dans les Andes du Haut Utcubamba', *Journal de la Société des Américanistes*, t. XXXIX, pp. 219–46. Paris.

REISS, Wilhelm, and Alphons STÜBEL (1880–7). *The Necropolis of Ancon in Peru.* 3 vols. Berlin.

Relaciones geográficas de Indias, Perú (1881–97). 4 vols. Madrid.

RICHARDSON, Francis B., and Alfred KIDDER II (1940). 'Publicaciones estadunidenses y británicas sobre la arqueología peruana', *Boletín Bibliográfico*, Año 13, nos 1–2, pp. 13–10. Lima.

RIVERO, Mariano E., and J. D. DE TSCHUDI (1851). *Antigüedades peruabas.* 2 vols. Vienna.

RIVET, Paul (1908). 'La Race de Lagoa-Santa chez les populations précolombiennes de l'Équateur', *Bulletins et Mémoires de la Société* (1924). *L'Orfèvrerie colombienne.* International Congress *d'Anthropologie de Paris*, Ser. 5, vol. 9, pp. 209–74. Paris.

(1924). *L'Orfèvrerie colombienne.* International Congress of Americanists, Sess. 21, The Hague, pp. 15–28.

(1926). 'Les Malayo-Polynésiens en Amérique', *Journal de la Société des Américanistes de Paris*, 18, pp. 141–278.

(1952). 'Langues américaines'. *In* Meillet et Cohen, *Les Langues du monde.* Paris.

RIVET, Paul, and H. ARSANDAUX (1946). 'La Métallurgie en Amérique précolombienne', *Travaux et Mémoires de l'Institut d'Ethnologie*, vol. 39. Paris.

RIVET, Paul, and Georges DE CRÉQUI-MONTFORT (1951–3). *Bibliographie des langues armará et kičua.* 3 vols. Paris.

ROMÁN Y ZAMORA, Jerónimo (1897). *Repúblicas de Indias; idolatrías y gobierno de México y Perú antes de la conquista.* Colección de libros raros o curiosos que tratan de América, vols 14–15. Madrid.

ROOT, William C. (1949a). 'The Metallurgy of the Southern Coast of Peru', *American Antiquity*, 15, 1, pp. 10–37.

(1949b). 'Metallurgy'. *In* Steward (Editor) (1949), pp. 205–25.

ROWE, John Howland (1942). *A New Pottery Style from the Department of Piura, Peru.* Carnegie Institution of Washington Notes on Middle American Archaeology and Ethnology, no. 8. Washington.

(1944). *An Introduction to the Archaeology of Cuzco.* Papers of the Peabody Museum of Archaeology and Ethnology, Harvard University, vol. 27, no. 2. Cambridge.

(1945). 'Absolute Chronology in the Andean Area', *American Antiquity*, vol. 10, no. 3, pp. 265–84.

(1946). 'Inca Culture at the Time of the Spanish Conquest'. *In* Steward (Editor) (1946), pp. 183–330.

(1948a). 'On Basic Highland Culture'. *In* Bennett (Editor) (1948), p. 20.

(1948b). 'On Absolute Dating and North Coast History'. *In* Bennett (Editor) 1948), pp. 51–2.

(1948c). 'The Kingdom of Chimor', *Acta Americana*, vol. 6, no. 1, pp. 26–49. Mexico.

(1950). 'Sound Patterns in Three Inca Dialects', *International Journal of American Linguistics*, 16, pp. 137–48.

(1954). 'Max Uhle, 1856–1944, A Memoir of the Father of Peruvian Archaeology', *University of California Publications in American Archaeology and Ethnology*, vol. 46, no. 1. Berkeley.

(1956). 'Archaeological Explorations in Southern Peru, 1954–1955'. *American Antiquity*, vol. 22, no. 2, pp. 135–51.

(1958). 'Tiempo, estilo, y proceso cultural en la arqueología peruana', *Revista Universitaria del Cuzco*. Cuzco.

(1960). 'Cultural Unity and Diversification in Peruvian Archaeology', *Fifth International Congress of Anthropological and Ethnological Sciences*, pp. 627–31. Philadelphia.

(1961). 'The Chronology of Inca Wooden Cups'. *In* Lothrop and others, pp. 317–41.

(1962). *Chavín Art, An Inquiry into Its Form and Meaning.* New York.

(1963). 'Urban Settlements in Ancient Peru', *Nawpa Pacha* I, pp. 1–28. Berkeley.

ROWE, John H., Donald COLLIER, and Gordon R. WILLEY (1950). 'Reconnaissance Notes on the Site of Huari, near Ayacucho, Peru', *American Antiquity*, 16, 2, pp. 120–37. Salt Lake City.

RUBIN DE LA BORBOLLA, Daniel (1961). *Los tesoros artísticos del Peru.* Museo Nacional de Ciencias y Arte, Mexico.

RYDEN, Stig (1947). *Archaeological Researches in the Highlands of Bolivia.* Göteborg.

(1957). 'Andean Excavations I. The Tiahuanaco Era East of Lake Titicaca'. *Publication* no. 4, Ethnographical Museum of Sweden, Stockholm.

(1959). 'Andean Excavations II. Tupuraya and Cayhuasi: Two Tiahuanaco Sites', *Publication* no. 6 (*id.*).

SAAVEDRA, Bautista (1913). *El ayllu.* La Paz.

SANCHO (DE LA HOZ), Pedro (1917a). *An Account of the Conquest of Peru.* Translated and edited by P. A. Means. Cortés Society, New York.

(1917b). *Relación para S. M. de lo sucedido en la conquista y pacificación de estas provincias de la Nueva Castilla, etc.* Colección de Libros y Documentos referentes a la historia del Perú, Ser. 1, vol. 5, pp. 122–202. Lima.

SANTILLÁN, Fernando de (1879). *Relación del origen, descendencia, política y gobierno de los Incas.* Edited by Marcos Jiménez de la Espada, *Tres relaciones de antigüedades peruanas*, pp. 1–133. Madrid.

SANTO TOMÁS, Domingo de (1891). *Arte de la lengua quichua, compuesta por Domingo de Sancto Thomás, publicado de nuevo por Julio Platzmann.* Edición facsimilar. Leipzig.

SARMIENTO DE GAMBOA, Pedro (1906). *Geschichte des Inkareiches.*

Abhandl. Königl. Gesellsch. Wissensch. Göttingen. Philologisch-historische Klasse, vol. 6, no. 4. Editor, Richard Pietschmann. Berlin.

(1907). *History of the Incas*. Translated and edited by Sir Clements R. Markham. Hakluyt Society, Ser. 2, no. 22. Cambridge.

SAUER, Carl O. (1936). 'American Agricultural Origins: A Consideration of Nature and Culture'. In *Essays in Anthropology*, presented to A. L. Kroeber, pp. 279–97. Berkeley.

(1950a). 'Geography of South America'. *In* Steward (Editor) (1950), pp. 319–44.

(1950b). 'Cultivated Plants of South and Central America'. *In* Steward (Editor) (1950), pp. 489–543.

(1952). *Agricultural Origins and Dispersions*. The American Geographical Society, New York.

SAVILLE, Marshall H. (1921). 'A Golden Breastplate from Cuzco, Peru', *Notes and Monographs*, no. 21. Museum of the American Indian, Heye Foundation, New York.

(1925). 'Balance-beam Scales in Ancient Peru'. *Indian Notes*, Museum of the American Indian, Heye Foundation, II, pp. 266–85. New York.

(1926). 'The Pottery Arybal of the Incas'. *Ibid.*, III, pp. 111–19. New York.

(1954). *The Nathan Cummings Collection of Ancient Peruvian Art*. Chicago.

(1961). 'Paracas and Nazca Iconography', *Essays in Pre-Columbian Art and Archaeology* by S. K. Lothrop and others, pp. 269–98. Cambridge, Mass.

SAWYER, Alan R. (1966). *Ancient Peruvian Ceramics; The Nathan Cummings Collection*. The Metropolitan Museum of Art, New York. New York Graphic Society, Greenwich, Conn.

SCHAEDEL, Richard P. (1948a). 'Monolithic Sculpture of the Southern Andes', *Archaeology*, vol. 1, pp. 66–73.

(1948b). 'The Callejón de Huaylas of Peru and Its Monuments', *ibid.*, vol. 1, pp. 198–202.

(1948c). 'Stone Sculpture in the Callejón de Huaylas'. *In* Bennett (Editor) (1948), pp. 66–79.

(1949). 'Uncovering a Frieze on the Peruvian Coast', *Archaeology*, vol. 2, pp. 73–5.

(1951a). 'Wooden Idols from Peru', *ibid.*, vol. 4, pp. 16–22.

(1951b). 'Mochica Murals at Pañamarca', *ibid.*, vol. 4, pp. 145–54.

(1951c). 'Major Ceremonial and Population Centers in Northern Peru', *Civilizations of Ancient America*, pp. 232–43. Selected Papers, 29th International Congress of Americanists, Chicago.

SCHMIDT, Max (1909). 'Uber altperuanische Ornamentik', *Archiv für Anthropologie*, VII, pp. 22–38. Brunswick.

(1910). 'Szenenhafte Darstellungen auf altperuanischen Geweben', *Zeitschrift für Ethnologie*, XLII, pp. 154–64. Berlin.

(1911). *Uber altperuanische Gewebe mit szenenhaften Darstellungen.* Baessler-Archiv, I, pp. 1–61. Leipzig and Berlin.

(1929). *Kunst und Kultur von Peru.* Berlin.

SCHMIDT, Wilhelm (1913). 'Kulturkreise und Kulturschichten in Südamerika', *Zeitschrift für Ethnologie*, 45, pp. 1014–1124.

(1939). *The Culture Historical Method of Ethnology.* New York.

SCHROEDER, Gerhard (1957). 'Hallazgos de artefactos de piedra en al Perú, y los problemas del poblamiento de América', *Revista del Museo Nacional*, vol. 26, pp. 290–94. Lima.

SCHWAB, Federico (1936). 'Bibliografíca de etnología peruana', *Boletín Bibliográfico*, Año 9, no. 1, pp. 1–26; no. 2, pp. 4–27. Lima.

SELER, Eduard (1893). *Peruanische Alterthümer.* Berlin.

(1912). 'Archäologische Reise in Süd- und Mittel-Amerika', *Zeitschrift für Ethnologie*, pp. 201–42.

(1923). *Die buntbemalten Gefässe von Nasca im südlichen Peru und die Hauptelemente ihrer Verzierung.* Edited by Caecilie Seler-Sachs in *Gesammelte Abhandlungen zur amerikanischen Sprach- und Altertumskunde*, IV, pp. 171–338. Berlin.

SELLARDS, E. H. (1952). *Early Man in America.* Austin, Texas.

SIEVERS, Wilhelm (1931). *Geografía de Bolivia y Perú.* Barcelona-Buenos Aires, Editorial Labor S.A., 221 pp. (Colección Labor, sección VII, no. 288.)

SINGER, Ernestine Wieder (1936). 'The Techniques of Certain Peruvian Hairnets', *Revista del Museo Nacional*, vol. 1, t. V, pp. 16–24. Lima.

SMITH, Grafton Elliot (1924). *Elephants and Ethnologists.* London.

SOLDI, P. (1956). *Chavín in Ica.* Ica.

SQUIER, E. G. (1871–2). 'Antiquities from the Huanu Islands of Peru', *Journal of the Anthropological Institute of New York*, vol. 1, pp. 47–56. New York.

(1877). *Peru. Incidents of Travel and Exploration in the Land of the Incas.* New York.

STAFFORD, Cora Elder (1941). *Paracas embroideries.* New York.

STEGGERDA. Morris (1950). 'Anthropometry of South American Indians'. *In* Steward (Editor) (1950), pp. 57–69.

STEWARD, Julian H. (1948). 'A Functional-Developmental Classification of American High Cultures'. *In* Bennett (Editor) (1948), pp. 103–4.

(1949a). 'Cultural Causality and Law: A Trial Formulation of the Development of Early Civilizations', *American Anthropologist*, 51, 1, 1–27.

(1949b). 'The Native Population of South America'. *In* Steward (Editor) (1949), 655–68.

(1949c). 'The Central Andean Peoples'. *In* Steward (Editor) (1949), pp. 731–42.

(1949d). 'Andean Culture Development'. *In* Steward (Editor) (1949), pp. 753–6.

STEWARD, Julian H. (Editor) (1946). 'Handbook of South American

Indians'. Bulletin 143, Bureau of American Ethnology, Smithsonian Institution, vol. 2, *The Andean Civilizations*. Washington.

(1949). 'Handbook of South American Indians'. Bulletin 143, Bureau of American Ethnology, vol. 5, *The Comparative Ethnology of South American Indians*. Washington.

(1950). 'Handbook of South American Indians'. Bulletin 143, Bureau of American Ethnology, vol. 6, *Physical Anthropology, Linguistics, and Cultural Geography of South American Indians*. Washington.

STEWART, T. Dale (1943a). 'Skeletal Remains with Cultural Associations from the Chicama, Moche and Virú Valleys, Peru', *Proceedings*, U.S. National Museum, vol. 93, pp. 153–85. Washington.

(1943b). 'Skeletal Remains from Paracas, Peru', *American Journal of Physical Anthropology*, N.S., vol. 1, pp. 47–61. Philadelphia.

(1950). 'Deformity, Trephining, and Mutilation in South American Indian Skeletal Remains'. *In* Steward (Editor) (1950), pp. 43–8.

STEWART, T. D., and Marshall T. NEWMAN (1950). 'Anthropometry of South American Indian Skeletal Remains'. *In* Steward (Editor) (1950), pp. 19–42.

STONOR, C. R., and Edgar ANDERSON (1949). 'Maize among the Hill Peoples of Assam', *Annals of the Missouri Botanical Garden*, 36, pp. 355–404. St Louis.

STRONG, William Duncan (1925). *The Uhle Pottery Collections from Ancon*. University of California Publications in American Archaeology and Ethnology, vol. 21, pp. 135–90. Berkeley.

(1943). *Cross Sections of New World Prehistory*. Smithsonian Miscellaneous Collections, 104, 2, Publication 3739. Washington.

(1948). 'Cultural Epochs and Refuse Stratigraphy in Peruvian Archaeology'. *In* Bennett (Editor) (1948), pp. 93–102.

(1957). *Paracas, Nazca, and Tiahuanacoid Cultural Relationships in South Coastal Peru*, Memoir 13, Society for American Archaeology. Salt Lake City.

STRONG, William Duncan, and John M. CORBETT (1943). *A Ceramic Sequence at Pachacamac*. Columbia Studies in Archeology and Ethnology, Columbia University, vol. 1, pp. 27–122. New York.

STRONG, William Duncan, and Clifford EVANS, Jr. (1952). *Cultural Stratigraphy in the Virú Valley, Northern Peru. Idem*, vol. 4. Columbia University Press, New York.

STRONG, William Duncan, and Gordon R. WILLEY (1943). *Archeological Notes on the Central Coast. Idem*, I, 1. New York.

STRONG, William Duncan, Gordon R. WILLEY, and John M. CORBETT (1943). *Archeological Studies in Peru, 1941–1942. Idem*, vol. 1. New York.

STÜBEL, A., and Max UHLE (1892). *Die Ruinenstätte von Tiahuanaco*. Leipzig.

STUMER, Louis Michael (1953). 'Playa Grande; Primitive Elegance in Pre-Tiahuanaco Peru', *Archaeology*, vol. 6, no. 1, pp. 42–8.

(1954). 'The Chillón Valley of Peru; Excavation and Reconnaissance, 1952–53', *Archaeology*, vol. 7, no. 3, pp. 171–8.

SULLIVAN, Louis R., and Milo HELLMAN (1925). *The Punin Calvarium.* Anthropological Papers, American Museum of Natural History, vol. 23, pt 7, pp. 309–37. New York.

TABIO, Ernesto E. (1957). 'Excavaciones en Playa Grande, costa central del Peru, 1955', *Arqueologicas*, I–I. Lima.

(1965). *Excavaciones en la costa central del Perú.* Academia de Ciencias. Habana.

TELLO, Julio C. (1912). *Prehistoric Trephining among the Yauyos of Peru.* International Congress of Americanists, XVIII, pp. 75–83. London.

(1917). *Los antiguos cimenterios del valle de Nasca.* Washington.

(1918). *El uso de las cabezas artificialmente momificadas en el antiguo arte peruano.* Lima.

(1921). *Introducción a la historia antigua del Perú.* Lima.

(1923). 'Wira Kocha', *Inca*, vol. 1, pp. 93–320, 583–606, Lima.

(1927). 'Bibliografía de antropología del Perú', *Bol. Bibl. Univer. San Marcos*, vol. 3, no. 3, pp. 31–6. Lima.

(1928). *Los descubrimientos del Museo de Arqueología Peruana en la península de Paracas.* International Congress of Americanists, XXII, pt 1, pp. 679–90. Rome.

(1929). *Antiguo Perú; primera época.* Lima.

(1930). *Andean Civilization. Some Problems of Peruvian Archeology.* International Congress of Americanists, Sess. 23 (1928), pp. 259–290. New York.

(1937). 'La civilización de los Inkas', *Letras*, no. 6, pp. 5–37. Lima.

(1938). 'Arte antiguo peruano', *Inca*, vol. 2. Lima.

(1939). *Las primeras edades del Perú por Guamán Poma.* Lima.

(1942). *Origen y desarrollo de las civilizaciones prehistóricas andinas*, Lima.

(1943). 'Discovery of the Chavín Culture in Peru', *American Antiquity*, vol. 9, pp. 135–60.

(1956). *Arqueología del Valle de Casma; Culturas Chavín, Santa o Huaylas Yunga y Sub-Chimú. Informe de los trabajos de la Expedición Arqueológica al Marañon de 1937.* Lima.

(1959). *Paracas, Primera Parte.* Lima.

(1961). *Chavín, Cultura Matrix de la Civilización Andina.* Universidad Nacional Mayor de San Marcos, Lima.

TELLO, Julio C., and Próspero MIRANDA (1923). 'Wallallo', *Inca*, I, pp. 475–549.

TEN KATE, Herman F. C. (1885). 'Sur les crânes de Lagoa-Santa', *Bulletin de la Société d'Anthropologie de Paris*, Ser. 3, vol. 8,240–4.

THOMPSON, J. Eric (1936). *Archaeology of South America.* Field Museum of Natural History, Anthropology Leaflet No. 33. Chicago.

TITO CUSI YPUANQUI, Diego de Castro (1916). *Relación de la conquista del Perú y hechos del Inca Manco II.* Colección de Libros y Documentos referentes a la historia del Perú, vol. 2.

BIBLIOGRAPHY

TOLEDO, Francisco de (1940). *Informaciones que mandó levantar el Virrey Toledo sobre los Incas*. Ed. Roberto Levillier, *Don Francisco de Toledo, supremo organizador del Perú*, vol. 2, pp. 1–204. Buenos Aires.

TORRES-LUNA, A. (1923). 'El vestuario en la época incáica', *Revista de Arqueología*, I, pp. 50–64. Lima.

TORRES RUBIO, Father Diego de (1603). *Gramática y vocabulario en la lengua general del Perú, llamada Quichua*. Seville.

TOWLE, Margaret Ashley (1952a). 'Description and Identification of Plant Remains from Certain Sites in the Virú Valley'. *In* Strong and Evans.

(1952b). 'Plant Remains from a Peruvian Mummy Bundle', *Botanical Museum Leaflets*, vol. 15, no. 9, pp. 223–46. Harvard University, Cambridge, Mass.

1961. *The Ethnobotany of Precolumbian Peru*. Viking Fund Publications in Anthropology, No. 30. New York.

TRIMBORN, Hermann (1923–4). 'Der Kollektivismus der Inkas in Peru', *Anthropos*, XVIII, pp. 978–1001. Vienna.

(1925). 'Straftat und Sühne in Alt-Peru', *Zeitschrift für Ethnologie*, LVII, pp. 194–240. Berlin.

(1927). 'Die Gliederung der Staende im Inka-Reich', *Journal de la Société des Américanistes de Paris*, XIX, pp. 303–44.

(1936). *Quellen zur Kulturgeschichte des präkolumbischen Amerika*. Strecher und Schröder, Stuttgart.

TROLL, Von C. (1931–2). *Die geographischen Grundlagen der andinen Kulturen und des Incareiches*. Ibero-Amerikanisches Archiv, vol. 5, pp. 257–94. Berlin.

(1958). *Las culturas superiores andinas y el medio geográfico*. Instituto de Geografia de la Universidad Nacional Mayor de San Marcos. Lima.

TSCHOPIK, Harry, Jr. (1946). 'Some Notes on Rock Shelter Sites near Huancayo, Peru', *American Antiquity*, vol. 12, no. 2, pp. 73–80.

(1950). 'An Andean Ceramic Tradition in Historical Perspective', *American Antiquity*, vol. 15, no. 3, pp. 196–218.

TSCHOPIK, Marion Hutchinson (1946). *Some Notes on the Archaeology of the Department of Puno, Peru*. Papers of the Peabody Museum of American Archaeology and Ethnology, 27, 3. Cambridge.

TSCHUDI, Johann Jakob von (1847). *Travels in Peru, during the Years 1838–1842*. Translated by Thomasina Ross. London.

(1853). *Die Kechua-Sprache*. 3 vols. Vienna.

(1869). *Reisen durch Süd-Amerika*, vol. 5. Leipzig.

(1891). *Culturhistorische und sprachliche Beiträge zur Kenntniss des alten Peru*. Vienna.

TUDELA Y VARELA, Francisco (1905). *Socialismo peruano*. Lima.

UHLE, Max (1889–90). *Kultur und Industrie der südamerikanischen Völker*. 2 vols. Berlin.

(1897). 'A Modern Kipu from Cutusuma, Bolivia'. *Bulletin of the Free Museum of Science and Art*, vol. 1, no. 2, pp. 51–63. Philadelphia.

(1898). 'A Snuffing-tube from Tiahuanaco', *ibid.*, vol. 1, no. 4, pp. 159–77. Philadelphia.

(1903). *Pachacamac; Report of the William Pepper, M.D., LL.D., Peruvian Expedition of* 1896. Trans. C. Grosse. University of Pennsylvania, Department of Archaeology, Philadelphia.

(1906a). 'Los Kjoekkenmoedings del Perú', *Revista histórica*, 1, pp. 3–23. Lima.

(1906b). 'Las llamitas de piedra del Cuzco', *ibid.*, 1, pp. 388–92.

(1906c). *Bericht über die Ergebnisse meiner südamerikanischen Reisen.* International Congress of Americanists, XIV, pt 2, pp. 567–79. Stuttgart.

(1906d). *Aus meinem Bericht über die Ergebnisse meiner Reise nach Südamerika* 1899–1901. *Idem*, pp. 581–92.

(1907a). 'La estólica en el Perú', *Revista histórica*, II, pp. 118–28. Lima.

(1907b). 'La masca paicha del Inca', *ibid.*, pp. 227–32. Lima.

(1908a). *Ueber die Frühkulturen in der Umgebung von Lima.* International Congress of Americanists, Sess. 16, pp. 347–70. Vienna.

(1908b). *Zur Deutung der Intihuatana. Idem*, pp. 371–89.

(1909). 'Peruvian Throwing-Sticks', *American Anthropologist*, XI, pp. 624–7.

(1910). 'Tipos de civilización en el Perú', *Boletin de la Sociedad Geográfica, de Lima.*

(1912). *Los orígenes de los Incas.* Congreso Internacional de Americanistas, Sess. 17 (Buenos Aires, 1910), vol. 1, pp. 230–53.

(1913a). 'Die Ruinen von Moche', *Journal de la Société des Américanistes de Paris*, vol. 10, pp. 95–117.

(1913b). 'Zur Chronologie der alten Culturen von Ica', *ibid.*, pp. 341–367.

(1913c). 'Muschelhügel von Ancon, Peru'. International Congress of Americanists, *Proceedings*, Sess. 18 (London, 1912), pp. 22–45.

(1917a). 'Fortalezas incaicas', *Revista chilena de Historia y Geografía.* Santiago de Chile.

(1917b). *Los aborígenes de Arica.* Santiago de Chile.

(1919a). 'Fundamentos étnicos de la región de Arica y Tacna', *Boletín de la Sociedad Ecuatoriana de Estudios Históricos Americanos*, II, pp. 1–37. Quito.

(1919b). 'La arqueología de Arica y Tacna', *ibid.*, vol. 3, pp. 1–48.

(1920a). 'Apuntes sobre la prehistoria de la región de Piura', *ibid.*, vol. 4, pp. 165–7.

(1920b). 'Los principios de las antiguas civilizaciones peruanas', *ibid.*, vol. 4, no. 12, pp. 448–58.

(1920c). 'Los principios de la civilización en la sierra peruana', *ibid.*, vol. 4, nos. 13–14, pp. 44–56.

(1922). *Fundamentos étnicos y arqueología de Arica y Tacna.* 2nd edn. Quito.

(1924a). *Explorations at Chincha.* University of California Publications in American Archaeology and Ethnology, XXI, pp. 58–94.

(1924b). *Notes on Ica Valley. Idem,* pp. 121–3.

(1924c). *Notes on Sites and Graves excavated. Idem,* pp. 123–7.

(1924d). *Ancient Civilizations of Ica Valley. Idem,* pp. 128–32.

(1926). 'Los elementos constitutivos de las civilizaciones sudamericanas', *Anales de la Universidad Central. Quito, Ecuador,* vol. 36.

(1928). *Späte Mastodonten in Ecuador.* International Congress of Americanists, Sess. 23, pp. 247–58. New York.

(1935). *Die alten Kulturen Perus im Hinblick auf die Archäologie und Geschichte des amerikanischen Kontinents.* Berlin.

(1939). 'Procedencia y origen de las antiguas civilizaciones americanas', *Actas y Trabajos científicos del xxvii Congreso Internacional de Americanistas,* t. I, pp. 355–68. Lima.

URTEAGA, Horacio H. (1909). 'El antiguo Perú a la luz de la arqueología y de la crítica', *Revista histórica,* IV, pp. 200–23. Lima.

(1921). 'La organización judicial en el imperio de los Incas', *ibid.,* IX, pp. 1–50. Lima.

(1931). *El imperio incáico. En el que se incluye la historia del ayllo y familia de los Incas.* Lima.

VALCÁRCEL, Luís E. (1924). 'El Cuzco precolombiano', *Revista Universitaria del Cuzco,* no. 44.

(1930). *Metallarbeiten aus dem nördlichen Peru. Ein Beitrag zur Kenntnis ihrer Formen.* Mitteilungen aus dem Museum für Völkerkunde in Hamburg, vol. 15. Hamburg.

(1932). 'El Gato de Agua, Sus Representaciones en Pucara y Nazco', *Revista Museo Nacional de Antropología y Arqueología,* vol. 1. Lima.

(1933). 'Esculturas de Pikillajta', *Revista del Museo Nacional,* vol. 2, pp. 21–48. Lima.

(1934–5). 'Sajsawaman redescubierto', *ibid.,* vol. 3, pp. 3–36, 211–23; vol. 4, pp. 1–24, 161–203. Lima.

(1935). 'Litoesculturas y cerámica de Pukara', *ibid.,* vol. 4, no. 1, pp. 25–8.

(1939). *Sobre el origen del Cusco.* Lima.

(1943–9). *Historia de la cultura antigua del Perú.* Lima, Imprenta del Museo Nacional y del Ministerio de Educación Pública, t. 1, 2 vols. Lima.

(1946). 'Cuzco Archeology'. *In* Steward (Editor) (1946), pp. 177–82.

(1953). *Altiplano andino. Programa de historia de América.* Instituto Panamericano de Geografía e Historia, México.

VALDEZ DE LA TORRE, Carlos (1920a). 'El ayllu', *Mercurio peruano,* V, pp. 187–209. Lima.

(1920b). 'Régimen de la propiedad durante los Incas', *ibid.,* V, pp. 399–413.

VALERA, Blas (1879). *Relación de las costumbres antiguas de los naturales del Perú*. Ed. Marcos Jiménez de la Espada, *Tres relaciones de antigüedades peruanas*, pp. 135–227. Madrid.

VALETTE, M. (1913). 'Note sur la teinture de tissus précolombiens du Bas-Pérou', *Journal de la Société des Américanistes de Paris*, x, pp. 43–6.

VAN STAN, Ina (1955). 'Peruvian Domestic Fabrics from Supe; A Study of the Uhle Collection of Painted Cloths', *Notes in Anthropology*, vol. 1, no. 3. Florida State University, Tallahassee.

(1958). 'Problems in Pre-Columbian Textile Classification', *Florida State University Studies*, no. 29. Tallahasee.

VARGAS UGARTE, Rubén (1939). *Historia del Perú; Fuentes*. Lima.

VEGA TORAL, Tomás (1841–4). *Historia del reino de Quito*. Edited by Don Agustín Yerovi. 3 vols. Quito.

(1921). *La Tomebamba de los Incas*. Cuenca.

VERGER, Pierre (1950). *Indians of Peru*. New York.

VESCELIUS, Gary S., and Edward P. LANNING (1963). 'Some New Finds at San Nicolas', *Nawpa Pacha* I, pp. 43–6. Berkeley.

VILLAR CÓRDOVA, Pedro Eduardo (1923). 'Las ruinas de la provincia de Canta', *Inca*, I, pp. 1–24.

(1935). *Arqueología peruana. Las culturas prehispánicas del departamento de Lima*. Lima.

VON HAGEN, Victor Wolfgang (1949a). 'Hiram Bingham and His Lost Cities', *Archaeology*, vol. 2, pp. 40–6.

(1949b). *Guides to Peru: Cusco, Sacsahuaman, Machu Picchu, Lima, etc.* New York.

(1952a). 'The Mystery of Pisac', *Archaeology*, vol. 5, pp. 33–8.

(1952b). 'The Highways of the Inca', *ibid.*, vol. 5, pp. 104–9.

Highway of the Sun, New York and Boston, 1955.

(1957). *Realm of the Incas*.

(1965). *The Desert Kingdoms of Peru*. New York Graphic Society.

WALLACE, Dwight T. (1963). 'Early Horizon Ceramics in the Cañete Valley of Peru', *Nawpa Pacha* I, pp. 35–8. Berkeley.

WALTER, H. V., A. CATHOUD, and Anibal MATTOS (1937). 'The Confins Man – A Contribution to the Study of Early Man in South America', *Early Man*, ch. 34, pp. 341–8. Philadelphia.

WARDLE, H. Newell (1936). 'Belts and Girdles of the Inca's Sacrificed Women', *Revista del Museo Nacional*, vol. 1, t. v, pp. 25–38. Lima.

(1939). 'An Ancient Paracas Mantle', *University Museum Bulletin*, vol. 7, no. 4, pp. 22–5. Philadelphia.

(1940). 'Fictile Art of the Mochicas', *ibid.*, vol. 8, no. 1, pp. 15–24. Philadelphia.

(1944). 'Triple Cloth; A New Type of Ancient Peruvian Technique', *American Anthropologist*, vol. 46, pp. 416–18.

(1948). *False Heads of Peruvian Mummy-bales*. International Congress of Americanists (Seville, 1935). pp. 208–17. Madrid.

(1949). *A Rare Peruvian Tapestry Bonnet*. International Congress of Americanists (New York, 1949), pp. 216–18. New York.

BIBLIOGRAPHY

Wassén, Henry (1931). 'The Ancient Peruvian Abacus', *Comparative Ethnographical Studies*. Gothenburg (Göteborg) Museum, vol. 9, pp. 189–205. Göteborg.

(1940). 'El antiguo ábaco peruano según el manuscrito de Guamán Poma', *Ethnological Studies*, no. 11, pp. 1–30. Göteborg.

Wassermann-San Blas, B. J. (1938). *Cerámicas del antiguo Perú; de la colección Wassermann-San Blas*. Buenos Aires.

Wauchope, Robert (1954). 'Implications of Radiocarbon Dates, from Middle and South America', *Middle American Research Records*, II, 2. Middle American Research Institute, Tulane University, New Orleans.

Weberbauer, Augusto (1945). *El mundo vegetal de los Andes peruanos*. 776 pp. Lima, Editorial Lumen.

(1962). 'Cerrillos, An Early Paracas Site in Ica, Peru', *American Antiquity*, vol. 27, pp. 303–14.

Wendt, W. E. (1964). 'Die präkeramische Siedlung am Rio Seco, Peru', *Baessler Archiv*, n.s., Band 11, No. 2, pp. 225–75. Baessel.

Whitaker, Thomas W., and Junius B. Bird (1949). *Identification and Significance of the Cucurbit Materials from Huaca Prieta, Peru*. American Museum Novitates, no. 1426. American Museum of Natural History, New York.

Wiener, Charles (1880). *Pérou et Bolivie*. Paris.

Wiesse, Carlos (1913). *Las civilizaciones primitivas del Perú*. Lima.

Willey, Gordon R. (1943a). 'Excavations in the Chancay Valley', *Columbia Studies in Archaeology and Ethnology*, 1, 3. New York.

(1943b). 'A Supplement to the Pottery Sequence at Ancón', *ibid.*, 1, 4. New York.

(1945). 'Horizon Styles and Pottery Traditions in Peruvian Archaeology', *American Antiquity*, vol. 11, no. 1, pp. 49–56.

(1947). 'A Middle Period Cemetery in Virú Valley', *Journal of the Washington Academy of Science*, vol. 37, pp. 41–7. Washington.

(1948). 'Functional Analysis of "Horizon Styles" in Peruvian Archaeology'. *In* Bennett (Editor) (1948), pp. 8–15.

(1949). 'Ceramics'. *In* Steward (Editor) (1949), pp. 139–204.

(1915a). 'Peruvian Settlement and Socio-Economic Patterns', *The Civilizations of Ancient America* (Selected Papers of the xxixth International Congress of Americanists), pp. 195–200. University of Chicago Press, Chicago.

(1951b). 'The Chavín Problem: a Review and Critique', *Southwestern Journal of Anthropology*, 7, 2, 103–44. Albuquerque.

(1953a). *Prehistoric Settlement Patterns in the Virú Valley, Peru*. Bulletin 155; Bureau of American Ethnology, Smithsonian Institution, Washington.

(1953b). 'Archaeological Theories and Interpretations'. In *Anthropology Today*, pp. 387–80. Chicago.

Willey, Gordon R., and John N. Corbett (1954). *Early Ancon and Early Supe Culture; Chavín Horizon Sites of the Central Peruvian*

Coast. Columbia Studies in Archaeology and Ethnology, 3. Columbia University Press, New York.

WORMINGTON, H. M. (1949). *Ancient Man in North America.* Popular Series, 4. 3rd edn. The Denver Museum of Natural History, Denver.

(1953). *Origins; Indigenous Period.* Program of the History of America, 1, 1. Instituto Panamericano de Geografía e Historia; Comisión de Historia. Mexico.

WRIGLEY, G. M. (1917). 'The Travelling Doctors of the Andes, the Callahuayas of Bolivia', *Geographical Review*, 4, 183–96.

XÉREZ, Francisco de (1872). *Reports on the Discovery of Peru.* Translated and edited by C. R. Markham. Hakluyt Society, London.

(1917). *Verdadera relación de la conquista del Perú y provincia del Cuzco llamada la Nueva-Castilla.* Colección de Libros y Documentos referentes a la historia del Perú, Ser. 1, vol. 5, pp. 1–121. Lima.

YACOVLEFF, Eugenio (1931). 'El Vencejo (*Cypselus*) en al arte decorativo de Nasca', *Wira Kocha*, vol. 1, pp. 25–35. Lima. (1932). 'Las falcónidas en el arte y en las creencias de los antiguos peruanos', *Revista del Museo Nacional*, vol. 1, no. 1, pp. 33–111. Lima.

(1933). 'Arte plumaria entre los antiguos peruanos', *ibid.*, vol. 2, pp. 137–58. Lima.

YACOVLEFF, Eugenio, and Fortunato L. HERRERA (1934–5). 'El mundo vegetal de los antiguos peruanos', *ibid.*, vol. 3, no. 3, pp. 241–322, vol. 4, no. 1, pp. 29–102. Lima.

YACOVLEFF, Eugenio, y Jorge C. MUELLE (1932). 'Una exploración en Cerro Colorado. Informe', *ibid.*, vol. 1, pp. 31–59, 81–9. Lima.

(1934). 'Un fardo funerario de Paracas', *ibid.*, vol. 3, nos 1 & 2 pp. 63–163. Lima.

ZARATE, Agustín de (1853). *Historia del descubrimiento y conquista de la provincia del Perú.* Biblioteca de Autores Españoles, vol. 26, pp. 459–574. Madrid.

ZIMMERN, Nathalie Herman (1944). 'The Tapestries of Colonial Peru', *Brooklyn Museum Journal*, 1943–4, pp. 25–52. New York.

ZURKALOWSKI, Erich (1919). 'Observaciones sobre la organización social del Perú antiguo', *Mercurio peruano*, II, pp. 337–52, 480–95. Lima.

INDEX

INDEX

INDEX

Chosen Women (*acllacuna*), 152,
184–6, 208, 212, 213, 217, 241,
242
Chuquimancu 'empire', 105
Chullpas, Bolivia, 107; Pl. 16B
Chumpivilca tribe, 123, 184
Chuñu, 146
Cieza de León, 96, 200
Cinchona, 225
Cinnabar, use of, 55, 64
Circumcision, 78
'City Builder Period', 100. *See*
Cultural Period (Urbanist)
City Planning, 100–102, 106–8,
120–21
Civic organizations, 99, 101, 121
Clans, 101, 112, 113, 174. *See also*
Ayllus
Climate, 2–4. *See also* Rainfall
Cloth, 34, 35, 42, 66, 67–8, 78, 85,
86, 103, 106, 240, 249–56,
259–61, 262; Pl. 47
as armour, 196
See also Bark Cloth; Cotton;
Textiles; Weaving
Clothing, 55, 63, 67–8, 78, 81, 85,
147–50, 183, 189, 190, 200, 216,
241, 259
emperors, 189, 190
See also Cloth; Dress; Textiles
Coca, 9, 23, 62, 76, 141, 146–7, 216,
218, 224, 227
Colla tribe, 114, 118, 119, 123, 124,
127
Collahuaya, 226
Collasuyu, 178
Colombia, 65, 131, 166
Colour, in pottery, 85, 94, 98, 99,
109, 235, 266
in textiles, 86, 103, 148, 246, 253
See also Dyes; Painting; Pigments
Communication, 171
Community life, 27, 59, 65, 83, 84,
175
Compounds (village), 161
Concubines, 154, 156, 158, 177, 186
Condor, 9, 53, 94
Conduits, 168
Confessions, 215–16. *See also* Religion
Confins skull, 25–6
'Convents', 185, 213, 214
Cooking, 34, 42, 141, 145, 146.
See also Food
Copper, use of, 79, 90, 93, 103, 196,
227, 267, 268, 269, 270
Coricancha (Temple of the Sun,
Cuzco), 113, 120, 136, 162, 207,
211–14; Pl. 13
See also Priests; Religion;
Shrines; Temples

Corn. *See* Maize
Cotabamba, battle of, 134
Cotton, 19, 23, 30, 32, 33, 35, 36, 57,
67, 76, 86, 97, 141, 148
cultivation in America, 23
in textile manufacture, 35, 86, 97,
245–8
See also Weaving
Crafts, craftsmanship, 17, 103, 177,
184, 239, 263–72
See also Pottery; Weaving
Crime, penalties of, 202–5
Crops, 3, 5, 23, 27–8, 53, 63, 76, 92,
94, 141–3, 181, 182
Cucurbits, 23, 33–4, 36. *See also*
Gourds, Squashes
Cuismancu 'empire', 104, 105
Cultural Eras, climatic, 16–17,
96–109
Developmental, 16–17, 38–72
Florescent, 16–17, 73–95
Incipient, 16–17, 19–37
See also Cultural Periods
Cultural Periods, 14–18
Chancay White-on-Red, 61, 69,
83
Chavín, 16, 39, 44, 47–53, 60, 62
Chimú, 15, 16, 75, 100–105
Chiripa, 71, 72
Cultist, 15, 16, 39, 43, 59, 60, 61, 63
Cupisnique, 16, 43, 48, 50, 52, 63
Early Agricultural, 16, 31–7, 39
Early Lima, 83
Expansionist, 15, 16, 96–9
Experimental, 15, 16, 39, 60–72, 83
Florescent, 15, 16, 60, 63, 72, 73, 83,
89
Formative, 15, 16, 39–43
Gallinazo, 16, 62, 64, 65, 73
Guañape, 16, 39–43
Huaraz White-on-Red, 61, 69
Huari-Tiahuanaco, 16, 44, 74, 86
90, 96, 97
Ica, 16, 105–6
Imperialist, 16, 107, 108–9
Inca, 15, 16, 17, 44, 74, 106–9,
111–238
Interlocking, 72, 83
Intermediate, 83
Moche, 15, 16, 56, 63, 65, 75, 82,
90, 97–8
Nazca, 66, 83–8, 97, 242
Paracas Cavernas, 16, 66, 67, 68, 84,
85, 252
Paracas Necropolis, 16, 66–8, 84,
242
Pre-agricultural, 16, 19–37
Pucara, 70–72
Recuay, 16, 65, 89–90
Salinar, 16, 61, 62–4, 65, 69, 73

327

INDEX